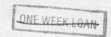
Social Theory and Sociology

In Memory of Edward Shils, 1910–1995

Social Theory and Sociology

The Classics and Beyond

Edited by Stephen P. Turner

BLACKWELL
Publishers

Copyright © Blackwell Publishers Ltd 1996, except for those chapters listed in the
Acknowledgments. Editorial matter and management copyright © Stephen P. Turner
1996

First published 1996

2 4 6 8 10 9 7 5 3 1

Blackwell Publishers Inc
238 Main Street
Cambridge, Massachusetts 02142,
USA

Blackwell Publishers Ltd
108 Cowley Road
Oxford OX4 1JF
UK

Library of Congress Cataloging-in-Publication Data

Social theory and sociology : the classics and beyond /
  edited by Stephen P. Turner.
      p.   cm.
    Includes bibliographical references and index.
    ISBN 0–631–19192–5. — ISBN 0–631–19193–3 (pbk.)
    1. Sociology—History. 2. Sociology—Philosophy. I. Turner,
Stephen P., 1951–
HM19.S52 1996
301'.01—dc20   96–3615
                                                           CIP

British Library Cataloguing in Publication Data

A CIP catalogue record for this book is available from the British Library.

Typeset in 10^1/2 on 12 pt Garamond 3
by Graphicraft Typesetters Ltd, Hong Kong
Printed in Great Britain by T.J. Press Limited, Padstow, Cornwall

This book is printed on acid-free paper

Contents

Figures and Tables

Figures

Tables

Contributors

Peter Abell is one of the leading figures in British Sociology, and one of its most creative thinkers about empirical social research. His books include *Model Building in Sociology* and *The Syntax of Social Life: The Theory and Method of Comparative Narratives*.

Jeffrey C. Alexander is Professor of Sociology at the University of California, Los Angeles. His most recent books are *Fin-de-Siècle Social Theory: Relativism, Reduction, and the Problem of Reason* and *Neofunctionalism and After* (forthcoming Blackwell).

Pierre Bourdieu holds the Chair of Sociology at the Collège de France where he directs the Center for European Sociology. His major works include, *Outline of a Theory of Practice, Distinction, Reproduction in Education, Society, and Culture, Homo Academicus*, and *The Rules of Art*.

Craig Calhoun is Professor of Sociology and History at the University of North Carolina at Chapel Hill, editor of the journal *Sociological Theory*, and author of *Critical Social Theory: Culture, History and the Challenge of Difference* and editor of *Social Theory and the Politics of Identity*.

John R. Hall is Professor of Sociology at the University of California, Davis. He is the author of *The Ways Out: Utopian Communal Groups in an Age of Babylon* and *Gone from the Promised Land: Jonestown in American Cultural History*.

Sandra Harding, Professor of Philosophy at the University of Delaware and Adjunct Professor of Philosophy at the University of California, Los Angeles,

is a major feminist thinker. Her creation of "standpoint analysis" was forma-
tive in the development of feminist epistemology. Her books include *The
"Racial" Economy of Science: Toward a Democratic Future, Whose Science? Whose
Knowledge? Thinking from Women's Lives*, and *The Science Question in Feminism*.

Anne E. Kane is Assistant Professor of Sociology at the University of Texas,
Austin. Her articles on cultural theory, politics and historical sociology have
been published in *Sociological Theory* and *Social Science History*. She is working
on a book about meaning construction, political alliance, and social movements in Ireland.

Gianfranco Poggi, formerly of the University of Edinburgh, is Professor of
Political and Social Theory at the European University Institute (Fiesole,
Italy). His books include *Calvinism and the Capitalist Spirit: Max Weber's
Protestant Ethic* and *The State: Its Nature, Development, and Prospects*.

Alan Sica, Professor of Sociology and Director of the Program in Social
Thought at Pennsylvania State University, is a former editor of *Sociological
Theory*, and the present chair of the Theory Section of the American Socio-
logical Association. He is the author of *Weber and Irrationality and Social
Order*. His *Max Weber* is forthcoming with Blackwell.

Stephen P. Turner is Professor of Philosophy at the University of South
Florida. His recent books include *Max Weber: The Lawyer as Social Thinker*
(with Regis Factor), and *The Social Theory of Practices*.

Loïc J. D. Wacquant is Associate Professor of Sociology at the University
of California, Berkeley. He is a close collaborator of Pierre Bourdieu, with
whom he co-authored *An Invitation to Reflexive Sociology*, and author of the
forthcoming *The Passion of the Pugilist*.

Peter Wagner is Professor of Sociology at the University of Warwick. He
has been involved in a major project on the relation between the develop-
ment of social science and the modernizing state in the nineteenth century.
His work in English includes *Social Sciences and Modern States: National
Experiences and Theoretical Crossroads* and *A Sociology of Modernity: Liberty and
Discipline*.

Immanuel Wallerstein is President of the International Sociological Association and the author of *The Modern World-System*, one of the most influential

books of modern social science, which created the field of worlds system-analysis. He is Distinguished Professor of Sociology at Binghamton University.

Steve Woolgar, Professor at Brunel University, is one of the creators of social constructionism in science and technology studies. He is co-author, with Bruno Latour, of the classic *Laboratory Life: The Social Construction of Scientific Facts*.

Erik Olin Wright is Professor of Sociology at the University of Wisconsin, Madison. Wright was the leader of a major international comparative study of class structure, and is one of the most prominent contemporary Marxist thinkers.

Acknowledgments

Chapter 2 is an abridgement of Jeffrey Alexander, "The centrality of the classics," which was originally published in *Social Theory Today*, edited by Anthony Giddens and Jonathan Turner, Blackwell, 1987. Chapter 7, "Marxism after Communism," by Erik Olin Wright, was published as "Class analysis, history and emancipation" in *New Left Review*, 202 (Nov.–Dec.), 1993, pp. 15–35. Chapter 11, Loïc Wacquant's interview with Pierre Bourdieu, is a small part of "Toward a reflexive sociology: a workshop with Pierre Bourdieu," published in *Sociological Theory*, 7(1), 1989, pp. 26–63. Chapter 12, Peter Abell's "*Homo Sociologicus*: do we need him/her?" was published in *Sociological Theory*, 9(2), 1991, pp. 195–8. The manuscript was prepared with the help of Eileen Kahl. Norma Walker and Nancy Stanlick also contributed to the work. I am grateful for their efforts.

1

Introduction: Social Theory and Sociology

Stephen P. Turner

Social theory is made with the heart as well as the head. But heart and head respond in different ways. They run on different clocks, clocks that are often out of synch. One model of the relations between the two holds that the heart is a kind of early warning system. Novel ideas, for example, of justice, derive from a basic untheorized or undertheorized experience of injustice – theories follow, as reason cools passions. Rudolph von Ihering, a source for both Durkheim and Weber, placed great stock in this process. Recent feminists have also embraced it. Durkheim had a somewhat different model. He saw the – usually brief – moments of "collective effervescence" in which heart and head work together as the formative periods of new collective understandings.

Sometimes the process is prolonged into a long moment of mutuality between heart and head. The thought of Marx developed and was first received in an atmosphere of this sort: a general sense of the onset of radical change, punctuated by political events that give substance and direction to thought, and that prize open the minds of potential audiences. Feminist theory is produced and read in such circumstances today. These periods have great significance, excitement, and drama, and produce a feeling, though often not the reality, of creativity. Some thinkers have sought to capture the secret of these moments and to ensure that they continued. Lukács coined the notion that the proper relation between theory and practice was one in which practice, meaning the self-realizing activity of the proletariat, and theory would develop in continuous mutual interaction driven by the practice of struggle.

Where are we today? What do head and heart have to say to each other now? The permanent revolution, the continuation of concert between theory and reform or revolutionary practice aspired to by 1960s radicalism, has now passed into the history of political failure and illusion. A few hearts may still be with the idea of the imminent overthrow of the "bourgeois order," but few heads are. "Radical action" is a subject for nostalgia, at best. Even in feminism, the moment of greatest mutuality between head and heart has passed. But these moments have their own drama, and they cast a long shadow, for it is the intellectualizations and corrections of the themes born of the moments of high excitement that become the intellectual mountains that later thinkers must climb. There is an analogue in the history of social theory. The period of Weber and Durkheim, the thought we now know as "classical social theory," was a time in which head and heart were separating, in which reflection took center stage. The first flush of optimism about the possibility of comprehensive reform in response to the "social question," as it was called in Germany, had faded in the face of recalcitrant events and forces, and the need for analysis was clear.

If feminism is perhaps coming into such a period, the situation for social theory generally seems to be quite different. It seems as though we are at the cusp of a new moment of confusion, a moment when identities and attitudes are up for discussion, but in which the heart provides little guidance. Anxieties about environmental risk, which are at the same time socially variable (and thus open to sociological analysis) and a tangible force promoted by an active social movement, provide another potential base. Ulrich Beck's account of the inequities of the "risk society" attempts to use these inequities to extend the life of "critical theory," which had originally attempted to extend the life of Marxism (Beck 1992). The early Frankfurt School grasped that misery would not produce the proletarian revolution, and turned to the supposed role of mass culture in the production of false consciousness and the deadening of the revolutionary impulse. Beck and the heirs of critical theory see that the traditional moral demands of socialism have lost their force for a comfortable electorate more concerned with preserving their advantages than risking them through political experiments. Beck's extension of the life of the critical edge of critical theory involves the recognition of new moral demands. It is a time when the need for reflection is clear, but it is also a time in which the heart pulls in new and various directions, and produces new conflicts.

The Marxian idea of class still has a precarious hold. But today its emotional force and intellectual interest is greatest where some very old forms of thought, especially the notion of the fundamental significance of class identity, exploitation and struggle, have been transposed to relations of race and gender. What anti-Marxists often counterpoised to the identities of class were the supposedly primordial ties of language, culture and nation. But these ties seem, at the end of the cold war, to have a newly problematic character. The problem of nationalities in Eastern and Central Europe, the problem that contributed to the instability of Europe in the interwar years, has now been revived; but the nationalisms of Western Europe, themselves being undermined by the creation of a European identity, seem to be at their lowest ebb in modern history. The ideas of community and civil society are candidates, and theorists of community and civil society would like to tap into, or promote, a corresponding sentiment. But there is an air of desperation about all of this. The sentiments of environmentalism, the desire for community, and of the attachment to an idealized vision of civil society seem too weak, short lived, and fluid to be captured by the heavy theories that have been constructed around them. Nor does it seem that the sentiments are much helped by being articulated as elaborate social theories.

The core identities of the past have been intellectual representations of clusters of facts about life-chances, mutual interests, and possibilities for the future realization of those interests. Class struggle was a characteristic source for identity: classes were the political base for hopes, the locus of shared experience and interest, and of culture. Members of a class suffer and prosper together. The same holds, of course, for communities, nations, and ethnic and religious groups. These older identities seem no longer to serve. Interests and the identities that embody those interests are shifting or evaporating. Often these changes can be readily understood in terms of the concepts of social theory. In the United States, for example, one effect of the massive strategy of transferring funds from the young to the old has been a kind of generational warfare. For demographic reasons, the same kinds of conflicts are certain to arise in Western Europe, where the ratio of productive employees to pensioners is inexorably rising as a result of lower birth rates.

New identities and new struggles to define interests dominate the matters of the heart that figure in present political life and social discourse. If this was all that was going on, today would be a fertile moment for the application of the traditional explanatory strategies of social theory. These are the kinds of changes to which these traditional strategies were successfully applied in the past. But there have been other changes, which seem to undermine these applications. New technologies have replaced the traditional "modern" means by which truth was shaped to fit the perspectives of class and nation. In Western Europe, major newspapers were associated with either political parties or political viewpoints, and took their audiences from particular groups. These narrow, audience-specific world interpretations have lost potency in relation to the television imagery, which is more powerful than the printed word, however ideologically and culturally coherent, could ever be. The "world" to which democratic politics responds is now, in large part, the world that is refracted through these media.

This change has its own implications. "Cultural" struggles that, in the past, occurred over centuries and could be mapped in detail in time and space across Europe and the United States now occur quickly and in ways that defy the simple model of lifestyles integrated with attitudes represented by symbols that confer identities. To be, for example, a Scandinavian fan of American Country and Western music is to *choose* an identity, and perhaps to some extent a "lifestyle": one participates in certain distinctive activities, valorizes certain emotions, and identifies with a new group of co-participants. It is an open question whether this kind of voluntary choice of identity is the model for future identity formation, but it is evident that movements such as feminism have provided an important source of identity across borders, classes, and lifestyles, in a way that would have been difficult to imagine in previous centuries apart from a highly developed organizational structure meeting a wide variety of human needs. Thus the socialist movement was made up of national Socialist parties each of which provided a large part of the social life and cultural experience of its members; the Catholic church did the same for its adherents. As recently as the 1930s, in the case of Nazism, bureaucratic demands and realities governed such movements to the extent that the bureaucracies undermined the cultural ideals and made the movements into servants of the bureaucracies. "Cultures" and viewpoints now seem to be freed from these cumbersome organizational requirements. Identities can be "socially constructed" without the efforts of large bureaucratic machines, such as churches, schools, parties, or similar organizations. The life world in which culture is transmitted and politics is experienced is a world that is altogether more fluid.

What are the implications of these changes for social theory? One view is that the project of social theory is simply out of date, a relic of the "modern project" and of the older forms of social movement with which social theory was originally associated. But are we in a "post-modern" condition in which the attempt to theorize on the basis of stable social "realities" like class is itself retrograde and pointless? The role of race, class and gender, and the ubiquity of variant forms of the model of class struggle and class standpoint in the writings of post-modernist thinkers suggests that there is no simple answer to these questions. One thing, however, is striking. The old forms of theorizing, however dead they might be in connection with the projects of directed social change they were originally associated with, are nevertheless indispensable to thinking – even the thinking of theorists of post-modernity.

This is a mysterious suggestion. How are the old forms relevant? Can they simply be renovated by inserting new objects and forms of oppression and exploitation in place of the old, as feminist Marxism has sometimes done? Or is there a fundamental conflict between the continued use of notions like class, which represent relatively fixed and stable realities, and the idea that identities, interests, cultural commitments, and the like, have become unstable and short lived. Is theoretically self-conscious rethinking of the basic categories of social theory needed, with perhaps a more ruthless selectivity about the inheritance from the past of social theory? Or should the inheritance be expunged in favor of an enterprise of cultural analysis that does not rely on them, or that understands the "facts" of classical social theory as powerful social constructions?

The papers in this volume are considerations of various aspects of the question of the current state of social theory and of the relevance of the past of social theory. Some of them represent, in part, attempts to use the tools of social theory to address the question of the future of social theory. Others are concerned with the way in which particular theoretical traditions can be relevant to present issues. They embody the changes which social theory, at the end of the century, is undergoing. The authors recognize that social theory is caught between its past successes and a situation that threatens to make its achievements irrelevant, and deal, in various ways, with the prospects of change and continuity.

The Relevance of the Classics

In the first paper in this volume, Alexander makes the case for the continued significance of the classics for sociology. His argument is that the classics are the intellectual core of disciplinary sociology and serve a continuing function as a common reference point for sociologists. He has defended the use of the classics as sources to be creatively plundered, an attitude shared by Parsons, who practiced a form of purposeful misinterpretation of the classics to produce his own best results (cf. Wearne 1989: 43). Gianfranco Poggi, in the following chapter, argues, against this, that the classics are intellectually significant apart from any function in relation to present sociology. It is not their utility for sociology that makes them important but their value as intellectual productions that makes them worth studying. He compares the study of the classics to the study of the law, which on the continent means the "Roman" law, a system of conceptual distinctions capable of endless, but highly disciplined, refinement. This refinement is not closely connected with "uses." Like the primitive peoples described by Lévi-Strauss in *The Savage Mind* (1964), the intellectual elaboration of the categories of the law proceeds out of intellectual motivations. Uses, such as defining disciplinary boundaries, or for providing a common reference point for disciplines, are beside the point of this refinement. Neither should we treat the writings of the classics as mere sources of hypothesis to be appropriated, or as icons of the sociological tribe. They are, Poggi argues, intrinsically intellectually significant and their classic status derives from the fact of their intellectual quality which itself justifies their study.

The authors in the next section pose important reflexive questions about the whole body of ideas that makes up the classical social thinkers' historical context. Immanuel Wallerstein argues that the trilemma of liberalism, conservativism, and socialism, which provided the impetus for the intellectual efforts of the classical sociologists, may now be understood historically as a product of a single underlying project, the project of modernity, which each of these ideologies extended in a somewhat different but fundamentally similarly motivated manner. The demise of "real existing socialism" in Eastern Europe, he suggests, is but a sign of a larger social change, namely the end of the modern project itself. These three ideologies and the passions they once depended on and validated thus belong to an epoch that is drawing to a close or perhaps has already ended. By implication this makes the classics of sociology into museum pieces. And if one sees such anti-sociological theoretical strategies as rational choice theory as extensions of, or ideological/analytic scientifications of, the liberal idea of the sovereign individual, one must see them too as trapped within an ideological field that is no longer meaningful.

The decreasing relevance of the models of classical social theory has not gone unnoticed within disciplinary sociology, of course, and a number of solutions have been proposed. Craig Calhoun argues that social theory can and should transform itself to meet the new challenges of the diversity of identities that is characteristic of the present. This entails the abandonment of some old intellectual attachments, notably the attachments of left wing intellectuals to the concept of class. The most promising venue for a radical development of social theory, Calhoun suggests, is to be found in considerations linking diverse identities to selfhood. He draws from the philosopher Charles Taylor the idea that social identities are sources of the self which are themselves transformed by their role in the creation of selves. People are not merely dupes who take on the identities that have been socially constructed for them, passive consumers of identities marketed to them, but rather users of identities in their individual projects of selfhood. Peter Wagner continues this focus on identities at a more macrosociological level by applying it to the subdiscipline of political sociology. He argues, as I have also suggested above, that today we are in a situation of change that parallels in its significance the situation of classical social theory. The rise of highly mobile and diverse identities largely undermines the applicability of classical social theory which rested on the apparent stability of ties of nationality and class. But he does not think that this spells the end of social theory. The theory one needs now, however, is one that accounts for the development and success of identities.

Classical social theory is not without intellectual resources to deal with such topics. A substantial renovation and extension of the ideas of classical theory might well serve to make sense of these changes. In the following section, a series of proposals for the intellectual extension or renovation of the themes of classical social theory and the project of scientific sociology are presented. John Hall begins the section with a discussion of the problem of method that has resulted from the decay of the project of a scientific sociology and the recent emergence of a new form of comparative historical social inquiry. Hall recognizes that the fissures that have opened up during the last few decades between social theory, empirical sociology, and narrative social history are vast. Indeed, the temptation is to regard them as having now become entirely separate and incommensurable forms of inquiry. Distinguishing them, Hall agrees is indeed an important first step. But in fact, Hall argues, these forms of inquiry are mutually dependent in many ways that are rarely properly acknowledged, and none of these modes can stand alone. Hall concentrates his discussion on problems of measurement and particularly on the problem of the historicity of measures. This discussion raises and attempts to answer a quite fundamental question about the relationship between social theory, history, and empirical or statistical sociology as it is presently practiced.

Where Hall turned to Weber for an account of the problems of methodological pluralism, Erik Olin Wright reconsiders the basic structure and appeal of Marxism. Wright notes that Marxism in its classic form involved tight links between three elements: the moral project of emancipation, claims about the trajectory of history, and a distinctive analytic procedure in which class was central. These tight links, he argues, have been loosened, and cannot be restored. But the three elements may be made to work, separately, if each is reconstructed. The moral imperative of emancipation can be reconstructed as a call for less exploitation and less power to owners. Dogmatic reductions of particular problems, such as gender oppression, to a supposed class basis can be replaced by the empirical study of the links between class and gender oppression. The basic idea of exploitation, meaning a relationship in which the exploiter needs the exploited, can be preserved.

Marxian ideas, modified and extended in an epistemic direction, are the basis of Sandra Harding's contribution as well. Harding discusses the idea, earlier developed in Lukács, that socially advantaged groups are blinkered in their apprehension of social reality, and that consequently disadvantaged groups, such as women and oppressed minority group members, have a "standpoint" which enables them to more successfully apprehend social reality. "Standpoint epistemology" derives from the post-positivist denial of the ability of science to provide theory-free access to facts. But standpoint epistemology adds to this the idea that there are unacknowledged and inaccessible conditioning features of cognitive understanding that derive from social location. Values and interests are hidden features of social location that are especially difficult to recognize from the perspective of dominant frameworks. Consequently these frameworks appear to be, Harding argues, uniquely valid and uniquely value and interest free.

Feminists' concerns with gender linked advantage suggests a natural extension of Lukács' idea that the proletariat had an epistemically advantaged starting point for the understanding of bourgeois society. Social location in "a gender class race matrix," Harding asserts, provides epistemic advantages to the extent that a thinker's position in this matrix enables her to apprehend social life more fully than can a member of a dominant class. On the basis of a reflexive assessment of the successes of feminism in improving our understanding of social life, Harding argues that in fact the socially disadvantaged are epistemically superior: feminism does reveal aspects of power relations that traditional social theory failed to recognize and consequently is not merely *another* standpoint but a *less partial* standpoint which contributes to the improvement of our understanding of social reality. By the same token, recognizing the "northern" character of our social theories and their consequent limitations suggests a possibility for further improvement. Standpoint epistemology can thus be usefully employed in the reflexive criticism of social theories and points us to sources of insights into social reality that are less limited and less partial than our own.

For both Wright and Harding, the notion of disadvantage is central. A part of the enlightenment legacy, the idea of egalitarianism, is still a basic organizing idea for them. The effect of adding gender differences to class differences, as Harding points out, produced a remarkable effervescence of new ideas. Feminism, in this form, represents, as I have suggested, a kind of renovation of the classical tradition that preserves its basic explanatory strategies.

Anne Kane's chapter also preserves some basic explanatory strategies of Weber and Durkheim, but directs these toward phenomena that she takes to be less stable than the facts of oppression, difference, and disadvantage that Harding and Wright take as a starting point. For Kane, the fact that social structures are produced and reproduced through culture and the fact that people interpret their experiences through culture, are the keys to understanding the historical development of social structures. Weber is the source of the idea of meaning, Durkheim the source of the idea that meanings are constructed and reproduced through ritualistic events. The events in which meanings are constructed can be analyzed and understood, Kane argues, and provides the example of the Irish land war of 1879 in which meanings and identities were successfully constructed. The example shows quite strikingly how collective meaning formation is necessary to the recognition of oppression, and especially to the creation of a sense of what nonoppression would be. Exploitation, this suggests, is a cultural fact, but not accepted passively: the consumers have an active role in the creation of the fact.

Kane criticizes the "cognitive turn" in social theory, in this case embodied in the neo-institutionalist theory of DiMaggio and Powell, according to which patterns of practical action, particularly action within organizations, become "institutionalized" through repetition and habitualization, which turns cognitive effort into habitualized taken-for-granted typifications and expectations. Kane objects that this account minimizes the possibility of "change based on voluntaristic agency." In the theories of Giddens and Bourdieu, as well, she argues, collective interpretation is mistakenly replaced by habit and symbolic invention is minimized. Kane's argument thus provides some theoretical tools for dealing with the processes of identity formation that Wagner regards as central.

In the brief portion of an interview included here, Pierre Bourdieu responds to reflexive questions about sociology as an activity that is a field of struggle and responds to questions about his employment of the terminology of economic rationality and interests in his accounts of the formation of cultural fields and bodies of practice. Bourdieu's core concepts are deeply rooted in older ideas, as he points out. He develops them in a direction that provides a kind of theoretical solution to the problem of what is internal and what is external to agents. This problem could not have more distinguished antecedents: it is Durkheim's problem of the relationship between the collective consciousness and the individual consciousness in a guise influenced by twentieth-century continental philosophy.

A "field" is outside of the agent: *habitus* are within agents. We experience the distinction when we step out of our own "field" or familiar social world

into another "field" in which our ways of thinking and constructing reality
are challenged and ineffective. We can strive to reduce this new domain to
our own. The philosopher Hans-Georg Gadamer thought of the mutual
understanding between persons with different "horizons" as a process of
"fusing" these horizons, that is to say, developing a kind of interpretative
mutuality or equality. Bourdieu thinks of this process as a struggle to create
an external fact about whose ways of defining the subject are determinative
for agents, about who is alien and who is at home in the social world. The
boundaries of "fields" may thus be extended in the fashion of a kind of intellectual imperialism, the success of which does not depend at all on mutuality
and interpretative equality.

Social theory is itself a domain of struggle of this kind. Bourdieu distances
himself from the kind of purely abstract, reified "theorizing" that he believes
to be dominant in Anglo-American social science, and suggests that he is
more concerned with the construction of "thinking tools," such as the notion
"cultural capital." These tools are, he argues, closely bound to their usages
in empirical work, and advance by confronting new objects rather than engaging in theoretical disputes that lead to metatheoretical disputes which
themselves reduce to a kind of totemism. For this kind of enterprise, and
indeed the social sciences generally, to progress, what is required is that a
continual revolution against the reified vision of the social world offered by
the social sciences occurs, and this can best be done, he argues, by people
who are on the one hand masters of the scientific culture and on the other
are predisposed by their social background to reject this vision of the world.
Bourdieu consciously sets himself against rational choice or "rational action"
theory and argues that in his conception "interests" are historically variable
and never fixed. This is not to say, of course, that they are unconstrained.
They arise through the process of the boundary extension of fields and the
process of *habitus* formation. *Habitus* are dispositional facts which produce
"interests."

Bourdieu's account has been widely influential. But it is precisely with
respect to its extension of the concepts of past social theory that it has been
most brutally criticized. Jon Elster suggests that Bourdieu is unable to give
a plausible account of what it means to adopt a non-conscious strategy of the
sort that his uses of the notion cultural capital requires. At the very least,
Elster says, one would have to suggest a causal mechanism whereby behavior
designed to increase cultural capital was maintained by its supposed unintended and beneficial consequences (1983: 70).

The conflict with Bourdieu may be understood in terms of the program
of rational choice theory itself, discussed in the following chapter by Abell.

This program amounts to a rejection of the idea that "social constraints" represent some sort of distinct factual order, an idea that is certainly present in Marx and Durkheim, though almost certainly absent in Weber. Rational choice theorists attempt to *account for* such social constraints as normative expectations in rational choice terms, that is to say as products of processes of preference formation or expectation formation that are themselves ultimately governed by a calculus of choice that is not necessarily articulable by the agent but is capable of being revealed as the underlying mechanism of action.

There is a long running dispute among rational choice theorists as to whether normative constraints of the sort that are routinely found by sociologists to operate in various settings can themselves be accounted for in rational choice terms, or whether some normative expectations at least must be treated as beyond the reductive explanatory powers of rational choice analysis (cf. Elster 1989: 150). The issue here can be put most easily in terms of a simple example much discussed in this literature. Large numbers of people in Western democracies take off as much as an hour or so of their time every few years or even more frequently to vote. Yet in only a tiny number of cases does a single vote decide an election, and in no cases of great national importance does a single vote have any significance in determining outcomes. It would seem to be "rational" for the individual to invest this hour in a more pleasurable or profitable activity. But millions upon millions of voters behave "irrationally" and vote. What is the explanation of this?

One way of approaching this kind of problem would be to say that there is a "civic culture" in Western democracies that includes the normative expectation that citizens vote. One might add to this various considerations that would connect the actions of the individual to these normative expectations, for example by arguing that failing to vote exposes one to the "nuisance cost" of being pressured by party promoters to vote the next time or spares one the embarrassment of justifying one's failure to vote. But these considerations do not account for the basic "cultural" expectation of voting. One may get around these difficulties in various clever ways. One can, for example, argue that individuals' attachments to "civic cultures" are themselves the subject of rationally accountable preferences, for example a "constitutional preference," that is to say a preference to live in a democratic society in which voting is the means of electing leaders (cf. Vanberg and Buchanan 1988: 138–60). This preference may be claimed to outweigh the inconvenience of voting.

Are these, or similar, "explanations" acceptable? In the end, it seems, conflicts between rational choice theory and its critics turn on this question.

If the program of rational choice theory actually succeeded in generating "explanations" of normative expectations and other phenomena ordinarily thought to belong to the "social" that social theory is in some sense about, social theory as an autonomous enterprise of explanation would simply disappear. It is striking that the dispute that Abell discusses between Elster and standard rational action theory is a dispute over social identity. If rational choice theory is able to account for the phenomenon of the formation of social identities, that is to say to account for the development of preferences for particular social identities in terms of prior interests and in terms of familiar processes of preference formation, the problem that Peter Wagner and Craig Calhoun stress in their papers as the issue which has undermined the fixed points of classical social theory, would be accounted for. In a sense, the acceptance of rational choice explanations in these domains would represent a return to the *status quo ante* social theory, to the moment at which social theory presented itself as an alternative to the individualist model of classical economics and the atomistic calculating individuals of liberal political theory and utilitarianism.

If this conflict is the end point of debate in present day social theory, it is a peculiar and extremely revealing end point. It is appropriate to ask whether we are in social theory perpetually condemned to refighting the battle of the origin of social theory, the battle with liberal atomism. The chapter by Wallerstein suggests that we may not be, that by a *deus ex machina*, the "modern" period, defined by the trilemma of conservatism or traditionalism, liberalism, and socialism may be coming to an end, for reasons having nothing to do with the traditional themes of social theory, at least to the extent that they are based on fixed facts of exploitation, culture, or interests. This raises the question of whether there could be a social theoretical comprehension of the process of the ending of modernity.

Steve Woolgar's paper points to a solution, or at least an approach, to the problem. If modernity itself may be understood as a "project" it may be understood not only as the ideology dominating an era but as a project that like other projects is only partially successful in constituting the era it purportedly dominated. Works like Bruno Latour's *We Have Never Been Modern* (1993), no less than the writings of the political philosopher Leo Strauss and his followers, have argued precisely this. For the followers of Strauss, the failures of the modern project, which they understood to begin with Hobbes and Machiavelli, point to a reconsideration of the birth of the modern from the premodern tradition of classical *political* philosophy, and to an understanding of the modern project in light of and as a modification of the earlier projects of Plato and Aristotle. For them, as for Latour, "modernity" is a bastard form, incompletely realized because it is impossible – and it is because of this impossibility that we can turn it into an object of analysis.

Woolgar's chapter proposes the theoretical reconsideration of one of the constitutive distinctions of the modern project, namely the distinction between human and machine. It is striking that this distinction is central to such thinkers as Hobbes, whose concern is to distinguish the natural state of man missing in the artificial machine of society, to reconsider the individual as a kind of machine, and to account for the human world in mechanical terms. Woolgar proposes to reconsider the distinction itself and to show how some familiar episodes in western history may be understood using the conceptual vocabulary of "actor network theory," originating in the social study of science, to illuminate an important and odd episode in history – the Luddites, who destroyed machines during the industrial revolution. As he shows, such terms of art in classical social theory as solidarity and social bond can be given radically new meaning if they are extended to machines as well as people.

The arrival of new machinery was similar to the arrival of a large body of human workers with different customs and a distinct identity. The effects of the arrival of the machines varied according to the structure of the networks that they intruded into, and the response of the workers varied in consequence. Where networks were less heterogeneous, Woolgar argues, the disruptive effects, and consequently the resistance, increased. Whether Woolgar's approach represents a way forward, whether the non-human/human distinction is in fact, as Latour and Michel Callon have suggested, a kind of barrier to social theory's moving forward, is a question that cannot be answered here. However, Woolgar's discussion suggests that the transformation of social theory, even if it is extremely radical, may nevertheless involve the recycling of core concepts of social theory and thus ensure their preservation within a "theoretical" project that no longer shares the original substantive concerns of social theory nor its various epistemic goals.

Alan Sica's concluding chapter reflects on another temporal marker, the end of the first century of academic sociology in the United States. He concentrates on the story of the rise of Talcott Parsons, who put together a group of alliances on which a powerful academic empire was to be built. Sica describes the attitudes of the participants in this empire building effort from the inside. Parsons himself believed that with him sociology in a scientific and theoretical sense was about to begin. Moreover, by an accident of history he was about to be handed a loudspeaker with which to impose this message on the world of post-war Europe. The history of the ascendancy of Parsonian sociology has yet to be fully written, but the basic outlines are clear (cf. Buxton 1985). Parsons was able to influence the emerging disciplines of area studies and the study of political development, in conjunction with the expanded post-war American role in the world. He was instrumental in the creation of the Russian Research Center at Harvard, deeply influential in relation to studies of China, and part of a strategic initiative to create a unified "behavioral" science comprising psychology, social psychology, political science, and sociology, with social psychology as a bridge discipline and anthropology related to these disciplines through the study of culture and personality and socialization. This vision, one aspect of which has already been touched on in connection with Hall's paper, had a profound influence. As Sica makes clear, the vision now seems very much a relic of a dead past. Parsons of course is especially dead. But the effects of the Parsonsian development of the task and domain of social theory linger and are embodied in an institutional relation between academic sociology and social theory that now seems itself problematic. To use the jargon of the chapters by Calhoun and Wagner, social theory today has a problem about identity.

The contributors to this volume would reconstruct the identity of the activity of social theory in different ways, and the differences can be seen in their approaches to the problems they address. My own view would be this: the problems to which social theory is addressed are not "eternal"; nevertheless the ways in which the problems that do arise in social life, such as the emergence of a new technology that leads to the rearrangement of social relations or to the transformation of the technology into a particular direction of use, for example, are *not* usually addressed most successfully in terms of concepts created on the spot, or by practitioners. Even journalists find that the legacy of social theory is cognitively useful. For the more serious thinker, it provides standards against which interpretations of novel circumstances can be held and also provides clues to how to analyze them.

Having said this, it should be added that the single greatest or most spectacular failure in the business of making sense of social life has been "functionalism" or the idea that there is a teleological order to society. It must be said that such current commonplaces as "society reproduces sexism and gender oppression," have no real force unless one also holds that society (or language, or "practices") is a kind of directing intelligence making choices to bring about certain ends. These are examples of the sort of "functionalism" that the classic social theorists rejected (cf. Turner and Factor 1994). The fact that these images not only recur, but become, in the hands of thinkers like Michel Foucault, matters of high intellectual fashion, suggests that social theory has a permanent, and in this sense "eternal" job: the criticism and uncovering of implicit functional ideas. Intellectually, however, this sisyphean task is trivial.

A serious "identity" for social theory would begin with what we have learned from the failures of the past. Functionalism was one failure; scientism was another. The reach for scientific theoretical sociology was beyond the grasp of Parsons and Merton, and, a century's experience now suggests, beyond anyone's grasp. But their efforts, as Merton quoted Whitehead, to follow the dictum "a science which hesitates to forget its founders is lost" (Merton 1968: 1), are nevertheless instructive in a cautionary sense. They suggest that in social theory, it may be that it is precisely the forgetting of the founders that renders the enterprise trivial and unmeaning.

An analogy might be drawn with the history of philosophy. In the period after Plato and Aristotle wrote, circumstances changed, and their political philosophy lost its direct relevance. The political recipes of Plato and the ethical account of political action given by Aristotle could no longer be applied to the situation of Athenian politics or indeed of the politics of the Greek world without extensive interpretation and analysis. Yet no new account of the circumstances of Greek political life could surpass the reinterpreted thoughts of Plato and Aristotle. Philosophy became, to take another cliche from Whitehead, a series of footnotes to Plato. Twentieth-century "constructive" social theory has been unsuccessful in ways that suggest that a reinterpreted Weber and Durkheim, and a quite radically reinterpreted Marx, will always be superior to a novel "program" that attempts to construct a social theory from scratch in accordance with some intellectual ideal or political demand of the day.

If this is true, the vocation of social theorists is to be proprietors and preservers of a very rich junkyard. This situation doubtless could be described in more flattering ways. Nietzsche spoke of nearsighted librarians in a far-flung library. The tasks of Nietzsche's librarian and the junkyard proprietor are nevertheless the same: to be able to find the right elements to use in addressing the problems that arise, and the craft skill of recognizing what can be adapted to the needs of the present.

This "identity" is deeply at odds with the identities that professional sociology is attempting to construct for itself. In almost every country of the world, sociology is now concerned with justifying itself as useful. The funding policies of research agencies and higher education authorities demand this language. Social theory, however, stands in a peculiar relationship to this enterprise of justification. It is "useless" from the point of view of the usual rhetoric of application as service to the state. But it is also free of the need to defend itself in this way. Carlyle is said to have responded to a gentleman who ridiculed scribblers by commenting that there was once a man named Rousseau who wrote a book. They bound the second edition of his book, Carlyle said, in the skins of those who had laughed at the first.

Social theory has had this rather grim justification since the French revolution, and it is even more deserved in the twentieth century than it was in the nineteenth. Marxist social theory, itself a project of scientific theoretical understanding, was at least partly responsible for Communism. If Zeev Sternhell's meticulous intellectual genealogy of fascism is to be believed, the social theory of Georges Sorel, itself a critical appropriation and revision of Marxism, was the intellectual kernel of the fascist revolution (Sternhell 1994). To speak metaphorically, this means that social theory was prominent among the co-authors of the two great catastrophes of the twentieth century. Marxists were not the only contributors. Durkheim gave aid and comfort to syndicalism; Weber contributed to the "realism" that dominated American foreign policy in the cold war; Parsons to developmentalism and thus to American policy toward the Third World.

Social theory, to put it brutally, has blood on its hands. Even if, in the Great Accounting, its role in the great catastrophes of the twentieth century is judged to be relatively small, it will still bear a large burden, for there is a great deal of guilt to be allocated. Thus as heirs of the tradition of social theory, even if the legacy is a junkyard, we social theorists have a kind of grandeur. We are aristocrats – ruined by our spectacular errors and extravagant passions – living among parvenus and butterfly collectors. The best we can say for ourselves is that we have learned something from our errors. But no one can say that the errors were trivial, or the passions empty.

To be sure, much of what passes as social theory today still labors under delusions, and our nostalgia for our old extravagances often overwhelms us. But a serious understanding of our own past gives us the means to grasp the errors of our present enthusiasms. For the same reasons, the "social theoretical" views of our contemporaries in fields with less highly charged histories, such as cultural studies, can be seen by us as familiar errors. We have a vocation – but a very different one than our predecessors thought we had.

Part I

Of What Use are "the Classics"?

If one goes back to the beginning of the academic field of sociology in the United States, one finds departments instructing on three basic topics. The first and distinctively "sociological" area would be the history of social thought. There would typically be a second course or set of courses on charitable institutions, and one on social problems. More rarely, there would be a course on statistical material in social science. This list gradually changed. In the 1920s, the development of an academic field of social work and the beginnings of change in the role of charitable institutions, which in the 1930s gave way to public welfare institutions, led to the creation of schools of social work and to the professionalization of social work. Sociologists, including both theoretically and empirically oriented sociologists, were active in the creation of these social work programs, in part because they believed that sociology could develop more successfully if the burden of preparing students for careers in welfare was removed from sociology departments.

The 1920s also saw the beginnings of an active struggle between sociologists oriented toward theory and those oriented toward scientism and a purely empirical conception of sociology. By the end of the decade there was open hostility toward "theory" and the funding of empirical social research by the Rockefeller charities effectively bypassed many of the sociologists whose primary commitments were to theory (cf. Turner and Turner 1990: 83). The term "social theory" was typically used during this period rather than "sociological theory" and courses with the title "History of Social Thought" were still routinely offered in sociology departments. Indeed, at the beginning of the publication of the *American Sociological Review* in the late 1930s, the history of social thought was described as an area for which the journal took specific responsibility.

The 1930s saw some new developments in the way in which the history
of social thought was conceived. The older view, championed by such prolific
writers as Harry Elmer Barnes and Howard P. Becker, was a comprehensive
and somewhat unselective idea of the limits and character of social thought.
Titles of books in this era included *Social thought from Hamurabi to Comte*.
Barnes and Becker's own huge compendium of social theories was *Social
Thought from Lore to Science*. The imagery reflected Comte's own picture of the
development of the sciences, in which each science passed through stages of
development beginning with primitive thought, which was typically dominated by theological ideas, developing them into a "metaphysical" stage, dominated by questions about the existence and true nature of entitites, such as
"society," and culminating in a "positive" stage in which the science would
become predictive. Simply mastering the history and development of social
thinking was understood to be a basic part of the education of every analyst
of society and these requirements were rigorously enforced in the major
graduate programs of the day.

This model of education and the central role it granted to the history of
social thought were in fact doomed. During the 1930s another much more
narrow model of the history of social thought also developed in the hands
of Talcott Parsons, then a junior faculty member in economics at Harvard
University. Parsons, under the influence of various Harvard luminaries,
attempted to identify a distinctive domain for sociological thinking that was
not shared by the other social sciences and added something unique and
necessary to them. He found antecedents for this conception in the thinking
of Weber, Durkheim, and Pareto, and he found some legitimation for the
notion of a distinctive sociological contribution to the understanding of action
in the writings of Alfred Marshall, an economic theorist, who placed the
study of value outside of economics proper. Parsons also reflected on the
thinking of such German theorists as Tönnies and Simmel, both of whom
had roles in the more traditional and larger list of thinkers discussed by
Barnes and Becker. Parsons's quest for a distinctively "sociological" problem
for "sociological theory" to be about led him to ignore the large list of
thinkers that previously had constituted the canon, and the issues that they
had addressed, such as the influence of geographical factors and technology
on society.

In the post-Second World War period, a younger generation of sociologists, including Parsons, Robert K. Merton, and the empirical researchers
Paul Lazarsfeld and Samuel Stouffer, came into a special degree of influence
over sociology. Together they created a widespread conviction that sociology
was at last about to become a science, and that a series of theoretical ideas

and ideas about measurement and survey research would be the basis of this emergence into science. In fact, they agreed on little else, but one thing they did agree on was the irrelevance and wrongness of the older conception of the history of social thought. Parsons and Merton, the two "theorists" in this group, worked actively to attack this older conception and to exclude it from the new "scientific" sociology. The most important document in this effort is Merton's essay on the history and systematics of sociological theory. This polemical essay, like the best of Merton's writings, is subtle and indeed contains many remarks that might be interpreted as supporting the traditional form of the study of the history of social thought. However, the main message was simple: That the history of social thought could not be and should not be mistaken for the systematic creation of scientific social theory, which could only relate to the history of social thought by using past social thinkers as sources for ideas which could be built into a single systematic body of theory.

The idea of the educated sociologist as a person comfortable with and cognizant of the great thinkers of the past, an image that would be characteristic for example of the educated philosopher, was the target of this polemic. He complained that "almost all sociologists see themselves as qualified to teach and write the 'history' of sociological theory — after all, they are acquainted with the classical writings of an earlier day" (1968: 2). The acquaintance with past social thought which this conception prized was, Merton said, no substitute for the possession of the elements of a systematic social theory of the sort that the newly emerged science of sociology would need to employ and sought to develop. Merton's paper is now some fifty years old, but the attitudes it expresses are still commonplaces among American sociologists, and indeed the open hostility to social theory expressed in the late 1920s is perhaps even more common in conventional elite sociology departments. In the United Kingdom, this same dispute arose in a somewhat different way, with different results. British sociology is the product of the period after the Second World War, and it is a commonplace that the discipline combined scholars whose primary background was philosophical with scholars whose primary orientation was toward social statistics or amelioration. The two emphases have ever since sat somewhat uneasily with one another. British sociology took over Parsons's list, and, like American sociology, deleted Pareto and added Marx to the canonical figures of Durkheim and Weber. Thinkers like Anthony Giddens and Steven Lukes, in contrast to the students of Parsons, returned to the originals for inspiration, producing in British sociology a different but even more classics-oriented form of social theory within academic sociology, but with the same small canon.

In these two papers, Alexander and Poggi discuss the present significance of the classics. Alexander argues that the classics serve important disciplinary purposes for sociology and are indispensable in organizing sociological discourse. This is, of course, a quite different justification than Merton presented for the study of systematic sociological theory and in some respects returns to the point of view of Barnes and Becker, with this difference: Alexander regards the short list of classics established by Parsons and the critics of Parsons who added Marx and deleted Marshall and Pareto to be the genuinely canonical list that can in fact serve these purposes. Gianfranco Poggi argues that no such justification is required. The classics have by now, he thinks, established themselves successfully as a standard against which serious social thought can and should be judged, and the discipline of mastering the classics is essential for serious social thinking. It is not the "utility" of the classics for sociology as a discipline but their intrinsic intellectual merit that, for Poggi, justifies our attention to them.

The Centrality of the Classics

Jeffrey C. Alexander

The relationship between social science and the classics is a question which opens up the deepest issues not only in social science but in cultural studies more generally. In the essay which follows I argue for the centrality of the classics in contemporary social science. This position is challenged from what, at first glance, appear to be two entirely different camps. Among social science practitioners, of course, there has always been skepticism toward "the classics." Indeed, for those of the positivist persuasion the very question of the relation between social science and the classics leads immediately to another, namely, whether there should be any relationship at all. Why do disciplines which profess to be oriented to the empirical world and to the accumulation of objective knowledge about it need recourse to texts by writers who are long dead and gone? According to the canons of empiricism, after all, whatever is scientifically relevant in these texts should long ago have been either verified and incorporated into contemporary theory, or falsified and cast into the dustbin of history.

Yet it is not only "hard" positivists who argue against interrelating classical interpretation and contemporary social science; it is humanists as well. Recently there has emerged a powerful argument against the injection of contemporary concerns into the consideration of classical texts. Classical texts, so this argument goes (for example, Skinner 1969), must be considered entirely in historical terms. This historicist position on the classics converges with the empiricist, in so far as both camps argue against the intermingling of contemporary social science concerns with the discussion of historical texts.

To answer the questions about the relation between social science and the classics, then, one must think about just exactly what empirical social science is and how it relates to the science of nature. One must also think about what it means to analyse the classics and about what relation this kind of presumptively historical activity might have to the pursuit of contemporary scientific knowledge.

Before pursuing these questions further, however, I will offer a pointed definition of just what a classic is. Classics are earlier works of human exploration which are given a privileged status *vis-à-vis* contemporary explorations in the same field. The concept of privileged status means that contemporary practitioners of the discipline in question believe that they can learn as much about their field through understanding this earlier work as they can from the work of their own contemporaries. To be accorded such a privileged status, moreover, implies that, in the day-to-day work of the average practitioner, this deference is accorded without prior demonstration; it is accepted as a matter of course that, as a classic, such a work establishes fundamental criteria in the particular field. It is because of this privileged position that exegesis and reinterpretation of the classics – within or without a historical context – become conspicuous currents in various disciplines, for what is perceived to be the "true meaning" of a classical work has broad repercussions. Western theologians have taken the Bible as their classic text, as have those who practise the Judaeo-Christian religious disciplines. For students of English literature, Shakespeare is undoubtedly the author whose work embodies the highest standards in their field. For 500 years, Aristotle and Plato have been accorded a classical status in political theory.

Why There are No Classics in Natural Science: a Post-positivist View

The epistemology of science does not determine the particular topics to which scientific activity is allocated in any given scientific discipline.[1] Yet it is precisely the allocation of such activity which is responsible for any discipline's relative empirical "feel." Thus, even outspoken anti-empiricists have acknowledged that an explicit focus on empirical questions is what distinguishes natural from human sciences. For example, while Holton has painstakingly demonstrated that arbitrary, supra-empirical "themata" affect modern physics, he insists that it has never been his intention to argue for the introduction of "thematic discussions . . . into the *practice* of science itself." Indeed, he suggests that "only when such questions were ruled out of place in a laboratory did science begin to grow rapidly" (Holton 1973: 330–1, italics added). Even the forthrightly idealist philosopher Collingwood, who has insisted that scientific practice rests upon metaphysical assumptions, allows that "the scientist's business is not to propound them but only to presuppose them" (Collingwood 1940: 33).

The allocation of scientific activity depends upon what is considered by practitioners to be scientifically problematic. Because in the modern era natural scientists tend to agree about the generalized commitments which inform their craft, it is more empirical questions which usually receive their explicit attention. This, of course, is precisely what allows "normal science," in Kuhn's phrase (1970), to proceed as an activity of empirical puzzle-solving and specific problem-solutions. Taking normal science to characterize natural science as such, Habermas, too, has identified consensus as what differentiates "scientific" as compared to "non-scientific" activity.

> We term information scientific if and only if an uncompelled and permanent consensus can be obtained with regard to its validity . . . The genuine achievement of modern science does not consist primarily in producing truth, that is, correct and cogent statements about what we call reality. Rather, it distinguishes itself from traditional categories of knowledge by a method of arriving at an uncompelled and permanent consensus of this sort about our views. (Habermas 1972: 91)

Only if there is disagreement about the background assumptions which inform a science do these non-empirical issues come explicitly into play. Kuhn calls this a paradigm crisis. It is in such crises, he believes, that there is "recourse to philosophy and to debate over fundamentals" (Kuhn 1970).

It is because attention is usually directed to the empirical dimensions of natural science that classics are absent. The non-empirical dimensions are camouflaged, and it appears that speculative hypotheses can be decided by reference either to sense data which are relatively accessible or to theories whose specificity makes their relevance to such data immediately apparent. Classics, by contrast, imply a privileged position for earlier theories. Earlier theories, not just contemporary ones, are seen as having explanatory status; indeed, classical texts often are considered to be capable of supplying relevant data as well. My point is that natural science is no less *a priori* than its social counterpart. A non *a priori*, purely empirical stance is not the explanation for "classicless" natural science. Rather, it is a matter of the form which the mixture of prior and contingent knowledge takes.

Thus, rather than classics, natural science has what Kuhn called exemplars. With this term, Kuhn (1970: 182) means concrete examples of successful empirical work: examples of the kind of powerful problem-solutions which define paradigmatic fields. While exemplars embody metaphysical and non-empirical commitments of various kinds, they are in themselves models of how specifically to explain the world. Of necessity, they include definitions and concepts, but they direct those who study them to questions of operationalization and technique. Yet for all their specificity, exemplars themselves play an *a priori* role. They are learned in textbooks and laboratories before neophytes are capable of testing for themselves whether or not they are really true. They are, in other words, internalized because of their privileged position in the socialization process rather than because of their scientific validity. The learning processes are the same in social science; what is different is that social scientists internalize classics at least as often as they internalize exemplars.

The Post-positivist Case for the Classics

The ratio between exemplars and classics is so much different in social science because in its social application science produces so much more disagreement. Because there is persistent and widespread disagreement, the more general background assumptions which remain implicit and relatively invisible in natural science here come vividly into play.[2] The conditions which Kuhn defines for paradigm crisis in the natural sciences are routine in the social. I am not suggesting that there is no "objective" knowledge in the social sciences, nor even that there is no possibility for successful predictions or covering laws. It is possible, it seems to me, to gain real cumulative knowledge about the world from within different and competing points of view, and even to sustain relatively predictive covering laws from within general orientations which differ in substantial ways. What I am suggesting, however, is that the conditions of social science make consistent agreement about the precise nature of empirical knowledge – let alone agreement about explanatory covering laws – highly unlikely. In social science, therefore, arguments about scientific truth do not refer only to the empirical level. They cut across the full range of non-empirical commitments which sustain competing points of view.

There are cognitive and evaluative reasons for the vast differences in the level of consensus. I will mention here only the most fundamental.

(1) In so far as the objects of a science are located in the physical world outside of the human mind, its empirical referents can, in principle, more

easily be verified through interpersonal communication. In social science, where the objects are either mental states or conditions in which mental states are embedded, the possibility for confusing mental states of the scientific observer with mental states of those observed is endemic.

(2) Resistance to simple agreement on empirical referents also emerges from the distinctive evaluative nature of social science. There is a symbiotic relationship between description and evaluation. The findings of social science often carry significant implications for the desirable organization and reorganization of social life. In natural science, by contrast, "changes in the content of science do not usually imply changes in social structures" (Hagstrom 1965: 285). The ideological implications of social science redound to the very descriptions of the objects of investigation themselves. The very characterization of states of mind or institutions – for example, is society called "capitalist" or "industrial," has there been "proletarianization," "individuation," or "atomization" – reflects an estimation of the implication for political values of an explanation of that phenomenon which has not yet occurred. While Mannheim over-estimated evaluative as opposed to cognitive assumptions, he was certainly sensitive to this point. Every definition, he wrote, "depends necessarily upon one's perspective, that is, it contains within itself the whole system of thought representing the position of the thinker in question and especially the political evaluations which lie behind this system of thought." His conclusion, in this regard, seems accurate: "The very way in which a concept is defined and the nuance in which it is employed already embody to a certain degree a prejudgment concerning the outcome of the chain of ideas built upon it" (Mannheim 1936: 196–7).

(3) Needless to say, in so far as it is difficult, for cognitive and evaluative reasons, to gain consensus about even the simple empirical referents of social science, there will be even less about the abstractions from such concrete referents which form the substance of social theory. Hagstrom suggests (1965: 256–8) that possibilities for scientific consensus significantly depend upon the degree of quantification that is consistent with the discipline's scientific goals. In so far as empirical referents are not clear and abstractions subject to constant dispute, efforts to mathematicize social science can only be efforts at disguising or promoting particular points of view.

(4) In so far as neither empirical referents nor covering laws generate agreement, the full range of non-empirical inputs to empirical perception become objects of debate. Because there is such endemic disagreement, moreover, social science will invariably be differentiated by traditions (Shils 1970) and

schools (Tiryakian 1979). For most members of the social scientific community, it is apparent that such "extra-scientific" cultural and institutional phenomena are not simply manifestations of disagreement but bases upon which scientific disagreements are promoted and sustained. This realization further sensitizes social scientists to the non-empirical dimensions of their field.

For all of these reasons, discourse – not just explanation – becomes a major feature of the social science field. By discourse, I refer to modes of argument which are more consistently generalized and speculative than are normal scientific discussions. The latter are directed in a more disciplined manner to specific pieces of empirical evidence, to inductive and deductive logics, to explanation through covering laws and to the methods by which these laws can be verified or falsified. Discourse, by contrast, is ratiocinative. It focuses on the process of reasoning rather than the results of immediate experience, and it becomes significant when there is no plain and evident truth. Discourse seeks persuasion through argument rather than prediction. Its persuasiveness is based on such qualities as logical coherence, expansiveness of scope, interpretative insight, value relevance, rhetorical force, beauty, and texture of argument.

Foucault (1970) identifies intellectual, scientific, and political practices as "discourses" in order to deny their merely empirical, inductive status. In this way, he insists that practical activities are historically constituted and shaped by metaphysical understandings that can define an entire epoch. Sociology, too, is a discursive field. Still, one finds here little of the homogeneity that Foucault attributes to such fields; in social science, there are discourses, not a discourse. These discourses are not, moreover, closely linked to the legitimation of power, as Foucault in his later work increasingly claimed. Social scientific discourses are aimed at truth, and they are constantly subjected to rational stipulations about how truth can be arrived at and what truth might be. Here I draw upon Habermas' (for example, 1984) understanding of discourse as part of an effort that speakers make at achieving undistorted communication. If Habermas underestimates the irrational qualities of communication, let alone action, he certainly has provided a way to conceptualize its rational aspirations. His systematic attempts to identify modes of argument and criteria for arriving at persuasive justification show how rational commitments and the recognition of supra-empirical arguments can be combined. Between the rationalizing discourse of Habermas and the arbitrary discourse of Foucault, this is where the actual field of social science discourse uneasily lies.

It is because of the centrality of discourse that theory in the social sciences is so multivalent and that compulsive efforts (for example, Wallace 1971) to follow the logic of natural science are so misguided. Those of the positivist persuasion sense the tension between such a multivalent conception and their empiricist point of view. To resolve it they try to privilege "theory" over "metatheory," indeed, to exclude theory in favour of "explanation" narrowly conceived. Thus, complaining that "far too much social theory consists of the history of ideas and general hero worship of Marx, Weber, [and] Durkheim," Turner argues for "doing theory as opposed to . . . providing yet another metatheoretical analysis of the early theoretical masters"[3] (Turner 1986: 974). And Stinchcombe describes Marx, Durkheim and Weber as "those great *empirical* analysts . . . who did not work mainly at what we now call *theory*." He insists that they "worked out *explanations* of the growth of capitalism, or of class conflict, or of primitive religion." Rather than being concerned with discursive theory, in his view, "they used a wide variety of theoretical *methods*" (Stinchcombe 1968: 3, italics added).

These distinctions, however, seem more like "utopian" efforts to escape from social science than efforts really to understand it. Generalized discourse is central, and theory is inherently multivalent. Indeed, the centrality of discourse and the conditions which produce it make for the overdetermination of social science by theory and its underdetermination by fact. Because there is no clear, indisputable reference for the elements which compose social science, there is no neat translatability between different levels of generality. Formulations at one level do not ramify in clear-cut ways for the other levels of scientific concern. For example, while precise empirical measurements of two variable correlations can sometimes be established, it is rarely possible for such a correlation to prove or disprove a proposition about this interrelationship that is stated in more general terms. The reason is that the existence of empirical and ideological dissensus allows social scientists to operationalize propositions in a variety of different ways.

Let us briefly consider, for example, two of the best recent efforts to move from data to more general theory. In Blau's attempt to test his newly developed structural theory, for example, he starts with a proposition he calls the size theorem: the notion that a purely ecological variable, group size, determines outgroup relations (Blau, Blum, and Schwartz 1982: 46). Drawing from a data set that establishes not only a group's size but its rate of intermarriage, he argues that a relationship between intermarriage rates and group size verifies the size theorem. Why? Because the data demonstrate that "group size and the proportion outmarried are inversely related" (p. 47). But outmarriage is a datum that does not, in fact, operationalize "outgroup relations." It is one type of outgroup relation among many others, and as Blau himself acknowledges at one point in his argument it is a type into which enter factors other than group size. Outgroup relation, in other words, does not have a clear-cut referent. Because of this, the correlation between what is taken to be its indicator and group size cannot verify the general proposition about the relation between group size and outgroup relations. Blau's empirical data, then, are disarticulated from his theory, despite his effort to link them in a theoretically decisive way.

In Lieberson's ambitious study (1980) of black and white immigrants to the United States since 1880, similar problems emerge. Lieberson begins with the less formally stated proposition that the "heritage of slavery" is responsible for the different achievement levels of black and European immigrants. In order to operationalize this proposition, Lieberson takes two steps. First, he defines heritage in terms of "lack of opportunity" for former slaves rather than in cultural terms. Second, he identifies opportunity in terms of the data he has developed about varying rates of education and residential segregation. Both these operations, however, are highly contestable. Not only would other social scientists define the heritage of slavery in very different terms, but they might also conceive of opportunities in ways other than education and residence. Because there is, once again, no necessary relationship between the rates Lieberson has identified and differences in opportunities, there can be no certainty about the proposition relating achievement and heritage. While the measured correlations stand on their own, and constitute an empirical contribution in their own right, they cannot test the theories toward which they are aimed.

It is far easier to find examples of the contrasting problem, the overdetermination by theory of empirical "facts." In virtually every broader, more theoretically gauged study, the sampling of empirical data is open to dispute. In *The Protestant Ethic and the Spirit of Capitalism*, for example, Weber's equation of the spirit of capitalism with seventeenth- and eighteenth-century English entrepreneurs has been widely disputed (Weber 1958). If the Italian capitalists of the early modern city-states are conceived of as manifesting the capitalist spirit (that is, Trevor-Roper 1965), then Weber's correlation between capitalists and Puritans is based on a restricted sample and fails to substantiate his theory. In so far as this is true, Weber's empirical data were overselected by his theoretical reference to the Protestant ethic.

In Smelser's famous study, *Social Change in the Industrial Revolution* (1959), a similar distance between general theory and empirical indicator can be found. In his theory, Smelser argues that shifts in familial role divisions, not industrial upheavals *per se*, were responsible for the radical protest activities by English workers which developed in the 1820s. In his narrative historical account, Smelser describes fundamental shifts in family structure as having occurred in the sequence he has suggested. His specific presentations of archival data (Smelser 1959: 188–99) seem to indicate, however, that these family disturbances did not develop until one or two decades later. Smelser's theoretical concern with the family overdetermined the presentation of his narrative history (and his archival data in turn underdetermined his theory).[4]

In Skocpol's (1979) more recent effort at documenting her historical and comparative theory, the same kind of overdetermination is exercised by a very different theory. Skocpol (p. 18) proposes to take an "impersonal and nonsubjective viewpoint" on revolutions, which gives causal significance only to "the institutionally determined situations and relations of groups." Her search is for the empirical data of revolution and the only a-priority she acknowledges is her commitment to the comparative method (pp. 33–40). When Skocpol acknowledges at various points, however, that local traditions and rights do play a role (for example, pp. 62, 138), and that political leadership and ideology must (however briefly) be essayed (pp. 161–73), the theoretical overdetermination of her data becomes apparent. Her structural preoccupations have led her to ignore the entire intellectual and cultural context of revolution.[5]

Empirical underdetermination and theoretical overdetermination go hand in hand. From the most specific factual statements up to the most abstract generalizations, social science is essentially contestable. Every conclusion is open to argument by reference to supra-empirical considerations. Here is the specifically social-scientific version of the thematization which, Habermas (1984) has shown, must lay behind every effort at rational argument. Every kind of social scientific statement is subject to the demand for justification by reference to general principles. In other words, I need not – and social scientists as a community simply will not – limit an argument against Blau to an empirical demonstration that structural considerations are only one of several which determine outmarriage; I can, instead, demonstrate that the very stipulation of such structural causation rests upon presuppositions about action which are of an excessively rationalistic kind. In considering Lieberson's work I can bracket the empirical question of the relation between education and objective opportunity in a similar way. Instead, I can try to suggest through discursive argument that Lieberson's exclusive focus on the heritage of slavery reflects ideological considerations and a prior commitment to models generated by conflict theory. In turn, Smelser's work can be effectively criticized in terms of logical adequacy or by demonstrating that his early functionalist model over-emphasizes socialization. And Skocpol's argument – without any reference to empirical material – can be negatively evaluated for the implausible manner in which it limits "purposive theories" – which she applauds – to the instrumental model of purposive rationality that her theory implies.

To make such arguments – indeed, merely to engage in the kind of discussion in which I have just engaged – is to engage in discourse, not explanation. As Seidman (1986) has emphasized, discourse does not imply the abandonment of claims to truth. Truth claims, after all, need not be limited to the criterion of testable empirical validity (Habermas 1984). Each level of supra-empirical discourse has embedded within it distinctive criteria of truth. These criteria go beyond empirical adequacy to claims about the nature and consequences of presuppositions, the stipulation and adequacy of models, the consequences of ideologies, the meta-implications of models, and the connotations of definitions. Insofar as they become explicit, they are efforts, in short, to rationalize and systematize the intuitively grasped complexities of social analysis and social life. Current disputes between interpretative and causal methodologies, utilitarian and normative conceptions of action, equilibrium and conflict models of societies, radical and conservative theories of change – these are far more than empirical arguments. They reflect efforts by sociologists to articulate criteria for evaluating the "truth" of different non-empirical domains.

It is no wonder that the discipline's response to important works bears so little resemblance to the neat and confined responses that advocates of the "logic of science" suggest. Skocpol's *States and Social Revolutions*, for example, has been evaluated at every level of the sociological continuum. The book's presuppositions, ideology, model, method, definitions, concepts and, yes, even its facts have been clarified, disputed, and praised in turn. At stake are the truth criteria Skocpol has employed to justify her positions at each of these levels. Very little of the disciplinary response to this work has involved controlled testing of its hypotheses or the reanalysis of its data. Decisions about the validity of Skocpol's structural approach to revolution certainly *will* not be decided on these grounds.[6]

When I began this section, I suggested that the proportion of classics to contemporaries is so much greater in social than natural science because endemic disagreement makes the background assumptions of social science more explicit. It is this obvious quality of background assumptions, in turn, that makes discourse so central a quality of social scientific debate. What remains is to explain why this discursive form of argument so often takes a "classical" turn. The existence of generalized, non-empirical debate does not logically imply any privileged position for earlier works. None the less, the very conditions which make discourse so prominent also make the classics central. There are two reasons for this centrality: the functional, and the intellectual or scientific.

Because disagreement is so rife in social science, serious problems of mutual understanding arise. Without some baseline of minimal understanding, however, communication is impossible. For disagreement to be possible in a coherent, ongoing and consistent way, there must be some basis for a cultural relationship. This can exist only if the participants in a disagreement have a fair idea of what one another is talking about.

This is where the classics come in. The functional necessity for classics develops because of the need for integrating the field of theoretical discourse. By integration, I do not mean cooperation and equilibrium but rather the boundary maintenance, or closure, which allows systems to exist (Luhmann 1984). It is this functional demand that explains the formation of disciplinary boundaries which from an intellectual standpoint often seem arbitrary. It is the disciplines of social science, and the schools and traditions of which they are composed, which have classics.

To mutually acknowledge a classic is to have a common point of reference. A classic reduces complexity (cf. Luhmann 1979). It is a symbol which condenses – "stands for" – a range of diverse general commitments. Condensation, it seems to me, has at least four functional advantages.

In the first place, of course, it simplifies, and thereby facilitates, theoretical discussion. It does so by allowing a very small number of works to substitute for – to represent by a stereotyping or standardizing process – the myriad of finely graded formulations which are produced in the course of contingent intellectual life. When we discuss the central issues which affect social science in classical terms, we are sacrificing the ability to embrace this finely graded specificity. We gain, however, something very important. By speaking in terms of the classics, we can be relatively confident that those whom we address will at least know whereof we speak, even if they do not recognize in our discussion their own particular and unique position. It is for this reason that if we wish to make a critical analysis of capitalism we will be more than likely to draw from Marx's work. Similarly, if we wish to evaluate the variety of critical analyses of capitalism which exist today, we will probably typify them by comparing them to Marx's original. Only by so doing can we be relatively confident that others will be able to follow, and perhaps be persuaded by, our ideological and cognitive judgments.

The second functional advantage is that classics allow generalized commitments to be argued without the necessity for making the criteria for their adjudication explicit. Since such criteria are very difficult to formulate, and virtually impossible to gain agreement upon, this concretizing function of the classics is very important. Rather than having to define equilibrium and the nature of systems, one can argue about Parsons, about the relative "functionality" of his early and later works, about whether his theory (whatever that may be precisely) can actually explain conflict in the real world. Or, rather than explicitly exploring the advantages of an affective or normative perspective on human action, one can argue that such a perspective was, in fact, actually taken by Durkheim's most important works.

The third functional advantage is an ironic one. Because a common classical medium of communication is taken for granted, it becomes possible not to acknowledge the existence of generalized discourse at all. Thus, because the importance of the classics is accepted without argument, it is possible for a social scientist to begin an empirical study – in, for example, industrial sociology – by discussing the treatment of labor in Marx's early writings. While it would be quite illegitimate for him to suggest that non-empirical considerations about human nature, let alone utopian speculations about human possibility, form the baseline for industrial sociology, this is precisely what he has implicitly acknowledged by referring to Marx's work.

Finally, because the condensation provided by the classics gives them such privileged power, reference to the classics becomes important for purely strategic and instrumental reasons. It is in the immediate self-interest of every ambitious social scientist and every rising school to be legitimated *vis-à-vis* the classical founders. Even if no genuine concern for the classics exists they still must be criticized, re-read, or rediscovered if the discipline's normative criteria for evaluation are to be challenged anew.

These are the functional, or extrinsic, reasons for the privileged status accorded by social science to a small and select number of earlier works. But there are, I believe, intrinsic, genuinely intellectual, reasons as well. By intellectual, I mean that certain works are given a classical position because they make a singular and continuing contribution to the science of society. My argument here begins from the proposition that the more generalized a scientific discussion, the less cumulative it can be. Why? Because, while generalized commitments are subject to truth criteria, it is impossible to anchor these criteria in an unequivocal way. Generalized evaluations are sustained less by qualities in the object world – upon which minimum agreement can often be reached – than by the relative tastes and preferences of a particular cultural community. Generalized discourse, then, relies on qualities of personal sensibility – aesthetic, interpretative, philosophical, observational – which are not progressive. In this sense, variations in social science reflect not linear accumulation – an issue which can be calculated temporally – but the essentially random distribution of human ability. Producing great social science is a gift which, like the capacity for creating great art (cf. Nisbet 1976), varies trans-historically between different societies and different human beings.[7]

Dilthey wrote that "life as a starting-point and abiding context provides the first basic feature of the structure of the human studies; for they rest on experience, understanding and knowledge of life" (1976: 183). Social science, in other words, cannot simply be learned by imitating an empirical problem-solution. Because its object is life, it depends on the scientist's own ability to understand life. It depends on idiosyncratic abilities to experience, to understand and to know. There are, it seems to me, at least three different ways in which such personal knowledge distinguishes itself.

(1) *Through the interpretation of states of mind.* Any generalization about the structure or causes of a social phenomenon, an institution, religious movement, or political event, depends upon some conception of the motives involved. To understand motives accurately, however, requires highly developed capacities for empathy, insight, and interpretation. All other things being equal, the works of social scientists who manifest such capacities to the highest degree become classics to which those with more mundane capacities must refer for insight into the subjective inclinations of humankind. The strength of Durkheim's later "religious sociology" depends, to an important degree, on his remarkable ability to intuit the cultural meaning and psychological import of ritual behavior among the Australian Aborigines. Similarly, it is not Goffman's inheritance of interactionist theory or his empirical methods which has made his theorizing so paradigmatic for the micro-analysis of social behavior; it is his extraordinary sensitivity about the nuances of human behavior. Few contemporaries will ever be able to achieve Goffman's level of insight. His works are classical because one must return to them in order to experience and to understand just what the nature of interactional motivation really is.

(2) *Through the reconstruction of the empirical world.* Because disagreement on background issues makes even the objective empirical referents of social science open to doubt, the complexity of the object world cannot here be reduced via the matrix of consensual disciplinary controls. Hence the social scientist's singular capacity for selection and reconstruction becomes correspondingly important. Here, once again, one finds the same kind of creative and idiosyncratic capacity for representation typically associated with art. As Dawe writes about the classics, "through the creative power of their thought . . . they reveal the historical and human continuity which makes their experience representative of ours" (1978: 366).

It is not only insightfulness but that evanescent thing, "quality of mind," upon which the capacity for representation depends. Thus, contemporaries may be able to list the ideal-typical qualities of urban life, but few will be able to understand or represent anonymity and its implications with the richness or vivacity of Simmel himself. Has any Marxist since Marx been able to produce an economic–political history with the subtlety, complexity, and apparent conceptual integration of *The Eighteenth Brumaire of Louis Bonaparte*? Indeed, has any social scientist been able to communicate the nature of "commodities" as well as Marx himself in the first chapter of *Capital*? How many contemporary analyses of feudal society approach the complex and systematic account of economic, religious, and political interrelations which Weber produces in the chapters on patrimonialism and feudalism in *Economy and Society*? This is not to say that in significant respects our knowledge of these phenomena has not surpassed Marx's and Durkheim's own. It is to say, however, that in certain critical respects our knowledge has not. Indeed, the particular ideas I have just cited were so unusual that they simply could not be understood – much less critically evaluated or incorporated – by Marx's and Weber's contemporaries. It has taken generations to recapture, piecemeal, the structure of these arguments, with their intended and unintended implications. This, of course, is exactly what may be said for the most important aesthetic works.

(3)　*Through the formulation of moral and ideological evaluations.* The more general a social scientific statement, the more it must provide compelling self-reflection on the meaning of social life This is its ideological function in the broadest sense of that term. Even if such an ideological reference were undesirable – which in my view it is not – it would not be possible to cleanse even the most scrupulous of social scientific practice of its effects. Effective ideology, moreover (Geertz 1964), depends not only on a finely tuned social sensibility but on an aesthetic ability to condense and articulate "ideological reality" through appropriate rhetorical tropes. Ideological statements, in other words, can assume a classical status as well. The soulless character of rationalized modernity is not just reflected in Weber's concluding pages of *The Protestant Ethic*; it is created by it. To understand rationalized modernity, one cannot merely observe it: one must return to Weber's early work in order to appreciate and experience it once again. Similarly, what is oppressive and suffocating about modernity may never be quite so firmly established as in Marcuse's *One Dimensional Man*.

These functional and intellectual considerations make the classics – not just generalized discourse *per se* – central to the practice of social science. It is because of these considerations that earlier works are accorded a privileged status, that they are so venerated that the meaning attributed to them is often considered equivalent to contemporary scientific knowledge itself. Discourse about a work so privileged becomes a legitimate form of rational scientific dispute; investigation into the "new meaning" of such texts becomes a legitimate way to point scientific work in a new direction. Which is to say that once a work is "classicized," its interpretation becomes a key to scientific argument. Indeed, because classics are central to social science, interpretation must be considered as one major form of theoretical argument.

Merton was quite right to suggest that social scientists tend to merge the history and systematics of sociological theory. He was also thoroughly justified in attributing this merging to "efforts to straddle scientific and humanistic orientations" (Merton 1968: 29). He was wrong, however, to suggest that the merging, or the straddling which produced it, are pathological. In this sense Merton has not himself been empirical enough. From the beginning of the systematic study of society in ancient Greece, merging and straddling have been endemic to the practice of social science. To read this situation as abnormal reflects unjustified speculative preconceptions, not the empirical facts.

The first unjustified preconception is that social science is a youthful and immature enterprise in comparison to natural science, with the implication that, as it matures, it will grow increasingly to resemble the sciences of nature. I have argued, to the contrary, that there are endemic, irrepressible reasons for the divergence between natural and social science; moreover, the "maturity" of the latter, it seems to me, has been firmly set for quite a long time. The second preconception is that social science – again, supposedly like its natural science counterpart – is a purely empirical discipline which can shed its discursive and generalized form. I have argued, however, that there is nothing to suggest that such a pristine condition will ever be achieved. Indeed, I have suggested that the science of nature upon which such hopes are modeled can itself never be separated from (usually camouflaged) commitments of an equally generalized kind.

Merton complains that "almost all sociologists see themselves as qualified to teach and to write the history of sociological theory – after all they are acquainted with the classical writings of an earlier day" (1968: 2). This, it seems to me, is all to the good. If sociologists did not see themselves as qualified in this way, it would not be merely a "vulgarized" history of sociology which would be eliminated, but the very practice of sociology itself!"[8]

Notes

1 The distinction I am employing between natural and social science obviously can have only an ideal–typical status. My purpose is to articulate general conditions, not to explain particular disciplinary situations. At the general level, it is certainly fair to say that the conditions for and against having classics broadly correspond with the division between the sciences of nature and the sciences concerned with the actions of human beings. Specific analysis of any particular discipline would require specifying the general conditions in each case. Thus, natural science is typically broken down into the physical and the life sciences. The latter are less subject to mathematization, less consensual, and more often subject to explicit extra-empirical dispute. In some instances this can extend to the point where debate over the classics has a continuing scientific role, as in the dispute over Darwin taking place in evolutionary biology. In the human studies, too, disciplines differ in the degree to which they typically manifest the conditions I will describe. In the United States, for example, economics is less bound to classics than sociology and anthropology, and the relation of history to classics seems constantly in flux. The variation in these empirical cases can be explained in terms of the theoretical conditions I lay out below.

2 Mannheim puts this distinction well: "No one denies the possibility of empirical research nor does anyone maintain that facts do not exist . . . We, too, appeal to 'facts' for our proof, but the question of the nature of facts is in itself a considerable problem. They exist for the mind always in an intellectual and social context. That they can be understood and formulated implies already the existence of a conceptual apparatus. And if this conceptual apparatus is the same for all the members of a group the presuppositions (that is, the possible social and intellectual values), which underlie the individual concepts, never become perceptible . . . However, once the unanimity is broken, the fixed categories which used to give experience its reliable and coherent character undergo an inevitable disintegration. There arise divergent and conflicting modes of thought which (unknown to the thinking subject) order the same facts of experience into different systems of thought, and cause them to be perceived through different logical categories" (Mannheim 1936: 102–3).

3 This pejorative characterization of metatheory as hero worship recalls Merton's claim of "uncritical reverence" (1968: 30) toward the classics. Obsequiousness, of course, is the obverse of scientific scepticism, and it is ultimately in order to deny a scientific role to classical investigations that such negative claims are made. It seems clear, to the contrary, that what I earlier called historical systematics consists of the critical reconstruction of classical theories. Ironically, empiricists like Turner and Merton are able to gain some legitimacy for their accusations because such reconstruction does, in fact, often occur within a framework which explicitly denies any critical ambition.

4 It demonstrates Smesler's conscientiousness as a historical researcher that he

himself presented data that, as it were, went beyond his own theory (in this regard, see Walby 1986). This is not usually the case, for the overdetermination of data by theory usually makes countervailing data invisible, not only to social scientists themselves but often to their critics.

5 Sewell (1985) has forcefully demonstrated this gap in Skocpol's data for the French case.

6 In this section I have illustrated the overdetermination of social science by theory, and its underdetermination by fact, by discussing single important works. It could also be illustrated by examining specific "empirical" subfields. In social science, even the most narrowly defined empirical subfields are subject to tremendous discursive argument. Discussion at a national conference on the state of disaster research (Symposium on Social Structure and Disaster: Conception and Measurement, College of William and Mary, Williamsburg, Virginia, May 1986), for example, revealed that even in this very concrete field there is vast disagreement simply about the empirical object of study. "What is a disaster?" is disputed and argued about by the field's leading researchers. Some argue for a criterion related to objective and calculable facts but disagree over whether these costs should be related to the geographical expanse of the event, the numbers of people involved, or the financial costs of rebuilding. Others argue for criteria that are more subjective but disagree over whether it is the larger society's consensus that a social problem has occurred that is decisive or the perceptions of the victims themselves. Given the extent of such conflict over the simple empirical referent of the field, it is not surprising that sharp discursive disputes rage about every level of the scientific continuum. There are presuppositional disagreements on individual versus social levels of analysis and about economizing versus interpreting actors; there are ideological struggles over whether disaster research should be governed by broad responsibilities to the community or by narrower professional concerns; there are many disputes over definitions, for example, what is an "organization"?, and over the very value of exercises in definition and taxonomies. For a good summary of these disputes see Drabek 1986 and forthcoming.

7 It is idiosyncrasy in the capacity for creativity, of course, that is the usual reason cited for the centrality of classics in the arts. In his writing on the formation of canonical literary works, however, Kermode (1985) has shown that this view attributes too much to accurate information about a work and too little to uninformed group opinion and "irrational" value commitments. The artistic eminence of Botticelli, for example, was re-established in late nineteenth-century circles on grounds that have since turned out to be highly spurious. His defenders used arguments whose vagueness and indirection could not, in themselves, have justified his art on aesthetic grounds. In this sense, Kermode introduces functional reasons for canonical works. Indeed, he concludes that "it is hard to see how the normal operation of learned institutions . . . can manage without them" (1985: 78). At the same time, Kermode insists that some intrinsic dimension for canonization remains. Thus, while he acknowledges that "all interpretations are erroneous," he argues that "some, in relation to their ultimate purpose, are good

nevertheless" (1985: 91). Why? "Good enough interpretation is what encourages or enables certain necessary forms of attention. What matters . . . is that ways of inducing such forms of attention should continue to exist, even if they are all, in the end, dependent on opinion."

8 I should also acknowledge that there are significant ambiguities in Merton's essay which make it possible to construe his argument in significantly different ways. (I have found this to be true of his work on middle-range theory as well: see Alexander 1982: 11–14.) For example, on the penultimate page of his essay, Merton (1968: 37) suggests the following systematic "function for the classics": "changes in current sociological knowledge, problems, and foci of attention enable us to find new ideas in a work we had read before." He acknowledges, moreover, that these changes could stem from "recent developments in our own intellectual life." This could well be read as endorsing just the kind of systematic need for presentist references to the classics (that is, for historical systematics) against which the main part of Merton's essay was written. For this reason, perhaps, Merton immediately qualifies this suggestion with a new version of his empiricist, accumulationist argument. It is because "each new generation accumulates its own repertoire of knowledge" that "it comes to see much that is 'new' in earlier works."

3

Lego Quia Inutile: An Alternative Justification for the Classics

Gianfranco Poggi

First, my title. "*Lego quia inutile*" is a Latin sentence I made up to say, *à propos* of the classics, "I read them because they are useless." I patterned it after an ancient saying, *Credo quia absurdum*, meaning "I believe it because it is absurd." A source for this saying familiar to most sociologists is a passage in Weber's "Science as a vocation," which refers it (in a longer version, *credo non quod, sed quia absurdum est* − "I do not believe what is absurd, but believe it because it is absurd") to St Augustine. Augustine, apparently, thought he was quoting it from an earlier church Father, Tertullian − except that the wording cannot be found in the writings by Tertullian known to us. (Professor Hans Joas, of the Free University of Berlin, has mentioned to me an alternative source − Isidor of Seville.)

But back to my title, and my "alternative justification for the classics." This is possibly best captured by another saying I had on my mind while considering what to contribute to this volume. On an occasion whose precise time and place unfortunately I cannot presently recall, a famous mathematician, at the end of a banquet with his peers, raised his glass and proposed a toast "to Mathematics − and may it never be of any use to anybody!"

Essentially, I am saying that "the classics" deserve to preserve the place they have acquired in the standard curriculum for sociology majors and graduates whether or not they make a distinctive, substantial contribution to their *training as sociologists*. They are entitled to that place because they can uniquely contribute, additionally (or: alternatively) to their *intellectual education* − and that is justification enough. The classics matter, in this view, simply because their writings are (by definition) the best stuff the discipline of sociology has produced in the course of its history. We owe it to our students, and to ourselves, to establish as direct as possible a contact with those writings, primarily because of their unique intellectual texture and of the magnitude of their scholarly achievement.

Let me confess that this is to some extent a tongue-in-cheek position, or perhaps a fall-back one, one (that is) I would adopt *in extremis*, if I failed to articulate to a relevant audience any other, more tough-minded, more instrumental, justification for the classics. For such a justification, I might refer the reader, in particular, to Jeffrey Alexander's discussion which appears in the previous chapter. I still recollect the sense of admiration and of envy ("Why did I not think of this?") with which I read Alexander's argument, and how I found myself agreeing with most of it. Yet, even assuming away such an argument for the classics (or any other one emphasizing their contemporary "uses"), I would maintain that their place in the sociology curriculum should remain uncontested. Come to think of it I am not *really* saying that the classics should be read because they are useless – what, indeed, would be the use of *that*? What I am implying in fact, as Hans Joas has suggested to me, is a distinction between two types of usefulness which can be attributed to bodies of knowledge: a more instrumental one, intended to equip those who acquire it to perform further cognitive roles, and one more oriented to the shaping and broadening of awareness and perhaps of wisdom through the appreciation and critique of intellectual legacies.

But let me play devil's advocate here, and join Homans for a moment in objecting testily, "who *cares* what old Durkheim said?" It appears in fact unlikely that the classics have much to contribute to the contemporary advance of sociology. At bottom, as I sometimes tell my students, the classics, and perhaps the whole "sociological tradition," constitute an episode in Western intellectual history, characterized by the intensity and the creativity with which a small number of gifted authors grappled with the following problem: what *really* happened in Europe between 1750 and 1850?

If this is a tenable view of the original intellectual task of the classics, then one may well doubt that the contemporary sociological enterprise can find in them more than the last remnants of a largely exhausted legacy, or at best an inspiring but substantively irrelevant exemplar of past achievements. Nearly one century and a half since 1850, how much can we realistically expect to gain, in dealing with our own circumstances, by delving into that legacy or worshipfully revisiting that exemplar?

Already by the middle of our own century sociologists and other social commentators had begun to suggest the exhaustion of that legacy, or at any rate the necessity of transcending it. Recall, from the 1960s, the notions of "late capitalism" or of "neo-capitalism;" or, from the decades that followed, the various "post-" formulas: post-industrial, post-modern, post-history. In each case the argument implicitly or explicitly conveyed by those formulations was that the sociology classics were becoming ever more irrelevant. Or consider to what extent contemporary social life, especially but not exclusively in the West, is shaped by experiences of which for example Max Weber, the last of the universally acknowledged sociology classics to die, had no (or little) inkling. Consider, say, the demographic explosion; or computers; or mass consumerism; or fordism; or the welfare state; or nuclear power and nuclear weapons; or the decline of colonial empires; or the electronic media. How likely does it seem, to anybody however minimally familiar with Mannheim's notion of the *Seinsverbundenheit des Wissens*, of the bond that *being* lays upon *knowing*, that re-reading Weber and his contemporaries, let alone his predecessors, would make a positive, useful difference to our own intellectual dealings with such phenomena?

One might counter that, in point of fact, a number of conceptual legacies and empirical insights from the classics are still being put to good use in contemporary sociological work. To give just two examples on a different scale, Ritzer's 1993 book on *The Mcdonaldization of Society* derives much conceptual and empirical inspiration from Weber himself; and many contemporary revisitations of the problem of social change still draw, in however modified and qualified a way, on the Spencer/Durkheim differentiation model. Luhmann's conceptualization of modernity, in particular, does so to a large extent; and although he continues to object to the exegetical approach to theory-construction, Durkheim is in fact one of the few authors whom he has expressly treated not just as a resource but as a topic, in his preface to the belated German translation of *Division of Labor in Society*.

In my view, however, even if one could not refute Homans' contemptuous "who cares?" along these lines, a frankly non-instrumental recourse to the classics, at any rate in the context of *teaching sociology* (at both undergraduate and graduate level) would still justify itself as giving students (and, by the same token, instructors) an opportunity to contemplate the classics' intellectual achievement and to learn from them. Even if the historical developments characterizing, again, "Europe 1750–1850" are now very remote, in dealing with them the classics performed such heroic scholarly and imaginative efforts that reading them remains a uniquely rewarding, "learn-ful" experience, albeit in the context of a vastly different world, making sense of which requires resources which the classics cannot be realistically expected to supply.

Rather than rhapsodizing on the classics' distinctive qualities (I have tried to specify them in the preface to an old book of mine, dealing with Tocqueville, Marx, and Durkheim) I would like to recount two experiences, many years apart, which lie behind my "non-instrumental" advocacy of the classics.

The first experience goes back to my earliest contacts with sociology as a graduate student at Berkeley. For quite a few semesters, I remember, I was bothered by the contrast between two impressions. On the one hand, I was developing a neophyte's enthusiasm for the subject, a keen sense of its relevance, a rewarding awareness of the scope and significance of its themes. On the other hand, it seemed to me that most of the reading I was doing (practically all of it from contemporary American sociology) did not display much intellectual muscle. There was something shallow and meager about its texture; the stuff was interesting, but very little of it displayed outstanding qualities of sophistication, excited me with its vigor and rigor.

It was the contrast between what I had studied for my first degree and what I was studying as a graduate student of sociology that called forth both my positive and my negative response to the latter experience. In my country, Italy, I had studied law – a very common subject for Italian university students of my generation (before, and since), not necessarily meant to prepare those graduating in it for the legal professions (although indispensable for entering them). I had been quite keen on most of the law courses I had taken, and had been a good student overall; but much in the content of my legal studies could not compete with sociology in terms of the intrinsic interest and the relevance of its contents. On the other hand, there was little doubt about the intellectual quality of the books we were made to read, and (more widely) of the continental tradition of juristic scholarship of which those books were part and in which we, as law students, were being initiated.

That "reading law" engages even undergraduate students in Italy (and in other continental countries) in a highly sophisticated, rigorous universe of discourse is not surprising, considering that the discourse in question had begun to develop over two thousand years ago in the Roman republic. Since that time juristic scholarship had been cultivated for generations (not without interruptions, the longest corresponding of course with "the dark ages") by some of the greatest talents in the history of Western intellectual culture. These had developed a rigorous form of distinctive juridical analysis, and self-consciously used it in rendering the content of a huge and diverse body of sources (Roman, Byzantine, ecclesiastical) into a comprehensive system of concepts. The point of their exercise was to construe the most diverse social phenomena (from commercial transactions to acts of liberality to crimes) according to a sophisticated form of literate reasoning, which addressed all and only the juridical aspects of those phenomena and sought to yield consistent, calculable resolutions of all related controversies.

Note that the social relevance of the discourse in question, as I began to familiarize myself with it in mid-twentieth-century Italy, was often minimal or non-existent – among other reasons because we had to take three-year long courses in Roman law, a body of rules and principles which had ceased to operate as a juridical reality centuries before. Furthermore, much intellectual effort was expended by contemporary jurists, including our teachers, in elucidating minute questions of very little consequence even from a legal standpoint, in splitting conceptual hairs. (French jurists, at the time, used to reproach Italian ones for being *enculeurs de mouches*, that is, for "buggering flies.") But the intellectual quality of that effort was sometimes sublime, the virtuosity of the analysis staggering, the vistas which our reading opened on that century-old tradition of sustained conceptual elaboration breathtaking. As I have suggested, in terms of sheer intellectual muscle, the sociology I was reading as a graduate had nothing to match the law I had read as an undergraduate; the former was, as I said, a damn sight more interesting because of its content, but did not evoke the same awe in contemplating the authors' achievement, the same feeling of accomplishment one derived from being able to understand them, to question them, occasionally to challenge them. In sum, as a sociology student I often felt somewhat intellectually deprived, in that my reading fare generally had a less refined texture than what I had read in law.

(Parenthetically, few things in American academia baffle me as much as what seems to me – as an outsider – the concerted effort by law schools to deprive the teaching and learning of law of the degree and kind of sheer intellectual sophistication I had experienced and enjoyed as an Italian law student. In fact, I have encountered this phenomenon also in Australia, where students apparently take it for granted that although in order to enter law school they must develop and exhibit high-grade intellectual skills and competences, once there they have to set them aside.)

The reader will have guessed what I am driving at. At Berkeley, only when I began to read the classics in a sustained way, which happened after I got past my graduate course work, did I satisfy myself that the price for learning interesting stuff need not be to absorb books of indifferent quality, to associate myself with a tradition of discourse unavoidably less scholarly, less rigorous, less sophisticated than law had been. By reading the classics I could have my cake and eat it too: huge, intellectually and morally exciting themes had been formulated and discussed by utterly superior minds, who had left behind writings of unsurpassed scholarly texture and intellectual substance, which on each reading revealed new dimensions of significance. It is this *frisson* of recognition, this humbling and at the same time heady and invigorating sense of conversing with great minds, that the sociology classics can still evoke in our students – and in ourselves.

If we give them – and ourselves – a chance, of course. And here I must relate the second experience behind my toast to "the classics – and may they never be of any use to anybody!" It has recently dawned on me that it is possible in a good American university (but this may apply also to other English-speaking university systems I am familiar with) for an undergraduate to get a liberal arts degree – say in political science, or in history, or in psychology, or in economics, or even (and this is a more recent, most perplexing development) in English or American literature – without having to read a single book written more than, say, twenty or thirty years ago. I must say that this realization rather upset me when it came upon me; that so far as I am concerned any university or indeed college that does not require its students to read a few books that are at least a century old has utterly failed in one significant aspect of its educational mission.

Be that as it may, it has also dawned on me that, *oddly enough*, if and insofar as its students are made to read the classics, the sociology department may have become one of the very few university departments (you can count them, as they say in England, on the fingers of a badly mutilated hand) whose majors do have to read books (or writings, anyway) which are more than eighty years old. I say "oddly enough" because of course sociology has always suffered from the reputation of being an upstart subject, a naive domestic discipline without any breeding by whose presumption the practitioners of most other, better established academic disciplines refused to be amused – to paraphrase a famous Thurber cartoon.

It seems endearingly odd to me that, if it *does* care what old Durkheim said, sociology, tainted as it is with the relative belatedness of its origins, and suspected of being intellectually meager, and historically shallow, should have become one of the last refuges of a certain form of scholarship, that consisting in reading, discussing, seeking to make sense of, *old books* of (perhaps) no contemporary consequence. By doing this (or rather, *insofar as* it does this) sociology is experiencing, and hopefully inducing in its students, a certain sense of reverent yet critical awareness of the past which I think all higher education should foster. Via the classics, it gives students an opportunity to develop a minimum of hermeneutical skill, a sense for the complexity, the preciousness, the intrinsic "open-endedness" of texts; it teaches them (well or badly) to inquire into the contexts, historical and geographical, of such texts, to identify their frames of reference, to acquaint themselves with their universes of discourse, to capture their sense of what is significant and valid. Furthermore, as Hans Joas has emphasized to me, the Great Books of the sociological tradition all have a significant empirical dimension; or, as Hans Freyer once insisted, sociology is a *Wirklichkeits* – not a *Geisteswissenschaft*.

This means that the hermeneutical engagement with those Great Books does not run the risk of becoming too self-involved and self-sufficient. In any case, if and insofar as the learning experience I am prospecting does take place for our students (and this applies to graduate ones as well) I think that it would be important (and rare) enough to make somewhat irrelevant the question of *what else, if anything* the sociology classics may be good (or bad) for.

My "alternative justification for the classics," besides being grounded in the two experiences above, has two corollaries which I would like to mention.

In the first place, the position I have taken presumably reflects my own skepticism that sociology has much of a chance to justify itself *as a science*. I feel that, rather than pursuing that will-o'-the-wisp, sociology would have done well, long ago, to characterize and justify itself instead as a distinctively modern yet historically aware form of *scholarship* (an expression, incidentally, that we do not use – and question – nearly as frequently as we should). I suspect, indeed, that by failing to do this sociology missed an attractive opportunity some decades back: the opportunity of becoming the intellectual fulcrum of a new form of humane learning, of establishing itself as a viable and attractive core component of a liberal education. As students ceased to learn classical languages in school, as philosophy in the universities either took a linguistic turn or developed an unrequited crush on the natural sciences, sociology could have gained a valid justification for itself by emphasizing its commitment to its own "Greats," by becoming more text-based. Furthermore, instead of either selling its soul to ideology, or deluding itself that it could become the scientific core of a post-ideological, technocratic approach to policy-making, sociology could have purposefully devoted itself to educating its students to "critical citizenship," taught them to observe, comment on, and to take part in, public affairs in an aware, informed, methodologically sound, intellectually sophisticated fashion. Had it done this, sociology might thus have gone upmarket in academia, gained the loyalty of more of the more sophisticated, better educated students, played a more visible and distinctive role in the formation of those going on to graduate study and the professional schools.

A second corollary to my own argument, closely connected with the first, is that our approach to the classics must resist the temptation of becoming fashionable, and associate itself instead, as far as possible, with the assumptions and the practices of, so to put it, pre-post-modern scholarship. In particular, it entails a commitment to the legitimacy of a canon, though that canon's composition may well vary from place to place and from time to time, and in any case should go beyond the usual Marx, Durkheim, Weber trio to include (at least) Tocqueville, Simmel, Pareto, Mead, and possibly

Freud. However, in the context of a given course, the canon adopted should probably select for attention no more than three or four among those authors, since covering more authors would make it very difficult to assign as readings whole books or substantial collections of readings from each author's *oeuvres*; it would compel instructors, instead, to assign unwieldy anthologies composed of a large number of short excerpts from those multiple authors' writings. The format proposed here, instead, emphasizes the fairly close reading by students of a relatively small number of writings, each sizeable in length, by a few authors selected within the canon. One might go as far as did an English Sociology Department years ago, where the required reading for the introductory course consisted exclusively in four books of Durkheim's: *Division of Labor*, *Rules*, *Suicide*, and *Elementary Forms*.

A preference for original texts over secondary writings, incidentally, was forcefully articulated a few years ago by the novelist Italo Calvino, in a piece entitled "Perché leggere i classici." (There is a translation in an American collection entitled *The Uses of Literature*.) The classics Calvino talks about are those of world literature; but much of what he says in the piece, both about what makes a classic and about how to read them, applies fairly straightforwardly to the "Greats" in the social disciplines – including, as I mentioned, an exhortation to read *them* rather than *about them*.

> One cannot recommend enough the direct reading of the texts themselves, leaving aside, as much as possible, secondary literature, comments, interpretations. Schools and universities ought to put it across that no book about a book says more than that book itself, whereas there is a conspiracy to convince the reader of the opposite . . . *A classic is a text which incessantly generates a myriad critical arguments about itself, but goes on shaking them off itself.* (Calvino 1986)

There is a personal corollary to this corollary. I have myself written on "the classics," but, even aside from the suspicion of futility that Calvino's injunction throws upon those writings, I have some misgivings concerning their scholarly significance. They appear, in retrospect, too marred by their "presentism," and they do not adequately represent the strictly text-based, hermeneutically sophisticated, philologically, and historically grounded approach to the classics I have, myself, recommended above.

I shall give one example of this fault. A couple of days before I drafted the outline of the talk on which this paper is based, I found in my mail a batch of reprints of a short essay of mine, a contribution to a symposium on Weber's *Protestant Ethic*. About three years before, when writing that essay, I had sought (I suspect) to at least end memorably an otherwise unmemorable piece, by closing it off with a ringing statement: "'The Protestant Ethic' is dead – long live *Economy and Society*!"

This ending strikes me today as unfortunate, at any rate from the stand-point of philologically correct scholarship. For, as I have since learned, the rigorous, painstaking editorial work on Weber's contribution to the *Grundriss der Sozialoekonomie* currently carried out in the context of the Max Weber *Gesamtausgabe* is doing considerable damage to *Economy and Society* as we know and love it, revealing it to be largely a doubtful product of first Marianne Weber's, then Johannes Winckelmann's editorial piety.

Be that as it may, I shall close *this* piece with a last quote from Calvino: "It should not be thought that the classics are to be read because they are 'useful' for some purpose. The only justification one may give is that to read the classics is better than not to read the classics." Amen.

Part II

Social Theory and Its Present

However we wish to regard the classics, whether as extraordinarily rigorous and important monuments of thought, or as useful common ground for the discipline of sociology, or in some other way, the problem of the relevance of the classics to the present is unavoidable. The circumstances under which Marx, Weber, and Durkheim wrote were obviously very different from the circumstances under which we currently think about society, because the societies they lived in and reflected on were very different from our own. And if the concepts of Weber and Durkheim, such as "Charisma" and the idea of society as collective consciousness enacted through ritual, may well be applicable and useful in analyzing particular events and patterns in current social life, it would be somewhat shocking if their concepts were sufficient to the creation of an adequate understanding of the present. This realization leads to two related kinds of questions about the classics. The first requires us to think about the differences between our circumstances and the circumstances that motivated their thinking. The second requires us to consider what is living and what is dead in their thought and what can be transformed to make it relevant to the present.

These two broad topics are considered in the next two parts. In the first part the question of the relationship between our time and theirs and our circumstances and theirs is considered. The cliché of the day is that we have now entered a period of a kind which is no longer comprehensible in terms of the idea of modernity. We have become "post-modern," meaning that there is no single coherent direction in either the development of our thought or in the direction of politics. As Wallerstein notes in his paper, we can now see the entire period under which the classics wrote as a period dominated by liberalism and by a particular model of human progress. The classics of course were not the authors of this model. They were instead the critics and reflectors upon the way in which the world constituted by this model had developed. If we have indeed come to the end of the fruitfulness of this model, we have perhaps come to the end of the meaningfulness of a discourse which is defined, even negatively, by this model.

To understand Wallerstein's point it is perhaps useful to go back to the famous slogan of August Comte, "order and progress." For Comte, the struggle of the modern age could be encapsulated in the formula "order and progress" because there were at all times two visible political alternatives, which Comte called the party of order and the party of progress. They may not have corresponded perfectly to actual political parties: it is common in American usage to speak of "progressive forces" and the image of progress and reaction is equally potent in European contexts. The problem, of course, is that we now, especially with the collapse of Communism, find it difficult to say who is progressive and who is not. In the United States, the "progressive forces" have ordinarily been identified with the redistribution of income, the regulatory welfare state, and the idea that the true representatives of progress in the electorate were the "oppressed," a group which was traditionally understood to include organized labor.

It now seems just as plausible that today's "progressive forces" are simply a faction of persons whose distinctive economic allegiances result from their dependence and association with the regulatory welfare state, and is largely unconnected to any substantial body of popular opinion or interest other than groups in society which have also been particularly benefited by state redistributive schemes, such as the elderly. Such an argument has in fact been presented by the sociologist of knowledge Peter Berger (1992: 47–62). The progressive forces, on this view, are no more "progressive" than the antebellum Whigs were. Like the Whigs, they were an interest faction with a distinctive culture, but neither the harbinger of a new form of social and political life nor would they long outlive the specific historical circumstances which brought them into temporary dominance. In the United Kingdom, similarly, the Labour party is difficult to cast as an unambiguously progressive force, and in any case the connection between the platform of the party today and its historical origins in the idea of state ownership of the industrial organization are now so tenuous as to raise questions about what Labour can coherently stand for today other than a kind of protest against the damaging effects of world capitalism.

One alternative to the "modern" image of social progress is provided by contemporary politics itself. A great deal of politics is now the politics of identity. The politics of membership in groups which are no longer the primary or exclusive determinants of one's life chances but which can be aligned with more or less at will. The way in which identity politics has characteristically emerged in American politics is in the assertion of rights or demands for specific recognition of distinctive group interests, such as interests in education oriented toward particular group needs and particularly the need for group pride. This kind of identity politics is the theme of Calhoun's paper and the theme of one of the thinkers on which he comments, Charles Taylor, the Quebec political philosopher, who has devoted much of his recent work to the justification of the demand for the preservation of a Quebecois identity.

The very idea that identities require states or political validation is rooted in the liberal Wilsonian ideal of national self-determination but is contrary to the equally Wilsonian political idea that democracy is the form in which all nations can find their fullest and most peaceful realization in a world of peaceful democratic self-determining regimes. The recognition of the destructive side of the doctrine of self-determination is no novelty. In the period between the First and Second World Wars it was the source of enormous mischief in Eastern Europe and continues to be now that the Soviet domination of Eastern European states has ended. But it is in the "developed" world that identities have become the most mobile and the most varied and problematic. Peter Wagner points out that this situation of disordered identities is parallel to the situation at the time Durkheim and Weber wrote, and that some lessons may be drawn from these similarities. If classical social theory was made possible by the fact that in its unique historical moment a novel spectrum of political possibilities was revealed, the same may be true for the present.

4

Three Ideologies or One?
The Pseudo-battle of Modernity

Immanuel Wallerstein

The story-line of modern times, in terms of the history of ideas or of political philosophy, is a familiar one. It can be briefly stated in this way: there emerged during the nineteenth century three great political ideologies – conservatism, liberalism, and socialism. Ever since, the three (in ever-changing guises) have been in constant struggle with each other.

Virtually everyone would agree to two generalizations about these ideological struggles. First, each of these ideologies represents a response to the fact that new collective outlooks had been forged in the wake of the French Revolution, which gave rise to the feeling that specific political strategies were necessary to cope with this new situation. Second, none of the three ideologies has ever been encrusted in one definitive version. Quite the contrary; each has seemed to take on as many forms as there have been ideologists.

No doubt, most people believe that there are some essential differences between these ideologies. But the closer one looks either at the theoretical statements or at the actual political struggles, the more disagreement one finds about exactly what these presumably essential differences are.

There is even disagreement about how many different ideologies there are. There are quite a few theoreticians and quite a few political leaders who have argued that there are in reality only two and not three ideologies, although the pair to which it is possible to reduce the trio is itself debated. That is to say, there are conservatives who have seen no essential difference between liberalism and socialism, socialists who have said the same thing about liberalism and conservatism, and even liberals who have argued that there is no serious distinction between conservatism and socialism.

This is in itself strange, but the story does not stop there. The term, ideology, in its many usages, has never been a word persons or groups have liked to use about themselves. Ideologists have always denied being ideologists. Not, of course, Destutt de Tracy who is said to have invented the word. But Napoleon quickly used the word against him, saying that political realism was to be preferred to ideology (by which he meant a theoretical doctrine), a sentiment shared by quite a few politicians then and since.

A half-century later, in *The German Ideology*, Marx used the word to characterize a worldview that was both partial and self-serving, the view of a class (the bourgeoisie). Ideology, said Marx, was destined to be replaced by science (reflecting the views of the working class, which was the universal class). Mannheim, in the period between the two world wars, went still further. He agreed with Marx about the partial and self-serving nature of ideologies, but added Marxism to the list of such ideologies. He wanted to replace ideologies with utopias, which he saw as the creation of classless intellectuals. And after the Second World War, Daniel Bell expressed the weariness of precisely Mannheim's intellectuals with both ideologies and utopias. When Bell proclaimed the end of ideology, he was thinking primarily of Marxism, which he saw giving way to a sort of gentle, non-ideological liberalism, based on an awareness of the limits of politics.

Thus, for the two centuries of its existence, the concept of ideology has been perceived negatively, as something one had to reject or supersede. But does this allow us to understand what an ideology is, what people have intended to accomplish by means of ideologies? I shall treat this subject via five queries, none of which I shall answer totally, but which represent an attempt to understand the concept of modernity, and its links with the concept of ideology.

1 What is the difference between an ideology and a *Weltanschauung* (or worldview)?
2 Who is the "subject" of an ideology?
3 What is the relation of ideologies to the state(s)?
4 How many different ideologies have there really been?
5 Is it possible to supersede ideology, that is, can one operate without one?

Weltanschauung and Ideology

There is an anecdote, probably apocryphal, about Louis XVI who, upon hearing from the Duc de Liancourt about the storming of the Bastille, is said to have asked "Is it a riot?" "No, Sire, it's a revolution" (Brunot 1937: 617). This is not the place to discuss once again the interpretation of the French

Revolution, except to indicate that one of its principal consequences for the world-system was that it made acceptable for the first time the idea that change, novelty, transformation, even revolution, were "normal," that is, not exceptional, phenomena of the political arena, at least of the modern political arena. What was at first perceived as statistically normal quickly became perceived as morally normal. This is what Labrousse was referring to when he said that Year II was "a decisive turning-point," after which "the Revolution took on a prophetic, annunciatory role, bearing within it an entire ideology that would eventually fully emerge" (1949: 29). Or, as Watson (1973: 45) said: "The Revolution [was] the shadow under which the whole nineteenth century lived." To which I would add, the twentieth century as well. The Revolution marked the apotheosis of seventeenth-century Newtonian science and eighteenth-century concepts of progress; in short, what we have come to call modernity.

Modernity is the combination of a particular social reality and a particular *Weltanschauung* or worldview that has replaced, even buried, another pair which, precisely to indicate how outdated it is, we now designate as the *ancien régime*. No doubt, not everyone reacted in the same way to this new reality and this new worldview. Some welcomed them, some rejected them, others were unsure how to react. But very few were unaware of the degree of change that had occurred. The anecdote about Louis XVI is very telling in this regard.

The way in which people within the capitalist world-economy reacted to this "turning-point" and dealt with the enormous discombobulation resulting from the shock of the French Revolution – the "normalization" of political change, which had now come to be seen as something inevitable, occurring regularly – is an essential component of the cultural history of this world-system. Might it not be useful therefore to think of "ideologies" as one of the ways in which people coped with this new situation? In this sense, an ideology is not itself a *Weltanschauung* but rather one response among others to the coming of this new *Weltanschauung* we call modernity.[1]

It is obvious that the first ideological reaction, an almost immediate one, had to come from those who were most profoundly shocked, even repelled, by modernity, by the cult of change and Progress, by the persistent rejection of whatever was "old." Thus it was that Burke, Maistre, and Bonald invented the ideology we have come to call "conservatism." A great British conservative, Lord Cecil, in a booklet written in 1912 and intended to be a popular statement of the doctrine of conservatism, specifically emphasized the role of the French Revolution in the birth of the ideology. He asserted that there had always existed a sort of "natural conservatism," but that before 1790 there was nothing "resembling a consciously held body of Conservative doctrine" (1912, p. 39). Certainly, in the view of conservatives,

> the French Revolution was but the culmination of the historical process of atomization that reached back to the beginning of such doctrines as nominalism, religious dissent, scientific rationalism, and the destruction of those groups, institutions and intellectual certainties which had been basic in the Middle Ages. (Nisbet 1952: 168–9)

Conservative ideology was thus "reactionary" in the immediate sense that it was a reaction to the coming of modernity, and set itself the objective either (the hard version) of reversing the situation entirely or (the more sophisticated version) of limiting the damage and holding back as long as possible the changes that were coming.

Like all ideologies, conservatism was first and foremost a political program. Conservatives knew full well that they had to hold on to or reconquer state power, that the institutions of the state were the key instrument needed to achieve their goals. When conservative forces returned to power in France in 1815, they baptized this event a "Restoration." But, as we know, things did not really go back to the *status quo ante*. Louis XVIII had to concede a "Charter," and when Charles X tried to install a true reaction, he was ousted from power and in his place was put Louis-Philippe, who assumed the more modern title of "King of the French."[2]

The next stage in the story was the construction of liberalism, which defined itself as the opposite of conservatism, on the basis of what might be called a "consciousness of being modern" (Minogue 1963: 3). Liberalism always situated itself in the center of the political arena, proclaiming itself universalist.[3] Sure of themselves and of the truth of this new worldview of modernity, liberals sought to propagate their views and intrude its logic within all social institutions, thereby ridding the world of the "irrational" leftovers of the past. To do this, they had to fight conservative ideologues whom they saw as obsessed with fear of "free men,"[4] men liberated from the false idols of tradition. In other words liberals believed that progress, even though it was inevitable, could not be achieved without some human effort, without a political program. Liberal ideology was thus the belief that, in order that history follow its natural course, it was necessary to engage in conscious, continual, intelligent reformism, in full awareness that "time was the universal friend, which would inevitably bring greater happiness to ever greater numbers" (Schapiro 1949: 13).

Socialism was the last of the three ideologies to be formulated. Before 1848, one could hardly yet think of it as constituting a distinctive ideology.

The reason was primarily that those who began after 1789 to call themselves "socialists" saw themselves everywhere as the heirs and partisans of the French Revolution, which did not really distinguish them from those who had begun to call themselves "liberals."[5] Even in Great Britain, where the French Revolution was widely denounced and where "liberals" therefore laid claim to a different historical origin, the "radicals" (who were more or less the future "socialists") seemed to be primarily merely somewhat more militant liberals.

In fact, what particularly distinguished socialism from liberalism as a political program and therefore as an ideology was the conviction that the achievement of progress needed a big helping hand, without which it would be a very slow process. The heart of their program, in short, consisted in accelerating the course of history. That is why the word "revolution" appealed to them more than "reform," which seemed to imply merely patient, if conscientious, political activity and was thought to incarnate mostly a wait and see attitude.

In sum, three postures toward modernity and the "normalization" of change had evolved: circumscribe the danger as much as possible; achieve the happiness of mankind as rationally as possible; or accelerate the drive for progress by struggling hard against the forces that were strongly resisting it. It was in the period 1815 to 1848 that the terms conservatism, liberalism, and socialism began to be used to designate these three postures.

Each posture, it should be noted, located itself in opposition to something else. For conservatives, this was the French Revolution. For liberals, it was conservatism (and the *ancien régime* whose revival they were thought to seek). And for socialists, it was liberalism that they were rejecting. It is this fundamentally critical, negative tone in the very definition of the ideologies that explains why there are so many versions of each ideology. Affirmatively, as a positive credo, many varied, even contradictory, propositions were put forward in each camp. The true unity of each ideological family lay only in what they were against. This is no minor detail, since it was this negativity that succeeded in holding together the three camps for 150 years or so, at least until 1968, a date to whose meaning we shall return.

The "Subject" of Ideology

Since ideologies are in fact political programs to deal with modernity, each one needs a "subject," or a principal political actor. In the terminology of the modern world, this has been referred to as the question of sovereignty. The French Revolution asserted a crystal clear position on this matter: against the sovereignty of the absolute monarch, it proclaimed the sovereignty of the "people."

This new language of the sovereignty of the people is one of the great achievements of modernity. Even if for a century thereafter there were lingering battles against it, no one has since been able to dethrone this new idol, the "people." But the victory was hollow. There may have been universal agreement that the people are sovereign, but from the outset there was no agreement on who the "people" are. Furthermore, on this delicate question, none of the three ideologies has had a clear position, which has not stopped them from refusing to admit the murkiness of their respective stances.

The position that seemingly was least equivocal was that of the liberals. For them, the "people" was the sum of all the "individuals" who are each the ultimate holder of political, economic, and cultural rights. The individual is par excellence the historic "subject" of modernity. As it is impossible to review here the vast literature on individualism, I confine myself to noting the three conundrums around which the debate has been waged.

1 All individuals are said to be equal. But can one take such a declaration literally? Obviously not, if one is speaking of the right to make autonomous decisions. No one would dream of authorizing a newborn to take autonomous decisions. But then how old does one have to be to have such a right? The answers have at all times been multiple. But if we agree to leave "children" (however defined) out of the exercise of these rights on the grounds of the immaturity of their judgment, it follows that the autonomous individual is someone who others believe has the capacity to be autonomous. And thereupon, once the possibility of someone else making a judgment as to whether an individual has the capacity to exercise his/her rights, other categories may be designated as incapable: the senile aged, imbeciles, psychotics, imprisoned criminals, members of dangerous classes, the poor, and so forth. This list is quite obviously not a fantasy. I am not here taking a position on whether each of these groups should or should not be eligible say to vote but simply pointing out that there is no self-evident dividing line which separates those who ought to be eligible for the exercise of their rights from those who might legitimately be denied this.

2 Even if we limit the discussion to those persons socially recognized as being "responsible" and therefore legitimately eligible for the full exercise of their rights, it may be that one individual exercising his/her rights may prevent another from doing the same. What are we to think about this possibility? That it represents the inevitable consequence of social life with

which we have to live, or that it involves an assault on the rights of the second person which we must prevent or penalize? A very knotty question which has never received more than a partial and imperfect answer both at the level of political practice and at the level of political philosophy.

3 Even if all individuals who are eligible for the full exercise of rights (the "citizens") never impinge on the rights of other citizens, they still might not all be in agreement about some collective decision. Then what? How can we reconcile the differing positions? This is the great debate concerning political democracy.

One can credit the liberals at least with having debated extensively this question of who this individual is in which sovereignty is located. Conservatives and socialists ought in principle to have been debating this issue as well, since each proposed a "subject" quite different from the individual, but their discussion was far less explicit. If the "subject" is not the individual, who then is it? It is a bit difficult to discern. See for example Edmund Burke in *Reflections on the Revolution in France*:

> The nature of man is intricate; the objects of society are of the greatest possible complexity; and therefore no simple disposition or direction of power can be suitable either to man's nature, or to the quality of his affairs. (cited in White 1950: 28)

If one didn't know that this was a text attacking French revolutionaries, one might have thought it was intended to denounce absolute monarchs. The matter becomes a bit clearer if we look at something Burke stated ten years earlier in his "Speech on Economic Reform": "Individuals pass like shadows, but the Commonwealth is fixed and stable" (cited by Lukes 1973: 3).

Bonald's approach is quite different, because he insists on the crucial role of the church. His view shares however one element common to all the varieties of conservative ideology – the importance they confer on social groups, such as the family, corporations, the church, the traditional "orders" – which become for them the "subjects" that have the right to act politically. In other words, conservatives gave priority to all those groups that might be considered "traditional" (and thus incarnating continuity) but rejected identifying conservatism with any "totality" as a political actor. What has never in fact been clear in conservative thought is how one can decide which are the groups that incarnate continuity. After all, there have always been arguments around contending royal lineages.[6]

For Bonald, the great error of Rousseau and Montesquieu had been precisely to "imagine . . . a pure state of nature antecedent to society." Quite the contrary, "the true nature of society . . . is what society, public society, is at present" ([1802] 1988: 87). But this definition was a trap for its author, because it so legitimated the present that it virtually forbade a "restoration." But precise logic has never been the forte or main interest of conservative polemics. Rather, they were concerned to issue warnings about the likely behavior of a majority constituted by adding up individual votes. Their historical subject was a far less active one than that of the liberals. In their eyes, good decisions are taken slowly and rarely, and such decisions have largely already been taken.

If conservatives refused to give priority to the individual as historical subject in favor of small, so-called traditional groups, socialists refused it in favor of that large group which is the whole of the people. Analyzing socialist thought in its early period, G. D. H. Cole remarked:

> The "socialists" were those who, in opposition to the prevailing stress on the claims of the individual, emphasised the social element in human relations and sought to bring the social question to the front in the great debate about the rights of man let loose on the world by the French Revolution and by the accompanying revolution in the economic field. (1953: 2)

But if it is difficult to know which individuals constitute the problem, and even more difficult to which of what "groups" the people is constituted, the most difficult thing of all is to know how to define the general will of the whole people. How could one know what it is? And to begin with, whose views should we take into account – those of the citizens, those of the persons resident in the country? Why limit the people in this way? Why not take into account the views of all humanity? By what logic can a restriction be justified? What is the relationship in actual practice between the general will and the will of all? In this set of knotty questions we find the source of all the difficulties encountered by socialist movements once they came to power.

In short, what the three ideologies offered us was not a response to the question who is the appropriate historical subject, but simply three starting-points in the quest for who incarnates the sovereignty of the people: the so-called free individual, for the liberals; the so-called traditional groups, for the conservatives; the entire membership of "society," for the socialists.

The Ideologies and the State

The people as "subject" has as its primary "object" the state. It is within the state that the people exercises its will, that it is sovereign. Since the nineteenth century, however, we have also been told that the people form a "society." How might we reconcile state and society, which form the great intellectual antinomy of modernity?

The most astonishing thing is that when we look at the discourses of the three ideologies in this regard, they all seem to take the side of society against the state. Their arguments are familiar. For staunch liberals, it was crucial to keep the state out of economic life and to reduce its role in general to a minimum: "*Laissez-faire* is the nightwatchman doctrine of state" (Watson 1973: 68). For conservatives the terrifying aspect of the French Revolution was not only its individualism but also, and particularly, its statism. The state only becomes tyrannical when it questions the role of the intermediate groups who command the primary loyalty of people – the family, the Church, the corporation.[7] And we are familiar with the famous characterization by Marx and Engels in the *Communist Manifesto*:

> [T]he bourgeoisie has at last, since the establishment of modern industry and of the world market, conquered for itself, in the modern representative state, exclusive political sway. The executive of the modern state is but a committee for managing the common affairs of the whole bourgeoisie. ([1848] 1973: 69)

These negative views of the state did not stop each of the three ideologies from complaining that this state which was the object of their critique was out of their control and said to be in the hands of their ideological opponents. In point of fact, each of the three ideologies turned out to be in great need of the services of the state to promote its own program. Let us not forget that an ideology is first and foremost a political strategy. Socialists have long been under attack for what has been said to be their incoherence in that most of them, despite their anti-statist rhetoric, have always striven in the short run to increase state activity. Anarchism has always been a very minority viewpoint among socialists.

But surely conservatives were more seriously anti-statist? Haven't they been regularly opposed to achieving reforms by state action? Not at all, in reality. For we must take into account the question of the "decline of values" which conservatives have seen as one of the central consequences of modernity. To struggle against the current decadence of society, to restore society as it was before, they have needed the state. What has been said of one of the great English conservatives of the 1840s, Sir Robert Peel – "he believed that a constitution issuing in a strong executive was essential to the anarchic age in which he lived" (Gash 1951: 52) – in fact applies more generally.

Note the way in which Halévy explains the evolution of the conservative position *vis-à-vis* the state during the "Tory reaction" in England at the beginning of the nineteenth century:

> In 1688 and in the years following, the King regarded himself, and was regarded by public opinion, as the Sovereign. It was always to be feared that he would make his sovereignty absolute, and the independence of his authority enjoyed by all the powers of the State constituted a deliberate limitation of the prerogative, a system of constitutional guarantees against royal despotism. At the opening of the nineteenth century it was the people who in America, in France, in England even, had asserted, or were about to assert, the claim to be supreme; it was therefore against the people that the three powers now maintained their independence. It was no longer the Whigs, it was the Tories who supported institutions whose significance had changed, while their form remained the same. And now the King presided over the league formed by the three powers for the defence of their autonomy against the new claimant for sovereignty. (1949: 42–3)

The analysis is limpid. Conservatives were always ready to strengthen the state structure to the degree necessary to control popular forces pushing for change. This was in fact implicit in what was stated by Lord Cecil in 1912: "[A]s long as State action does not involve what is unjust or oppressive, it cannot be said that the principles of Conservatism are hostile to it" (1912: 192).

Well, at least the liberals, champions of individual freedom and of the free market remained hostile to the state? Not at all! From the outset, liberals were caught in a fundamental contradiction. As defenders of the individual and his rights *vis-à-vis* the state, they were pushed in the direction of universal suffrage, the only guarantee of a democratic state. But thereupon, the state became the principal agent of all reforms intended to liberate the individual from the social constraints inherited from the past. This in turn led them to the idea of putting positive law at the service of utilitarian objectives. Once again, Halévy pointed clearly to the consequences:

> The "utilitarian" philosophy was not solely, nor even perhaps fundamentally, a liberal system; it was at the same time a doctrine of authority which looked to the deliberate and in a sense scientific interference of Government to produce a harmony of interests. As his ideas developed, Bentham, who as a young man had been an advocate of "enlightened despotism," was converted to democracy. But he had reached that position by what we may call a long jump, which carried him at a bound over a number of political doctrines at which he might have been expected to halt – aristocracy, a mixed constitution, the

balance of powers, and the doctrine that the stateman's aim should be to free the individual by weakening the authority of the Government and as far as possible dividing its powers. In Bentham's view, when the authority of the state had been reconciled by a universal or at least a very wide suffrage with the interests of the majority there was no further reason to hold it suspect, it became an unmixed blessing.

And thereupon, the Conservatives were now the upholders of the genuine Liberal tradition, the old system of aristocratic self-government with its un-paid officials against a new system of bureaucratic despotism administered by salaried officials. (1950: 100, 99)

You may think that Benthamism was in fact a deviation from liberalism, whose optimal expression is to be found rather in the classical economists, the theoreticians of *"laissez-faire."* Let us then remember that when the first Factory Acts were passed in Great Britain, all the leading classical economists of the time supported the legislation, a phenomenon spelled out (and ap-proved) by none other than Alfred Marshall (1921: 763–4). Since that time, the great bureaucratic state has never stopped growing, and its expansion has been sponsored by successive liberal governments. When Hobhouse wrote his book on liberalism as an answer to that of Lord Cecil on conservatism, he justified this expansion in this way: "The function of State coercion is to overcome individual coercion, and, of course, coercion exercised by any associa-tion of individuals within the State" (1911: 146).

No doubt the justifications each ideology invoked to explain its somewhat embarrassing statism were different. For socialists, the state was implement-ing the general will. For conservatives, the state was protecting traditional rights against the general will. For liberals, the state was creating the condi-tions permitting individual rights to flourish. But in each case, the bottom line was that the state was being strengthened in relation to society, whilst the rhetoric called for doing exactly the opposite.

How Many Ideologies?

All this muddle and intellectual confusion involved in the theme of the proper relation of state and society permits us to understand why it is that we have never been entirely sure how many distinct ideologies came into existence in the nineteenth century. Three? Two? Only one? I have just reviewed the traditional arguments that there were three. Let us now look at how one can reduce the three to two.

In the period from the French Revolution to the revolutions of 1848, it seems clear that for contemporaries the "only clear cleavage" was between those who accepted progress as inevitable and desirable, and thus "were globally favorable" to the French Revolution and, on the other hand, the Counter-Revolution which took its stand against this disruption of values, considering it as profoundly wrong (Agulhon 1992: 7). Thus the political struggle was between liberals and conservatives, and those who called themselves radicals or Jacobins or republicans or socialists were regarded as simply a more militant variety of liberals. In *The Village Cure*, Balzac has a bishop exclaim:

> We are compelled to perform miracles in a manufactory town where the spirit of sedition against religious and monarchical doctrines has put forth deep roots, where the idea of close scrutiny, born of Protestantism and today known as Liberalism, with liberty to adopt another name tomorrow, extends to everything. (1898: 103)

Tudesq reminds us that in 1840 a Legitimist newspaper, *l'Orléanais*, denounced another newspaper, *Le Journal de Loiret*, as a "liberal, Protestant, Saint-Simonian, Lamennaisian paper" (1964: 125–6). This was not completely wild since, as Simon notes: "The Idea of Progress, in fact, constituted the core and central inspiration of Saint-Simon's entire philosophy of thought" (1956: 330; cf. Manning 1976: 83–4).

Furthermore, this liberal–socialist alliance has roots in liberal and egalitarian thought of the eighteenth century, in the struggle against absolute monarchy (see Meyssonier 1989: 137–56). It continued to be nourished in the nineteenth century by the ever-increasing interest of both ideologies in productivity, which each saw as the basic requirement for a social policy in the modern state.[8]

With the rise of utilitarianism, it might have seemed that the alliance might become a marriage. The conservatives did not fail to argue this:

> When the Tories wished to discredit Utilitarianism, they denounced it as an unpatriotic philosophy, inspired by foreign ideas, and especially by French ideas. Were not the political principles of the Benthamites the democratic principles of the Jacobins? Did they not derive their ethics and their jurisprudence from Helvétius and Beccaria, their psychology from Condillac, their philosophy of history and their political economy from Condorcet and Jean Baptiste Say? Were they not irreligious Voltairians? Had not Bentham composed in French and published at Paris his *Traités de Législation*? But the Utilitarians could reply with truth that all these so-called French ideas, of

whose importation they were accused, were in reality English ideas which had found a temporary home abroad. (Brebner 1948: 583)

Once again, the conservative view was not incorrect. Brebner speaks with sympathy of the "collectivist" side of Bentham, concluding "What were the Fabians but latter-day Benthamites?" And he adds that John Stuart Mill was already in 1830 "what might be called a liberal socialist" (1948: 66).

On the other hand, after 1830, a clear distinction begins to emerge between liberals and socialists, and after 1848, it becomes quite deep. At the same time, 1848 marks the beginning of a reconciliation between liberals and conservatives. Hobsbawm thinks that the great consequence of 1830 was to make mass politics possible, by allowing the political triumph in France, England, and especially Belgium (but even partially in Switzerland, Spain, and Portugal) of a "moderate" liberalism, which consequently "split moderates from radicals" (1962: 117). Cantimori, analyzing the issue from an Italian perspective, thinks that the question of a divorce was open until 1848. Until then, he notes, "the liberal movement . . . had rejected no path: neither a call for insurrection nor reformed political action" (1948: 288). It was only after 1848 that a divorce was consummated between these two tactics.

What is crucial to note is that after 1848, socialists stopped referring to Saint-Simon. The socialist movement began to organize itself around Marxist ideas. The plaint was no longer merely poverty, susceptible to repair by reform, but the dehumanization caused by capitalism, whose solution required overturning it completely (see Kolakowski 1978: 222).

At this very time, conservatives began to be conscious of the utility of reformism for conservative objectives. Sir Robert Peel, immediately following the Reform Act of 1832, issued an electoral manifesto, the Tamworth Manifesto, which became celebrated as a doctrinal statement. It was considered by contemporaries as "almost revolutionary" not merely because the manifesto announced the acceptance of the Reform Act as "a final and irrevocable settlement of a great constitutional question" but because this position was announced to the people rather than to Parliament, which caused a great "sensation" at the time (Halévy 1950: 178).[9]

In the process, conservatives noted their convergence with liberals on the importance of protecting property, even though what interested them about property was primarily the fact that it represented continuity and thus served as the foundation for family life, the church, and other social solidarities (see Nisbet 1966: 26). But beyond this philosophical convergence, there was the concrete menace of real revolution, a fear they shared, as Lord Cecil noted:

"For it is an indispensable part of the effective resistance to Jacobinism that there should be moderate reform on conservative lines" (1912: 64).

Finally, we should not entirely neglect the third possible reduction of three to two: conservatives and socialists joining hands in opposition to liberals, even if this seems the least likely theoretically. The "conservative" character of Saint-Simonian socialism, its roots in Bonaldian ideas, has often been remarked upon (see Manuel 1956: 320; Iggers 1958: 99). The two camps could come together around their anti-individualist reflex. Equally, a liberal like von Hayek denounced the "socialist" character of the conservative Carlyle's thought. This time, it was the "social" side of conservative thought that was in question. Lord Cecil did not in fact hesitate to declare this affinity openly:

> It is often assumed that Conservatism and Socialism are directly opposed. But this is not completely true. Modern Conservatism inherits the traditions of Toryism which are favourable to the activities and the authority of the State. Indeed Mr. Herbert Spencer attacked Socialism as being in fact the revival of Toryism. (1912: 169)

The consequence of liberal–socialist alliances was the emergence of a sort of socialist liberalism. The consequence of liberal–conservative alliances was a sort of conservative liberalism. In short, we ended up with two varieties of liberalism. The conservative–socialist alliances, more improbable, were originally merely passing tactics. But one might wonder whether one might not think of the various "totalitarianisms" of the twentieth century as a more lasting form of this alliance, in the sense that they instituted a form of traditionalism that was both populist and social. If so, these totalitarianisms were yet another way in which liberalism remained center stage, as the antithesis of a Manichean drama. Behind this facade of intense opposition to liberalism, one finds as a core component of the demands of all these regimes the same faith in progress via productivity that has been the gospel of the liberals. In this way we might conclude that even socialist conservatism (or conservative socialism) was, in a way, a variant of liberalism, its diabolical form. In which case, would it not be correct to conclude that since 1789 there had only been one true ideology, liberalism, which has displayed its colors in three major versions?

Of course such a statement has to be illustrated in historical terms. The period 1789 to 1848 stands out as a great ideological struggle between a conservatism that failed in the end to achieve a finished form and a liberalism in search of cultural hegemony. The period 1848 to 1914 (or 1917) is notable as a period in which liberalism dominated the scene without serious opposition, while Marxism was trying to constitute a socialist ideology as an independent pole, but not being entirely able to succeed. One might then argue (and this assertion would be the most controversial) that the period 1917 to 1968 (or 1989) represented the apotheosis of liberalism at the world level. In this view, although Leninism was making the claim that it was an ideology violently opposed to liberalism, it was actually being one of its avatars.[10]

Beyond Ideologies?

Is it now at last possible to go beyond ideologies, that is, to go beyond the dominant liberal ideology? The question has been explicitly put, and repeatedly, since the world revolution of 1968. For what were the revolutionaries of 1968 attacking if not liberalism as an ideology, as that ideology among the three which served as the ideology of the capitalist world-economy?

Many of those engaged in the confrontations in 1968 no doubt clothed their demands in a Maoist discourse, or that of some other variant of Marxism. But that did not stop them from putting the Marxists into the same liberal pot, rejecting both official Soviet Marxism and the great Communist parties of the industrialized world. And when, in the period after 1968, the most "conservative" elements sought to formulate a response to the revolutionaries of 1968, they gave themselves the name of "neo-liberals."

In reviewing a book by Kolakowski, *Publisher's Weekly* resumed his thought in the following way: "'Conservatism,' 'liberalism' and 'socialism' are no longer mutually exclusive political positions" (*N.Y. Review of Books*, March 7, 1991, 20: advertisement). But if our analysis is correct, we may wonder if there ever was a moment when these ideologies were mutually exclusive. What is new is not that there reigns confusion concerning the meaning and validity of liberalism, the great hegemonic ideology of the capitalist world-economy. This has always been the case. What is new is that for the first time in its history as a dominant ideology since 1848, liberalism, which is at heart nothing but modernity, has been once again fundamentally questioned. What we should conclude from this will go beyond what we can deal with here. I believe, however, that liberalism as an effective political project has had its day, and that it is in the process of collapsing under the impact of the structural crisis of the capitalist world-economy.

This may not be the end of all ideology. But now that one is no longer so sure that political change is necessary, inevitable, and therefore normal, one no longer needs to have an ideology to deal with the consequences of such a belief. We are entering a period of transition, which may go on for some fifty years, and which can be described as a major "bifurcation" (*vide* Prigogine) whose outcome is uncertain. We cannot predict the worldview(s) of the system(s) that will emerge from the ruins of our present one. We cannot predict what ideologies will be born or how many there will be, if any.

Notes

1 Ideologies were only one of three ways of coping. The other two were the social sciences and the antisystemic movements. I discuss this in detail in Wallerstein (1991), and seek to specify the interrelations between the three modes.

2 The Charter conceded by Louis XVIII was politically crucial to his "restoration." In his declaration at St.-Ouen, the future king announced that he was determined to "adopt a liberal constitution" which he designated as a "charter." Bastid (1953: 163–4) observes that "the term Charter, whose meanings in former times had been multiple and varied, above all brought to mind the memory of communal liberties." He adds that, "for those of liberal bent, it evoked quite naturally the English Magna Carta of 1215." According to Bastid, "Louis XVIII would never have been able to win public acceptance had he not satisfied in some way the aspirations for liberty." When, in 1830, Louis-Philippe in turn also proclaimed a Charter, this time it had to be one that was "assented to" (*consentie*) rather than one that was "bestowed" (*octroyée*) by the king.

3 "It is to mankind as a whole that liberals have, without major exception, addressed themselves" (Manning 1976: 80).

4 In *The Charterhouse of Parma*, the revolutionary Ferrante Palla always introduces himself as a "free man."

5 Plamenatz argues that, although there were four factions among those opposed to the July Monarchy that one might designate as being on the "left" and who later supported the Revolution of 1848, the term used to refer to them collectively was not "socialists" but "republicans" (1952: 47 and *passim*).

6 As Tudesq notes (1964: 235): "The Legitimist opposition to the July Monarchy was an opposition of notables to established authority." Were the Legitimists not thus contradicting Bonald's dictum that "the true nature of society . . . is what society, public society, is presently"?

7 See the discussion of Bonald's views in Nisbet (1944: 318–19). Nisbet uses "corporation" in the sense of "associations based on occupation or profession."

8 "Both Saint-Simonism and economic liberalism evolved in the direction of what we call today economic rationalisation" (Mason 1931: 681).

9 Halévy quotes an article (no. x) that appeared in the *Quarterly Review* of April 1835 (Vol. LIII, p. 265), entitled *Sir Robert Peel's Address*: "When before did a Prime Minister think it expedient to announce to the *People*, not only his acceptance of

office, but the principles and even the details of the measures which he intended to produce, and to solicit — not from parliament but from the people — that they would so far maintain the prerogative of the king as to give the ministers of his choice not, indeed, an implicit confidence, but a fair trial?" (1950: 178, fn. 10).

10 As Leninism reconstructed itself from being a program for the revolutionary overthrow of the governments by the organized working class to being a program for national liberation followed by national development (of course a "socialist" one), it was in fact following a parallel path to Wilsonianism, which was the official version of liberal ideology. See Wallerstein (1992).

5

Whose Classics? Which Readings?
Interpretation and Cultural Difference in the
Canonization of Sociological Theory

Craig Calhoun

I

Histories of sociology commonly tell us how the discipline was formed in the nineteenth-century struggle to understand the combined upheavals of the great political revolutions and the industrial revolution. These overturned the established order and posed a variety of questions that remain with us still: questions about class, community, the nature of social integration, and processes of social change. This version of disciplinary history is true enough, but most tellings leave out important causal factors: the impact of voyages of discovery, of long-distance trade and colonization, of nationalism, and of easier travel and communications on the transformation of European consciousness. Sociology, in other words, was born partly as comparative sociology, seeking to understand the ways in which societies (or cultures or peoples) differed from one another. A variety of dimensions were of interest, but perhaps none more so than differences in political system. Partly because Europeans were in the process of challenging absolutist authority and the divine rights of kings, they were particularly interested in contrasts that pointed up the extent to which certain countries enjoyed liberty, rule of law, and government in the interest of the people that were denied to others. The contrasts could be between France and Britain, between the Old World and the New, historically between the *ancien régime* and its successors, and perhaps most tellingly between Western Europe and "the East." Montesquieu and Tocqueville stand as the great "founding fathers" in this tradition. That they are less central than others in canonical disciplinary histories and the teaching of new sociologists is due, in significant part, to the marginalization of certain important concerns – especially political struggle and cultural difference – within the discipline.

Given the way we represent the history of sociology, it is easy to forget how powerful the East–West contrast was in constituting early modern social thought. Its *locus classicus* lay in accounts of Persia, such as Montesquieu's *Persian Letters*. But the East could also be Ottoman Turkey, India, China and even Russia, and on occasion Eastern or Central Europe. These views were generally "orientalist," as Edward Said has argued (1976), but the most crucial point for present purposes is not the prejudiced view early social thinkers had of the "East," but that they looked at other countries and epochs not only to learn about those places and peoples for their own sakes but to draw lessons for the contemporary West. As so many of us do all the time and at all levels of analysis, the founders of sociology looked at others to learn about themselves. When they looked at the "others," thus, scholars often took as obvious what it meant that some people were cannibals, or ruled by sultans, or married to multiple partners at once. This was as true of early anthropologists like James Frazer and Edward Tylor, with their vast apparatuses of classifications and interpretations of practices and myths divorced from their cultural contexts. It was in its revolt against this sort of thinking that anthropology (led perhaps above all by Bronislaw Malinowski) made itself into the discipline that argued that the meaning of such things was not obvious but had to be explained in the context of an account of a whole "indigenous" society or culture. But sociology (not altogether a separate discipline at the outset) was not entirely ethnocentric, and also developed traditions that problematized the cross-cultural constitution of meaningful interpretations.

If sociologists, and modern social theorists more generally, started with a concern for difference, however, they also projected it outward in "them–us" contrasts. From very early on, European thinkers approached human diversity with a vision of differences among types, not a ubiquity of cross-cutting differentiations.[1] This affected not only their views of others, but their views of themselves. Especially under the influence of nationalist ideas, they developed notions of societies as singular, bounded, and internally integrated, and as realms in which people were more or less the same. On this basis, a great deal of modern social theory came to incorporate prereflectively the notion that human beings naturally inhabit only a single social world or culture at a time.[2] People on borders, children of mixed marriages, those rising through social mobility and those migrating from one society to another were all constituted for social theory as people with problems by contrast to the presumed ideal of people who inhabited a single social world and could therefore unambiguously place themselves in their social environments. The implicit phenomenological presumption was that human life would be easier if individuals did not have to manage a heterogeneity of social worlds or modes of cultural understanding. An ideal of clarity and consistency prevailed. This ideal of course reflected broadly rationalist thinking, but it should not be interpreted as limited to rationalistic (or Enlightenment) views. Much of the jargon of authenticity in Romantic and later anti-rationalist thought shares the same idealization of the notion of inhabiting a single self-consistent lifeworld (see Adorno 1973). This notion of the external world mirrored a preFreudian (not to mention preBakhtinian) notion of the potential self-consistent internal life of the individual – one represented in the very term "individual" with its implication that the person cannot be internally divided.

This notion of inhabiting singular social or lifeworlds as integral beings reflected both assumptions about how actual social life was organized and ideals about how social life ought to be organized. It invoked, in other words, an idea of normality. But the early theorists did not for the most part see their contemporary world as unproblematic on this dimension. Rather, they recognized that people around them faced challenges in trying to come to terms with differences, border crossings, and interstitial positions. This led to an understanding of the past as one in which singular social worlds more completely enveloped people; in which society was less differentiated and less complicated. This was for some a golden age, but most social scientists emphasized that for better or worse modernity meant parting with such visions. One powerful version of this argument was Weber's notion of the differentiation of value spheres, itself an elaboration of a Kantian distinction.[3] In modern societies, Weber suggested, the realms of truth (theory), morality (practice), and aesthetics (judgment) must be differentiated; dedifferentiation is a pathology. This view carried forward directly into the work of Horkheimer and Adorno and continues to shape that of Habermas (among many others).

Durkheim took a partially similar tack when he contrasted mechanical to organic social solidarity (Durkheim 1893). He stressed that the older, mechanical form of social solidarity was one rooted in sameness and consensus. The modern organic form was rooted in the division of labor and presupposed functional interdependence based on difference. But, actually existing modern societies were pathological on Durkheim's account, for they lacked the necessary means of reconciling individuals to these differentiated societies. Durkheim conceptualized these means, first, in social terms – the need for strong groups of intermediate scale-like occupational associations – and, second, in cultural terms – the need for some overarching ideology or collective representations that would reveal the nature of the singular whole of their social world to individual members.

There are obviously senses in which the view that modern social life is distinctively characterized by differentiation makes sense. Social life is organized on an extremely large scale and subgroups that have a high level of autonomy in some respects are at the same time closely interdependent with each other. Whether because it is necessary or simply because it has been historically produced, the distinction among truth, goodness, and beauty (and/or its analogs) does indeed structure a great deal of contemporary discourse.

Yet there is problematic baggage packed into this way of understanding epochal change. Along with an appreciation of the scale, differentiation, and intensification[4] of modern social life this account presents us with the presumption that earlier modes of life were basically organized in terms of internal sameness or dedifferentiation. This is what gives Weber's account its special pathos, for example, because Weber sees the differentiation of value spheres as essential to maintaining rationality and as both part of what produces the iron cage and simultaneously a fragile arrangement constantly vulnerable to collapse. His successors who lived through the Nazi era were even more impressed with the threat of dedifferentiation. Durkheim too saw the pathologies of modern people as stemming significantly from the difficulties of coping with this internally differentiated world. And both Durkheim and Weber saw differentiation producing these challenges even without seriously questioning the notion that people would live inside one social world, one society (or subculture) at a time.

Both Durkheim and Weber in this way reflected some emerging features of modern thought that were closely associated with nationalism, though neither produced more than fragmentary analyses of nationalism. They saw human life as "naturally" involving social worlds of internal sameness and only contingently and with difficulty adapting to worlds of high differentiation. Within the worlds of high differentiation they saw people managing by locating themselves firmly within one or another sphere of social relationships and orientations to action. In Weber's most classic contrast, thus, one opted for science or politics as a vocation, not for both.

But of course Weber's own life suggested otherwise.[5] He wrote purely academic treatises and entered directly into public life and practical action. He revealed that it was indeed possible to inhabit multiple social worlds and to manage their conjunctures and disjunctures (if not always happily). Modernity may present a number of distinctive challenges of this kind, but we should also be careful not to follow the many classical social theorists whose examination of "other cultures" was conducted in a way that hypostatized both the otherness and the integral unity of cultures. People have long inhabited multiple social worlds at the same time. Multilinguality is as "natural" as monolinguality. Trade has established linkages across political and cultural frontiers. The great religions have spread across divergent local cultures and maintained connections among them. Even in the relatively small scale, low technology societies that most informed Durkheim's notion of mechanical solidarity, people inhabited multiple horizons of experience, for example as members simultaneously of local lineages and far-flung clans. In great civilizations like India that were not organized as singular political units, this was all the more true.

It is important, thus, both that we recover from the traditional histories of sociology the extent to which the discipline was formed in the challenge of confronting difference and that we recognize the way in which difference was constituted for most sociologists as a problem when it came to be manifest inside putatively singular social worlds. Comparative sociology for the most part reinforced the presumption of internal integrity by taking presumptively "whole" societies as its units. From its beginning, in short, sociology posed basic questions about how to interpret the meaning of different ways of life, but it tended not to grasp how much and how often those different ways of life could be inhabited simultaneously by the same persons.

It is important today to recover the sociological tradition of addressing the challenges of cultural and historical difference, but to do so in ways that do not render observed differences the bases for hypostatizing contrasting "whole" societies or cultures as though they were internally integral. It is in something of this spirit that, generations ago, Sorokin criticized those who studied cultures with the presumption that these were necessarily cognitively or logically integrated units, rather than seeing such integration as an empirical variable (Sorokin 1957). We need to see not only that empirical variable, however, but the practical activity by which ordinary people manage cultural complexity and the interfaces among social worlds.[6] The issue is not just to avoid "essentialist" invocations of integral identity, but to see that just pointing to "social construction" offers little if any analytic purchase. It is not just that collective identities and ways of life are created, but that they are internally contested, that their boundaries are porous and overlapping, and that people live in more than one at the same time.

II

None of this, of course, makes the more straightforward issues of how to undertake interpretation and comparison across lines of difference any less important. It is a serious deficiency that contemporary sociologists (especially in the US) recognize the deep relation of their discipline to the historical challenge of interpretation and difference mainly in terms of vague references to Weber's notion of *Verstehen* and his involvement in the *Methodenstreit*, the turn of the century German struggle over the nature of historical knowledge, science, and the claims of social science. Still, even if stopping the story at this point is a problem, this is not a bad place to begin. It was in this context, arguing against Schleiermacher's notions of historical recovery, that Weber claimed "one does not need to be Caesar to understand Caesar."[7]

In the rest of this chapter, I want to discuss something of the ways in which sociologists have struggled with the challenge of understanding Caesar – or others different from themselves. I will first explore further some of the conditions that initially both made this problematic and opened certain particular intellectual approaches to it. I will then turn to some of the different theoretical nexes in which the problem of interpretation has been posed for sociologists, and finally to the ways in which this issue is addressed – or more often avoided – in the contemporary sociology of culture. I will suggest that grappling successfully with the set of issues thus posed is crucial not only for comparative or cross-cultural sociology as a general pursuit of knowledge, but specifically and vitally for the development of a critical sociology able to break with the received categories of social understanding, to engage not simply in an endless production of different interpretations but in dialogue across lines of difference, and thus to inform normative discourse. Taking interpretation seriously, in short, is essential to developing sociology as part of our human capacity for practical reason.

Discourse that takes interpretation seriously is typically called "hermeneutics." The term "hermeneutic," in this discussion, is both a general term for the study of interpretation, and therefore for sociology's struggle with interpretation, and the label for one particular historical tradition of tackling the problems posed by interpretation – that of Biblical scholars, Schleiermacher, Dilthey, Heidegger, and Gadamer. At the present time, a variety of different analytic traditions are bringing forward serious accounts of interpretation, and of the effects of different ways of framing and presenting social analysis: Hans-Georg Gadamer is by far the most important figure, but in addition to hermeneutics narrowly conceived there are rhetoric, which is enjoying a resurgent influence (exemplified in the social sciences by D. McCloskey's work in economics and more generally by that of Wayne Booth), new understandings of legal argument and change such as that of Ronald Dworkin, new trends in the philosophy of science from Kuhn through Feyerabend, the post-structuralist movement in cultural theory and the revitalized interest in the American tradition of pragmatism.

Hermeneutic problems are of significance for social theory primarily because of historical distance and cultural difference. We are especially apt to become aware of difficulties and uncertainties in the interpretation of meaning, in other words, when we attempt to understand social actions whose meaning is embedded in contexts very different from our own. The relevant differences of context may stem from either material conditions or differences in the symbolic production of meaning. By material conditions I mean those various concrete pressures and possibilities that shape action and meaning in different settings whether or not they are recognized by actors or exert their influence through discourse. We face a hurdle, thus, in understanding those whose lives and actions never involved printed texts, widespread literacy, or electronic communications technologies, for example, since these are ubiquitous in our own lives and constitutive of our own understanding of social life. Variance in population density also shapes communication and other meaningful aspects of social life, even when it is not made into an object of discourse or cultural meaning. Differences of context may also stem from the internal cultural construction of meaning. Such differences arise in language, in schemes of identification and valuation, and in orientations to social practice. They bear on the fact that understanding human beings is not just a matter of interpreting their action, but also of understanding the ways in which their own interpretations and constructions of meaning shaped their action. This is what Anthony Giddens famously dubbed the "double hermeneutic."[8]

In both these senses, then, we face difficulties in interpreting social life that is differently constituted from our own. In a nutshell, our resources for making sense of it, for giving meaning to what we can observe of it, derive from our own culture (including intellectual traditions) and from previous experience. These are the only resources we have, but in applying them we necessarily run the risk of failing to grasp meanings operative in other contexts while constituting for ourselves meanings that were not at work there.

In a very general sense, the problem of interpretation across lines of difference is at work in any conversation; it is implied by the philosophical problem of how we know other minds. It is, therefore, no accident that many approaches to this problem focus on a model of conversation. Hans-Georg Gadamer, for example, presents a hermeneutics built around the notion of dialogue, the reciprocal process of questioning and learning from each other by which two or more parties move toward consensus at least on certain aspects of what they have discussed. This dialogical model is rooted in Gadamer's appreciation of the earlier Socratic dialogues in which all parties participate actively and each learns from the others (by contrast to Socrates' domination of the later dialogues). Jürgen Habermas, by contrast, worries that

Gadamer's conversational model does not distinguish adequately between consensus based on persuasion and that based on truth. In an account of the "ideal speech situation" and similar regulative ideals he attempts to ground an account of discourse on validity claims implicit in all speech. These claims – to truthfulness, sincerity, and rightness – propel discourse forward in a cumulative development toward truth and certainty, even if these are only approached asymptotically.[9]

But there are problems with this whole approach to interpretation and dialogicality through the model of conversation. It grasps a good deal, to be sure, and we can learn from both Gadamer's and Habermas' analyses. But both, and especially Habermas, tend to focus so completely in interpersonal conversation that they do not recognize the full significance of intrapersonal dialogue. One of the key resources we have for communication with others (it is more or less redundant to say "others who are different from ourselves" since this is always a matter of degree, however radical) is that we are not entirely "self-same." Freud and Bakhtin in different ways stressed the internal complexity of the person. Whether in object–relations or ego–analytic terms, thus, psychoanalysis points out the extent to which being a person means coping with a variety of different identities, identifications, and objects; balancing impulses, self-criticism and sense of reality. Much of what Bakhtin saw in the modern novel was a reflection of a human capacity to carry on an interior dialogue, indeed the constitution of the human being through this dialogicality.[10] Because we already engage ourselves through interior dialogue, we are better placed to come to understandings of others and to bridge significant differences than if we were only monological speakers of self-sameness.[11]

Habermas approaches internal complexity mainly through recognition of the importance of intersubjectivity. That is, he sees that people are not self-identical in any simple sense because each is constituted as a person both through relations to others and through participation in more or less impersonal but social processes such as language. Our very capacity to speak of ourselves thus draws on resources partially outside ourselves. This is a crucial, but significantly different insight from recognition of the centrality of internal dialogue.

Habermas remains within an approach that presumes consensus as its goal. If one takes the notion of interior dialogicality seriously – if one grants that people are constituted by tensions within themselves, as well as by their definitely held views or propensities – then one cannot quite imagine perfect consensus as a desirable social goal. Certainly we do seek consensus about various matters of truth and practical action. We hold more or less rational and in any case discursively available values and understandings of the world that we wish to be confident that others share. But creatures who had only such discursively available and definite understandings and values, and who were altogether or even basically self-consistent about them, would not be recognizable as humans.

Part of the problem is that Habermas has adopted a strong version of the widespread assumption of social theorists (noted at the beginning of the chapter) that human beings naturally inhabit a single horizon of experience, a single social world, at a time. This informs a view in which establishing consensus is the program both for living within that social world and for building bridges to other social worlds. But if we start from the view that human beings can and indeed very commonly do inhabit multiple social worlds (as well as highly differentiated social worlds) then we are led less to see consensus as the orientation of all communication. For one thing, we are led less to rely on sender–receiver models that presume the issue is one of adequate translation between "thoughts" that start out in one head and are transmitted to another. Beyond this, we can recognize that each of us develops various practical skills for managing our lives in multiple social worlds, and for constituting ourselves against multiple horizons of experience. These practical skills are basic to meeting the challenge of communicating across lines of difference. What we seek – and indeed often achieve – is not consensus as such, but adequate mutual understanding for the pursuit of various practical tasks in which we are jointly engaged. Just as we do not come to complete self-understanding or complete "consensus" among the voices in our interior dialogues, so we do not do so in exterior, interpersonal or societal dialogues. Indeed, we cannot and it does not altogether make sense even to conceptualize this as a goal or regulatory direction for our efforts. This does not mean that consensus is not important, but: (1) that it is an account of the nature of mutual understanding appropriate to certain domains of rational critical discourse and not to all of social life, and (2) even those restricted domains (for example, law courts) in which the rational critical pursuit of consensus is what we would want rest on foundations not just in language but in less discursive and less consensual practical agreements.

The conversation model for interpretation and mutual understanding also has other limits. Notably, accounts like Habermas' and Gadamer's tend to posit participation in conversation as a given and recognize inequalities and power only as distortions and intrusions. It is hard to relate such model discourses to those settings in actual social life where conversation itself is imposed by force and maintained by unequal power. Perhaps the most obvious of these is colonialism. Even more generally, the whole modern problem of interpretation across lines of differences has been constituted by the processes of state-building and capitalist expansion. Both within Europe and throughout the world, the challenges of cross-cultural relations did not arise and still do not arise either as mere intellectual pursuits or as results of the unconstrained choices of free and equal partners to engage in conversation. They are produced in large part by the exercise of power, whether that power appears in the form of a centralizing state suppressing subordinate ethnicities, of a colonial state backed by an army, of a multinational corporation, or of the dominance of Western communications media. Power is not simply a distortion of the conversation, it is its occasion. Yanomamo in the Amazon basin and Papuans in New Guinea generally have not simply sought out Europeans for dialogue aimed at mutual understanding.

Now of course Habermas and Gadamer can both answer to the effect that they were not analyzing actual conversations (and still less cross-cultural relations) but proposing accounts of how we might understand conversation to be able to move toward mutual understanding and truth. Nonetheless, the problem is a serious one. In the first place, it simply poses an unrealistic notion that meaning can be separated from distorting influences rather than appearing always and only in relations constituted in part by power (as well as by other determinations not reducible to meaning, such as social structure). Approaches such as Gadamer's and Habermas' are superior to the idea of a pure semiotics; at least they locate the pursuit of meaning in dialogue rather than in the external point of view of a semiotician. They do not advocate the kind of science of pure meaning suggested by semiotics (and attacked for example by Bourdieu).[12] Their views are plausible accounts of the pursuit of understanding – and thus can represent viable contending positions in the philosophy of science, or inform accounts of legal processes. The catch is that cross-cultural relations are not occasioned primarily by the pursuit of understanding. The efforts of social scientists to interpret other cultures are never free from the larger structures that bring the different cultures into relationship. Much the same could be said of many interpersonal relations – they are crucially constituted by power. This is, for example, the crux of Nancy Fraser's criticism of Habermas' tendency to ground his notion of a lifeworld free from systemic distortions of communication in appeals to idealizations of family life. Families are hardly realms of free and uncoerced mutual pursuit of understanding.[13] Habermas' appeals to the model of psychoanalysis are similarly problematic.[14] It is not clear how one could establish a collective analog to the roles occupied by analyst and analysand. We can learn from the importance of intersubjectivity to achieving self-understanding, from ideas about systematically motivated blockage and distortion, and from how a mixture of strategic and pure communicative action is required, but it is hard to figure out what sort of collective *project* is strictly analogous to psychoanalysis, and especially what sort of project *between different cultures*.

Not least of all, the very notion of difference with which social scientists work is constituted by the way in which the modern world has developed. "Cultures" and "societies" are not simply given as units in the nature of things, nor is this an arbitrary construct of social scientists, a sort of unmotivated mistake. Cultures and societies have been constituted as putatively bounded units in a world-system that is presumed to divide into an exhaustive and more or less mutually exclusive set of such categories. Conditioned by state-building and the global expansion occasioned above all by capitalism, moderns have come to see the world through the lenses of nationalist discourse – that is, in terms of the kinds of collective identities and divisions defined paradigmatically by the notion of nation. "Nation" is a particular construct informed by power relations; it shapes not just the specific interpretations of those who use the concept but the very idea of difference between discrete cultures that is implicit in all our discussions of cross-cultural relations.

Similarly, the social scientist's standpoint of observation is constituted as the synoptic view of a representative of an international culture. Institutionalizing this notion of an international culture was one of the achievements of the Enlightenment; at the same time, the Enlightenment itself depended on an infrastructure of networks across lines of cultural difference to provide the social organizational basis for its discourse. It is only from the vantage point of "international culture" that seemingly disinterested accounts of particular cultures or of the general problem of cultural difference can be posed. International culture constitutes the ground of a specifically social scientific equivalent to the Cartesian "view from nowhere" that informs the modern notion of science and epistemology generally. But of course it is a view from somewhere, even if not precisely spatially located. And it is a view that preforms the supposedly brute facts of social science observation – for example by constituting nations as appropriate units of comparative research.

This construction of "cultures" and "nations" as basic units of modern collective identity and of comparative social science research has significant implications. In the first place, it implies that each one is somehow discrete and subsists as an entity unto itself rather than only as part of a world-system or some other broader social organization or discourse that defines it as a constituent unit or part. This boundedness is suggested, in large part, by the sharp boundedness of modern states; the ideology of nationalism promotes the notion that each state has or should have its own singular culture (and vice versa). We extrapolate from archetypal examples. French culture is claimed as something clearly distinct from German (never mind the Alsace); Norwegian culture is something clearly distinct from Danish (no matter how much they have been joined historically, how mutually intelligible their languages, or how similar they seem by comparison with Borneo). This way of constructing cultures as objects of our study, however, obscures interconnections. It implies, to expand the last example, that Scandinavian is purely an aggregate term; that it refers to the sum of Norwegian, Danish, Swedish, Finnish, and possibly Icelandic cultures, while only these four or five are primary units. Or to take an example of more practical moment, it makes it hard for us to figure out the relationship between the term Europe and the various putative nations that also have claims on the identities of Europeans. This idea of discreteness is also a key factor in constituting the modern problem of ethnicity, minorities, or subcultures. In a nutshell, these are terms we apply when we want to deny that some collection of people constitutes a fully autonomous and/or modern culture because this would imply that they constituted a nation which would imply that they had a legitimate claim on a state. We do not leap to list Sami (Lapps) as one of the constituent cultures of the term Scandinavian, I think, largely because Sami have played little role in the history of contentions over the proper constitution of nation-states in the region.[15]

The Sami not only confound our notion of a discrete Norway, secondly, they confound the notion that Norway has a completely unified, integrated culture. Yet referring to "cultures" and "nations" as integral is a second key implication of our typical usage. We refer to each as though it constitutes a single thing to which determinate reference can be made, rather than a cluster of tensions, contradictions, and agonisms. Thus we assume that with an appropriate sample, we can compare Japanese culture to Norwegian culture. We take it as given in such studies that the "culture" can be an object of unitary reference rather than a term needing to be deconstructed. We assume that it is something "out there" to be revealed to us by the responses of a set of individuals, and that the main issue before us is the methodological problem of accurately constituting a "representative" set of individuals. This reflects, in part, our characteristic understanding of the nation as comprising a set of individuals rather than subordinate powers or communities; national identity is understood as inscribed directly into individual identity, the relation between the two terms is unmediated (Calhoun 1993a; 1993b). At the same time, thinking of cultures as integral, we tend both to hypostatize them and to direct attention away from the ways in which they are internally complex and continually reshaped by struggle.

Third, in speaking of "cultures" and "nations" as units, we tend to imply that they are equivalent. This is sometimes a practical, political issue – for example, San Marino with its 24,000 citizens enjoys the same formal status in organizations like the United Nations as do Germany, the United States, and Brazil. It is also a prejudgment that shapes our understanding of ways of life different from our own. We attempt to understand their putatively discrete, integral cultures on analogy to our own, assuming that they must be functional equivalents. This sort of assumption – along with those of discreteness and integrity – has been challenged in a good deal of recent anthropology. Famously, for example, Jack Goody challenged attempts to define a set of discrete, equivalent and internally unitary cultures in northern Ghana. He pointed out the ways in which language, religious observance, mythology, and kinship patterns varied along a continuum in certain locales. Previous British observers, thus, had developed a categorization of "Lo" and "Dagaa" as separate and distinct cultures. This was a misunderstanding, Goody argued, for Lo and Dagaa are really more like poles to a continuum. Those in the middle were not marginal to each of two different cultures, or representative of some confusion between them. They were full participants in a way of life defined in varying degree by different forms of practice – not unlike the children of Norwegian immigrant mothers and Irish Catholic fathers who in the US are just as American as anybody else (Goody 1967).

The point here is not that we must abandon the notions of culture or nation, assuming that such a thing would be possible. It is that we need to recognize the ways in which such units: (1) preform our empirical observations of the world, (2) constitute central dimensions of the modern idea of difference that informs our problems of cross-cultural understanding, (3) are deeply embedded in the sociological thinking we inherit from the "classics," and (4) constitute the premise of our own putatively synoptic understanding of the world of such differences on the basis of our position in an international culture. This last, for better or worse, does not remove us from the play of practical concerns and allow us the universal view of free-floating intellectuals. It positions us within a socio-historical process (or set of processes) that by virtue of expanding throughout the globe pose us certain problems and open certain paths for solving them.[16]

III

Obviously both differences and interrelationships among people – and peoples – existed long before what we call the modern epoch. Ancient Greeks commented on the differences among their city-states and between Greeks generally and various other people with whom they came in contact. The great empires of world history all involved long-distance trade, tributary legations, and military recruitment that established contact among diverse people; many created cosmopolitan cities in which cross-cultural relations were a matter of daily contact. What then made the problem of difference and consequent problems of interpretation distinctively modern? The philosopher Wilhelm Dilthey gave one important answer when he described the birth of modern hermeneutics as the "liberation of interpretation from dogma" (Warnke 1987: 5). Dilthey referred to the Protestant Reformation with its attack on the authority of the ecclesiastical hierarchy to dictate proper interpretation of the Bible. The Roman Catholic church had attempted to impose theological uniformity; Protestants were inherently schismatic. Martin Luther was not the first heretic, of course; indeed, the Catholic church had only achieved its capacity to enforce a certain orthodoxy in the late patristic era – fighting a host of heretical sects – and it was never complete. But Luther and the Protestant Reformation generally helped to expose orthodoxy as an imposition of force and so – contrary to the intentions of many – to encourage a basic presumption of heterodoxy.

Pierre Bourdieu has usefully discussed the movement of *doxai* – opinions or beliefs – from being simply the taken-for-granted background conditions of life – what he calls *doxa* – through *orthodoxy* with its recognition but implicit condemnation of otherness and *heterodoxy* with its sense of the unavoidability of multiple views. The Protestant Reformation figured prominently in this story. This is not because Protestants were necessarily tolerant; many were as quick to discover heretics or witches as their Catholic brethren. What Protestants did was (1) to create conditions in which Catholic orthodoxy could not appear as taken-for-granted and was likely to be seen as imposed, (2) to offer a series of competing orthodoxies which predisposed their followers to some acceptance of the heterodox nature of the world (even despite their leaders' best intentions), and (3) to make religious faith a matter of active choice, bringing forward disputes over a variety of particulars from the proper mode of communion to the status of the Trinity and the legitimacy of priestly marriage. In this context, the interpretation of Biblical texts took on a new significance – and a new excitement and danger. At the same time, once people began to inquire in this way into the significance of Biblical teachings, they were led to note certain distances between the historical conditions portrayed in the Bible and their own lives. For the first time, Christians faced on a large scale the challenge that had long been posed to Jews, and which had helped to occasion the Talmud – that of adapting a manifestly historically specific set of sacred texts to serve as guides to lives lived under historically different conditions.

Similar issues have shaped relationships to classical or sacred texts in other traditions – to Vedic lore in India and to Confucian texts in China, for example. Once the distance between the texts and present-day life was established, once they could not be fitted immediately into the same unproblematic background *doxa*, then interpretation became problematic. Attempts could be made to impose orthodoxy, but social change always brought the prospect of heterodox challenges.[17]

Protestants, of course, lapsed back into dogma and orthodoxy of their own, but they established the basic principle of hermeneutics – the idea that sacred texts are to be understood on their own terms and for themselves. It was this idea that posed problems of interpretation. It suggested the need for direct access to the sacred texts, of course, thus occasioning a pressure for printing, for widespread literacy, and for refusal of priestly restrictions on reading the Bible. But it also suggested the need for some rules of interpretation to help in the reading. For example, efforts to understand the Bible would need to be guided by the principle of trying to achieve consistency among its many diverse parts and seemingly conflicting statements.[18]

The Reformation was but one moment or phase in a long series of transformations that helped to inaugurate the modern era as one crucially constituted by the interplay of orthodoxy and heterodoxy, sameness and difference. As Gadamer has written:

> When then remoteness of the lofty and the remoteness of the recondite needed to be overcome not simply in specialized domains such as religious documents, texts of law, or the classics in their foreign languages, but when the historical tradition in its entirety up to the present moment moved into a position of similar remoteness, the problem of hermeneutics entered intrinsically into the philosophic awareness of problems. This took place in virtue of the great breach in tradition brought about by the French Revolution and as a result of which European civilization splintered into national cultures. (1981: 97)

It is perhaps best to think of the French Revolution as a symbol for a cluster of decisive events, including not least of all the Protestant Reformation, rather than the sole and sufficient cause of this momentous transformation. Nonetheless, Gadamer's point is strong. The problem of radical otherness is constituted as a problem of the universality of interpretation across lines of difference because modernity appears: (1) as a break with tradition, turning tradition into history, and (2) as a breaking-up of the broad social and civilizational commonality within which (at least European) ways of life were loosely differentiated, replacing Western Christendom with bounded nations (and reified cultures). Of course, modernity is not the first occasion of a break in tradition. Once more or less unitary, Islam has been divided into theologically and ethnic or nationally distinct variants starting very early on – and leaving the occasion for the project of reunification which helps to inform contemporary Islamic fundamentalism. In another vital sense, the literate, orthodox "big traditions" of religious and cultural transmission already constituted major breaks with the "little traditions" of every passing on of information and reproduction of the social world in all its immediate identities and relationships (Redfield 1957). The unity of Christendom broke with the grip of numerous local cultures and traditions, both religious and secular. Indeed, in the hermeneutic tradition and in modern Western thought more generally, "tradition" is too easily identified with Catholic orthodoxy and other aspects of medieval Europe rather than with the more radically traditional social organization characteristic of many ways of life around the world. Like other literate "big traditions," Christianity was always subject to hermeneutic problems and self-conscious interventions in reflected understandings not typical of traditions passed on locally, face-to-face, without the mediation of textual experts – such as those of acephalous African societies, village India before Mughal rule, or elsewhere (including alongside or beneath the very gaze of "big traditions").

In very much the same sense that Dilthey thought the Protestant Reformation liberated Biblical interpretation from dogma, the development of the social sciences – especially sociology and anthropology – might be taken as liberating cross-cultural comparison from established European accounts of the heathen world. This does not mean that sociologists or anthropologists were free from prejudices, any more than Protestants were. Many reproduced the attitudes of colonists toward colonized, for example. More generally, as I have hinted and Gadamer has argued at length, there is no such thing as an understanding free from prejudices: we are always shaped by our origins, our thought is always situated, we are unable to think without taking some things for granted. What we take for granted is determined by our own cultural backgrounds, and more specifically by our academic training. Nonetheless, whether biased or not, sociologists and anthropologists set about attempting to make sense of other ways of life, other forms of social organization or culture, in terms of the way they worked internally. Functionalist analysis obviously reflected this, but so in a different way did Weber's adoption of the notion of *Verstehen*. What this meant was that in a central way, especially insofar as it was essentially comparative, sociology took on the task of interpreting contrasting ways of life. This was fundamentally different from the practical understanding of other ways of life occasioned, for example, by living in the same imperial city. In such a case, say, in Istanbul, Jews might be in daily contact with Muslims and Christians but have no reason to develop a sociology of the gentile world. Neither, in this example, would it have been necessary to choose between absolutizing the difference between Jews and others as "nations," or reducing their differences to mere ethnic variation among the citizens of a single nation. Among other reasons, though they would have needed to interact, they would not have been called upon to deliberate or to confer legitimacy on a government.[19]

Confronted with other cultures, sociologists could find no access to these contrasting ways of life through "brute facts" not needing some manner of interpretation. This was perhaps equally true of sociology's domestic analyses, but more easily ignored.[20] At the very least, looking abroad, it was necessary to translate from one language to another in order to make study possible. Generally, translation depended on some level of more general interpretation. Usually, this more general level operated at least partially in its own terms and understandings; it was, in the currently fashionable term, a "metadiscourse." How could one make sense of kin relations, for example, without situating a variety of indigenous terms in relation to one another in order to construct analogies between the set of relationships being studied and those described in the analyst's language? Translation adequate to comparative analysis requires, however, an interpretation of a whole organization of activity, not just the matching of vocabulary. Indeed, the very metaphor of translation may be of limited value in explaining how cross-cultural understanding is achieved. Even within a single cultural setting, interpretation of practical activity faces significant inherent problems, since most practical activity is not directly amenable to discursive rendering. It is difficult, that is, to put into words the embodied understandings and practical skills by which a host of everyday activities are made possible. To think all human action reducible to rules, and therefore to potentially decontextualized explication, is one of the fallacies Pierre Bourdieu criticizes as characteristic of "objectivism." "The logicism inherent in the objectivist standpoint leads those who adopt it to forget that scientific construction cannot grasp the principles of practical logic without changing the nature of those principles: when made explicit for objective study, a practical succession becomes a represented succession" (1977: 117). A large part of the role of theory in sociology is providing the guidelines for these efforts of interpretation. This is one reason why so much of the most influential "classical" theory is hard to reduce to testable propositions; it is rich with empirical description and offers frameworks for interpretation.

Neither theories nor specific interpretations can be proved or checked for correctness by reference to a set of methodological principles. They must be constructed and evaluated in relation to a range of empirical knowledge through a process of judgment and practical reason. They are judged by whether they are persuasive, whether they seem to make sense, whether they seem adequate to various practical projects. The criteria for this include systematicity, parsimony, scope, intuitive insight, and the like. But these are never conclusive. They do not establish which theory is right when two theories clash, or which of two conflicting interpretations we should believe. The same problems arise in deciding which of the criteria to prefer when they themselves clash. Above all, we evaluate complex empirical interpretations in relationship to the range of other such interpretations we have accepted and in general what we know of the world. One of the best examples of this as an aspect of academic training is the way in which anthropologists master (or at least used to master) a variety of ethnographies from all over the world. These formed the context for their evaluation of new studies.

Despite what I have argued is the centrality of the interpretative task to the history and role of sociology, we do not try to teach it or thematize it very directly as a problem in sociology. The discipline has long been characterized by efforts to repress it or reduce it to a minor and seemingly unproblematic preliminary stage of research. These efforts have been occasioned largely by attempts to make sociology more "scientific." Indeed, a good deal of the relationship of hermeneutics to sociology in recent years has been focused on the philosophy of science question of how similar to the natural sciences sociology is or should be. Unfortunately, regardless of the merits of the arguments, they have often cast hermeneutics (and similar lines of argument) in a negative role. That is, arguments about the centrality of interpretation to sociology have appeared largely as critiques of prevailing scientism and empiricism. The point has been made over and again that positivist sociology fails to attend to the essentially meaningful, preinterpreted character of human life, and by attempting to reduce human beings to mere objects misses something fundamental to their nature. I will not repeat such arguments now. The problem is not to make this negative point better, or more often, but to focus attention on how better to do the actual interpretative work of sociology.

IV

Rather than simply expostulating on my ideas of what a good sociology would look like, however, let me turn for a moment to the sociology of culture as it already exists. A great deal of sociology has been conducted as though culture were a separate field of study that could unproblematically be left to anthropologists, literary critics and others. Recently, however, culture has returned to sociology, sometimes with a vengeance. Where sociology has seemed to have little to say about culture, moreover, it has often been excluded from or devalued in exciting and influential interdisciplinary discourses (to the loss of both sociology and those other discourses). To a surprisingly large degree, however, the sociological subfield of cultural analysis is not a particularly good place to look for serious hermeneutical engagement. One could say the glass is half full, that after years of repressing culture sociologists are studying it in increasing numbers. But those who see the glass as half-empty will have to retort that too many sociologists of culture are doing so in ways that avoid serious hermeneutical (and sociohistorical or theoretical) questions in order to maximize their newfound legitimacy.

There are several senses in which attention to culture has been urged on sociologists. First, and with fewest transformative implications, it has been argued that as a set of more or less objective social products – books, films, paintings – culture deserves more sociological attention than it has received. Culture, in this sense, is understood as a special domain of objects, social actions and institutions. Studies aim to understand who produces these objects and how, who gets access to them and why, what processes determine the fate of different producers and products, how formal organizations shape, select, or disseminate cultural products, and so forth. Though some of these studies are more creative, it is quite possible to contribute to this literature by applying conventional sociological research techniques, conceptualizations, and theories to this specific domain. Thus one might ask about the socio-economic status of those who go to museums, or the structural position of those who make decisions about arts programming, or the ways in which artistic producers forge a community or subculture. Two common threads unite work in this approach: (1) culture is treated in terms of more or less objectified indicators, and (2) attention to culture is compartmentalized within sociology as the study of a specific domain of social life, analogous to law or medicine. These two characteristics remain distinctive and in force even when this approach is expanded beyond the study of the arts in which it originated and includes studies of popular culture.

A second claim about the importance of culture has more central sociological significance. This turns on the argument that social research in general requires paying attention to culture as a sort of methodological propaedeutic. In constructing surveys, thus, sociologists must be concerned to avoid or control for cultural bias. In developing categories of analysis, sociologists must be clear that they are often working with culture-specific categories that they have induced as though they were obvious in their meaning and non-problematic. Thus sociologists using the term race need to worry about the "cultural baggage" that comes with the use of this term, the extent to which it represents a historically specific and possibly prejudicial understanding of certain social phenomena, the number of different meanings that it bundles together (though analysis might fruitfully unpack them and make them several separate dimensions or variables) and the extent to which its meaning is inherently contestable. This series of arguments can be presented narrowly as a critique of specific terms and part of a project of finding better, less problematic terms, or more broadly as an argument for the necessarily unstable and multivocal character of sociological concepts and the need for them to be analyzed as parts of broader cultural contexts.[21]

Recognition of this led to a new wave of cross-cultural research, still designed largely as part of an effort to uncover universal processes or laws. Researchers assumed accordingly that cross-cultural variation, while possibly interesting at a surface level, was not deeply problematic; it was in some combination: (1) a matter of residual variance, (2) a matter of extraneous factors to be controlled for, or (3) a "black box" standing in for proper structural or other variables that had not yet been discovered. Culture became the object of somewhat more serious study within this tradition, perhaps ironically, as the result of methodological problems rather than substantive interest. Researchers found that translating survey instruments was more than merely technically difficult, more than simply a matter of finding the right words, since people in different cultures apparently thought differently about various issues, used different schemes of evaluation, and categorized their experiences in different ways.

Attention to this cluster of issues is valuable for all sorts of sociological work, of course, but it has been brought forward because of sociologists' increasing awareness of cultural diversity. This constitutes a third program of increasing sociological attention to culture. One could call it the "culture as a variable" approach. Many sociologists have attempted to expand operationalizations of their conventional sociological problematics by asking whether cultural difference is a significant intervening variable changing the relationship between, say, fathers' class positions and sons' educational attainment, or between environmental complexity and span of control in organizations.[22] Many of these new studies involve cross-national comparisons, though they are logically similar to others comparing subcultures or ethnic groups. Such studies generally do not begin with the idea that cultural differences might prove internally very problematic. Culture is a label for social groups or categories that become units in the analysis; to the extent that culture becomes significant in explanations it is generally as a kind of residual category putatively accounting for variance that cannot be explained by other, more clearly identified and better understood variables.

In trying to deal with these methodological problems, some of these "culture as a variable" researchers have begun to touch on the most basic and potentially transformative of the ways in which culture has demanded the attention of sociologists. This fourth agenda starts with the recognition that social life is inherently cultural, that is, inherently shaped and even constituted in part by differences in the ways in which people generate or recognize meaning in social action and its products. It is fitting that methodological concerns should drive one sociological effort to connect with culture as both basic to sociology and basically a matter of meaning. This is so because positivist methodological concerns to stick to an "objective" way of studying social life have been responsible for much of the repression and/or marginalization of interpretative methods and concerns in post-war sociology. Interpretative, culturally oriented sociology has of course existed since the beginning of the discipline. It appears in every lineage of classical theory from Marx to Durkheim to Weber and Mead. It has maintained a continuous tradition in symbolic interactionism, in the sociology of knowledge and cultural sociology of scholars like Mannheim and Elias, and in variants of Marxist sociology, especially in the Frankfurt tradition and the new Gramscian currents in and after the 1960s. Yet though culture never quite disappeared from sociological attention, it was banished to the margins of the field wherever positivist methodological concerns reigned, especially in America.

Even in the course of reviving the subfield of sociology of culture during the last fifteen years, for example, many researchers have felt constrained to make sure that their work did not focus on the problem of interpreting meaning, lest it appear to be unscientific.[23] The result, of course, was that they were obliged to interpret the social world as one in which meaning was not problematic. It is precisely in taking meaning as problematic, often under the pressure of trying to cope with manifest differences in interpretations of texts or of actions, that some strands of empirical sociology opened the possibility of a more fruitful relationship with hermeneutics.[24]

In a sense, the split between positivist, empiricist sociology and more interpretative, cultural sociology mirrors the divide between Anglo-American philosophy and its continental counterparts. This offers only cold comfort for positivists, since the last several years have seen even analytic philosophers (like Quine and Popper) demolishing empiricism and related conventional views of science even for the natural sciences (even if they weren't as radical as Feyerabend and Lakatos); Kuhn's and others' historical studies carried similar import. It is no longer just that there are doubts as to whether the social sciences can be more like the natural sciences, it is widely recognized that the natural sciences as practiced are much more deeply culturally (and theoretically) constructed – more dialogical and multi-perspectival – and therefore much less positive, than textbook accounts of science have suggested. It is not just the alleged relativism of Gadamer or Derrida that positivist sociologists have to fear, in other words, it is Einstein with his idea of relativity.[25]

Neither Gadamer nor Derrida holds all the answers. On the contrary, each brings the deep problems of difference and interpretation forward in a problematic form. In the first place, both intellectualize, both treat as essentially cognitive a field of knowledge that owes more than they recognize to embodied practice and structures of social relations. Second, while Gadamer is inattentive to power and the difference between the sway of ideology and the more general fact of prejudice or situatedness, Derrida universalizes power and ideology, making it hard to distinguish whether any specific intellectual claims can be said more to warrant acceptance on their intellectual merits than others. Even more for the crasser followers of Derrida and other post-structuralists, because there is no absolute foundation for judging truth, there is no relative basis for judging "epistemic gain" or partial improvement either (as there is in Gadamer and Taylor) (Taylor 1989a). If Gadamer is insufficiently critical, as Habermas suggests, then deconstructionism is critical in so undifferentiated a manner as to lose practical, especially constructive, purchase. Both Gadamer and Derrida leave us with the knowledge that we can never escape from our interpretative traditions or communities. Yet this has less force than at first appears. All knowledge, justifications and interpretations may indeed be internal to traditions or interpretative communities, but there is never *a* singular and unitary tradition or interpretative community. Membership must always overlap. Such traditions or communities must be internally differentiated and at least at odds on some significant issues, and will be the more so as there is a break between "big" and "little" traditions.

V

As I stressed at the outset, it is important to recognize how much of our approach to problems of difference, and therefore interpretation, is contingent on the way in which we have tacitly accepted the notions that cultures (and even intellectual traditions and interpretative communities) are discrete, integral, and equivalent. But this is a construct we can re-examine. As we work to develop a more complex cultural sociology, it will be only one of many cases in which the meaning of the basic objects we study is reconstituted by critical, theoretically informed reflection, historical and cultural analysis, and the effort to make better sense of as broad a range of empirical observation as we can.

The role of theoretically informed interpretation is basic to this project. The first of the sociologist's tasks – and perhaps the most important and problematic – is the constitution of the object of study. As Bourdieu and his colleagues have written, social facts do not just appear, they must be won (Bourdieu, Chamboredon, and Passeron 1991: ch. 1). When taken seriously, this effort always situates objects within broader contexts, generally theories of social life, interpretations of specific ways of life (including epochs or socio-geographic and cultural settings), and their comparison. This was an important part of the empirically rich work of many "classical" sociologists, but it is largely lost in approaches to canonical theory that work by trying to abstract their concepts and formal propositions from their comparative and historical analyses. There is always room for variation in approaches to constitution of objects of study, for tradeoffs between more local detail and wider comparison, for example, or for emphasizing different aspects of social life – structure, action, culture, power, function, and so on. The point is to see the process as basic and never ending, and to subject it to our continuing critical attention, rather than to imagine that it is somehow settled once and for all, or merely a matter of operational definition.

The objects of sociological study do not present themselves in nature any more than farmland presents itself. Farmers may look at plains that have never been tilled, as some Norwegian immigrants to the American middle west did a century ago, and see rich fields. But this vision is one shaped by their tradition and one rooted in their practical orientation. Just as the farmers must win the fields from nature (or from previous inhabitants who are sometimes dismissed by assimilating them to the category of nature), so too sociologists must win the objects of their research. In this struggle, interpretation is always central. It can be informed by theory, and guided by wise precepts, but it can never be settled by method in such a way as to guarantee the fertility of the fields or to make sure in advance that they grow the scientifically correct crops. Taking interpretation seriously in research, recognizing how deep its problems run, restores the connection of even the most methodologically sophisticated social science to the grounding of judgment and practical reason, and saves it from worshipping the illusions of scientific self-sufficiency that offer the future to the putative certainty of those experts who would be social engineers.[26] Precisely because problems of interpretation cannot be solved in advance but only lived through in history, science does not preclude choice. It is up to us to create a discourse in which choices are made on the basis of knowledge, practical reason, and judgment, challenged by criticism, and open not just to the range of social interests but to the novelty of contending understandings.

Notes

In addition to the ASA session on which this book is based, an earlier version was also presented to the Norwegian Sociological Association summer conference at Lofoten, June 1992. Members of both audiences made helpful comments.

1 See Todorov (1993), *On Human Diversity* for an evocation of how exoticism in French portrayals of non-Western peoples dovetailed with racism and nationalism.
2 On the idea of "social world" see Strauss (1978), "A social world perspective," and for the phenomenological notion of lifeworld that informs Strauss's account, but also puts the notion of social world on a somewhat different theoretical basis, see Schutz and Luckmann (1976), *The Structures of the Lifeworld*.
3 See "Science as a vocation," and "Politics as a vocation," among a number of Weber's works; Kant's three critiques are distinguished on just these lines.
4 By "intensification" I mean something like Durkheim's notion of "dynamic density," the capacity for human beings not just to live near each other but to carry on manifold significant relations with each other.
5 This is evident immediately from recognition of the substantial public and political work he did – for example, helping to draft the Weimar constitution – alongside his scientific or scholarly production. For a deeper sense of the extent to which Weber did not in fact choose sharply between these vocations see Marianne Weber's (1975) excellent (and very sociological) biography, *Max Weber*.
6 See Hannerz (1992), *Cultural Complexity* for a nice contemporary suggestion of this issue. Also, Hannerz (1958), "The world in Creolisation."
7 Compare Arendt's ([1954] 1977: 182) contemptuous formulation of a central theme in pragmatism (which she understands more broadly than just the American philosophical school, and which she charges with deeply pernicious effects on modern education): "that you can know and understand only what you have done yourself."
8 See Giddens (1977), *Studies in Social and Political Theory*, following Charles Taylor ([1971] 1985), "Interpretation and the sciences of man" and Gadamer (1975), *Truth and Method*.
9 Gadamer, *Truth and Method* (1975), *Philosophical Hermeneutics* (1976), *Reason in the Age of Science* (1981); Habermas, *On the Logic of the Social Sciences* (1988), *Theory of Communicative Action* (1984).

10 I will not attempt to lay out the range of appropriate references to Freud and
    psychoanalysis. The most accessible of Bakhtin's texts is probably (1981) *The
    Dialogical Imagination*. The work of Vygotsky (also published under the pseudo-
    nym Voloshinov) helps to open up related themes. See Holquist and Clark (1986)
    on Bakhtin; Wertsch (1990) on Vygotsky.

11 This insight is partially suggested in George Herbert Mead's (1934) notion of
    taking the role of the other (*Mind, Self, and Society*), but not really developed in
    the same way.

12 Bourdien (1990), "Lecture on the lecture," in *In Other Words*.

13 Fraser ([1986] 1989), "What's critical about critical theory." Part of the problem
    is that Habermas does not see the need for a specifically gendered analysis but
    tries to achieve universality by transcending gender (which keeps it from being
    thematized but not from being relevant).

14 Habermas is certainly aware that there are problems with applying the model of
    doctor and patient to large-scale subjects such as classes; he indicates in *Theory
    and Practice*, p. 30, that the key is to distinguish strategic confrontations (to
    which the psychoanalytic model does not apply from normative reflection and
    communication to which it does, though this still seems both to strip psychoana-
    lytic therapy of its strategic dimension and to imagine an improbable sort of
    social encounter.

15 Though the formation of a Sami Parliament appropriates nationalist rhetoric and
    (like other mobilizations of subordinate nationalities and regional identities) poses
    a question about distributions of power among the constituent identities of a
    potentially unified Europe.

16 The international intellectual discourse thus does not attain objectivity, though
    it attains salutary diversity, from the inclusion of the voices of post-colonial
    intellectuals. It is important also to remember that, for example, South Asian
    participants in this international discourse are not simply representatives of the
    anthropological other but elites empowered by education and/or class to enter
    into this realm.

17 Such attempts are often understandable from the point of view of priestly power
    as well as theology; see Bourdieu (1991), "Genesis and structure of the religious
    field."

18 Earlier Biblical redactors and copyists seem sometimes to have responded to
    internal inconsistencies by assuming them to be the result of previous transcrip-
    tion errors – and often trying to resolve them by altering texts to achieve con-
    sistency and to accord with prevailing doctrine. See Ehrman (1993), *The Orthodox
    Corruption of Scripture*.

19 See discussion in Weintraub (1994), "Introduction"; Eisenstadt, *The Political System
    of Empires* (1962), *The Decline of Empires* (1964).

20 Bourdieu, Chamboredon, and Passeron (1991), *The Craft of Sociology*, offer a strong,
    though not explicitly cross-cultural, analysis of this in their discussion of "win-
    ning the social fact."

21 It also reveals the limits of the idea of a "pure structuralism" in sociology, such

as that advocated by Peter Blau. Blau's sociological structuralism involves study-ing interaction rates between various categories of persons – for example, rich and poor, black and white. Inescapably, though, Blau must begin with inductions of such categories from some cultural framework. If they are objectified in data sources (such as census items) it is easy to treat them as though they were objective and forget that they were not only chosen by individuals but consti-tuted by culture. Whether or not this is the case, Blau's reliance on these categor-ies implicitly calls not just for tests of their salience (that is, their ability to predict interaction rates), which is his own main concern, but for an account of how they are derived and why they are the most appropriate representations of the cultural factors that make the variance in interaction rates meaningful (which Blau does not offer). Blau (1977), *Inequality and Heterogeneity*; see also discussion in Calhoun and Scott (1990), "Introduction."

22 A somewhat similar style of research introduces gender as a variable into analytic models that had previously ignored it – but without undertaking a more general rethinking of the importance of gender as a category constitutive of both the social world and sociological problems.

23 See, for example, Robert Wuthnow's (1987) attempts to move "beyond the prob-lem of meaning;" *Meaning and Moral Order* and (1989) *Communities of Discourse*, and my (1992a) response in "Beyond the problem of meaning."

24 It is also, by the way, in taking meaning as infinite and lacking any intrinsic relation to "truth" or application that "post-structuralist" and "post-modernist" lines of thought have differed most decisively from hermeneutics.

25 Or even more, with his understanding of the transformative implications of Planck's work. Or consider Heisenberg (quoted from Arendt's 1954/1977), *Be-tween Past and Future*, p. 47): "The most important new result of nuclear physics was the recognition of the possibility of applying quite different types of natural laws, without contradiction, to one and the same physical event. This is due to the fact that within a system of laws which are based on certain fundamental ideas only certain quite definite ways of asking questions make sense, and thus, such a system is separated from others which allow different questions to be put." But the implications of this should not be overstated. In particular, social scien-tists should not collapse the issue of interpretation completely into the contrast between quantitative and qualitative methods – equating quantitative techniques with analysis and viewing interpretation as either an imprecise version of analysis or somehow its opposite. First, quantitative sociology also depends on interpre-tation and this is sometimes done with great sensitivity. Second, much quanti-tative sociology is essentially descriptive; the use of numbers does not guarantee causal or other forms of analysis, let alone relation to theory. Third, while some qualitative sociology is overwhelmingly descriptive in aim, much focuses on analyses aimed at clarifying the conceptual constitution of phenomena under study. Finally, a good deal of qualitative sociology is in fact model-building and shares both the use of abstraction and the goal of precision with quantitative analysis – or even more, with mathematical model-building. If there is a real

issue in this sociological debate, it is the question of whether meaning is constituted by a rich relation of the specific objects of study to a broad socio-cultural context, or narrowed and even violated by wrenching variables from their contexts.

26 In Kantian language, the social sciences depend largely on judgment, for the social world is not accessible to pure reason. But since social scientists are not passive, external observers but engaged social actors, their work is necessarily guided by the ethical imperatives of practical reason as well.

6

Crises of Modernity: Political Sociology in Historical Contexts

Peter Wagner

The Problem of Political Sociology

This essay will offer some elements of a comparison of current sociology with classical sociology, that is, sociological work around the turn of the nineteenth century. Far from being exhaustive in any respect, it will focus on one main intellectual and political problematic, though one which can indeed be regarded as constitutive of what is often called the sociological tradition. The problem I try to define is the one of the relation between social identities, social practices and modes of collective rule-setting. To put it crudely, for a beginning, I shall argue that political sociology has mostly dwelt on the idea of a need for – as well as a tendency toward – a neat coherence of identities, practices and rules in a society. Coherence, in this sense, means that there is a collectivity of human beings, forming a "society" by virtue of the fact that they share common understandings about what is important in their lives (identities), that they mostly interact with each other, inside this collectivity (practices), and that they have ways to determine how they regulate their lives in common (rules of the polity).[1] However, it has been notoriously difficult to argue under which – empirical – conditions such coherence can be said to exist, why and to which degree it is needed as well as how it would actually be brought about and maintained. To lay the groundwork for the search for an adequate understanding of this issue, I shall first try to exemplify what is meant by identities, practices, and rules of the polity.

Self-identity I take to be the understanding somebody has of her or his own life, the orientations one gives to one's life. Mostly, self-identities are composed of a number of elements, such as being father to a family, loyal employee to a company and good citizen of a nation. And, as this example shows, its elements may have different width, referring to others or groups of others at smaller or greater distance from oneself. Under modern conditions, it is often argued, self-identity is closely linked to the idea of self-realization. Again, self-realization may be conceived in quite different ways. In romantic terms, it could mean the discovery of an inner self and the attempt to live up to that inner self's exigencies. In more profane terms, it can be read as giving priority to one's own goals at the possible neglect of "higher" values.[2] In the latter variant, self-identity appears as highly individualistic, referring to the possibility of a choice of identity and of being responsible for that choice to oneself only. However, it is important to recognize that every process of identity-formation is a social process. Even a highly individualistic concept of self-identity relates to, and is to a certain extent dependent on, an individualistic culture in which it can be realized.

By *social identities*, specifically, I refer to the effective rooting of individual identities in social contexts of others. To see oneself as part of a larger group may be the crucial element of one's self-identity. The classical examples are national identities and class identities. Thus, natives of German parents on German soil may feel part of a greater group of "Germans" to whom they consider themselves tied by historical fate even though they will not actually meet most of them ever during their lives. Or, workers may have felt united with other workers anywhere in the world by defining their social situation as a common one and seeing themselves as engaged in the same struggle. More recently, gender and "non-national" ethnic identities have explicit foci in the formation of social groups, such as in the women's movement and among Afro-Americans and Hispano-Americans in the US.

By *social practices* I mean to refer to the activities people pursue and, importantly, to the effective links such activities provide to others – by sharing a residential location and meeting each other frequently, by exchanging goods, or by communicating with each other and exchanging information. Some of such practices are direct, involving face-to-face-interaction. However, people are also linked to each other indirectly through widely extended chains of interaction. The global circulation of goods through what has become known as the world-market, or the wide transmission of information by electronic means are among the currently widely debated of those chains of interaction. We may note already here that social practices may be related to social identities; thinking of environmentalists buying organically grown foods, of workers reading journals of the workers' movement, or of socially and ethnically homogeneous neighborhoods where you mostly meet others to whom you feel some affinity. However, very often they are not; many of the human activities in contemporary societies – buying food in supermarkets, salaried work for a big company – have no or very thin links to the self-conception of those who pursue them.

Finally, by *modes of collective rule-setting* I mean what is conventionally called politics, namely communication and deliberation over rules that apply to a collectivity of human beings with a view to regulating what they have in common. Key issues in the determination of such modes are the extension of the group to which they apply; the rules for participation in their deliberation; and the definition of the realm of practices collective rules may legitimately cover. Liberal politics used to claim that it has neat solutions for all these issues: the nation-state setting the natural boundary of the polity; universal adult suffrage in regularly recurring elections of representatives being the major rule of participation; and the distinction of the private and the public sphere limiting the legitimacy of political intervention to the latter. However, as some of the preceding examples show, these solutions may be not all that neat. In world-market exchanges, for instance, social practices may exceed the boundaries of the nation-state in politically relevant ways. Migration has changed the composition of many nation-states so that sizable minorities are often excluded from participation rights. Or, bringing gender identities to the political agenda violates the public–private distinction as it was commonly understood.

It is here that we approach the question of coherence of identities, practices, and rules of the polity. A common way of putting the argument is as follows: a nation-state is a viable polity only if most, or the most important, social practices link the people inside its boundaries to each other, and if these people share a sense of their being part of one collectivity.[3] In more generic sociological terms, one would speak of "society" instead of the nation-state. However, due to the historical coincidence of the emergence of sociology and the strength of the nation-state, both terms tend to be conflated in sociological reasoning. And, in some variants, the idea of a *need* for coherence is replaced by the analytical argument on an *inclination* toward coherence. By this move, though, the emphasis is merely shifted to the question how such coherence should come about.

Let us briefly trace this argument through social thought. First, by way of delimitation, it is important to note that the question is meaningful only within a conceptual space whose boundaries are marked by two extreme political possibilities: regimes which are based exclusively on some external reasoning or force rather than consent, or cooperative orders of free individuals which do not rely on political force that does not arise from consent. The former conception assumes either some natural interlocking of the polity with identities and practices or a complete suppression of "deviant" identities and practices. The latter, based on the assumption of an automatic production of a harmonious coherence of identities, practices and the rules of the polity, is the basic conception of a self-sustained individualist liberalism. Whereas some may regard this view as describing a desirable state, most observers of nineteenth- and twentieth-century societies did not consider it to have been achieved by any actual society, and many regarded it as illusory and unreachable. The ideal remains, however, as a key to the self-understanding of Western societies, to what one might call, following Castoriadis (1990), the imaginary signification of modernity.

In the case of these two possibilities, the problem of this paper does not arise. For other societies, the question of the relation of identities, practices and modes of collective rule-setting is a highly general formulation of the object of political sociology. At the same time it describes an inescapable key *political* problematic of modernity, and, as such, one of the most time-honored problems of social thought. In the beginnings of political modernity, Adam Smith, Auguste Comte, and Georg Wilhelm Friedrich Hegel, among others, dealt with it each on their own terms, offering self-interest and market, science and the state respectively as means to reconcile tensions in these relations (or rather, to evaporate them conceptually). Talcott Parsons, a towering figure of modernist sociology, called it the problem of social order, ascribed it to Hobbes, and later formulated it in terms of the integration of the cultural, the economic and the political "systems." Zygmunt Bauman (1992: 53) has recently spoken of a new relation of "individual life-world, social cohesiveness, and systemic capacity for reproduction" as the key to understanding post-modernity, that is, our own time.

The issue, then, has an impressive genealogy. The different historical terms in which it has been cast indicate divergences in the ways in which social relations are perceived in intellectual discourse as well as, to some extent, how they are actually lived. My own exercise of reconceptualization, in this chapter, will proceed by comparing two different ways of conceiving this relation, each of which occurred at a different point in the social history of modernity. The first dates from the period broadly around the turn to this century, 1890 to 1920; and the second period is the present, which may be said to have begun at some time between 1968 and 1973.[4] Both periods were critical periods of sociological thought, critical in the double sense of being highly fruitful and in the sense that in each period the sociological project came to the verge of collapse.[5] Both were also periods of major transformations of a social formation, or "crises of modernity"; the intellectual reorientations were ways to critically reflect on, and actively deal with, these transformations.

Classical Sociology and the First Crisis of Modernity

In political terms, classical sociology needs to be understood against the background of the discursive hegemony of liberalism. During most of the nineteenth century, the century after the democratic revolutions in the United States and in France, liberalism and liberal theorizing had been at center stage of intellectual debates on politics. Even the adversaries of liberalism saw themselves in relation to it – as progressives who went beyond liberalism, or conservatives who resisted it. At the end of that century, however, intellectuals were generally well aware of the failure of liberal theory, in politics as well as in economic matters, to either understand the changes in societal practices or to provide criteria for their regulation. In those *fin-de-siècle* debates, the position of the classical sociologists was marked by the fact that they agreed that societal developments had superseded classical liberalism, but insisted that revisions had to be made within that political tradition (Seidman 1983: 278). What was it that had brought about this shift in politico-intellectual climate, and how did the sociologists fare in the process of rethinking?

Mostly, liberal theory is known for its claim to have resolved the questions of political expression, economic interest, and scientific validity. In principle, democracy, efficiency, and truth were to be achieved by leaving them to open contestation and competition. However, a closer look reveals that most early nineteenth-century liberals did not actually advocate a fully inclusive liberal society. Restrictions based on criteria such as gender, race, culture, or social standing persisted. The ideas of liberalism were restricted to male household and property-owners, who alone were reasonable and responsive enough to be free. All others, most notably women, workers, and "savages," needed to be taken care of and/or excluded from free activities. One might say that the guiding representation of society was of a dual nature: "domestic" relations prevailed between women and men as well as between workers and entrepreneurs, whereas "market" relations were dominant between free citizens (see Boltanski and Thévenot 1991). This representation showed a certain coherence, as long as the practices of women and workers remained confined to the house and the factory respectively, and as long as they regarded these as the right places to be. Even if one may accept, with many qualifications, that such was broadly the case early in the nineteenth century, much of the social history of the second half of that century can be analyzed as the erosion and active destruction of that coherence.

This is not the place to repeat accounts of the dislocation of large parts of the population, of the growth of industry and the industrial cities, of the struggles for the extension of the suffrage, of the phrasing of the social question or labor question, or of the formation and rising strength of the workers' movement, its parties, and social theories.[6] Suffice it to say that these processes, reordering social practices and disembedding individuals from the social contexts in which they had grown up, uprooted social identities and created widespread uncertainty about individual life chances – about the place in society of those who were disembedded, and among the elites about the order and stability of society as a whole. Classical liberalism proved absolutely unable to deal with these questions and a rather radical reconceptualization of society was at stake.

Reform movements during the latter half of the nineteenth century tried to re-establish some solidity and certainty into the social fabric. Many reformers came from the bourgeois elites, and their idea was not least to safeguard order; they often drew on the idea of the nation as a collective of people who shared a common history and had developed a collective social identity. But an equally important element was the self-constitution of the working class as a collective body capable of defining and representing its own interests. Socialism, trade unions, and labor parties spring from this attempt at developing organized responses to social change on the part of a new collective, the working class. Besides their political and economic objectives, the movement also created a new social identity as an industrial worker, an identity at struggle for a full place in society or in the combined forces of the future of humankind.

In very broad outlines, this was the political context of those writings that we know as classical sociology. Their authors saw the contemporary situation as one in which a major political restructuring was occurring without a clear objective or guiding vision. They turned this into their major theme: unable to stick to the idea of a quasi-automatic regulation of social conflicts but similarly unwilling to move completely away from the tenets of bourgeois liberalism, they devoted their analytical efforts to the search for those phenomena which might provide for a sustainable development of society (Rossi 1982: 199). Theories of "organic solidarity" and the relation of religion and morality as in Durkheim, of forms of legitimate domination and "charisma" in Weber, of the political class and the "circulation of elites" in Pareto were the products of such attempts at reconceiving somehow orderly relations between extended social practices, uprooted social identities, and polities in need of adaptation. I shall return to the type of these responses below, but before doing so, I shall sketch how political thinking in sociology went on.

A key feature of the sociological tradition, well worth remembering, is its discontinuity. From the turn of the century onwards and especially during the inter-war years, the classical sociological reappraisals of the liberal tradition lost their persuasiveness. In the larger crisis of the liberal utopia, both the intelligibility of society by the classical sociological means and the manageability of social order by drawing conclusions from such means were increasingly doubted (see Wagner 1991). The disillusion was far more profound in Europe than in the United States. In Europe, sociological discourse fell to pieces: one piece, its considerations on a theory of action, was taken up by highly voluntarist philosophies of action, often referred to as "philosophy of the deed." Another piece, what was later to be called empirical social research, developed a practical orientation toward the use of such information on people's opinions and behavior, and was often on the fringes of or outside academia. Both parts of the broken discourse flourished under the fascist regimes. Philosophies of action underpinned the idea of a strong man and his will and power to rejuvenate the nation. Empirical social research was often specifically organized to acquire strategically useful knowledge about the state of the population. But both pieces flourished separately. Taken together they might have formed an empirically supported social theory of collective action that could have been inscribed into a normative theory of democracy.

At least elements of such latter discourse existed in the United States. If the political philosophy of John Dewey is linked to the social theory of George Herbert Mead and the empirical sociology of the Chicago School (Joas 1993), we have a body of theoretical and empirical knowledge which emphasizes the human ability to create and recreate one's own life individually and collectively. These thinkers did not fall into voluntarism, much less irrationalism, but instead studied empirically the enabling and constraining conditions under which such creative action occurred. One might say that such reasoning tried to offer ideational and empirical tools for people to construct coherent identities, practices, and polities on their own.[7]

But pragmatism did not become the dominant discourse of American society. Its broader social and political theory remained undeveloped and even its continuation within sociology, as symbolic interactionism, provided no strong theoretical impetus after the Second World War, but rather moved to the periphery of the discipline (Joas 1987; Manicas 1987: 214, 275). The shift of hegemony in American sociology was from the Chicago School in the 1920s and 1930s, to the Columbia School in the following decades, to social policy research in the 1960s. Neither continental European nor North American academics and intellectuals were successful in interpreting social transformations in such a way as to enable individuals to interactively reconstruct a meaningful set of social relations. In contrast, one might say that political sociology after the Second World War moved to prefabricate a well ordered representation of society for people to accept ready made.

Organized Modernity and the Consolidation of Sociology

The "modernization" of the social sciences went a third way, which bypassed the problems of either classical European or pragmatist sociology of linking identities to practices and political orders. In the United States, Talcott Parsons tried to reappropriate the classical European heritage by showing that there were elements in those works of a social theory that could deal with entire social formations while at the same time being able to account for the rationales of human action. Parsons gradually developed these selectively appropriated ideas into a theory of modern societies as systems which became differentiated into functionally related subsystems whose combined workings would safeguard system integration.

System integration is nothing but the term for a coherent and stable relation of identities, practices and collective rules. The theory of modernization works with a foundational distinction between two coherent forms of society, traditional and modern; and the transition from the one to the other is a coherence-seeking movement called development. Once this process is started, it entails modernization. It is only at the stage of "modern society" that a new coherence is reached..

Some works inside the modernization paradigm have shown how such coherence is achieved. It did not escape these observers that the imaginary signification of modernity as such, linked as it is to liberty and autonomy, was neither coherent nor a source of stability. An example relevant for understanding modes of collective rule-setting from the modernization perspective is provided by Gabriel Almond and Sidney Verba (1963) in their seminal study of civic culture as a political ideal of modernity. On the basis of their findings, the authors dissociated themselves from an activist, participatory ideal of the citizen. They emphasized that a certain degree of passivity and lack of involvement which is typical of so-called civic culture is functionally necessary to secure democratic processes. They ignored the liberal principle of political inclusion and its history of violation; for them "moderated" change, even if "moderation" necessitated restrictions to participation, was a legitimate objective. As they saw the modern state, participation in collective rule-setting was a privilege to be granted only to those whose orientations have adapted to the modern polity. This thinning out of the liberal ideal of inclusion and participation is reinterpreted as a sign of progress toward political modernity.

The core of this theory was not the liberal ideology of the open society, but the idea that a "fit" between societal requirements and individual strivings was characteristic for the modern order. Starting out from the assumption of the need for a basic overall coherence of society, it identified related substructures or subsystems in it, each of which would have its own logic or mode of operation, and which together could secure overall coherence. The activities of individuals were tied into these social phenomena via behavior-guiding norms and the learning of these norms or, in some variants, via structural constraints. These theories emphasized the organized, relatively closed nature of overall social relations but tended to see this as an achievement rather than a restriction.[8]

With hindsight, one may understand such reasoning against its historical background. After the Second World War, an unprecedented growth of production and consumption, that is, a strong dynamic in certain social practices, occurred parallel to relative tranquillity and stability of authoritative practices, while at the same time only limited formal restrictions were imposed to free political expression, especially compared to other times and places. The core problematic was to explain the co-existence of these features as a specific social configuration. This extraordinary conjuncture of dynamics, stability and nominal liberty was treated not only as "normal" but as the end state of all social change. Modernization was defined as the process leading to this end.

The representation of society in these discourses was not completely flawed. Modernization theory did make valid observations about some basic features of the advanced industrial societies of the 1950s and 1960s. I will call this "organized modernity" (see in more detail Wagner 1994). The general features of organized modernity are these: social practices were organized so that they moderately cohered on the level of national society and formed interlinking sets of institutional rules. A discursive image of these interlinking practices emphasized their coherence and long-term stability, and associated them with a solid developmental perspective. Such completion of modernity, in the sense that its imaginary significations reached the end of their effectiveness as an ideal, did occur historically, even if the order did not prove to be stable over the long run. What has largely been neglected in discussions of this order was that it had been constructed through intense struggles in the relatively recent past, and that its closure was not as complete as some post-Second World War theorists thought. To reopen their representations of society to consideration, one needs to examine the actual historical construction of this organized order.

The period between the First and the Second World War with planned (wartime) economy, fascism, National Socialism, and Soviet socialism seemed to witness the final demise of the liberal notions of politics, economy, and science. In the view of many participants and observers, the experience of the wartime economy and social management during the First World War meant that the full establishment or re-establishment of liberal institutions was neither possible nor desirable. Many of the proposals that were made in the protracted struggle over societal reorganization during the inter-war period called for a greater degree of social organization than any liberal political or economic theory prescribed (in the "moderate" versions predominant in the United States, the United Kingdom, or Sweden), or even for limited-diversity polities firmly based on class, cultural, occupational or ethnic identities (more strongly proposed in Germany, Italy, or the Soviet Union). The perceived instabilities of the post-liberal regimes motivated these proposals, which relied on the definition of a, mostly national, collective body and on the mobilization of the members of such a collective body under the leadership of the state. The program and practices of these political experiments of the period all restricted the notion of individual liberty in the name of some collectivity, though of course to highly varying degrees. Often, the political reorientation was seen, and portrayed in propaganda, as some new awakening, a new beginning, which signified collective liberation rather than the introduction of constraints to individual action.

In these political experiments, *liberal* practices, based on the free communication and association of a multitude of individual agents with a view to determining the degree and actual substance of collective arrangements in society, gave way to *organized* practices that relied on the aggregation of groups of individuals according to some social criterion before communication and decision-making about collective arrangements were made in and between the organizations whose leaders were speaking and acting on behalf of, that is, *representing*, their allegedly homogeneous memberships. The setting of boundaries and the social production of certainties is generally privileged against the liberal assertion of the unlimited autonomy of everybody to create and recreate oneself and one's social context.

The Second Crisis of Modernity and the Renewed Debate on the Possibility of Sociology

The "achievement" of organized modernity was that it transformed the disembedding and uncertainties of the late nineteenth century into a new coherence of practices and orientations. Nation, class, and state were the main conceptual and institutional ingredients to this achievement, which provided the substance for the building of collective identities and the setting of boundaries. They were materials that were all at hand, historically, to those who participated in building organized modernity. But they obviously did not cohere naturally. It took half a century of political struggle and of unprecedented violence and oppression to form a social configuration that seemed not only to satisfy major parts of its membership but also to develop a dynamic of its own. This dynamic was what came to be called the "long prosperity," the "thirty glorious years," or the "Golden Age of capitalism."

If the building of organized modernity can be understood in terms of the conventionalization of social practices within set boundaries, many recent changes can be seen as the erosion of boundaries and as processes of de-conventionalization. With very few exceptions, current analyses of the organization of sets of social practices stress the breaking up of established rules. In some cases, a terminology is chosen that leads to positive associations, such as flexibilization and pluralization. In others, when the emphasis is on disorganization, instability, or fragmentation, negative connotations prevail. We learn about the disorganization of capitalism, the decline of the nation-state, the crisis of political representation, and the like.

This second crisis of modernity reoriented the modes of intellectual representation of society, too. The questioning of the order of practices extended to a questioning of their imaginary representation, and ultimately to doubts over the very possibility of representation. Because the achievements of organized modernity were bought at the price of setting strict boundaries and conventions, the critique of organized modernity was directed at the constraining effects of those boundaries and conventions. Intellectually, the recognition of the social construction of conventions was the major tool of such critique. It is made visible that strong grounds are lacking for rules that are nevertheless universally applied and enforced within a polity.[9] Thus, during the past two decades, much critical intellectual energy has been devoted to attempts at de-conventionalization (some may call this deconstruction) and recreation of ambivalence in a social order that was regarded as over-conventionalized and closed to any freedom of action beyond pre-established channels.

Sociological critics started by questioning the accounts of a well ordered society that had dominated the discipline. Efforts at reopening the analysis of social relations focused on notions of action and interpretation as well as historicity. Such concepts reintroduced the potential for identifying forms of plurality and diversity in social relations that could not be accounted for in the language of structure and integration. The sociological critics also reapproached the activities of the sociologists to those of "ordinary" human beings. Both were capable, in principle, of reflexively monitoring their own activities and those of others. Sociology was increasingly seen as a reflexive enterprise, itself part of the society to the analysis of which it was devoted. The destruction of the boundary between sociological and lay discourse allowed the very possibility of a science of society to be questioned. It was at this point that sociological discourse on post-modernity emerged (for more detail, see Wagner 1992).

We may begin to draw the analogy between the era of classical sociology and our own – in the following way. The preceding turn of the century witnessed the emergence of classical sociology as a reasoning on society that was much more open, and less reliant on strong preconceptualizations, than earlier evolutionist, organicist and/or determinist social thought. Analogously, from the late 1960s onwards, comprehensive structural–functionalist or structuralist models of society lost their persuasiveness. In both situations, then, rather closed representations of the social world were profoundly questioned, and in both cases, the alternatives that were proposed were of broadly similar kinds (on the notion of closure, see Eisenstadt and Curelaru 1976: 102–4, 245–73, 347–50).[10]

Very schematically, I shall distinguish four such kinds of response.

1   Much of Durkheim's work can be regarded as the *modified continuation* of the project of a positive science of society, building on earlier views and trying to strengthen them at places where they had been found deficient, without altering their basic outlook and ambition. A similar attitude can be found today in self-labelled "neo-functionalist" or "neo-modernization" theories. All other responses view the "crisis" as touching the foundations of prior social science more deeply.

2   One view, which we may term *formalization*, acknowledges a basic difficulty in conceptualizing social phenomena, but also offers a clearcut solution. If nothing else is certain, then the isolated human individual, without assuming specific social ties, has to be taken as the sole methodological (if not also ontological) basis. Everything else will have to be derived from this starting-point. In the first crisis of social representation, this perspective was developed by authors of the marginalist revolution, which led to what we call today neoclassical economics. In current debates, the extension of rational choice theorizing far beyond the discipline of economics reflects a similar stand-point. While this approach sticks strongly to the possibility of a science of social phenomena, it offers a very asocial version of such a science.

3 If one shares the skepticism of rational choice theorists about the validity of other sociological concepts, but is also inclined to strongly reject the economistic idea of the autonomous subject, one will easily tend to the *abdication* of the entire project of "sociological theory." Historical approaches which emphasize the particular, or philosophical ones which focus on the general, may become more dominant, leaving between them, so to say, the space for a social science empty. The dissolution of the sociological discourse in Europe between the two great wars came close to such an abdication. Its present form goes most often under the name of post-modernism, a form of thinking that emphasizes diversity and singularity, on the one hand, and resists all universal statements, on the other, except the one that no well founded universal statements are possible.

4 The fourth response, which I would like to call *reconsideration*, straddles all three other ones. What I have in mind here is a form of thinking that takes all objections to social science seriously, but concludes with the possibility, though a very precarious one, of maintaining the project, even if under considerably changed assumptions. Most importantly, in the context of my argument, this approach reverses the question of the relation of identities, practices, and polities by rejecting any idea of a preconceived need of, or tendency toward, coherence. It is on this point in particular – and on epistemological and methodological thoughts that are related to it – that this response differs from the response I have called modified continuation. The remainder of this paper will try to understand what "reconsideration" would mean today by continuing to focus on this problem of political sociology.

The Sociological Task of Today: Social Identity and Political Community between Globalization and Individualization

Drawing an analogy between the problematic of classical sociologists and the current one, as I have tried to do, was possible in part because the former lived through, and tried to make sense of, a major social transformation that can be compared, in some respects, to the one we are going through. Weber and Durkheim faced societies whose members had broadly accepted, or could no longer escape, a basically liberal imaginary signification. By their time, it was obvious to them and many others that the restrictions that had been applied to the liberties – and which had radically divided each of these societies into "two nations" of included and excluded – could no longer be upheld. It seemed clear that these restricted liberal orders would have to be transformed to ones with fully inclusive social rules. How that would occur, however, was very much an open question. Many doubted that it could occur without immense social costs. The sociologists intended, among other things, to contribute to the viability of such an inevitable social transformation.

Classical social science intended to diagnose emerging phenomena such as the increasing individualization that appeared to result from the dissolution of *Gemeinschaft*, the formation of "society" as a larger order based on different rules, and the construction of bureaucratic apparatuses in the big industrial enterprises, state administration, and the mass parties. Some observers recognized in such new institutions and rules the potential for a new coherence – though others, notably Weber, remained skeptical. But the intermediate historical outcome of the transformation then underway – through political struggles and disasters – was "successful": an organized modernity that effectively focused "modernized" social practices was built. Focusing involved a double movement. On the one hand, theoretically global, open-ended practices were reduced to national, bounded ones. On the other hand, the potentially infinite plurality and diversity of people on a territory was ordered and bound by a relatively coherent set of conventions for action. The order of organized modernity was one which was fully inclusive within nation-state societies, the extension of equal suffrage to all adult people and the recognition of gender equality in the law being the most indicative examples. At the same time, however, possibilities for participation were channeled into the prestructured paths of mass parties and welfare bureaucracies, and the boundaries to the "outside," to people of other nation-states, were much more firmly controlled than before.

By drawing on institutional and cultural means that were available in the nineteenth century, the actual structure and extension of social practices (what came to be called *society*) was made to overlap strongly with the rules for collective deliberation (in the *polity*, defined as the nation-state) and many of the socially important means of individual orientation (*social identities*). With hindsight, the creation of *imagined* communities, such as nation and class, can be identified as a means by which the political problematic was *temporarily* fixed. For much of the twentieth century, national and class communities – being English or French, a worker or a *cadre* – appeared not as creations and imaginations but as the natural locations of human beings in a post-traditional society.

The last two or so decades can be read as the breaking-up – or active dismantling – of this three-layered coherence.[11] Analyses of our time again stress processes of dissolution and of individualization. Theorists of dissolution argue that "the world market [. . .] has erased the territorial inscriptions of the productive structures [. . .] The occidentalization of the world is a broad movement of uniformization of the imaginary involving the loss of cultural identities" (Latouche 1985: 39–40). Theorists of individualization claim that all stable social orientations, such as class, culture and family are breaking up, and leaving individual human beings in much greater uncertainty and at greater risk when shaping their lives. If these two observations are joined together, then a second-crisis-of-modernity equivalent of the theory of the mass society emerges. Theorists of the latter had argued that the bureaucratic nation-state is the grand individualizer and destroyer of social structures and collective identities, that it isolates human beings and makes them depend-ent on its own, anonymous, and machine-like organization. Currently, the same is said to occur on a global scale: the nation-state then appears as an almost homely, "intermediary" institution and container for authentic cultural expression. Such ideas are found both in those theories of post-modernity that have an air of the tragic, since they see these developments as losses *and* as inevitable (see Lyotard 1985: 63–4), and by conservatives who try to maintain or reconstruct bounded institutions based on substantive notions of culture. Significantly, a normatively opposed interpretation of the same observations is also possible, in which the trends toward globalization would be seen as enhancing enablements, as widening and easing the human capabil-ity to reach out widely in space and time. Individualization may be regarded as a liberation from social constraints which have limited and channeled the ways in which human beings could draw on the historically available enablements. These views can be found in continuations of the modernist perspective in social thought, in neo-modernization theory, but they are also found in those strands of post-modernism that hail the new liberations.

Where, though, do these opposed assessments of globalization and indi-vidualization leave us with regard to the current condition of modernity – and the sociological possibility at understanding it? Let me begin an assess-ment with the issue of social identities. The concept of the nation as a strong basis for social, namely cultural–linguistic, identity rested on an idea of the historical depth of community, of bonds and commonalities created over long periods. Such a concept tends to "naturalize" boundaries and distinc-tions with "others" outside the historical community and to limit cross-boundary exchange. The concept of class was lower than the one of the nation, and not least for that reason its identity-constituting potential was more short lived. However, it is probably generally valid to say, in spite of some resurgence of nationalism, that the hold of these quasi-natural identi-ties has been loosening over the past quarter of a century in the West. From the 1960s onwards, the cultural revolution against organized modernity emphasized the normative unacceptability of such limitations and under-mined the persuasiveness of the idea of any "natural" community. What we have witnessed since then is not individualization but rather the creation of communities on other substantive grounds, chosen by the acting human beings themselves, and possibly more fluid and open to reconsideration than the classically modern, national, and class, communities.[12]

How then are such modes of identity-formation related to the current organization of social practices? The quasi-naturalness of social identities during organized modernity stemmed from the overlap of social identities with coherent sets of practices and polity boundaries. Under such conditions, there may be very little choice of social identity, even if awareness prevails that identities are not ascribed but "only" socially determined. But this overlap was not natural, it had been produced by cultural policies emphasiz-ing national identity and by controlling and restricting cross-boundary travel of people, goods and ideas (see, for example, Noiriel 1991). At the end of organized modernity this overlap is much less pronounced, and the formation of social identities is freed from such pre-determination. Today there is a strong dissonance between social identities and social practices, each of which are highly diverse and variable.

What impact then does such a situation have for conceptions of the polity? Political agency during organized modernity resided in practices and iden-tities focused on the sovereign nation-state and its idea of representation, both of which are now strongly challenged. Thus, modern politics faces a radical dilemma. On the one hand, the very idea of political deliberation depends on concepts of boundaries, membership and representation (Walzer 1983). On the other hand, the social practices to which politics refers may become increasingly "a-topic" (Gilbert and Guillaume 1985: 92), that is, not confinable to any space, so that no possible definable membership group could be found for deliberation, far less any community with a significant degree of shared values and, thus, a substantive basis for common deliberation.

The split between the organization of social practices, boundaries of poli-ties, and modes of identity formation a century ago led sociologists to argue strongly for the need for the emergence of a new, coherent social order. They were not particularly successful in their predictions of what form it would take. The division of social labor did not produce "organic solidarity," contra Durkheim; contra Weber, the legitimacy of existing forms of domination remained in doubt in European societies during the first half of the twentieth century. But sociologists contributed to identifying the political problematic of the time as well as the social and cognitive resources that were available to bridge the splits between identities, practices, and polities.

In the current situation, it appears as if those splits are even wider and the social and cognitive resources to bridge them scarcer than in the earlier situation. Any attempt to forge a new coherence on the model of the late nineteenth-century European nation-states could hardly be other than very restrictive, if not repressive, with regard to the pursuit of social practices and the expression of identities. In the face of multiculturalism, and violent racism and nationalism, the dissolution of class structures and the emergence of new social barriers, and homogenizing globalization and heterogenizing tribalization, I think, one can formulate the basic task of a political sociology today as the analysis of the *current* relation of social identities, social practices, and polity boundaries. The objective would be, on the one hand, to understand the degree and form of overlap or cleavage, but, on the other, also to rethink the very idea of the need for coherence.

Earlier sociology and political thought have rarely been able to work without some assumptions on *tendencies toward* coherence, through mechanisms of adjustment of values and norms, or on the *need for* coherence, to be enforced and safeguarded by supraindividual entities as guardians of the common, like the state, "society" writ large, or a universalist discourse on morality. In their own time of social transformation, the classical sociologists took significant steps in opening up this issue.[13] But mostly, they have not been able, or have not dared, to free their thinking radically of such presuppositions. That is where the limits of their political sociology can be found.

The existence of a certain overlap between social identities, political boundaries, and social practices may be a precondition for (re-)establishing political agency, but the extent and its possible current forms need to be assessed sociologically by looking at the actual "relations of association" between human beings and the degree of social and moral contingency of their communities.[14] Relations of association have to be analyzed with regard to the extensions and permeations of practices which human beings share with others and therefore should want to regulate in community, and assessed with regard to the conditions for such a potential political community to emerge, that is, the possibility of proceeding with common deliberation in such a form that political rules meet the other social practices at their level of extension, reach and impact.

To start out from the actual relations of association and their – potential or real – plurality, diversity and even incompatibility, means to radically loosen both the analytical and normative presuppositions common in social thought. Such a sociology renews its ties to political theory. It recognizes the fallacies of self-sustained individualist liberalism and accepts the notion that rules and boundaries of polities are related to identities and practices. It does not preconceive, however, what the mode of such a relation would or should be. Sociologically, this question is left to empirical, strongly interpretative analysis; politically, it is left to the open deliberation of the people who enact these rules.

I have tried to describe the task of current sociological reconsideration in terms that made it comparable to earlier efforts, and translatable into their languages. This analogizing should not conceal that I see this task as a radical one indeed. Accepting diversity of practices and identities brings back an idea of politics as open, creative human action; the sociology that goes along with such a politics will be quite different from most of either classical or modernist sociology.

Notes

This essay was written during a summer stay at the Princeton Institute for Advanced Study. Once again, I wish to thank the Institute's School of Social Science for their hospitality. Discussions with Albert Hirschman, Bernhard Peters and Björn Wittrock have helped me clarify my thoughts.

1 My own choice of terminology is not guided by the desire for intellectual distinction, but by the need to avoid those, often more familiar, terms in other views which are strongly shaped by conceptual or historical presuppositions. The notion of society, for instance, makes an assumption on the coherence of social practices; the (economic) idea of interest, one of autonomy and rationality shaping the view on self-identity. An analysis of conceptual transformations over time is seriously hampered by maintaining such loaded terms.

2 For two different ways of putting the issue, see Rorty (1989: chap. 3) and Taylor (1989a).

3 It may be recalled that the 1994 German government denied immigrants the right to double citizenship on grounds of the possibility of "conflicting loyalties" in the case of a dispute between Germany and their native country.

4 I elaborate ideas here that were initially raised in Wagner (1992; 1994).

5 Broadly in the sense in which Turner and Wardell (1986: 161) use the term "sociological project."

6 For useful accounts of various aspects see Polanyi (1975); Katznelson and Zolberg (1986); Evers and Nowotny (1987); Brock (1991); Procacci (1993); Rueschemeyer and Skocpol (1996).

7 For a more detailed characterization of this divergence between Europe and the United States see Wagner (1994: 108–11).

8 Parallel to this theorizing, an alternative approach, the critical theories of mass society, was developed which regarded basically the same phenomenon, namely the closure of modernity, as a threat and a loss. I shall not deal in detail with this approach here, though.

9 Politically, the right to diversity – to be different and to handle things differently – is a claim that stems from such reasoning. Other than calls for equality, such claims have proven difficult to deal with under the rules of organized modernity.

10 A major difference between the two situations is that sociological debate proved to be more continuous and persistent in the later one. I would attribute this fact mainly to the firm institutional establishment of social science at universities and other academic institutions. Thus, a minimal precondition for the continuity of a discourse was provided. This continuity meant that much rethinking of theories, concepts, and methods could and would take place under the broad assumption of the possibility of a social science.

11 Alain Touraine's notion (1992: 164–5, 225, 409) of the "dissociation" of a former "correspondence" of modernity and the social actors seems to stem from a similar observation – which he, though, casts in terms of actors and systems.

12 Such as observed by Alain Touraine (1985) for social movements and Michel Maffesoli (1988) for what he calls tribes. Even if the substantive idea is related to an ascriptive criterion, such as being black or being a woman, there is today a strong element of choice in whether one would make this criterion important for one's own self-realization, that is, by making belonging to the respective community a part of one's self-understanding. This is also how I would rather discuss neo-nationalism in the West.

13 See, for instance, Frisby and Sayer (1986) on variations in the concept of "society."

14 See Offe (1989: 755); also Hindess (1991). Significantly, the debate among communitarians and liberals seems to have focused on exactly this question, with the communitarians arguing for reinforcing coherence, for building polities on identities. However, some of the most reflective contributions to the debate, such as Charles Taylor's (1989a: 532; 1989b) and Michael Walzer's (1990), have, while accepting the proposition, raised the issue of the degree to which such a strong relation is actually required – as well as normatively defendable. See Frazer and Lacey (1993) for a critical assessment of the debate in related terms.

Part III

Continuity and Revision

There is little question that the classics are still useful sources of insight for analysts of social life. A careful thinking through of the classics enables one to identify the salient features of social phenomena in all eras. But an intelligent application of the classics also requires us to do the work of criticism of the classics that they themselves did of their predecessors as well as to do their work of refining and extending as well as altering the concepts they inherited. This kind of use of the classics is distinct from the kind discussed in Part I, in that the focus is on what the classics can do for us rather than on what we must do to understand the classics. Nevertheless, it is in the work of extension and application that we often come to understand the classics in new ways. We can see how their attention to particular empirical phenomena misled them into premature abstraction or into the reification of the phenomena with which they dealt. Through this kind of engaged extension of the classics we arrive at an answer to the question of what is living and what is dead in their thought.

The classic most in need of this kind of rethinking is Marx himself. The rethinking has, in a sense, been continuous since the death of Marx, with revisionisms and reconstructions a characteristic part of Marxism. The immediate context of the rethinking of Marx's thought is dominated by two different developments. The first is the collapse of the real existing socialist regimes in 1989. Whatever else could be said about these regimes, they were the living embodiments of at least some of the ideas of Marx and represented uniquely in history the construction of political orders according to recipes derived theoretically. The fact that much of the world's population was living under regimes professing roots in the theories of Marx, and the fact that numerous "liberation" struggles also existed under the banner of Marxism, is a fact unique in history and lent the thought of Marx a significance unlike that of any of the other "classics." When the end of this world movement came, it was natural to ask whether the significance of the ideas of Marx depended essentially or largely on this historical fact, and in view of the long relationship between the historical phenomena of Marxism as a political reality and the popularity of Marx's theory in Western circles this was a particularly trying question. Marxist intellectuals could no longer see themselves as contributing in their theoretical work toward the kind of continuation and fulfillment of an ongoing world transformation. For the first time Marx's thought was forced to be evaluated and adhered to purely on the grounds of its intellectual significance. And the main evidence of its correctness, the revolutionary movements of the world, could no longer be employed in its support.

At the same time as real existing socialism was collapsing, came the second development. Many important Marxists were engaged in an effort to provide Marxism with intellectual foundations consistent with the standards of academic debate. In a sense, this effort, and particularly the branch of this effort called analytic Marxism, which sought to restate Marxism in rigorous economic terms, proved to be part of the intellectual undoing of Marxism as a scientific doctrine itself. Erik Olin Wright discusses the future of Marxism and the question of the continuing significance of Marx's ideas in the light of both these developments.

Wright's analysis concludes that the continuing significance of Marx's thought is a consequence of his analysis of the phenomena of oppression and exploitation, so it is perhaps not surprising that the most vivid employments of Marxian ideas have been by feminists. Issues of gender and the analysis of the nature of gender domination have become a central part of academic sociology, especially in the US. Sandra Harding, a leading feminist philosopher with a background in sociology, has been at the forefront of the application of ideas derived from the tradition of Marxist sociology of knowledge to the problem of the gender character of knowledge. One of the most important topics in feminism is the phenomenon of the exclusion of women from positions of power and from full participation in the political, economic, and public life of modern as well as past societies. Central to the problem of exclusion and the specific injustices done to particular women who have been unable to employ their talents is the question of whether exclusion makes any difference in the character of these institutions and activities themselves. Much of feminist theory and the women's movement has been concerned to establish that indeed there is a difference, that the character of these activities is distinctively gendered as a result of these exclusions not only with respect to the individuals engaged in public life or holding positions of power, but in terms of the character of the activities and thinking of the institutions themselves. If the law is distinctively gendered and science is distinctively gendered, as feminist theorists have argued, there should be some sort of alternative to a male dominated form of these bodies of thought. Harding describes the grounds for believing that alternatives are possible and gives the success of feminist analysis as evidence that there is indeed a distinctive standpoint that deserves not only consideration, but which we have reason to believe is less blinkered than the standpoint of the dominant male order.

The influence of feminism on contemporary thought has been closely related to the rise of the field of cultural studies. In some respects cultural studies seems to be the successor to social theory: studies of popular culture and media now have the fashionability that sociology had in the 1960s. Culture is of course a central concern of the classics, and specially of Durkheim. Anne Kane shows how their insights can be extended not only to illuminate the role of culture in a particular historical situation, but to show why the social theoretical analysis of culture has a continuing significance that a social theoretically uninformed cultural analysis cannot have.

One of the pressing questions about the classics pertains most directly to the project of a scientific sociology which emerged, as noted earlier, after the Second World War in the United States. The attempt to create a scientific sociology resulted in neither a clear cut victory nor a clear cut defeat. The quantitative machinery of social science did develop, though emphatically not in the way that the quantifiers of the post-war period had expected it to develop. Not measurement, but the methods of multiple regression analysis and partial regression, already an important part of sociology by the 1920s, emerged as standard methods not only for sociology but for policy analysts and in a related form for economic forecasters and policy makers. For technical reasons, the technology of causal modeling did not require or employ the kinds of theoretical ideas important to the classics, and similarly did not require the insights of interpretative sociology as practiced by academic sociologists.

This situation led to the emergence of what John Hall calls, following the famous essay by C. P. Snow, the two cultures of sociology, reconstituting the project of sociology in any form resembling the idea of Merton and Parsons of a theoretical sociology closely based on and informative to empirical social research requires some sort of reconciliation of or bridging of these two cultures. Hall argues that a link can be made through a proper understanding of the character of measurement which still remains as a practical problem for empirical sociology despite the technical development of means of analysis which enable their user to de-emphasize the problems of the validity of measurement by utilizing multiple measurements of and using the technology to select those measures which best define structure. Hall's concerns are central to the question of whether it makes sense to think of sociology as a meaningful collective enterprise. If Hall is wrong and if no attempt like Hall's to reconcile the two cultures is possible, the long institutional connection between empirical social research and social theory will be no more than a fragile historical relic, with no continuing intellectual purpose.

7

Marxism after Communism

Erik Olin Wright

Introduction

In both the popular press and the scholarly media we hear a lot about the crisis of Marxism, even of its death. Frequently the collapse of regimes ruled by Communist parties is equated with the collapse of Marxism as a social theory. However, while there is unquestionably a historical linkage between Marxism and capital-C Communism, they are not interchangeable. Marxism is a tradition of social theory, albeit a social theory that has been deeply embedded in efforts to change the world. What is more, it is a tradition of social theory within which it is possible to do social science – that is, identify real causal mechanisms and understand their consequences. Capital-C Communism, on the other hand, is a particular form of social organization, characterized by the eradication or marginalization of private ownership of productive resources and high levels of centralization of political and economic power under the control of relatively authoritarian political apparatuses, the party and the state. Such parties and states used Marxism as a legitimating ideology, but neither the collapse of those regimes, nor their failure to live up to the normative ideals of Marxism are, in and of themselves, proofs of the bankruptcy of Marxism as a tradition of social scientific practice.

Indeed, there is a great irony in the claim that the demise of Communist regimes based on command economies implies the demise of Marxism. The core ideas of classical Marxism as developed in the late nineteenth century would lead one to predict that attempts at revolutionary ruptures with capitalism in backward, non-industrialized countries would ultimately fail to accomplish their positive objectives. Orthodox historical materialism insisted that socialism only becomes possible when capitalism has exhausted its capacity for development of the forces of production – when it is a fetter on the future development of society's productive capacity.[1] All Marxists, including Lenin, believed this prior to the Russian Revolution. The anomaly from the point of view of classical Marxism, therefore, is not that the state bureaucratic command economies have failed and are in a process of transition to capitalism, but that they survived for as long as they did. This reflects a basic silence in classical Marxism: it contains no theory of the temporal scale of its predictions. But the important point in the immediate context is that the collapse of Communist states is not a refutation of Marxism; it is at most a refutation of Leninist voluntarism, of the belief that by revolutionary will and organizational commitment it is possible to build socialism on inadequate material foundations.

Yet, even though strictly speaking the collapse of Communist regimes does not imply a refutation of Marxism as a social theory, nevertheless the events of the late 1980s have helped to accelerate a growing sense of self-doubt and confusion on the part of many radical intellectuals about the viability and future utility of Marxism. I continue to believe that Marxism remains a vital tradition within which to produce emancipatory social science, but I also feel that in order for Marxism to continue to play this role it must be reconstructed in various ways. In the rest of this paper I want to sketch briefly the basic contours of this reconstruction focusing especially on the problem of class analysis.

Three Nodes of Marxism

Before discussing the project of reconstruction itself, it is first necessary to map out the central contours of what it is that is being reconstructed – that is, what is "Marxism"? The answer to this question, of course, can become an exercise in stupid doctrinal scholasticism: what is a *true* Marxist vs. a phony Marxist. The Marxist tradition is littered with the debris of battles over this kind of question. My intention here is not to define a set of beliefs which one must hold in order to be properly counted as a "Marxist," but rather to map out the basic coordinates of the Marxist tradition as a way of giving focus to the task of reconstruction.

To do this I think it is useful to see the Marxist tradition as being built around three conceptual nodes.[2] These I will call Marxism as *class analysis*.[3] These three nodes are illustrated in figure 7.1. Let me briefly define each of

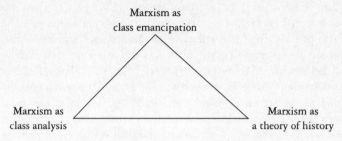

Figure 7.1 The three nodes of Marxism

these and their interconnections, and then indicate what I see to be the central tasks of reconstruction within them.

The contrast between Marxism as class analysis and Marxism as a theory of history can be clarified by the use of an analogy from medicine. Consider the following two disciplines: endocrinology and oncology. Endocrinology is what might be called an "independent variable discipline." If you are an endocrinologist you are allowed to study a vast array of problems – sexuality, personality, growth, disease processes, and so on – so long as you explore the relationship between the endocrine system and those explananda. Endocrinology is disciplined on its explanatory variables – the hormone system – but promiscuous on its dependent variables. Furthermore, in endocrinology it is not an embarrassment to discover that for some problems under investigation hormones turn out not to be very important. It is an advance in our knowledge of endocrinology to know what hormones do not explain as well as to know what they do. Oncology, in contrast, is a dependent variable discipline. As an oncologist you can study any conceivable cause of cancer – toxins, genetics, viruses, even psychological states. Oncology is disciplined on its dependent variable but promiscuous on its independent variables. And, in oncology, it is not an embarrassment to discover that certain potential causes of cancer turn out to be not very important.

In these terms, Marxism as class analysis is like endocrinology – it is independent variable Marxism – and Marxism as a theory of history is like oncology – dependent variable Marxism. As class analysts Marxists can study virtually anything. You can do a class analysis of religion, war, poverty, taste, crime. As in endocrinology, it should not be an embarrassment to discover that class is not very important for certain problems – this, too, is an advance in our knowledge about class. For example, in a recent study on the relationship between class and the sexual division of labor in the home in the United

States and Sweden, in spite of valiant efforts on my part to show that class was important, I concluded that the class composition of the household had very little to do with the distribution of housework between husbands and wives in either country. Yuppie husbands and working-class husbands did equally little work. The resulting paper, "The noneffects of class on the gender division of labor in the home" (1992), is, I hope, a contribution to class analysis by virtue of helping to clarify the limits of the explanatory reach of class.

The distinctive dependent variable of Marxism is history, or perhaps somewhat more precisely, *historical trajectory*. In its most ambitious form this is the overall epochal trajectory of human history from the prehistory of human civilization, through the present, and into the future. In its more modest form, it is the trajectory of capitalist development, from its origins within precapitalist feudal societies through its dynamic development and toward its eventual demise. In both cases Marxism attempts to theorize the inherent tendencies of historical change to follow a particular trajectory with a specific kind of directionality.[4]

Marxism as an emancipatory normative theory is the third, and in some ways the least elaborated, node of the Marxist tradition. Indeed, there have been Marxists – including Marx himself in places – who have denied the relevance of moral theory altogether. Nevertheless, the emancipatory dimension of Marxism is important and helps to frame much of what makes Marxist class analysis and Marxist theories of history distinctive. The heart of the emancipatory theory of Marxism is the idea that the full realization of human freedom, potential, and dignity can only be achieved under conditions of "classlessness" – the vision of a radically egalitarian society in terms of power and material welfare within which exploitation has been eliminated, distribution is based on the principle "to each according to need, from each according to ability" and the control over society's basic productive resources is vested in the community rather than in private ownership.

There are many different ways in which this egalitarian emancipatory ideal has been elaborated. Sometimes the stress is on the communitarian aspects of the ideal, sometimes on the issue of self-actualization and individual freedom, sometimes on the issue of material egalitarianism and the end of exploitation. In the strongest versions of the Marxist emancipatory vision classlessness is treated as the necessary and sufficient condition for the realization of emancipatory goals. Most contemporary Marxists would take a more modest position, seeing classlessness as a necessary, but not sufficient, condition, thus opening the door for an autonomous role for gender and other non-class issues in a project of human emancipation. In any case what makes the Marxist take on these normative issues distinctively Marxist is the commitment to classlessness as the necessary condition for the realization of these values.

Working-class politics – the collective organization of social forces in pursuit of working-class interests – has traditionally constituted the unifying link among the three nodes of Marxism. The emancipatory normative theory defines the ultimate values of radical working-class politics; the theory of history generates its broad, long-term objectives; and class analysis provides the basis for its strategies. If the point is to actively change the world, not merely interpret it, then Marxism is above all about using *class analysis* to understand the political processes for the realization of *historically* possible *emancipatory* goals.

The Interconnections among the Three Nodes of Marxism

The interconnections among these nodes are an essential part of what makes Marxism a distinctive intellectual enterprise.[5] Consider class analysis. What is most distinctively "Marxist" about Marxist class analysis? It is not the view that capitalists and workers exist in a class relation based on ownership of the means of production and sale of labor power. Nor is it the claim that this relation generates material inequalities and conflicts. This much one finds in Weber's class analysis. The crucial property of Marxist class analysis which differentiates it from Weberian analysis is its linkage to the normative problem of class emancipation and a theory of historical trajectory. The emancipatory normative theory is directly implicated in one of the core concepts of Marxist class analysis: exploitation. "Exploitation" is simultaneously an explanatory concept and a morally charged term. As an explanatory concept, exploitation is meant to identify one of the central mechanisms through which class structure explains class conflict. Class relations are thought to explain conflict in part because classes do not simply have *different* material interests which are contingently conflictual; their material interests are *intrinsically antagonistic* by virtue of being based on exploitation. Identifying such class relations as exploitative also implies a moral judgment about the inequalities generated within those relations. Exploitation does not simply define a "transfer of labor" from one social group to another, but a transfer that is deemed unjust or illegitimate. The emancipatory ideal of radical egalitarianism – ending class exploitation – is thus implicated in the very conceptualization of class itself.

One could, of course, construct a form of class analysis in which the concept of classlessness was simply a normative ideal of radical egalitarianism without any belief in the possibility of achieving this normative ideal. This would give the class analysis a moral edge, but there would be no implication that this alternative to capitalism was actively posed by capitalism itself. This is where the link between class analysis and the theory of historical trajectory comes in. The theory of history attempts to show that there are inherent tendencies inside of capitalism which pose socialism as an alternative. There are various forms of such claims, from highly deterministic ones (capitalism necessarily destroys itself through its own contradictions and is inevitably superseded by socialism) to much softer versions, in which the development of capitalism simply poses the possibility of socialism, perhaps making that possibility more and more viable, but not more and more of a necessity. In any case, this link between class analysis, class emancipation and historical trajectory is crucial for the distinctive, critical force of Marxism: class analysis is not just a moral condemnation of capitalism rooted in its link to an emancipatory ideal; it is also an empirical critique of capitalism rooted in its account of the historical generation of real alternatives.

In classical Marxism, these three theoretical nodes mutually reinforced each other in an extremely tight manner. Marxism as class emancipation identified the disease in the existing world. Marxism as class analysis provided the diagnosis of its causes. Marxism as the theory of historical trajectory identified the cure. Without class analysis and the theory of history, the emancipatory critique of capitalism would simply be a moral condemnation – what Marx derisively called "utopian socialism" – while without the emancipatory objective, class analysis would simply be an academic speciality. The three nodes constituted a unitary theory in which class analysis provided the necessary and sufficient explanatory principles for the theory of historical trajectory toward an emancipatory future. The enormous appeal of Marxism came in part from the unity of these three elements, for together they provided a seemingly firm basis for the conviction that eliminating the miseries and oppressions of the existing world was not simply a utopian fantasy, but a practical political project.

In recent years, along with a considerable deepening of our understanding of each of these nodes taken separately, there has been a gradual erosion of their unity and integration. Today, relatively few Marxists still believe that class analysis alone provides a sufficient set of causes for understanding the historical trajectory of capitalism, and even fewer feel that this historical trajectory is such that the likelihood of socialism has an inherent tendency to increase with capitalist development. From a comprehensive and relatively self-contained paradigm of social science which aspired to explain all social phenomena relevant to emancipatory social change, Marxism is moving toward a more loosely coupled conceptual framework that provides an account of a range of specific causal mechanisms that help explain those phenomena.

This decline in the integration of its theoretical components has contributed to the sense of intellectual crisis in the Marxist tradition. This loosening of its theoretical structure, however, need not signal the impending demise of Marxism; to the contrary, the less rigid framework may open up new avenues of theoretical development within each of the nodes of the Marxist tradition. Such a reconstruction is especially important given the intellectual climate created by the collapse of the command economies ruled by Communist parties.

The Challenge to Marxism Posed by the Collapse of Communism

Even though a good case can be made that the collapse of the command economies is consistent with the predictions of classical Marxism, nevertheless, these great historical transformations do pose a challenge for all three nodes of Marxism. The Marxist emancipatory ideal, the theory of history and Marxist class analysis all depend in one way or another on the plausibility of socialism as an alternative to capitalism. If the collapse of these regimes undermines the theoretical arguments about the feasibility of transcending private property and capitalist class relations, then these elements of Marxism are seriously threatened. While the demise of the command economies does not prove that there are no viable emancipatory alternatives to capitalism, it does potentially call such claims into question, depending upon one's diagnosis of exactly why the command economies reached such a crisis and impasse.

Neo-Marxists had been very critical of the Soviet Union long before the present attempt to construct capitalism. The guts of the standard neo-Marxist critique revolved around the problem of democracy: in the absence of meaningful democracy, socialist economic institutions could not be constructed and sustained. Many neo-Marxists thus felt that a profound democratization of social and political institutions would be able to generate viability to the socialist project, at least under conditions of highly developed forces of production. Rather than seeing the absence of private ownership of capital as the core problem, we argued that it was the absence of workers' democracy.

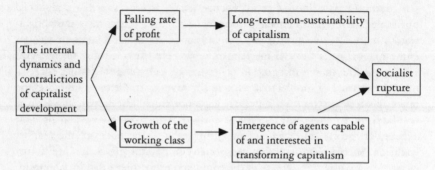

Figure 7.2   Traditional Marxist arguments for socialism

Hardly anyone in Russia and Eastern Europe seems to believe this. What is more, many radical intellectuals in the West who share the egalitarian values traditionally associated with Marxism are also today skeptical about the viability of democratic socialism, let alone communism.[6] Even if one believes that the empirical evidence remains highly ambiguous on these matters, nevertheless, it is difficult to sustain the concepts of socialism and communism with the certainty that once characterized Marxism. Without such concepts, however, the whole enterprise of Marxist class analysis falters.

Classical Marxism had a brilliant solution to the problem of establishing the credibility of socialism as a form of social production: it turned the problem upside down and tried to prove the long-term *non*-viability of capitalism. The story is quite familiar as illustrated in figure 7.2. It is based on two causal chains, both rooted in the internal dynamics of capitalist development. One causal chain leads from the contradictions of capitalist development through the falling rate of profit to the fettering of the forces of production within capitalism and thus the long-term non-sustainability of capitalism; the other causal chain leads through the growth of the working class to the increasing capacity of agents capable of transforming capitalism. The coincidence of these two causal chains makes a rupture in capitalism desirable and possible.

If this story were correct, then it would perhaps be less essential to have a positive theory of socialism as an alternative to capitalism. If capitalism is non-reproducible in the long run and if agents exist (workers) who have a clear interest in democratic control over social production and a capacity to seize power, then perhaps the problem of demonstrating the viability of socialism can be bracketed. Unfortunately, both of the causal chains in this argument no longer seem secure, even to many theorists still working within the Marxist tradition. The thesis of the long-term non-reproducibility of capitalism – the inherent, endogenous tendency toward deepening, and eventually catastrophic, crises rooted in the falling rate of profit – is certainly problematic, as is the claim that capitalism produces a sufficiently homogeneous class of proletarians to constitute its grave diggers. In this context, then, the failure of the command economies and the tentative embrace of capitalism by many people in those societies is troubling to democratic socialists. While these societies were not socialist in the sense of society's productive resources being democratically controlled by workers, they had suppressed capitalist property, and their failure is thus consistent with the claim that private ownership of capital is essential for incentives and efficiency in developed economies.

The future of Marxism thus faces two significant challenges: first, there is the theoretical challenge posed by developments within radical social theory, including the Marxist tradition itself, which have led to a rejection of totalizing versions of Marxism, and, second, there is the political challenge posed by the dramatic historical developments of recent years which call into question the feasibility of a critical theory normatively anchored in socialism. Some people might think that these challenges will ultimately lead toward a dissolution of Marxism as a coherent intellectual tradition. There are certainly voices in the post-Marxist, post-modernist camp who reject all explanatory pretensions for class analysis as epistemologically illegitimate and believe that efforts of reconstructing Marxism are last gasp efforts by recalcitrants unwilling to face the facts. Such councils of despair, I believe, should be resisted. While there may be no going back to the confident assurances of Marxism as a comprehensive paradigm of everything, it is also the case that any serious attempt to understand the causes of oppressions in order to enhance the political projects aimed at their elimination must include as part of its core agenda the analysis of class. And for this, a reconstruction of Marxism is essential.

In what follows I will briefly discuss ways of recasting the tasks of each of the nodes of the Marxist tradition and then turn to a more sustained discussion of certain problems in class analysis.

Reconstructing the Nodes of Marxism

MARXISM AS THE THEORY OF HISTORICAL TRAJECTORY

The central *function* of the theory of historical trajectory within Marxism is to provide a grounding for the claim that socialism – and ultimately communism

– are not simply moral ideals, but empirically viable alternatives to capitalism. Historical trajectory was taken as an explanandum not primarily for its own sake as an object of intellectual curiosity, but because it provided the foundation for scientific socialism.

The question, then, is whether this function can be satisfied without embracing the problems of trying to construct such an ambitious theory of history. Two departures from the traditional model are particularly promising.[7] First, the explanandum can be shifted from historical *trajectory* to historical *possibility*. Instead of trying to explain the overall trajectory of human history or even the trajectory of capitalism as a more or less determinate sequence of stages, it may be more useful to focus on the ways in which alternative futures are opened up or closed off by particular historical conditions. A theory of historical possibility might develop into a stronger theory of historical trajectories, but it does not presume that sequences follow a single trajectory as opposed to a variety of possible trajector*ies*.

Second, instead of understanding historical variation in terms of discrete, qualitatively discontinuous modes of production as in classical Marxism, historical variation can be analyzed in terms of more complex patterns of decomposition and recombination of elements of modes of production.

Consider capitalism and socialism. Capitalism is a society within which capitalists own the means of production and workers own their labor power; socialism is a society within which workers collectively own the means of production while still individually owning their labor power. In traditional Marxist conceptions of modes of production you either have one, or the other, except perhaps in periods of unstable transition. (Of course, in a socialist society one might still have vestiges of some capitalist enterprises and in a capitalist society there can be some state enterprises and even worker-owned enterprises, but any given unit of production would be capitalist or socialist.)

An alternative conceptualization sees the category "ownership" as consisting of a complex set of rights and powers, and entertains the possibility that these rights and powers can be broken apart, that they need not form a unitary gestalt. Within a given system of production, certain rights can be socialized and others remain private. Individual firms can therefore have a mixed ownership character. Even in American capitalism, the heartland of relatively pure capitalism, certain aspects of private property rights are partially socialized through such things as health and safety regulation and environmental protection. Such a situation might be termed an "interpenetration" of modes of production. Rather than seeing the historical trajectory of capitalism primarily in terms of the ruptural division of capitalism vs. socialism, this way of thinking about economic structure opens up the possibility for a much wider set of variations among capitalisms and socialisms in which different patterns of interpenetration become the salient problem for analysis. In analyzing the historical development of capitalist societies, then, the issue becomes one of trying to theorize the development of different trajectories (in the plural) of such interpenetrations of modes of production.

MARXISM AS A THEORY OF CLASS EMANCIPATION

The shift in the account of historical variation from a sequence of discrete modes of production to patterns of interpenetration of modes of production suggests a parallel shift in the normative theory of class emancipation. Instead of seeing "classlessness" as the practical normative principle motivating Marxist theory, this principle might better be thought of as "less classness." This implies a shift from an idealized end state to a variable process. Capitalisms vary in the degree of exploitation and inequality that characterize their class structures and in the extent to which socialist elements have interpenetrated the system of production. Private ownership of capital can be more or less constrained through democratic empowerment of workers, through socialized control over various dimensions of property rights. Classlessness still remains as a utopian vision, but the operative norm that provides the basis for the empirical critique of existing institutions is the reduction in classness.

A focus on less classness also opens the door for a much broader variety of theoretical models of practical emancipatory objectives. Let me give two recent examples. One proposal for the reform of the welfare state in advanced capitalism is to replace most income-support programs with what is called an unconditional "basic income grant" (or BIG).[8] The idea is quite simple: every citizen is given a subsistence grant of basic income sufficient to have a "historically and morally" decent standard of living, unconditional on the performance of any contribution to the society. The grant of basic income is like the grant of basic education and basic health, a simple right of citizenship. Such a grant effectively breaks the linkage between separation from the means of production and separation from the means of subsistence that is the hallmark of proletarianization in capitalism. Marxists, following Marx, have always assumed that it was inherent in capitalism that by virtue of the separation from ownership of means of production workers would also be separated from the means of subsistence and thus would be forced to work for a living. This is what it means to call workers "proletarians." What the BIG proposal hopes to accomplish is significant erosion of the coercive character of capitalism by making work much more voluntary and thus at least partially deproletarianizing the working class. There are, of course,

many possible objections, both ethical and practical, to BIG. The point here
is that this kind of proposal is opened up within a reconstructed theory of
class emancipation once the normative core is understood in terms of less
classness rather than exclusively in terms of classlessness.

A second illustration of the new kinds of models of emancipatory objectives is represented in John Roemer's controversial work on the problem of
public ownership and the meaning of "socialism" (1992a; 1992b). Roemer
argues that it is inconceivable that any technologically advanced society can
function with the minimum necessary efficiency without a substantial role
for markets in both consumption goods and capital. He therefore believes
that the idea of a centrally planned socialism is no longer viable. But how
can you have real markets, especially in capital, without having private
ownership? How can the idea of "market socialism" be made coherent? His
proposal is basically quite simple. Very briefly, it amounts to creating two
kinds of money in a society – money for the purchase of consumption goods
and money for the purchase of ownership rights in firms (stock-money).
Stock-money is initially distributed equally to all adults and a mechanism is
in place for the individuals in each new cohort of adults to receive their per
capita share of stock-money. The two kinds of money are non-convertible;
you cannot cash in your wealth in commodity money for stock-money. This
prevents people who have high income from their jobs becoming wealthy
owners. You are allowed to buy and sell stocks with your stock-money, and
thus there is a stock market. Firms obtain new capital through loans from
banks, which are publicly owned.

There are various other details and refinements of this idea, but basically
it amounts to creating a mechanism in which it becomes impossible for
people to become wealthy owners of the means of production. Ownership is
"socialized" in the sense that every person has close to the per capita share
of ownership of means of production and credit institutions are democratically controlled. In other respects, markets function with only the usual
kinds of regulations one finds in capitalist economies.

Is this socialism? Does it further the emancipatory goals that socialists
have traditionally supported? These are important and controversial questions. But again, as in the case of BIG, models of this sort enter the purview
of a normative theory of class emancipation once the preoccupation shifts to
less classness.

MARXISM AS CLASS ANALYSIS

To understand the tasks facing a reconstructed class analysis it is useful to distinguish between two understandings of what class analysis can realistically

hope to achieve. Consider the problem of explaining various aspects of gender oppression, let's say the unequal division of labor in the home. One view is that Marxists should aspire to a general class *theory* of gender and thus of gender inequalities. To return to the analogy between Marxism and medicine, this would be equivalent to proposing an endocrinological theory of cancer in which hormones would be viewed as the most fundamental determinants of cancer. Similarly, a class theory of gender oppression implies that class is in some sense understood as the most fundamental or important cause of gender oppression. This need not imply that all aspects of gender oppression are explainable by class, but that at an appropriate level of abstraction, class explains the most important properties of gender oppression.

An alternative view is that Marxists should engage in the class *analysis* of gender oppression without prejudging ahead of time whether or not a fully fledged class theory of gender is achievable. A class analysis implies examining the causal connections between class and gender and their mutual impacts on various explananda, such as gender ideologies, women's poverty, or sexual violence. This implies a provisional recognition that gender processes are rooted in autonomous causal mechanisms irreducible to class and the task of class analysis is to deepen our understanding of their interactions in explaining specific social phenomena. Now, it may happen that out of the discoveries of the class analysis of gender oppression, it may eventually be possible to construct a class theory of such oppression. While such an eventuality seems unlikely given our present knowledge of these processes, it is not logically precluded.

Reconstructing class analysis, therefore, involves a shift from an a priori belief in the primacy of class in social explanations to a more open stance toward exploring the causal importance of class. It might appear that this way of treating class analysis relegates class to the status of simply one factor among many. Does this not lead to a kind of causal pluralism characteristic of some currents in "post-modernist" social theory in which everything causes everything and nothing is accorded special explanatory importance?[9] Such a conclusion might be warranted if we had recently arrived from outer space and never studied anything about human social life. The fact is, however, that we know a great deal about social life, both from casual observation and systematic research, and one of the things we know is that class is massively important for understanding many social phenomena. Class is a powerful causal factor because of the way in which class determines access to material resources and thus affects the use of one's time, the resources available to pursue one's interests and the character of one's life experiences within work and consumption. Class thus pervasively shapes both material interests and

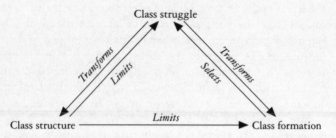

Figure 7.3   Macro-model of class stucture, class formation, and class struggle

capacities for action. This is not to suggest that class is universally the most important determinant of everything social, but that it is presumptively important for a very wide range of phenomena. More specifically, class is likely to be especially important in explaining the possibilities for and obstacles to human emancipation, since on virtually any construal of the problem, emancipation requires fundamental reorientations of the use of society's material resources, surplus, and time. Such projects, therefore, inevitably involve in a central way class politics – political struggles over property relations and control of the social surplus. The central task of class analysis, then, is to give greater precision to the causal structure of class phenomena and the relationship between class and other social phenomena relevant to the normative goals of Marxism.

ELEMENTS OF A RECONSTRUCTED CLASS ANALYSIS

My work on reconstructing class analysis has revolved around a relatively simple model of the interconnections among the core concepts of class analysis: class structure, class formation, and class struggle. This model is illustrated in figure 7.3. The basic idea of this model is that class structures impose *limits* upon, but do not uniquely determine, both class formations (that is, the collective organization of class forces) and class struggles; class formations *select* class struggles within the limits imposed by class structures; class struggles in turn have *transformative* impacts on both class structures and class formations.[10] This is not a purely structural model, for the conscious practices of actors – class struggles – transform the social structures which limit those practices. But it is also not an agent-centered model, for those struggles are seen as systematically constrained by the structures within which people live and act. Structures limit practices but within those limits practices transform structures.

This model defines, at best, an agenda of problems to be solved. Content needs to be put into each of the terms and mechanisms need to be elaborated for each of the connections specified in the model. My own work on these issues has been preoccupied primarily with one element of the model: class structure. I have argued that in order to have a solid foundation for understanding the relationship between class structure and class formation and both of these to class struggles, we first need a coherent concept of class structure. Traditional Marxist concepts of class structure suffered, I have argued, from two major problems. First, they were too *abstract* for many empirical problems. The conventional Marxist concept of class structure posits polarized, antagonistic classes defined within pure modes of production – slaves and slave masters, lords and serfs, capitalists and workers. But for many concrete empirical problems, many locations in the class structure, especially those loosely called the "middle class," do not seem to fit such a polarized view of classes. Second, traditional Marxist concepts of class structure tended to be too macro. They described the overall structures of societies, but did not adequately map onto the lives of individuals. My objective, then, was to produce a Marxist concept of class structure which would link concrete and micro levels of analysis to the more abstract macro concepts.

I will illustrate this problem of concept formation through three specific conceptual issues: the problem of the *middle class*, the problem of the (so-called) *underclass*, and the problem of *class alliances*.

THE MIDDLE CLASS

The "middle class" poses an immediate problem for Marxist class analysis: if the abstract concept of class structure is built around polarized classes, what does it mean to be in the "middle"? In the 1970s when I began work on this problem, there was, in my judgment, no satisfactory answer to this question. I proposed a new concept as a way of dealing with these kinds of locations: *contradictory locations within class relations*. The basic logic was quite simple. Previous attempts at solving the problem of the middle class all worked on the assumption that a given micro *location* within the class structure (a location filled by an individual) had to be in one and only one class. Thus the middle class was treated as part of the working class (a new working class), part of the petty bourgeoisie (a new petty bourgeoisie) or as an entirely new class in its own right (a professional–managerial class). I argued that there was no need to make this assumption. Why not entertain the possibility that some class locations – jobs actually performed by individuals – were simultaneously located in more than one class. Managers, for example, could be viewed as simultaneously capitalists and workers – capitalists insofar as they dominated the labor of workers, workers insofar as they did not own the means of production and sold their labor power to capitalists.

The idea of contradictory locations seemed to provide a more coherent solution to the problem of the middle class, a solution that was consistent with both the abstract polarized class concept and the concrete complexities of real class structures. Nevertheless, there were a number of significant conceptual problems with this approach.[11] This led me in the mid-1980s to propose a second solution to the problem of the middle class. This solution revolved around the concept of "exploitation." Exploitation can be loosely defined as a process by which one group is able to appropriate part of the social surplus produced by another group. Any society, I argued, is charac- terized by a variety of mechanisms of exploitation. Capitalist societies do not simply have distinctively capitalist forms of exploitation based on unequal ownership of means of production. They also contain what I called, based on the work of John Roemer, "skill exploitation" and "organization exploitation" (1982). In skill exploitation, owners of scarce skills are able to extract a rent component in their wages. This is basically a component of the wage above and beyond the costs of producing and reproducing the skills themselves.[12] It thus embodies part of the social surplus. In organization exploitation, managers are able to appropriate part of the surplus through the power which they command inside of the bureaucratic structures of capitalist production. Using this notion of differentiated mechanisms of exploitation, the "middle class" could be defined as those locations in the class structure which were exploited through one mechanism of exploitation, but were exploiters through another. Professional and technical employees, for example, can be seen as capitalistically exploited, but skill exploiters. They thus constitute "contra- dictory locations within exploitation relations."

Both of these proposals break with the idea that individual class locations must have a homogeneous class character, and in this way they introduce greater concrete complexity than earlier concepts of "class location." In other respects, however, both of these proposals still adopt a quite restricted view of what it means to occupy a class "location." In particular, they both define locations statically and they restrict the concept of class location to jobs. A fully elaborated micro-concept of how individual lives are tied to class struc- tures needs to break with these restrictions by developing the idea of *mediated* class locations and *temporal* class locations.[13]

The concept of mediated class location recognizes that people are linked to the class structure through social relations other than their immediate "jobs." People live in families, and via their social relations to spouses, parents and other family members, they may be linked to different class interests and capacities. This problem is particularly salient in households within which both husbands and wives are in the labor force but may occupy different job classes. A school teacher married to a business executive has a different "mediated" class location than a school teacher married to a factory worker. For certain categories of people – housewives and children, for example – mediated class locations may be the decisive way in which their lives are linked to class. For others, mediated class locations may be less salient. In any case, the patterning of mediated class locations is potentially an important way in which class structures vary.

Temporal class locations refer to the fact that many jobs are embedded in career trajectories which in various ways involve changes in class character. Many managers, for example, begin as non-managerial employees, but the fact that they are in a managerial career track changes the class interests tied to their statically defined location. Moreover, many middle-class employees have a sufficiently high rent component in their wage (that is, earnings above what is needed to reproduce their labor power) that they can turn a significant amount of savings into capital through various kinds of investments. Such a capitalization of employment rents is itself a special kind of temporal dimension to class locations for it enables highly paid middle-class employees over time to directly tie their class interests to the bourgeoisie. This does not mean that they become capitalists, but rather that their class location assumes an increasingly capitalist character over time.

All of these complexities are attempts at defining systematically the linkages between individual lives and the class structure in ways that enrich the general model of determination in figure 7.3. In that model class structures are seen as imposing limits on the process of class formation. There are two basic mechanisms through which this limitation occurs: first, class structures shape the material interests of individuals and thus make it more or less difficult to organize certain arrays of class locations into collective organizations; and, second, class structures shape the access to material resources and thus affect the kinds of resources that can be deployed by collective organizations within class struggles. Both of the proposed concepts of the middle class as well as the concepts of mediated class locations and temporal class locations attempt to provide a more fine-grained map of the nature of the material interests and resources available to individuals by virtue of their linkage to the class structure and thereby facilitate the analysis of the process of class formation.

THE UNDERCLASS

A second problem in the analysis of class structures that has become especially important in recent years is the issue of the "underclass." This concept was popularized in William Julius Wilson's work on the interconnection between race and class in American society (Wilson 1982; 1987).

Wilson argues that as legal barriers to racial equality have disappeared and as class differentiation within the black population has increased, the central determining structure of the lives of many African-Americans is no longer race as such, but class. More specifically, he argues that there has been a substantial growth of what can be called an urban "underclass" of people without marketable skills and with very weak attachments to the labor force, living in crumbling central cities isolated from the mainstream of American life and institutions.

How can this concept be given some precision within the framework of a reconstructed Marxist class analysis? One strategy for doing this is to introduce a distinction between what might be termed *non-exploitative economic oppression* and *exploitative economic oppression* (or simply "exploitation" for short). To get at this distinction, we first need to define the general concept of economic oppression. As a first approximation, economic oppression can be defined as a situation in which: (1) the material welfare of one group of people is causally related to the material deprivations of another, and (2) the causal relation involves morally indictable exclusion from access to productive resources. This is a fairly complex definition. Without (2), the losers in a poker game would be described as "oppressed." Without (1), we have economically gratuitous exclusion – exclusion from resources from which no one derives material benefit. "Economic oppression" is thus a situation in which the material benefits of one group are acquired at the expense of another and in which unjust exclusion is an essential part of the process by which this occurs. The introduction of (2), of course, renders judgments of the oppressive nature of a particular inequality highly contentious, since there will generally be disputes about the moral standing of the exclusions that back up the inequalities in question.

Economic oppression defined in this way can take many forms. Of particular salience to class analysis is the distinction between exploitative and non-exploitative economic oppression. Economic exploitation is a specific form of economic oppression defined by a particular kind of mechanism through which the welfare of exploiters is causally related to the deprivations of the exploitated. In exploitation, *the material well-being of the exploiter causally depends upon their ability to appropriate the fruits of labor of the exploited*. The welfare of the exploiter therefore depends upon the *effort* of the exploited, not merely the deprivations of the exploited. In non-exploitative economic oppression there is no transfer of the fruits of labor from the oppressed to the oppressor; the welfare of the oppressor depends on the exclusion of the oppressed from access to certain resources, but not on their effort. In both instances, the inequalities in question are rooted in ownership and control over productive resources.[14]

The crucial difference between exploitation and non-exploitative oppression is that in an exploitative relation, the exploiter *needs* the exploited since the exploiter depends upon the effort of the exploited. In the case of non-exploitative oppression, the oppressors would be happy if the oppressed simply disappeared. Life would have been much easier for the European settlers to North America if the continent had been uninhabited by people.[15] Genocide is thus always a potential strategy for non-exploitative oppressors. It is not an option in a situation of economic exploitation because exploiters require the labor of the exploited for their material well-being. The contrast between South Africa and North America in their treatment of indigenous peoples reflects this difference poignantly: in North America, where the indigenous people were oppressed (by virtue of being coercively displaced from the land) but not exploited, genocide was the basic policy of social control in the face of resistance; in South Africa, where the European settler population heavily depended upon African labor for its own prosperity, this was not an option.

This dependency of the exploiter on the exploited gives the exploited a certain form of power, since human beings always retain at least some minimal control over their own expenditure of effort. Purely repressive control is costly and often fails to generate the required levels of diligence and effort on the part of the exploited except under very special circumstances. As a result, there is generally systematic pressure on exploiters to elicit in one way or another some degree of consent from the exploited in order to gain at least a minimal level of cooperation from them.

In these terms, an "underclass" can be defined as a category of social agents who are economically oppressed but not stably exploited within capitalist production. People in the contemporary American underclass are oppressed because they are denied access to various kinds of productive resources, especially the necessary means to acquire skills and good jobs.[16] But they are not consistently exploited. They are thus largely expendable from the point of view of the rationality of capitalism, and as a result repression is the central mode of social control directed toward them. Their potential power against their oppressors – their capacity to force concessions of various sorts

– comes from their capacity to disrupt consumption, especially through crime and other forms of violence, not their capacity to disrupt production through their control over labor.

CLASS ALLIANCES AND MULTICLASS MOVEMENTS

One of the main objectives in elaborating these refinements in the concept of class structure is to facilitate the analysis of class formations and class politics. One crucial dimension of class formation is the problem of class alliances. Class alliances are situations in which people from different class locations come together to engage in collective action against a common class enemy by reaching, in one way or another, some kind of compromise on the differences in their class interests. A class alliance is thus to be contrasted with what can be termed a "multiclass movement" in which the actors agree to ignore class differences in order to form a solidaristic movement for some political objective. National liberation movements, for example, frequently place class differences among their supporters on a back burner in the name of "national unity." No real attempt is made to forge a class compromise between bourgeois, middle-class, working-class, and peasant participants in the struggle. They are united in their opposition to a colonial power, but their unity is not grounded in any significant attempts at reconciling their conflicting class interests.

This contrast between multiclass movements and class alliances is, of course, somewhat stylized. Many situations involve variable mixes between these two ideal types. Nevertheless, the analytical distinction is important politically and theoretically. In many situations, multiclass movements are easier to form than class alliances, but equally, they frequently founder by virtue of the unresolved class tensions within them. Class alliances, on the other hand, may be harder to forge, but once forged may be more durable since conflicts of interest have been compromised rather than ignored.

The various complexities in the analysis of class structure we have been discussing can help to illuminate specific problems in the formation of class alliances. Consider the problem of alliances involving the middle class with either the capitalist class or the working class. People in the middle class and the working class are both exploited by capitalists; they are both employees dependent upon the labor market for their livelihoods. They thus share some common class interests *vis-à-vis* capital which constitutes a basis for a class alliance. On the other hand, as skill and organization exploiters, the wages of middle-class employees contain a component of surplus which they are interested in protecting. Particularly when this component is large, people in the middle class have the capacity to capitalize their surplus and thus link their class interests directly to those of capitalists. These conflicting forces mean that within class struggles the middle class will be pulled between class formations involving alliances with workers or with capitalists. There are historical moments when the middle class seems to strongly ally with the bourgeoisie, as in Chile in the overthrow of the Allende regime, and other circumstances in which segments of the middle class forge fairly durable alliances with workers, as in Sweden in the period of the heyday of Social Democratic Party rule. An important task of class analysis is to sort out the conditions under which one or other of these patterns of alliance occurs.

The underclass poses quite different problems for the analysis of class alliances. It might seem natural that the underclass and the working class would tend to form class alliances, but there are many obstacles to this occurring. In their efforts to protect the jobs of workers and increase their wages, the labor movement often creates barriers within labor markets which act to the disadvantage of people in the underclass. In many historical cases, the underclass has been a source of scab labor in strikes and in other ways are manipulated by capitalists against workers. Thus, while both workers and the underclass share an interest in the state providing job training, regulating capital and increasing employment opportunities, in many contexts they see each other on opposing sides. Again, one of the tasks of class analysis is to understand the conditions which make solidaristic movements combining the working class and the underclass feasible.

Conclusion

Since the early 1970s there has been an extraordinary development of theory and research within the Marxist tradition. Our understanding of a host of Marxist problems has been fundamentally transformed, including such things as the labor theory of value, the theory of history, the dynamics of capitalist development, the transition from feudalism to capitalism, the contradictions of the capitalist state, the mechanisms of consent formation within production and the problem of the middle class in capitalist societies. These are solid achievements.

It is ironic, then, that in the context of such advances, Marxism should be pronounced dead as an intellectual force in the world. Mark Twain once remarked on reading his own obituary in the newspaper, that "the reports of my death are highly exaggerated." What looks like the death throes of Marxism to hostile critics may be simply growing pains as Marxism matures as a social scientific theory of class and its effects. One thing, however, is certain: class politics will continue to be a central dimension of social struggles, since the forms of ownership and control of society's productive resources has such a pervasive impact on so many social issues. And, if class politics is a central dimension of social struggle, then class analysis will have an important role to play in developing adequate theoretical tools for radicals. What remains to be seen, however, is the extent to which such class analysis will be embedded in a broader theoretical configuration that contains the normative commitments of class emancipation and the explanatory aspirations of a theory of historical possibilities.

Notes

This paper reflects, in part, a series of lectures given in South Africa in June, 1992. An earlier version of the first part was prepared for the American Sociological Association, August 20, 1992. The ideas in the paper have benefited greatly from the intense discussions I had in conjunction with the South African lectures.

1 For the clearest and most systemic elaboration of this claim, see Cohen, *Karl Marx's Theory of History: A Defense* (1978).

2 There are other ways of defining the contours of the Marxist tradition. From different sides of the methodological fence Alvin Gouldner in *The Two Marxisms* (1979) and Louis Althusser in *For Marx* (1977), for example, see the central line of demarcation within the Marxist tradition lying between deterministic–scientific Marxism and voluntarist–humanist Marxism. Others have distinguished between "vulgar Marxism" and non-reductionist Marxism. In contrast to such schemas which analyze the Marxist tradition in terms of epistemological and methodological commitments, the proposal that the Marxist tradition should be mapped in terms of these three nodes emphasizes the substantive preoccupation of different styles of Marxism. For a more elaborate discussion of these nodes of Marxist theory, see Wright et al., *Reconstructing Marxism* (1992: ch. 8). It should be noted that in that earlier treatment the "theory of historical trajectory" node was referred to as "Marxism as scientific socialism."

3 Robert Brenner has argued (personal communication) that "class analysis" is too narrow a characterization of the "explanatory node" of Marxism. In particular, class analysis does not adequately encompass the problem of *alienation*. While alienation generated inside of the capitalist labor process might be subsumed under class analysis, alienation rooted in markets and competition (also theorized under the rubric "commodity fetishism") cannot. Such alienation would exist even if we had a market economy consisting entirely of worker-owned and run cooperatives. In Brenner's view, market-generated alienation is as powerful an

explanatory principle within Marxism as class-generated exploitation. He thus proposes substituting the concept of "social property relations" for "class analysis" as the encompassing term to capture the core explanatory logic of Marxism. Class analysis would then be one among several aspects of the analysis of social property relations. In my usage of the terms here, the analysis of market competition within capitalism is treated as one dimension of class analysis, namely the analysis of the forms of competitive interaction among agents *within* specific classes – labor markets for the working class and commodity markets for the capitalist class Marxism as a *theory of historical trajectory* and Marxism as an *emancipatory normative theory*.

4 In these terms, Marxism is much more ambitious than Darwinian evolutionary biology in its attempts to explain historical change. Darwin never attempted to treat the trajectory of biological history as having any directional tendency of development. Its trajectory is the result of the contingent connection between accidental environmental factors and universal laws of adaptation. Classical Marxism, in contrast, argues that human history in general – or at least the history of capitalism in particular – has a relatively determinate trajectory. In this sense, the Marxist theory of history is more like the theory of the development of a single organism from conception to birth through maturation, than it is like the theory of evolution. For a systematic comparison of the Marxist theory of historical materialism and the Darwinian theory of biological evolution, see Wright et al. (1992: ch. 3).

5 Not all Marxists would accept this characterization of the "terrain of Marxism." Some Marxists, especially those who work in the more Hegelian tradition of theorizing, would object to the language of "mechanisms," "independent variables," and "dependent variables." Instead, Marxism's core concepts are seen as rooted in a notion of totality which cannot be meaningfully decomposed into "causes" and "effects." Still, even in Hegelian Marxism, class analysis figures prominently in the conceptualization of the totality and the central point of theorizing the totality is to understand the "unfolding of history" toward the emancipation of the proletariat. Hegelian Marxism can therefore be seen as engaging these three nodes albeit with a very different philosophical stance toward the problem of theoretical construction than the one I am using here.

6 The issue here is not socialism as an immediate political project, but its viability as a successful, sustainable alternative to developed capitalism under any plausible historical conditions.

7 For an extended discussion of these and other modifications of classical historical materialism, see Wright et al. (1992: ch. 5).

8 A particularly lively discussion of basic income was launched by the publication of an essay by Van der Veen and Van Parijs (1986), "A capitalist road to Communism," pp. 635–55. For a provocative collection of essays evaluating the normative and practical issues involved in basic income, see van Parijs (ed.) 1992, *Arguing for Basic Income: Ethical Foundations for a Radical Reform*.

9 Or, in some versions of post-modernist social theory, nothing explains anything and everything is simply a matter of perspective.

10 The model in figure 7.3 can be considered the core macro-model of class analysis. There is a parallel micro-model which links class *locations* to class *consciousness* and class *practices* of individuals.

11 These problems are discussed at length in Wright, *Classes* (1985: ch. 2). The most salient of them is that the concept of domination replaced exploitation as the core criterion for class locations within the concept of "contradictory locations."

12 The concept of "surplus" is not easy to define rigorously. The conventional idea in the Marxist tradition is that the total social product can be divided into two parts. One part – the necessary product – is the part needed to cover all of the costs of production, including the costs of producing workers (or, as Marxists have traditionally called it, the "value of labor power"). The surplus, then, is the difference between the total product and the necessary product. The difficulty with this definition comes in when we try to define precisely the "costs of producing labor power." If such costs are equated with the empirical wages of employees, then by definition, no employee can be an exploiter. If, however, wages are seen as potentially containing "rents" derived from various kinds of barriers to entry in labor markets, then wages can contain pieces of surplus.

13 For a more extensive discussion of the concepts of mediated and temporal class locations, see my essay "Rethinking, once again, the concept of class structure," chapter 8 in Wright et al. (1989).

14 It might be argued that criterion (2) is not strong enough to capture what is normally meant by an oppressive economic relation. Oppression is usually taken to imply more than simply a morally illegitimate inequality, but one that also involves some kind of power relation between the oppressor and the oppressed. Cheating in an economic exchange (or even a poker game) would count as a form of oppression under some interpretations of (2), since it results in the exclusion of the cheated from economic resources. But cheating, while surely morally illegitimate in most circumstances, would not generally be considered a form of oppression since there is not necessarily a power relation of domination and subordination between the cheater and cheated. Indeed, in many cases the cheater may be dominated by the cheated. To strengthen (2), we could add an additional criterion that the exclusion in question be backed by coercion, typically in the form of protection of property rights. In any case, for the present purposes we need not fine-tune this definition since the main point is to give some clarity to the distinction between exploitation and non-exploitative oppression.

15 This is not to deny that in certain specific instances the settlers benefited from the knowledge of native Americans, but simply to affirm the point that the displacement of the indigenous people from the land was a costly and troublesome process.

16 It is perhaps controversial to amalgamate the exclusion of the contemporary urban underclass from human capital and other job resources with the exclusion

of Native Americans from the land. In the latter case there was a zero-sum character to access to the resource in question and massive coercion was used to enforce the exclusion, whereas in the case of education, skills, and even good jobs, it is not so obvious that the resources in question are a fixed quantity and that access is being denied through force. Thus the factual inequalities of access to these resources may not in fact be instances of coercively enforced "exclusion." For present purposes, therefore, it should be viewed as a hypothesis that the underclass is "economically oppressed": that is, that there is indeed a process of morally indictable exclusion from access occurring here, an exclusion which has the effect of benefiting certain groups of people at the expense of others. This, of course, leaves open the crucial question of who, precisely, is benefitting from this exclusion.

8

Standpoint Epistemology (a Feminist Version): How Social Disadvantage Creates Epistemic Advantage

Sandra Harding

What is the relation between social and epistemic advantage? Most social theorists and philosophers act as if they assumed that persons like themselves – socially advantaged professionals, experts, in the production of knowledge – had epistemic advantage. The dominant paradigms and conceptual schemes of social theories, including theories of knowledge and philosophies of science, lead to such assumptions for they emphasize disinterested, dispassionate, rational, objective methods, and the susceptibility of the regularities of nature and social relations to explanation through such processes. These paradigms and conceptual schemes construct professionals as model knowledge producers. In societies valuing such rational, objective methods, professionals in knowledge production get high social status.

However, one strain of feminist epistemology, borrowing from older Marxian insights, has argued that it may be the case that, in limited but important respects, such *socially advantaged* people and their institutions are, in fact, *epistemically disadvantaged*, and that *social disadvantage* creates a certain kind of limited but important *epistemic advantage*. These standpoint theorists depart in significant respects from the Marxian arguments, and they reject interpretations of their own arguments that regularly are offered by philosophers and social theorists working in the liberal/empiricist traditions. They enable us to gain a more accurate understanding of the epistemic authority of knowledge-claims that originate "from below," and they suggest guidelines, a "method," for everyone to follow in seeking better to understand nature and social relations.

Here I will first briefly summarize the particular failures of Enlightenment confidence that provide an important context for understanding the standpoint arguments, and then outline the relation between social and epistemic advantage proposed by standpoint theories in general and feminist ones in particular. Finally, I shall show how standpoint theories challenge several common assumptions about the social that diminish the usefulness of many contemporary social theories and their associated theories of knowledge.

Post-Enlightenment Enlightenment in the Philosophy of Science

Late twentieth-century social theories have produced an impressive array of arguments that undermine confidence in the Enlightenment vision. By the end of the 1960s, even mainstream US philosophy of science had come to recognize that scientific claims could not, in principle, provide a glassy mirror of a reality that is out there and ready-made for such reflecting, and that the desire to do so was itself epistemically disadvantaging. This point is relevant to social theory because when the latter is constructed within liberal/ empiricist assumptions, in some form or other it takes this ideal as a model of the natural sciences that it tries to emulate or reject. And it is not only liberal/empiricist theorists whose conceptual frameworks are in these respects Enlightenment ones. In an important sense, leading strains of Marxian social theory made assumptions about the value-neutrality of the "standpoint of the proletariat," the way it expressed a truly human standpoint, that are not too different from those that empiricists make about "the rational mind." Echoes of Enlightenment assumptions can be heard even in social theory approaches that lodge epistemic authority in rational reconstructions of phenomenologies of life worlds.

It turned out that observations are necessarily theory laden. Moreover, our beliefs form a network such that none in principle are immune from revision. Even the laws of logic could come to be reasonable candidates for revision, as Quine argued in pointing to the untenability of the analytic/synthetic distinction, if scientists could come up with no more satisfying ways to bring their theories and observations in line with each other. Consequently, our theories are underdetermined not just by any actual evidence for them, but by any possible evidence (Feyerabend 1975; Kuhn 1970; Quine 1953). Scientific processes, both micro and macro, are not transparent; their culturally local features contribute to and sometimes even constitute our descriptions and explanations of nature's order.

One consequence of the failure of that part of the Enlightenment vision is the emerging understanding that more than one scientific theory or model can be consistent with any given set of data, and each such theoretical representation can come to have more than one reasonable interpretation. Indeed, this "slack" in scientific explanation, far from being the unmitigated defect that it appears in older philosophies of science, turns out to be a major source of the growth of scientific knowledge, permitting scientists to "see nature" in new ways that advance the increased accuracy and comprehensiveness of their claims (Van Fraassen and Sigman 1993).

These older admissions of the failure of Enlightenment hopes show that there is plenty of room in our very best, most rigorous belief sorting – even in the natural sciences – for different values and interests to construct different, reasonable representations or models of reality, and different, reasonable interpretations of those representations. Our knowledge systems could not be the dynamic, flexible, creative, empirically sensitive ones that they are were this not the case. It is against this background that standpoint theorists meditate on the links between social power and cognitive authority. They do not "import" political values and interests into sciences or social theories that were otherwise "pure"; they try to identify those ways in which such values and interests are already there that are especially hard to see from the perspective of the dominant paradigms, conceptual frameworks or epistemes.

Standpoint Theory

Standpoint theorists begin from the observation that social power and cognitive authority are not merely accidentally linked. The production of knowledge is a social matter, and what gets to count as knowledge is shaped in part by what the socially advantaged groups in any society want to know and how it benefits them to understand and explain it. Standpoint theorists question the legitimacy of that link on both cognitive and historical grounds. They argue that in societies stratified by gender, class, race, ethnicity, sexuality, and any other subjugating politics, the activities of those at the top both organize and set limits on what those people can understand about themselves and the world around them. "There are some perspectives on society from which, however well intentioned one may be, the real relations of humans with each other and the natural world are not visible" (Hartsock 1983: 159).

In contrast, the activities of those at the bottom of such hierarchies can provide starting points for everyone's research and scholarship, not just knowledge production *by* or *about* the socially disadvantaged, from which less partial and distorted perspectives become available. It is not that thought arising from the lives of the disadvantaged mirrors reality, since there are various kinds of cognitive limitations to it also. Rather, everyone should learn to start off their thought from the lives of the socially disadvantaged in order to detect the paradigms and conceptual practices of power that get to count as legitimated knowledge, and to shape social policy and everyone's thought. It is this distinctive kind of knowledge that cannot be made visible from within those paradigms and conceptual practices, but the outlines of which become visible from lives that are in significant respects outside them. Thus all knowledge is shaped by power relations in stratified societies, but not all such knowledge claims are equally false: some are less false than their competitors because of the greater comprehensivity, accuracy, and criticism that starting off thought from disadvantaged social locations makes possible.

Of course no one in the educated classes in modern societies, ones that hold scientific rationality as an ideal, would ever claim that legitimacy *should* accrue to knowledge claims simply because those who make them are socially advantaged. No one in such groups would defend "might makes right" in sorting knowledge claims. Nevertheless, two kinds of evidence have appeared to support the assumptions that cognitive advantage accrues to socially advantaged professionals in the production of knowledge, and not to the socially disadvantaged. First, there was the apparent "silence" of the weak. Of course the weak never really were silent; they were always trying to make their voices heard. Sometimes they managed to gain access to publicly recognizable speech so as to write books, deliver manifestos, or articulate the perspective from their lives in other forms that the strong found difficult not to hear. At other times the refusal of attentive listening by the powerful reduced the speech opportunities of the weak to such desperate forms as strikes, armed revolts, running away, street begging, going mad, or dying early. What counts as silence and speech is itself a matter of social interpretation. In the case of women's speech, the objective cognitive successes of feminist analyses in the sciences, social sciences, humanities, and public policy have eliminated any plausible imputation of "silence" to them.

Second, the powerful produced various theories to explain why social disadvantage was under certain circumstances linked to cognitive disadvantage. Most effective here have been theories of how biological inferiority explains both social and cognitive inferiority, for example, that women's uncooked semen (Aristotle), brain lateralization, hormones, or lower moral development, or Africans' inherent lazy and brutish nature, smaller cranial capacity, lower IQ or lower evolution in Darwinian struggles, and so on, were responsible both for these groups' lower social status and legitimate lack of cognitive authority. Social explanations have also been advanced that link lower social status to lesser cognitive authority – for example, middle-class women's purported preference for and happiness in restriction to the domestic realm, or the African–American "culture of poverty."

However, a long history of social theories have by now convincingly argued that there is no legitimate justification for social advantage. Moreover, it is clear that the social advantage of the powerful often enables them to continue to legitimate false claims that they perceive to advance their interests – for example, about their biological superiority, and how that justifies their social advantage. There is nothing inevitable about the plausibility of less false claims; many false but socially advantageous ideologies can be maintained presumably indefinitely, even if others may sooner or later lead their followers and, these days, the rest of us into extinction. Furthermore, such reflections suggest another possibility, namely that social advantage is, indeed, systematically linked to legitimate cognitive authority, but inversely so. In limited but important ways, social advantage creates epistemic disadvantage, and social disadvantage creates the possibility for epistemic advantage.

How has the specifically feminist form of standpoint theory developed? Its intellectual history is conventionally traced to Hegel's reflections on what can be known about the master–slave relationship from the standpoint of the slave's activities, and to the way Marx, Engels, and Lukács subsequently developed this argument into the standpoint of the proletariat from which were produced theories of how class society operates. The mechanisms of the class system cannot be detected if one starts off thought from bourgeois or managerial/administrative activities. From the perspective of the activities of workers and other socially disadvantaged groups, how capital is accumulated, profit generated, wages kept low, labor deskilled, and so on, becomes visible. A *social* history of standpoint theory would focus on what happens when marginalized peoples begin to gain public voice. They point out that from the perspective of their lives, the dominant accounts are less than maximally objective. Institutions designed to serve the needs of professional managerial classes have favored conceptual frameworks and paradigms that reflect not universally valid human problems, but only those the solutions to which will advance the values and interests of those classes.

In the late 1970s, several feminist thinkers independently began reflecting on how the Marxist analyses could provide resources for identifying effects of the structural relationship between the genders on the production of knowledge. (Harding 1983; 1986; Hartsock 1983; Rose 1983; Smith 1987; 1990; cf. also Jaggar 1983.)[1] How have favored conceptual frameworks and problems in the disciplines and public policy disproportionately represented only the values and interests of men in the dominant groups? How are values and interests unexpressed in our dominant institutions, their practices and cultures, that arise from women's assigned responsibilities for children, the elderly, the sick and disabled; from women's positions in intimacy relations, violence against women, domestic work, wage labor, the maintenance of community food supplies, health and the environment; from women's assigned positions in nationalism, imperialism, and capitalist expansion?

Feminist standpoint theory proposes a kind of "logic of discovery": start off thought from women's lives to be able to detect androcentric conceptual frameworks within which the prevailing research, scholarship, and social policy generated by the dominant groups are formulated. These frameworks are otherwise invisible. Why does this "logic of discovery" work? What makes women's activities more valuable than the activities of men in the ruling groups for generating fruitful research agendas? Diverse features of women's socially disadvantaged positions in gender relations, familiar to social theorists in other contexts, can be identified as sources of epistemic advantage for research and scholarship guided by feminist concerns.[2] For example, knowledge is supposed to be based, however complexly, on *human* experience, but women's half of human experience has been ignored or devalued as an origin of problematics and data. (What new questions are we led to ask about the law, about "normal" social relations between the genders, if we start off our thought from women's experiences of sexual harassment, rape, incest, or battery?) Moreover, women are "strangers" to social orders that have not been designed with their interests in mind; thus their lives can provide a more critical, less "nativist," perspective from which to seek causal accounts of social relations. (Why does the double day of work that most women in the world do appear to require no comment or explanation from self-styled progressive *social* theorists? Do they take women's situation to be determined by "the natural"? How are their analyses of social relations that ignore women's social situation functionally any different from those of sociobiologists?)[3]

Women's daily resistance to their oppression makes their lives better places from which to begin to understand how "the battle between the sexes" works at institutional as well as individual levels; thus women's struggles and feminist politics become part of "research methods" for understanding nature and social relations. (Try to put a sexual harassment policy in place in a university in order to be led to fresh understandings about how ancient ideals of mentoring and of the "great teacher" are based on assumptions of an erotically charged, all male, teaching community.) Another argument is that the perspective from women's lives reveals how women's activities in everyday life provide the necessary conditions for men in the ruling groups to engage in the illusion that they are self-made, autonomous, individuals, who owe no debts to anyone for their achievements. Moreover, it shows the material conditions that make appear plausible the excessively abstract conceptual schemes favored by Western social theory. Finally (for this only illustrative list), women are "outsiders within," whose presence inside a society from which they are nevertheless in some respects estranged makes their lives uniquely valuable positions – "borderlands" – from which to understand causal social relations that are not visible from the lives of people who are more solidly either outsiders or insiders.[4]

In its directive to "start thought from marginal lives," standpoint approaches of course contrast with the natural (or social) superiority arguments; they deny that what counts as knowledge is maximally responsible to the way things are. They deny that legitimate epistemic authority matches de facto social power. But they also are in opposition to the liberal/empiricist arguments to the effect that the solution to such problems lies in ad hoc adjustments to existing knowledge communities, their practices, and culture. "Including" members of excluded groups in knowledge institutions, encouraging more vigorous criticism in these communities, practicing existing methods more carefully – such adjustments certainly are very good things to do for all kinds of reasons. But they fail to address the fundamental issue standpoint theory raises: the problem of the paradigm. Those members of socially disadvantaged groups who get "included" into advantaged groups usually are marginalized and silenced within such groups, their silence often a condition of their inclusion. Moreover, the members of socially disadvantaged groups who are selected for inclusion in the first place are usually exactly those who have been most socialized into working within the dominant paradigms; they are the ones who are perceived most to exhibit the prevailing standards of excellence. To say this is not to impugn the high quality of their work or devalue the importance of their inclusion in socially advantaged institutions and cultures; it is only to question how effective such a strategy can be for the standpoint project of learning to identify more clearly the dominant paradigms of research, scholarship and policy. Finally, there is little reason to think that the already preferred methods of research, no matter how rigorously pursued, can detect values and interests that are *shared* by an entire research community. The effectiveness of methods at detecting values and interests depends upon less than the entire legitimated knowledge community sharing the latter (Harding 1991: ch. 6; 1992).

Standpoint approaches are also in opposition to what we could call the "identity epistemology" argument. Standpoint approaches are not claiming that the experience of the disadvantaged naturally or automatically generates knowledge. This would obviously be false, since women disadvantaged by their gender have had experiences since time immemorial, but socially legitimated articulations ("knowledge") of the perspective from their lives are rare indeed. Nor could standpoint epistemologies be claiming that everything the disadvantaged say is incorrigible. After all, women, too, have made androcentric assumptions about their own and men's natures and abilities; and they have also made racist and class-distorted assumptions. Finally, standpoint approaches are not claiming that *only* the disadvantaged can start off thought from their own lives and so generate knowledge; sometimes men, too, have been able to start their thought from women's lives, and so to grasp regularities of nature and social relations and their underlying causal tendencies in ways prohibited by the dominant conceptual paradigms. Few would challenge that this is a fair description of important insights by John Stuart Mill, Marx, Engels, and a good number of present-day historians, anthropologists, economists, literary critics, and so on.

I have discussed elsewhere other misreadings of this new epistemology (Harding 1992). Here I want to turn to some aspects of "the social" visible in standpoint theory that could improve social theory more generally. These are that socially located knowledge is located in a gender/class/race matrix; that it can also be regarded as universally valid; that standpoint theories show us how to locate our own thought "in the North"; and, in conclusion, that socially located knowledge maximizes "strong reflexivity": it moves us toward principled, Northern, ethnotheories.

What is "Socially Located Knowledge"?

First of all, it is *socially located in a gender/class/race matrix*. In contrast to the Marxian and liberal legacies, standpoint epistemology's subject of knowledge is not homogeneous and coherent but, instead, heterogeneous and contradictory. It is not "the rational man" or "the proletarian," but the Chicana feminist, Marxist–feminist, woman philosopher, or male feminist. This is a claim with complex implications; here I can only draw attention to two of them.

However, first I must clear the ground by recalling that standpoint theory is concerned with gender relations – social relations between the genders – rather than biological differences. Moreover, gender is fundamentally structural and symbolic relationships, not a set of fixed properties of individuals.

It is often assumed that by inspecting women (or men) we can tell what are the characteristics of that gender, though, as the anthropologists and historians report, gender is organized in different ways in different cultures (just as class is not inherently a property of individuals but a consequence of their location in class relations). Gender is fundamentally created and maintained through structural relations between the activities assigned to different groups, so societies in which such activities are more highly segregated and hierarchicalized have more gender than others. It is also created and maintained through oppositionally organized meanings, through "symbolic gender," so diverse natural and social objects and relations – hurricanes, nations, the processes of science – are perceived to carry masculine or feminine meanings. Additionally, these appearances are not always coherent; sexist rhetoric (symbolic gender) tends to increase not when women's structural position is worsening but, to the contrary, exactly when women are beginning to occupy social positions that had been forbidden them. Here it appears as an expression of cultural malaise in which anxieties about changes in familiar gender activities or meanings express more general anxieties about the loss or breakdown of a familiar social order (Bordo 1987; Merchant 1980).

Now we can come to the main point here, which is that all three kinds of expressions of gender relations are interlocked with such other ways systematically of organizing individual identity, human activity, and social meanings as class, race, and sexuality. Several African–American feminist theorists have discussed this phenomenon as a "matrix of domination" (Patricia Hill Collins 1990; hooks 1983). Thus each appearance of manliness or womanliness is always also distinctively African–American or European–American, working or middle class, gay or straight (or bisexual, or transgender), and so on. In this sense, there are no men or women *per se* any more than there are humans who transcend a class location. Nor is there any pure masculinity or femininity; there is only that characteristic of particular cultural locations. And social relations between two white women are race and gender relations no less than are ones between any other two individuals in cultures stratified by race and gender. Standpoint theory's socially located knowledge is situated at determinate places in a complex network of individual, structural, and symbolic social relations.

Finally, though we each think and speak from a determinate location in a network of mutually supporting hierarchies, our consciousnesses are not determined by such locations. For one thing, there are white racists and white anti-racists, female feminists and female sexists, and far subtler complexities of consciousness within such categories. For another thing, it is widely recognized that the most illuminating feminist research and scholarship has flowed from the "internally" heterogeneous and contradictory consciousnesses of women: from the dissonance arising from attempting to think and act as a liberal–feminist, black–feminist, Jewish–feminist, woman–scientist, woman–filmmaker, and so on. Perhaps it has also arisen from the contradictory consciousnesses of male–feminists. It is the dissonances that generate the research problematics, but feminist research and theory, not "what women think" or experience, that produces the resulting knowledge claims. Feminist theories provide frameworks alternative to the dominant ones in our disciplines and daily social life – alternative discourses – within which men and women can gain less distorted and partial understandings, descriptions and explanations of natural and social relations (Hennessy 1993).

The second point about the social that standpoint theory raises is that *socially located knowledge can also be perceived to be, and to be, universally valid*. This argument emerges from current feminist and post-colonial studies of the natural sciences, but at least some of its points are relevant also to social theory. According to the legacy of modern science assumed by most social theory (including by those theorists who reject it for thought about the social), a claim cannot be universally valid if it bears the cultural fingerprints of its origins – the individuals, groups or era that declared or found it a legitimate knowledge claim. Natural sciences "work," they are universally valid, it is said, because they transcend culture. To refer to a claim as "knowledge" rather than merely as "opinion" marks the divide between the universally and only locally valid. Scientific knowledge "works" because it can tell us how nature really functions instead of only how the British, Native Americans, or Chinese fear or want it to work. This universal science view also shapes much social theory – especially that most closely modeled on natural sciences, such as neo-classical economics, and many areas of psychology, but including also less determinedly empiricist fields.

I shall make the argument here by following the challenges to the universal science view for the natural sciences to stress how seriously this view requires revision even for such "hard cases" (Harding 1996). For one thing, the metaphors and models within which conventional knowledge is generated clearly are culturally distinctive, and yet the claims produced do permit accurate predication and explanation of how nature works. For example, Newtonian physics and Copernican/Galilean astronomy substituted a mechanistic model for the earlier organicist one. Both the organicist and mechanistic models were permeated by religious, political, social, psychic, and sexual meanings, as many feminist and pre-feminist analysts have pointed out (Leiss 1972; Merchant 1980). Moreover, scientific metaphors, analogies, and models are not mere pedagogical or heuristic devices that can be eliminated without residue but, instead, fundamental constituents of scientific theories; they tell scientists how to extend and revise their theories (Hesse 1966). But nobody would deny that modern physics and biology work universally, even though to this day they continue to carry such distinctive cultural fingerprints. The laws of gravity and of antibiotics will "work" on one whether one is in Peru or Britain, a Confucian or a Catholic.

Second, the total image of nature and social relations that is provided by the sciences of a particular era reflects what the groups directing those sciences – those in or aspiring to power – do and do not want to know. Such a seventeenth-, late nineteenth-, or late twentieth-century image provided by Northern sciences clearly reveals its cultural features if one looks at it from the perspective of other eras or other cultures with which it is in conflict (if one tries to maximize objectivity by taking a standpoint outside the dominant culture). It works and is universal, we could say, precisely *because* it sets out to provide solutions to a culturally distinctive set of social projects. For example, natural or social sciences that conceptualize their subject matter, natural or social, as composed of autonomous parts only externally connected to each other work well to advance groups that do not care how their interventions in nature or society affect others. But such sciences are ineffective at predicting how the interventions they make possible in industrialization, imperialism, or militarism will affect the environment or social relations. They are both universal and culturally distinctive.

Third, in some cases sciences become universal precisely because of their cultural features. For example, Northern sciences have always benefited from their intimate association with European expansionism. Thus, not only do they work well to describe and explain how to advance such expansionism; they also assist in eliminating or dedeveloping alternative scientific traditions (Pettijean et al. 1992). Their cultural specificity is thus hidden by the advantages provided by their alliance with power.

Thus, there could be other universally valid social theories that "work" at different projects, for example, anti-sexist, anti-Eurocentric, ones to increase democratic social control and to maximize sustainable resources.[5] They would be "encultured" by the social distinctiveness of those projects no less than existing theories are encultured with what critics would call sexist, Eurocentric, or anti-democratic purposes. Thus the *uniqueness* of the universal validity that social researchers and theorists seek and attribute to their best knowledge claims is a function of how successfully they destroy any viable alternative accounts; it does not necessarily signify the absolute adequacy of those accounts or of the standards by which adequacy is conventionally measured. The unique validity of a social theory and its claims all too frequently is an empirical consequence of the social power of the groups making the claims, not an *a priori* feature of the research process, as Northern science enthusiasts claim. Standpoint epistemology enables us to think more clearly about the relation between the philosophical claim that sciences succeed because/when they are universally valid, and the historical and sociological descriptions of sciences' constitution through cultural projects.

Finally, it must be pointed out that there is yet another sense in which sciences or social theories can be universally valid in the sense of making successful predictions, and yet they are clearly culturally distinctive. Even if modern Western sciences bore none of the above cultural fingerprints, their actual and claimed value-neutrality would itself mark them as distinctively Western (and masculinist). Of course this is a contradiction ("If it's value-free, then it's not value-free"), or at least highly paradoxical. The point is that trying to maximize cultural neutrality, as well as claiming it, expresses a culturally distinctive value. Most cultures do not value neutrality, they value their own cultures' values; so one that does is easily culturally identifiable. A number of feminists have located the origins of the preference for abstractness, formality and decontextualization in psychic consequences of the construction of masculinity; for the educated classes in the modern "North," manliness and neutrality help define each other's practices and meanings (Hartsock 1983; Lloyd 1984; MacKinnon 1982). Others have located it in the exchange relations of class societies (Sohn-Rethel 1978).

Thus standpoint theory insists that the best knowledge claims can be universally valid and yet always will remain distinctively socially located, and this argument challenges various forms of objectivism and relativism.

Third, standpoint theories, like the rest of European and North American produced social theories, are themselves socially located "in the North." One dimension of the social location of conventional and feminist knowledge deserves a bit more discussion. The new multicultural, post-colonial, and other anti-Eurocentric studies both challenge and create opportunities for us to understand the culturally distinctively *Northern* ("Western") features of European and North American sciences and social theories (cf. Harding 1993; 1994; 1996). As one of the post-colonial science critics puts the point, why is there no (or so few signs of) "europology" of Northern social sciences and theories (Goonatilake 1992)? That is, Northern theorists have constructed "orientologies," "Africologies," and the like for centuries; we have generated Eurocentric descriptions and explanations of what we take to be the culturally distinctive features of the cultures that have constituted Europe's Other.

(Primitive, static, regressive, savage, and otherwise generally inferior are central terms in the European accounts of Others.) It is time for Northern social theory to engage in the parallel project of examining critically Northern social theories, their historical legacies and present culture and practices, critically to map their distinctively Northern features (Said 1978; Mudimbe 1988).

Some fields of social theory have already begun this project – anthropology and history most obviously. (Is it relevant that these fields are centered on the geographically and temporally distant? That these are the two fields of social theory where feminist theory earliest blossomed most richly?) North-ern feminist epistemologies, like the rest of Northern thought, need to be relocated onto the less partial and distorted map of global history that is being created by such post-colonial studies. We need to understand North-ern history, including the legacies of social theory that have been critically reused by contemporary feminist theorists, as one thread in the map of global history, in constant encounter and exchange with the intellectual and politi-cal histories linking thinkers and their cultures around the globe. To do so is to use the lens of standpoint theory critically to examine standpoint theory itself (along with the rest of Northern social theory) in order to locate it, too, in the history in which it argues every theory is located.

This leads to the last point I wish to make here, which will also serve as my conclusion.

Conclusion: "Strong Reflexivity" – toward Principled, Northern Ethnotheories

We can learn in another way from the post-colonial science critics. One strategy they propose is to construct fully modern sciences within their cultural legacies of Islam or regional African cultures rather than within ours, as they point out that the universality arguments expect of them. These theorists have begun critically to re-examine their cultural legacies to identify the ele-ments that will be useful in such a project today and those that will not. But we, too, can engage in such a project. We can begin to explore how to construct "fully modern social theories" – that is, post-modern ones for today – within the cultural legacies of the North. How can such notions so central to Northern institutions as objectivity, rationality, progress, method, and sciences linked to democracy be modernized so that they become useful in the world of today and tomorrow, where the North and its gender and class elites hopefully will no longer be able to design the world and the dominant images of it to suit only their own desires? Any social theories that are created in the North will be distinctively Northern ethnotheories whatever their purposes and methods – all knowledge is and must be socially located. But these theories could be principled ones. They could conscientiously retrieve those elements of the modern European and North American cultural legacy that can provide appropriate resources for the post-colonial and post-patriarchal world that, we hope, is beginning to emerge, and they could reject those that are not.

To engage in this project is to generate a "strong reflexivity" to replace the only weak forms of it that have appeared in social theory. It is to demand a kind of symmetry between the agent and object of knowledge in the sense that the conceptual framework shaping our theory, research, and policy be subjected to the same critical scrutiny on which we insist for the objects of our knowledge. It is to place the subject in the same critical plane as the object of knowledge. Natural scientists and social theorists have tended to respond to the "problem" of reflexivity either with dejection and stoicism, personal confessions of their individual social values, interests, and location, recommendations about submitting the results of one's research for approval or at least comment by the "natives" one was studying (in appropriate cases of social research), or moral exhortations to "be more critical." I do not mean to suggest that all of these responses are entirely wrong, but only that they are all inadequate to the problem. In contrast, standpoint theory inserts the reflexive moment into the ongoing research process. Maximizing the objectivity of our accounts requires that the conceptual frameworks within which we work – the assumed and/or chosen ones of our discipline, culture, and historical moment – be subjected to the same critical examination that we bring to bear on whatever else we are studying.

Social disadvantage can create epistemic advantage for those courageous enough to be willing to try to identify the paradigms, conceptual frameworks, and epistemes that have shaped our most cherished social theories. To do so requires starting off our thought from the lives of those most disadvantaged by those paradigms, lives revealed through their speech – whether explicit or implicit. It requires social theory and political struggle to manage to start off our thought from lives whose outlines the dominant ideologies have systematically obscured – and this is as true for those who live those lives as for those who do not. It requires dialogues that cannot occur between individuals or groups that are social unequals, that are not yet ideal speech communities. But it is the first attempts at such dialogues, and then the next, and the many following that are required to create the ideal speech communities. Standpoint epistemology refuses clear and certain foundations for beginnings, uncontroversially true endings, and the relativist theories of knowledge that usually accompany such refusals. We are always, already only in the middle of our knowledge projects.

Notes

1 Smith was already publishing on the topic in the mid-1970s.
2 The following arguments are drawn from chapter 5 of my 1991 text.
3 Rose makes this point in another context (1983).
4 Patricia Hill Collins (1990) developed the concept of the outsider within to explain the importance of rethinking sociology from the perspective of African–American women's lives. Gloria Anzaldua (1987), bell hooks (1983), and other feminists of color have emphasized what can be seen from "borderlands," and by looking "from margin to center." Similar characterizations of epistemically advantaged social locations from which to start thought appear in Dorothy Smith's (1987; 1990) "bifurcated consciousness" of women, for whom the dominant accounts of social life do not accommodate their understandings of their lives; from such bifurcated consciousnesses have arisen all feminist analyses of women's bodies (of beauty ideals, violence against women, biology and health care issues, and so on). To think out of the contradictions of being a woman philosopher or scientist or a great woman artist, and so on, is also to think critically from this "outsider within" borderlands about womanliness, manliness, the philosopher, the scientist, the greatness of artists.
5 Just how democratic social control will best be achieved will and should vary in different circumstances; the practices that maximize it in small community groups will be different from those that are effective in international energy policy. Nevertheless, we can call on John Dewey's very general principle to guide the design of the institutions, practices, and cultures of democracy: those who bear the consequences of decisions should have a proportionate share in making them. (Is this a principle that can achieve universality because the aspects of world it is about are not chartable by cultural variation, or because it does or can eliminate all competing principles?)

9

The Centrality of Culture in Social Theory: Fundamental Clues from Weber and Durkheim

Anne E. Kane

Introduction: the Development of Cultural Theory

The evolution of current cultural theory and analysis has made the most profound contribution to a new wave of social theory which instructs us to look to the "formulation," "structuration," and "transformation" of temporally and spatially situated social structures: in other words, at the specific social action which fabricates society.[1] Indeed, developments in cultural theory have finally given theoretical teeth to the interpretative mode of sociological inquiry, which can now effectively challenge the structural approach. Cultural theory has been built through an interdisciplinary effort. First, social historians empirically studying the role of culture in historical development realized the implication of the simple but powerful precept that culture is collectively constructed: they had to study events in which cultural construction occurred (for example, Thompson 1963; Sewell 1980; 1985; Darnton 1984; Hunt 1984).

This theoretical exigency was buttressed by the method of historical narration, especially event analysis. The narrative method presupposes that history is a process, constituted by sequences of events, the latter being the "moments of becoming," in which action and structure meet (Abrams 1982). Likewise, in events of cultural construction, historically specific social conditions and structures, interests, experience, and contingencies meet, interact, and culminate in producing or reproducing cultural formations. But how? Social historians and cultural sociologists learned from anthropological theory and research, as well as Durkheim's study of pre-modern religion, that ritual is the primary process of symbolic production and reproduction. It was not long before study of secular historical events – such as demonstrations, riots, association meetings – revealed their ritualistic quality, empirically indicating that cultural and social structuring occurs at the same time, in the same locations, and that the relationship between the culture and social structure was one of mutual formulation with ritualistic processes guiding both (Kane 1991).

In addressing the question that the work of social historians implicitly raised – "how is culture structural?" (an essential question whose answer counters the reductionist vision of culture) – cultural sociologists plumbed cultural anthropology even further. They drew on the structuralism of Lévi-Strauss, then turned to linguistic and semiotic theory and began to conceptualize culture as autonomous structures of symbolic patterns and sets.

Demonstrating analytically the independent structure of culture does not, however, specify its concrete relationship to social institutions and processes. To understand a culture structure and its causal importance in historical development, it is necessary to systematically reconstruct it by investigating the historical events in which the original formulation occurred (Kane 1991). Which brings the cultural theorist back to ritual. The work of people like Marshall Sahlins and William Sewell, Jr, has shown that though ritual is the internal process through which culture is maintained and transmitted from generation to generation, it is also the means by which culture is constructed and transformed, in concert with and as part of social system structuring.

But cultural theory has done more than reaffirm the wider "constructionist turn" in wider social theory.[2] Cultural theory has reoriented our understanding of the world and how we ought to study it by revealing culture to be central to social life. Because culture provides the structure through which people interpret experience, it informs and guides both intention and action. It is through culturally mediated social action and interaction, often in ritualistic events, that social structures, including culture, are produced and reproduced. Thus culture ultimately provides the link between the most perplexing sociological dichotomy, agency and structure.

Despite advances, theories of social structuring are yet inadequate because many sociologist still do not acknowledge culture as a central component in the social structuring process. However, the two are intimately related, as Sewell points out: "Events . . . shape history by changing the cultural meanings or significations (of) political and social categories and consequently changing people's possibilities for meaningful action" (1990: 548). The primary reason for the disregard or minimalization of culture, even in most action-oriented and event-centered analyses, is that most sociologists do not adequately theorize the meaning which underlies all action, nor how meaning is constructed, maintained, and transformed. Furthermore, cultural structuring continues to be viewed as separate from social structuring, when in fact the two occur simultaneously.

I argue in this paper that only by thus theorizing culture can sociologists fully understand social action and structuring, as well as transcend the dictates of transhistorical conceptual frameworks and false analytical dichotomies. I propose a theoretical framework for doing cultural analysis based on the presupposition that the construction of meaning structures is part and parcel, and thus central, to social action and the social structuring process. The theory is fundamentally based on two classic concepts: from Weber, the central importance of *meaning*; and from Durkheim, *ritual* as the site of meaning construction. The principles of the theory are: first, meaning underlies all social action (Weber 1978); second, meaning is embodied in "autonomous" symbolic structures; and third, meaning and symbolic structures are collectively constructed through social interaction, often in ritualistic events (Durkheim 1965). Thus, action and culture are interdependent; culture and social structuring are reciprocal processes. These principles need to be rejuvenated and reintegrated into contemporary sociology even as it strives to overcome obstacles, such as the assumption of a basic split between subject and object, bequeathed by classical theory.[3]

Weber and the Structure of Meaning

Weber's foundational definition of sociology posits subjective meaning as the basis of social action and structure (1978: 4). Weber claims that the basis of meaning and its construction is the human compulsion to understand the world as a meaningful cosmos and to take up a position in it (1978: 499). Subjective meaning is a person's understanding of the world and the significance he gives to his experience in that world. Personal interpretation of experience and attitudes about action is derived from collectively structured symbolic systems providing "images of the world." Weber drew these theoretical conclusions from his study of world religions, which have historically been the most important form of symbolic structures.

In ancient religions, systems of meaning were constructed through prophetic revelation. Weber's analysis of prophecy provides two related insights for cultural theory. By attributing the construction of meaning to prophets, Weber contends that symbolic structures used by individuals are not of their own making. However, prophetic revelation itself was a collective construction: the charismatic power and legitimacy of the prophets is tied to intense and continual interaction with his followers, and the revelation is based on the emotional needs of the followers.

Weber shows that most religious systems are based on conceptions of redemption and salvation. Like all religions, redemptory systems express coherent explanations of the world; but redemptory religions allow people to confront their specific reality via secular activity in the pursuit of salvation. The foundation of redemptory religion is the "conflict between empirical reality and [the] conception of the world as a meaningful totality [which] produces the strongest tensions in man's inner life as well as in his external relationship to the world" (1978: 451). In other words, people need a coherent, if not harmonious, explanation about the world: yet the brutality of life continually shatters that system of meaning, unless it provides for ultimate salvation.

This contradiction between cosmological symbolic systems and concrete reality is also the basis for symbolic innovation and change. People will always give meaning to life through symbolic systems; yet, because life is always challenging those systems innovation is inevitable. In *Ancient Judaism*, Weber points out that the "prerequisite to new religious conceptions is that man must not yet have unlearned how to face the course of the world with questions of his own" (1967: 206). Questions come from lived experience and are put to the structure of meaning on which people operate; new ideas also come from experience and help transform meaning structures.

Despite Weber's insight, social analysts inadequately theorize action because meaning is not theorized. And a number of prominent culture theorists have explicitly rejected the importance of meaning.

In *Meaning and Moral Order* (1987), Robert Wuthnow prescribes giving up the "problem of meaning" in cultural analysis in order to eradicate subjectivity and thus avoid "idealism." Yet if we abandon trying to understand the significance of symbolic structures in the interpretation of concrete experience, we cannot understand either the reciprocal process of formulation between culture and social structure, or why people embrace a particular meaning system.

Ann Swidler has recommended that culture be seen as "a 'tool kit' of symbols, stories, rituals and worldviews, which people may use in varying configurations to solve different sets of problems" (1986: 273). This vision of culture denies both the structural logic of cultural systems, as well as the role a coherent and collectively constructed meaning system plays in concrete social action during specific historical situations.

In *Culture and Agency*, Margaret Archer's theoretical goal is the unification of structural and cultural analysis (1988). To achieve this end, she correctly calls for a more structural analysis of culture. Her approach is based on a dualism – the separation of the "cultural system" from "social-cultural inter-action." Unfortunately, in Archer's conceptualization culture is reduced to true/false propositions about the world; and the process of cultural creation is conceived of primarily as the domain of interests and group solidarity based on those interests. Hence, "meaning" becomes cultural agency based on maneuvers of interest and power.[4]

In short, meaning is often conceived of by contemporary sociologists as the internal world of the individual, a person's beliefs and attitudes about the surrounding world, inherently unknowable to the social analyst. If this were a valid conceptualization, then we truly would have a "problem of mean-ing."[5] However, the individual's internal structure of knowledge is not pri-vate and particular; it is derived from publicly and collectively constructed systems of meaning.

Therefore, we should think of meaning as the *significance collectively given to experience*. Individuals do not conceptualize experience on their own: they filter their thoughts, feelings, and responses through conventional (which has a double definition of collectively constructed and established) meaning systems in order to interpret experience and decide how they should act.[6] As soon as thoughts are articulated, they are transformed into a collectively shaped form, and thus made public and recoverable. Without this process of transformation, perception of experience holds no meaning.

The collective interpretation of individual experience leads to the con-struction of structures of meaning which in turn mediate action and social structuring. The most persuasive theoretical work on meaning structure begins with *symbols*, that is, signs which represent generalized meaning and provide categories for understanding the elements of social, individual, and organic life.[7] Signs are "arbitrary" in the sense that their significance cannot be deduced from their referent alone. Symbolic systems possess this arbitrary characteristic inasmuch as meaning is produced not by an immediate and intrinsic bond between the symbol and its interpretant, but by the internal play of signs in complex patterns of similarity and difference, or *codes*, built up from simple binary opposition, such as sacred and profane. On the other hand, this production of meaning occurs over time and space and is built on inherited meanings. Thus "there is a rudiment of a natural bond between the signifier and the signified [such as a] symbol of justice, a pair of scales" (de Saussure 1985: 38). To the degree that they are, and are not, arbitrary, symbols and meanings are subject to change (1985: 40–6). Because the relationship between a symbol and the meaning it represents is not forever fixed, but evolves generationally from a specific basis, this means that cultural change is possible.

Finally, symbolic sets function as *discourses*, relating binary symbolic associations with social forms. Discourses provide a vocabulary for social interaction, whether harmonious or conflictual (Alexander 1992b: 297–8; Alexander and Smith 1993). Furthermore, as a structured code set, a discourse constitutes a general grammar from which historically specific sub-cultures are configured (Alexander and Smith 1993; Jacobs forthcoming), or against which new cultures may emerge (Hwang 1993).

The intervening structures are *narratives*, stories through which a discursive structure is made socially available, often in ritual, and a society comes to understand and identify itself. These stories, or myths, specify and stereotype a society or group's founding and values, its critical events, and its aspirations (Alexander and Smith 1993; Sherwood 1993). Narratives place actors and events into plots, allocate moral responsibility, causality and agency, and often provide exemplary models for action (Smith 1993; see also Calhoun 1991; and Somers and Gibson 1994).

Meaning and Action

How does the structure of meaning influence individual action? Desires, decisions, intentions, and actions, that is agency, are based on a double interpretation: an interpretation of experience and circumstances using a socially constructed code of meaning, and an interpretation of the code itself. This act of double interpretation demonstrates the social basis of meaning and action, but also the agentic quality of action and the contingent character of culture. In interpreting the cultural code an actor engages in typification, categorizing experiential impressions according to his developed understandings of the world, that is, an already interpreted and internalized code (Alexander 1988a: 312–15; Rambo and Chan 1990: 638). Out of the typification process, the actor invents. Because reality is always new, there is always something different in each typification of reality; hence, meaning classifications are shifted if only slightly (Alexander 1988a: 312–15; 1992a). The contingency of reality forces constant reinterpretation of the cultural code.

The interpretation of experience demands strategization, "not merely understanding the world, [but] transforming and acting upon it" (Alexander 1988a: 314). Marshall Sahlins has brilliantly specified the interpretation of experience via cultural codes.[8] While a sign has *conceptual value* in a symbolic structure, it represents a *differential interest* to actors according to its place in their specific life schemes. A person may act upon the conventional value of a sign in the culture-as-constituted; but in action, the generalized/abstract meaning of the sign is given contextual meaning by the actor as it is brought into referential relations to the objects of action. Thus, socially constructed meaning guides but does not determine action or its outcome because each actor's specific experience, interpretative process, and arrangement of signs in relation to concrete objects leads to contingent outcomes.

This conceptualization of individual action points out mechanisms true in any circumstance of social action: how individuals internalize the meaning of symbols, the effect of action on structure, and symbolic transformation due to constant individual rearrangement of signs. Sahlins' account of the Hawaiians' reception of Captain Cook and the Europeans exemplifies how people, individually and collectively, employ their cultural system in confronting an extraordinary event, yet in so doing change that system forever.

The Hawaiians received Captain Cook directly through ritual classification as he happened to land in the islands during the ritual festival of Makahiki and was perceived as the god Lono. And the islanders continued to relate to the Europeans in terms of the ritual narratives about the gods. For example, in accordance with ritual the women gave of themselves sexually to the sailors, seeing them as gods. However, the sailors soon imputed a tangible value to the "services" of the women, and began materially compensating them. This conjuncture of structure thus led to a rearrangement and transformation of cultural categories among the Hawaiians (1981: 17–43).

In an insightful article entitled "The discourse of American civil society," Alexander and Smith chart the "pervasive nature of the same culture structure across time, type of events, and differing political groups" (1993: 17). Yet, demonstrating the continuity of the United States' "discourse of civil society" in the face of contingent events and crises does not disallow its transposability,[9] which is a form of transformation. Rather, Alexander and Smith assert and demonstrate that the discourse of civil society "constitutes a general grammar from which historically specific traditions draw to create particular configurations of meanings, ideology and belief . . . that have historically characterized American political debate" (p. 16). By examining the use of the symbolic binary codes – democratic/counter-democratic – constituting the discourse of civil society through 200 years of political crisis and scandal from Teapot Dome to Iran–Contra, Alexander and Smith show how "conflicting parties within the civil society have drawn on the same symbolic code to formulate their particular understandings and to advance their competing claims" (p.

47). Though Alexander and Smith do not show how the outcome of these political crises have led to transformations of political culture and structure, the fact that different groups use the same codes to formulate particular and competing understandings implies that transformation took place, even though the basic structure remained intact. Furthermore, as theorized by Alexander and Smith, reproduction of the culture structure is dependent on the meaning derived from specific interpretations of specific experience in specific contexts by specific groups, which implies that culture is transposable, and transformable.

Both these examples of cultural continuity and transformation illustrate that "the same reproductive biases of structures that explain the powerful continuities of social relations also make it possible to explain the paths followed in episodes of social change" (Sewell 1992: 16). Furthermore, both essays demonstrate that cultural change is usually gradual and that "new" structures are founded on the old. People use their cultural understandings to interpret experience and formulate strategies of action. If "a sharp disjunction exists between our perceptions and the categories provided by our schemas" the latter are likely to be revised or even rejected, and new meanings collectively constructed (Kertzer 1988: 82). This collective construction and reconstruction occurs through ritual.

The Construction of Meaning –
Social Interaction and Ritual

My argument for the primacy of meaning in cultural and social theorizing has thus far assumed an established system of meaning, as well as the process of meaning construction and reconstruction. However, both theoretically and empirically it is critical that the process of meaning construction not be conjectured, but explored in detail. As Clifford Geertz lamented some twenty years ago, "The link between the causes of ideology and its effects seems adventitious because the connecting element – the autonomous process of symbolic formulation – is passed over in virtual silence" (1973: 207). In this section I will show how we can reconstruct the process of meaning formulation. While I concur with Geertz that the process is analytically autonomous, it occurs in concrete social interaction; thus, the process of meaning construction is both highly contingent on non-symbolic elements, and is in a mutually influencing relationship with extra-cultural structuring.

As a host of cultural theorists have been claiming for some time (Turner 1969; Moore and Myerhoff 1977; Alexander 1988b; Kertzer 1988),

Durkheim's theory of ritual remains the paradigm for understanding the cultural structuring process, both because rituals are the primary site of cultural production and maintenance, and because much social interaction is ritualistic to varying degrees.

In *The Elementary Forms of Religious Life*, Durkheim theorizes that the designation of the sacred as the center of social cosmology, and the reproduction and transmission of beliefs through communal rites, leads to social solidarity and order. Durkheim demonstrates that the beliefs people hold regarding the world are organized according to the opposition of the sacred and the profane. Beliefs must be tangibly represented through symbols so that members of the society can use and transmit them. Designating the sacred is a collective process, as is giving beliefs symbolic expression. "Sacred beings exist only when they are represented as such in the mind . . . the sacred character which makes objects of the cults . . . is added to them by belief [and] it is in the communal life that they are formed" (1965: 386). Durkheim contends that every society must regularly reaffirm and regenerate itself through collective symbolic activity (p. 474). Finally, ritual "is the school of collective life" where the individual learns how to formulate ideas about social life and her place in it (p. 470).

What exactly happens in collective events that leads to symbolic construction? Durkheim claims that the intensity of social contact reproduces a "state of effervescence" (p. 469). "It is in the midst of these effervescent social environments and out of this effervescence itself that the religious idea seems to be born" (p. 250). Durkheim points out that the dramatic character of rituals, created through the enactment of myth (narratives) both produces and channels the communal fervor into symbolic construction and reproduction (p. 417).

Durkheim tells us that symbolic construction or reproduction is not dependent on the reasons why the group is assembled, but on the fact that it is assembled and "that sentiments are felt in common and expressed in common acts" (p. 431). In other words, all sorts of collective events contain the process of meaning construction. To enlarge on Durkheim's conceptualization of ritual, we can envision an action continuum, extending from practical action to ritual (Bloch 1989: 22; Moore and Myerhoff 1977: 22; Alexander 1988a: 327; Collins 1988a: 111). At every point on the continuum, action contributes to meaning construction and social (and cultural) structuring, and ritual theory helps us understand the process in any variation. Across the continuum we can identify three types of action (or events): on the one end, ritual; on the other end, non-ritual (or practical) action; and in between, ritualistic action. We can distinguish between the three based on the following criteria: ritual action is specifically and intentionally performed for symbolic reasons as discussed above; ritualistic activity is not specifically symbolic or originally intended to be, but shares the same characteristics and outcomes; non-ritual action is highly routine and practically motivated, with little or no ritualistic features. I conceptualize a continuum not to demonstrate that action fits neatly into one of these three categorical boxes, but rather to show that action and events usually "slide" between these ideal types, and that ritual, ritualistic, and non-ritual action are interrelated in terms of meaning construction.

Ritual Action

Ritual is fundamentally the location of intense social and symbolic interaction between people, and can be defined as "a set of formal acts which deal with or refer [symbolically] to postulated matters about society" (Moore and Myerhoff 1977: 22). Rituals address sacred matters, whether religious or secular, not mundane reality or everyday life. Rituals therefore have a high moral, or normative, dimensionality. Rituals tend to be institutionalized, and ritual action prescribed.

Ritual is the central internal process of a cultural system. By making meaning evident, rituals infuse members of the group with an understanding of experience, a prescription for action in life, and a bond of solidarity to the group. Secondly, ritual maintains the symbolic system, and through narrative, drama, and myth transmits it from generation to generation. In other words, ritual provides a particular, and collective, narrative structure through which groups can understand their world and their place in it.

Ritual is structured by three phases: separation, liminality, and reaggregation.[10] During separation, the transition from mundane to sacred time is constructed through "liminal agents," highly-charged symbolic activity, and "passageways" (Turner 1969: 123). During the middle phase of transition or "liminality," there is a period of ambiguity, what Turner refers to as "anti-structure" (Turner 1974: 27). During the final period, reaggregation, the ritual closes. With reaggregation, whether the culture is reproduced or transformed, solidarity increases among members of the group. These ritual functions and processes that renew the meaning system and peoples' commitment to it are evidence of cultural autonomy (Kane 1991).

In ordinary times, once the symbolic system is created and institutionalized, its reproduction is the primary function of ritual. But ritual is also the process of symbolic creation and recreation in which individual sentiments are given collective significance, identities are developed and interests articulated. In ritual or collective events, the beliefs, interests, experience, and differences among and between participants coalesce and collide. During the liminal phase the interactional, emotional, and symbolic intensity provides a space for scrutiny of old values and symbols, struggles over meaning, and the creation or transformation of symbols (Hwang 1993).[11] These struggles are played out in dramas and narratives. Typically, these ritual dramas are symbolic enactments of two types of stories: the "lived," or common experience and myths, and the "imagined," visions of alternatives and of the future.[12] Thus, in extraordinary times ritual often becomes the vehicle for cultural and social change.

In the transformation of symbolic systems, it is most common that the rituals of the extant culture are the mechanisms by which that culture is changed. Meetings of the French National Assembly were political rituals of the *ancien régime*, but in the course of the Assembly's meeting on the night of August 4, 1789 the ideological structure of privilege was dismantled and the "uncluttered Enlightenment ideal of equal individual citizens" was set in its place (Sewell 1985: 69).

In Iran, the overthrow of Shah Reze Pahlavi in 1978 began with a series of mass protests, many scheduled and conducted according to the Islamic ritual practice of commemorating deaths, the latter being those of regime opponents killed by agents of the Shah (Burns 1992). The traditional ritual celebrates the martyrdom of Mohammed's grandson Hussein by the evil Yazid in the year 680. Re-enacting the ritual, through song, the demonstrators injected a list of wrongs suffered by the Iranian people under the Shah into the traditional story (Kertzer 1988: 168).

As all these examples demonstrate, rituals are not always tightly controlled or bound practices, nor do they exclusively reproduce and reinforce established symbolic systems. Ritual outcomes are highly contingent on external events and circumstances, the agency of participants in the ritual, and the ritual process itself. Thus, as in the French and Hawaiian case, cultural transformation may unintentionally occur during traditional rituals; and as in Iran, traditional rituals can be manipulated against the existing social system. Symbolic rearrangement leads to new meanings, new interpretation of experience, and new forms of social action.

Ritualistic Events and Action

Ritualistic events are theoretically and empirically more enigmatic than rituals. Empirically, they are more difficult to perceive: they may be over-categorized as rituals, or their ritualistic quality may be overlooked. More importantly, because ritualistic events are not institutionalized, as are rituals, the environment in which they occur is less rigid structurally but more complex in terms of social objects and contingency encountered in the event. Following from this, in ritualistic action "(t)ypification is less standard; strategization is more ramifying; invention is more dramatic" (Alexander 1988a: 327). Moreover, ritualistic events possess a high affective dimension.[13] More than ritual and non-ritual events, ritualistic events occur most often in episodes of social instability and/or crises. Thus, ritualistic events retain the most capacity for cultural innovation (the construction of meaning) and social structuring. By analyzing ritualistic events we can best see the reciprocity between cultural and social structuring. In demonstrating this through the example of the ritualistic land meetings of the Irish Land War, I further explicate how symbolic meaning is collectively constructed in ritual, often out of conflicting beliefs, thus leading to solidarity among different social groups.[14]

The Irish Land War which erupted in 1879 on the heels of an agrarian crisis can best be described as a militant constitutional anti-landlord social movement. The immediate result of the Land War was the Land Act of 1881 which eventually led to peasant land purchase from landlords. The long-term achievement was an enduring alliance between Irish nationalists, farmers, and Catholic clergy, crucial to the struggle for Ireland's independence.

The Irish Land War combined two powerful movements: the agrarian revolution against the landlord system, and the nationalist revolution against English domination. From the outset the ideology intertwined symbolic codes and patterns concerning land and nation. Not only was the logic of the interconnection of the land and national movements reflected in the emergent Land League ideology, it was to a great extent crystallized, that is, became understood and embraced by movement participants, through their active construction of it in ritualistic events – most prominently, the hundreds of land meetings which took place from 1879 to 1881.[15]

Constantly scrutinized in the ritual of the land meetings were the three central pillars of nineteenth-century Irish social structure – the union with Britain, property rights of landlords, and the tenant farmers' attitude of deference to landlords. There were five main narratives of the "lived": the story of the conquest, the famine, the horrors of British domination and the landlord system, and the here-to-fore impotent response of the Irish people to the last two. As narratives dramatized experiences and myths common to all movement participants, they were immediately unifying. The struggles that occurred in the liminality of land meetings were over the "imagined" – alternative forms of government, property rights, and class structure, how these alternatives should actually work, and how they ought to be reached. Contention between competing narratives of the imagined was the primary force driving the construction of land movement ideology; and the ideological resolution of competition led to goal and strategy definition. This is demonstrated in the following example of the dynamics of symbolic construction at one land meeting.

At the crucial Westport land meeting on June 8, 1879, the principle that tenants unable to pay "unreasonable" rents had a right to hold on to their farms was firmly established as land movement doctrine and strategy. This meeting was momentous, primarily because of the open and explicit tension between the participating social groups. At this early point, the Catholic clergy opposed the fledgling agitation. More critical, the ideological rift between radical and constitutional nationalists, as well as the conflicting interests of large and small farmers, threatened the movement. In the narrative of the speeches we can see both the clash of beliefs, and the possibility of symbolic resolution.

Radical nationalist Michael Davitt challenged the constitutional, and federalist (Home Rule), vision of independence from England. Davitt encouraged the audience to:

> define what you mean by self-government . . . [the] term self-government
> . . . may be employed in a truly national sense, or made to subserve to a party
> purpose. . . . Some there are who would be content with less than complete
> independence in the belief that the full measure of our rights is unattainable.[16]

Davitt drew a symbolic line for the audience between separatists and Home Rulers. He imputed to the latter profane motives: as federalists, they either had self-serving interests in a union with England, or they lacked the courage and conviction to fight for all that is rightfully Ireland's, that is, national and economic sovereignty. The true and sacred cause of nationalists could only be complete separation and independence from England.

Switching from imagery of political revolution to social revolution, the radical agrarian activist Matthew Harris tapped the tension between large and small tenant farmers. "The people are beginning to revolt – to feel that if they did not stand up against such iniquity, they would be almost as criminal as the landlords and graziers."[17] In this brief drama, the audience is drawn into the fervor of revolution, and forced to decide on which side they stand. If they do not fight for their rights, they are as bad as landlords and graziers. This was also a direct assault to the Home Rule vision of unity between classes in attaining national independence, and symbolically proclaimed the priority of the land question over the national question.

The "advanced" Home Ruler, Charles Stewart Parnell, leader of the Irish Parliamentary Party and soon to become Land League President, managed to use these radical challenges to the advantage of the constitutionalist agenda. For example, he agreed with Davitt about Parliament: "I should be deceiving you if I told you that there was any use in relying upon the exertions of the Irish members of Parliament on your behalf."[18] However, with forethought to a probable upcoming general election, Parnell quickly posed an alternative condition that would make parliamentary action viable: "I am as confident as I am of my own existence that if you had men of determination, of some sort of courage and energy, representing you that you could obtain concessions (hear, hear)." This vision of courageous and determined MPs achieving results in Ireland's favor, a vision which would be repeated constantly in the coming months, helped to transform the negative view the Irish had of parliamentary representatives and the possibility of constitutional change. Concomitantly, with this dramatic vision Parnell began to lay the political foundation for the election of advanced Irish nationalists and land reformers into the House of Commons.

However, it was on the question of land that the audience most wanted to hear him speak, and on which he was most triumphant. After affirming his commitment to peasant proprietary as the final settlement, Parnell electrified the audience by combining elements of the "lived" and the "imagined," admonishing the tenant farmers to: "hold a firm grip of your homesteads and lands (applause). You must not allow yourselves to be dispossessed, as you were dispossessed in 1847. You must not allow your small holdings to be turned into large ones."[19]

The symbols were simple yet powerful. In associating the present crisis to that which precipitated the Famine, Parnell dramatically offered an alternative outcome, if only the farmers would act resolutely on their own behalf. "Hold a firm grip on your homesteads" became a rallying cry and core principle of Land League ideology and strategy, and a concrete form of political action by tenant farmers during the Land War.[20]

Practical Action[21]

"Practical Action" occupies the non-ritual end of the continuum. The term refers, variably depending on school of thought, to: (1) ordinary but instrumental activities, (2) modes of action that are learned, made more proficient with repetition, and rooted in particular knowledge, and (3) "practice" which implies habit, routine, and rules. Practical action is situated in day-to-day life; and retains a high cognitive quality. Alexander's suggestion that practical action be conceptualized as "fixed" above and "open" below encompasses the contingency of everyday life and the agency of individuals, while acknowledging the structured nature of social life (1988a: 327). This notion, like most dealing with practical action, stems from Harold Garfinkel's ethnomethodology.

According to Garfinkel,[22] social order, though greatly maintained within social institutions, originates from shared understandings among social actors. Shared understandings, or "knowledge held in common" to use Garfinkel's terminology, derives from shared practices by which individuals produce and recognize social reality as meaningful. Thus, shared understandings, or culture, are a product of practice, emerging from the everyday activities of society's members. What then is practice based on?

Through innovative "breaching" experiments, Garfinkel demonstrated that social action, like games, is based on social rules which must be internalized by individuals (1963). However, actors must "work at" rules, as rules are only effective when operating in conjunction with the order-creating "consciousness" of individual actors. One of Garfinkel's most important contributions was showing how actors make sense of, interpret, everyday situations through accommodative work.[23] Confronted with continuously changing events and situations, people "normalize," that is, depict new events as normal and consistent with past events and with overarching rules; "index," that is, categorize new objects in terms of prior knowledge; and "ad hoc," that is, use new experience to document prior expectations based on dominant rules, thereby reproducing the rules. A vast set of collectively held cognitive categories, emotional appeals and evaluative symbolic elements underlies individual accommodative work. Thus, through agency the shape of social order is maintained or modified as individuals struggle, constrained or enabled by internalized collective rules, to satisfy the demands of everyday contingency.

An example of how accommodative work (agency) on the part of individuals reproduces structural rules (culture) is provided in *Language and Social Reality* (1974) by D. L. Wieder. In his study of a halfway house, Wieder described how drug offenders used a set of rules, the "convict code," to interpret and act in their institutional situation. Wieder thus demonstrated how rules retain their sense-making quality despite constant social conflict, precisely because of individual accommodative work.

Through what Garfinkel termed the "documentary method of interpretation," "actors understand individual objects of perception in terms of the context in which the objects appear, and at the same time, they understand context on the basis of particular objects occurring within it" (Roth 1994: 3). Thus according to ethnomethodologists, both social objects and contexts must be theoretically understood as actively constructed by social actors themselves. Though this conceptualization often leads to an individualist turn theoretically, it in fact confirms the centrality of collective understandings, contingency, and individual interpretation and agency in social action and structuring. This is demonstrated in Melvin Pollner's *Mundane Reason: Reality in Everyday and Sociological Discourse* (1987), especially his study of conflicting testimonies in traffic court. Pollner explicates how people sustain their belief of what the reality of their world is, especially when confronted with competing, divergent accounts of those events in that world, through enormous interpretative efforts based on shared understandings.

Meaning, interpretation, collectively constructed meaning systems, and agency, then, are at the heart of practical action. As they are central to all types of action, these elements clearly relate the three landmarks – ritual action, ritualistic action, and practical action – on the continuum. Thus the continuum allows us to distinguish and compare different types of meaning constructing action and events, but also to understand how one type can "slide" into another.

Recently however, theorists connected with the current "cognitive turn" in social theory, especially neo-institutionalists in sociology, have expanded upon, and subverted, Garfinkel's early work on practical action. This new theorizing abandons meaning and agency in individual action, compromises the notion of culture, and sees "structure" as ultimately determinative of social processes.[24]

According to neo-institutionalist theory, practical action occurs primarily within institutions and organizations; in fact, practical action creates institutions. According to Meyer and Rowan social behavior is determined by "reciprocated typifications or interpretations" which actors must take into account in social situations. Then when "social processes, obligations or actualities come to take on a rule-like status in social thought and action . . . institutionalization takes place" ([1977] 1991: 42), and day-to-day action becomes routine, taken for granted, and constitutive of social structure. Contrary to continuum expectation, the environment of action is highly structured: coercive, mimetic and normative pressures limit the range of action choices individuals can make (DiMaggio and Powell [1983] 1991: 67–74). Ultimately, the pattern of institutional ideas and beliefs which determines behavior in organizations becomes the template guiding action throughout society, creating "modern worldwide myths of rationality" (Meyer and Rowan 1991: 46; Kully 1994, for the phrase). How does this theory of practical action square with the agency/culture/structure nexus, and how is meaning theorized?

In a telling passage summarizing new institutionalism, DiMaggio and Powell define institutionalization as the "process by which certain social relationships and actions come to be taken for granted and a state of affairs in which shared cognitions define 'what has meaning and what actions are possible' (Zucker 1983: 2)" (1991: 9). Deconstructing this definition we can find the core of this new practical action theory, shared not only by neo-institutionalists but among other social theorists, such as Pierre Bourdieu and Anthony Giddens.

Social relationships (based on interests) and the routine interaction and actions they generate, become taken-for-granted behavior. The taken-for-granted becomes habit or "preconscious" processes, schema, and rules. Rules and habits constitute both individual and collective cognition, that is, ideas and beliefs, that is, culture.[25] Thus, shared cognition[26] defines meaning, and possible action. According to this logic, culture is key to the social structuring process; however, culture is ultimately reducible to structure (in the materialist sense). Once the pattern of cognition is institutionalized, it overwhelmingly tends to reproduce its structuralist foundation; hence, change based on voluntaristic agency is limited.[27]

Anthony Giddens and Pierre Bourdieu are perhaps the most prominent social theorists espousing the processual analysis of social structuring within theories of practical action. Both Giddens' theory of "structuration" and Bourdieu's "theory of practice" laudably look to the constitutive, and contingent, nature of action – time, place, strategy, improvisation – in conjunction with the rules and schemes of social structure in order to understand social structuring. However, something major has been left out of both their efforts to interconnect agency and structure: namely the subjective meaning of action. Because meaning systems (rules of habitus and social knowledge) are directly referential to social structure, meaning is not transformable. In the theories of Giddens and Bourdieu, as in neo-institutionalism, individual and collective *interpretation* is mistakenly replaced by *habit*. Thus, there is little chance of symbolic invention and rearrangement in individual and collective interpretation of experience.

So tightly is practice and structure connected that there is no room for either real agency or structural change. As I have outlined above, to make the agency/structure connection the intervening element of culture must be thoroughly theorized, analyzed, and integrated into concrete event analysis.

Conclusion

Most sociologists now agree that agency and structure constitute a reciprocal relationship, and that culture is not reducible to social structure. However, the contention made a few years ago that "most historical analyses attend to the interplay of meaningful actions and structural contexts in order to make sense of the unfolding of unintended as well as intended outcomes in individual lives and social transformation" (Skocpol 1984: 1) is still wishful thinking. We are woefully inadequate at theorizing meaningful action because meaning itself is not theorized. Implementing the theoretical and methodological proposals outlined above – jointly, examining the processes of historical events and episodes instead of long-term evolutionary trends, and making meaning and meaning construction the central foundation of the cultural analysis that ought to be part of every study of the social structuring process – will allow, indeed force, us to attend to the interplay of agency, culture, and structure.

In contending that meaning and its ritual construction are the central pillars of cultural theory and analysis, I assert the profound relevance of Weberian and Durkheimian theory to contemporary social theory. The classical traditions of Weber and Durkheim are very much alive. Though most theoretical concepts – such as class, states, and nations – must be empirically proven in every historical analysis, the principles of meaning-driven action and the collective construction of specific meanings are transhistorical. However, these principles are not static. The vitality of these classic concepts, much like culture, derives greatly from their flexibility and transformability in the face of changing historical circumstances and innovations in social theory.

Notes

I would like to thank the members of the UCLA sociology culture group, especially Andrew Roth, Ronald Jacobs, and Hannah Kully, for commenting on the many drafts of this paper. I also thank Stephen Turner for asking me to write it.

1 This new social theorizing has emerged from a diverse group of sociologists: historical/comparative sociologists (Calhoun 1992b; Sewell 1991; 1992), practical action theorists (Giddens 1984; Bourdieu [1972] 1977; 1984) sociologists trying to make the "micro/macro" link (Collins 1981; 1988b), cultural sociologists (Alexander 1987b; 1990; Wuthnow 1989), and "new institutionalists" (Powell and DiMaggio 1991), as well as Alfred Schutz, Harold Garfinkel, Peter Berger, and Thomas Luckman, and Erving Goffman, the so-called micro-theorists from whom macro-theorists have drawn so heavily.

2 I am aware that the term "constructionist" is used for a social theory of social problems. What I am calling constructionist social theory is not related. I use the term because it implies the *process* of building structures, and that the social analyst must analyze and interpret the process in order to explain the structure.

3 Some readers may object to the neglect of Marx in this essay on the classics and cultural theory. While I certainly acknowledge Marx's contribution to cultural analysis, it tends to come in through the back door (cf. Wuthnow 1987: 26–7). Weber and Durkheim's cultural concepts are much more straightforward, and have the potential to be mated in a very robust cultural theory.

4 This analysis is derived from Rambo and Chan 1990: 635–48.

5 Despite Wuthnow's theoretical conclusion that the concept of meaning should be abandoned in cultural analysis, the chapter "Beyond the problem of meaning" in *Meaning and Moral Order* is very illuminating on the issue.

6 Ethnomethodologists, beginning with Harold Garfinkel, demonstrate how this happens in the day-to-day context of social action. I discuss this fully below.

7 The exposition in this paragraph is derived from Alexander and Smith 1993: 6–7 who draw upon semiotics, post-structuralism, new cultural history, hermeneutics, symbolic anthropology, and Durkheim.

8 The following discussion is derived from *Historical Metaphors and Mythical Realities*, 1981: 68–70. Sahlins points out that interpretation is defined as "classification within a given system"; therefore a person's perception of something becomes a fact of their consciousness "insofar as it is embedded in a concept of which the perceiver is not the author" (pp. 6–7).

9 I lean here on Sewell's definition and conceptual use of transposability: to change the form, content, or meaning of something in the process of applying it in a new domain (1992: 8 and 17). However, my use of the term may be somewhat different.

10 The ritual process does not move deterministically from separation to reaggregation; rather, the onset of ritual implies the expectation of an eventual reaggregation. I credit Ronald Jacobs with suggesting this paragraph and helping to construct it.

11 Jin Lin Hwang (1993) has reworked Turner's concept to show that liminal states are not just characterized by feelings of relief and escape from a culturally ordered world, but can be full of tension and confrontation.

12 The concept of "lived" and "imagined" dramas is from Geertz (1973: 112). It is Hwang's suggestion that through these dramas new cultural symbols can be created (1993).

13 For documentary film evidence of emotional power in the ritualism of labor strikes and union meetings, and civil rights movement meetings, rallies and marches see, respectively: *American Dreams*, 1991, Barbara Koepple and Arthur Cohen, HBO Video; and *Eyes on the Prize: America's Civil Rights Years* (series 1), 1987, Blackside Productions, PBS Video.

14 The Irish land meetings could have been categorized just as easily as rituals: for example, they were often formalistic, addressed sacred matters, and action in them was often structured and prescribed. That I have designated the land meetings as ritualistic events instead of rituals demonstrates the concrete "drift" of action and events between analytical categories.

15 The following discussion of ritual in the Irish Land War is derived from my

dissertation, "Culture and social change: symbolic construction, ideology, and political alliance during the Irish Land War" (1994).

16 *Connaught Telegraph*, June 14, 1879, p. 3.
17 Ibid.
18 Ibid.
19 Ibid.
20 Calhoun's account of identity formation among the student protesters in Tiananmen Square also exemplifies ritualistic social interaction (1992b). The protesters occupying the sacred Chinese place did not re-enact traditional rituals in furthering the democracy movement; but they did draw on traditional heroic narratives to guide their action (pp. 62–3). The hunger strikes, as well as other single and repeated actions, were highly symbolic gestures generating much solidarity, and transforming consciousness among the protestors and in wider Chinese society. In fact the six weeks of the Tiananmen protest was a very liminal period whereby institutionalized meanings and norms China were suspended and scrutinized, and new meanings and identity created through the struggle.
21 I am indebted to Andrew Roth for redirecting my previous thinking on the issues of this section. However, this does not necessarily associate him with any of the ideas and contentions put forth.
22 The exposition in the following paragraph is derived from Roth (1994).
23 The following exposition is based on Alexander (1988a: 233–45), and Kully 1994: "Where is agency and meaning in neo-institutionalist theory?"
24 It is argued, and generally acknowledged, that Garfinkel himself abandoned the centrality of meaning and collectively constructed signification to focus on situated material practices of individuals (Alexander 1988a: 236–45). Indeed, it is Garfinkel's later work that neo-institutionalists primarily embrace (Powell and DiMaggio 1991: 19–22).
25 To verify that I haven't misinterpreted DiMaggio and Powell's conceptualization of culture, note the contention that "cultural elements are taken for granted beliefs and widely promulgated rules that serve as templates for organization" (1991: 27).
26 Note the difference between "shared understandings" in Garfinkel's conceptual framework, and "shared cognitions" in neo-institutionalism. By embracing the cognitive turn, neo-institutionalists neglect the normative and affective dimensions of culture.
27 Neo-institutionalist theory does conceptualize ritual: as a process which perpetuates, in an almost sinister manner, institutional culture. Neo-institutionalists generally (though there are exceptions, for example, Friedland and Alford 1991) do not accept the contingency in ritual which allows it to be susceptible to collective reconstruction.

10

Measurement and the Two Cultures of Sociology

John R. Hall

> Or, again, may there not be some danger that the physicist of to-day may treat his [sic] electron, as he treated his old unchangeable atom, as a reality of experience, and forget that it is only a construct of his own imagination, just so far useful as it describes his experience, and certain to be replaced by a wider concept as his insight expands?
>
> Karl Pearson *The Grammar of Science*

Sociology today may be described by two cultures – scientific and relativistic. In this chapter I explore the problem of measurement as a way of marking a "third path" in which the claims on each side can be taken seriously. That path reaches an understanding of measurements as social actions that construct our perceptions about manifold features of socio-historical phenomena, and it opens up a new vista of sociological reasoning in relation to inquiry under such conditions.

The divide between the two cultures of sociology is formidable. On one side, the *scientific* culture, what in the US is often called "mainstream" sociology – is oriented toward explanation of socio-historical regularities by use of formal and replicable methods of inquiry. Scientific sociology encompasses quantitative empirical analysis of social processes, organizations, populations, public opinion, and the like, as well as the quantitative testing of formal theory – practiced today by rational-choice, network, population-ecology and formal Marxist theorists, among others. Legitimated by logical positivism until the epistemological crisis, scientific sociology now is widely seen to require some sort of post-positivist epistemology to account for its procedures and knowledge (Hall 1990). This shift, however, has not dampened the commitment to a science of society.

The other culture of sociology – the *relativist* one – now can be called post-modern, even if, just as much as scientific sociology, it has modernist sources (cf. Lyotard 1984: 79). Historically, there have been many sociological accounts of relativism, but paradoxically, the diverse ways of accounting for the absence of any single, privileged form of knowledge have recently converged. Both action-centered phenomenological and structuralist symbolic traditions now share a post-structuralist recognition about the reflexive historicity of social life and its emergent mediation by cultural categories and their social appropriation (Bourdieu 1977; Wuthnow 1987). Philosophically, relativism implies the absence of any foundational epistemology, and is thus open to charges of self-contradiction in any assertion of its "truth." But post-modern culture draws on perspectivism and pragmatism rather than scientism or logic, and it does not take its project to be the search for ultimate truth or the elimination of all logical contradictions.

I believe that the long-standing challenge of transcending this scientific–relativist divide can be confronted in a direct way by reconstructing the philosophical basis of quantification in concept formation and measurement. The division between the two cultures can be framed in terms of multiple binary divisions – for example, between theory and historicity, and between claims about social structure and about social actors' agency. But the most institutionally compelling of these many fractures, especially in American sociology, separates the so-called "quantoids" from so-called "soft" sociology. If we could somehow transcend this divide, we might arrive at a reconstruction of the culture of sociological inquiry that is both clear cut and fundamental. The task is formidable, however, for it is impeded by the cultures of inquiry themselves: quantitative sociologists have been mostly concerned with the newest issues and techniques, not with questioning fundamental assumptions, while most non-quantitative sociologists have lacked the interest in pursuing the technical expertise on which critical accounts of measurement and statistics might be based (but see Blumer 1956; Cicourel 1964).

Indeed, the quantitative and non-quantitative cultures of sociological inquiry developed in relative autonomy from one another during the twentieth century. Quantitative sociology was initiated under modern positivist claims for science, and today, sociologists such as Jonathan Turner (1985), Randall Collins (1989), and Edgar Kiser and Michael Hechter (1991) continue to defend scientific sociology against the relativist implications of emergent historicist, philosophical and post-modernist critiques of science (for example, Kuhn [1962] 1970; Winch 1959; Rorty 1979; Lyotard 1984). Yet the substance of these latter critiques is hardly new to sociology. The destabilization of meaning in texts and discourse, the crisis of foundational epistemology, and assertions about the reflexive historicity of social phenomena already have been anticipated among "classical" sociological thinkers like Max Weber (C. Turner 1990) and Georg Simmel (Levine 1985). In different ways, Weber and Simmel engaged in efforts to establish sociology as an interpretative discipline of inquiry based on a neo-Kantian recognition about the role of values in formulating topics of cultural significance.

Briefly, the neo-Kantian problem that confronted Weber and Simmel was this. Because Kant treated benchmarks of interpretation as value constructions, his philosophy opened up issues of value disjuncture that nineteenth-century German neo-Kantians sought to address. Kant's philosophy depends upon a constructionist approach to concept formation: what we know about the world is mediated by our concepts. Although examining experience by use of reason offers considerable room for finding out about the world, there is no hope for knowledge of the world as such. It follows that radically alternative ways of knowing about the world may be constituted by their distinctive frames of reference. Only the formulation of an objective value orientation would seem to allow for the communal exercise of reason, and this project has proved elusive. Put differently, objectivity would be possible only *within* a given value frame of reference, not *between* them. Pushed to its full implications, the identification of alternative value spheres of knowledge sustains a neo-Kantian perspectivist relativism that acknowledges alternative, equally viable, ways of conceptualizing socio-historical phenomena – for example, by encompassing meanings in relation to social structural phenomena, as Weber did, or by separating structural form and social meaning, as Simmel proposed. It was this broad circumstance of multiple crosscutting approaches to conceptualization – driven by what I will call the socially constructed character of concepts – that Weber and Simmel confronted.[1] But there is an important difference between how Weber and Simmel and to-day's post-modern relativists construe the circumstances of relativism: post-modernists, intoxicated by rhetorical and poetic critiques, too easily dismiss rigorous inquiry *tout à fait*, without puzzling through how any knowledge, including theirs, might be achieved. By contrast, neither Weber nor Simmel allowed the difficulties to paralyze empirical inquiry. They thus offer a point of departure for a third path, one that transcends either a narrowly procedural science or the more hopeless versions of post-modernist relativism that deny any possibilities of shared knowledge.

How might quantitative sociology be brought along the third path? Recent efforts at reconstructing quantitative sociology have concentrated most on critique and transformation of its techniques and analytic strategies. This rethinking of quantitative practice – initiated on a programmatic basis by

Stanley Lieberson (1985; 1992) – is increasingly premissed on a recasting of "variables sociology" – what Andrew Abbot (1988) has called "general linear reality" – within a more general framework of measurement attuned to comparative, configurational, and event-transitional analyses of historically situated and socially embedded cases (Ragin 1987; Isaac and Griffin 1989; Griffin and Isaac 1992; Griffin 1993; Tuma and Hannan 1984; Mayer and Tuma 1990). These efforts demonstrate that a reconstruction of quantitative sociology can proceed without leaving the discipline stranded in a wasteland of texts, unable to engage in empirical analysis, forbidden to use computer software.

The third path that I propose here is meant to extend these efforts at reconstruction by addressing the relation of measurement to theoretical reasoning in a way sensitive to both the claims of relativism and the interests of science. This third path does not deny that there are sometimes coherent (constructed) social realities. However, it does insist on a neo-Kantian understanding about the significance of concepts for bringing into view some (and by the same stroke, potentially submerging other) aspects of the manifold social realm. This neo-Kantian account emphasizes that an act of naming may prove "meaningful" even if it does not "correspond" to any underlying reality or property of things identified by naming. In this critical and skeptical account of the status of concepts, terms like "class," "deviance," "organization," and "socialization" do not bear any necessary relation to any coherent and bounded realities, even if such terms "colligate" – that is, draw together – perceptually parallel aspects of actual social phenomena. Such terms are simply (more or less) useful for gaining analytic leverage on social complexity. To be quite clear, however, even if sociological concepts are perspectival rather than "real," they need not condemn us to a narrow hermeneutic circle. To the contrary, the problem of circularity that arises in post-positivist inquiry can be addressed by adopting on a more general basis a modified version of an approach to measurement originally applied to philosophical realism (Pawson 1989). In effect, this approach acknowledges quantitative sociology as a specialized cultural practice of reading and writing texts, and nevertheless proposes ways of improving that cultural practice.

In this chapter, I will explore the third path as a basis for quantitative sociology by addressing two issues: (1) the problem of value and theory relativity in sociological inquiry, and (2) post-positivist efforts to salvage a scientific basis for concept formation and measurement. These discussions set the stage for: (3) a consideration of an alternative approach to concept formation that acknowledges measurement as an activity of social construction under conditions of value and theory relativism, and (4) exploring the prospects of scientific sociology within this approach.

Value and Theory Relativity

The assertion of relativity involves two quite different important claims: first, about the *theoretical character of the objects* to which inquiry is directed, and second, about *criteria of explanation*. The first claim is the more familiar: it advances the view that conceptualization, observation and measurement of empirical phenomena are not autonomous activities. Rather, they are held to be theory-dependent, with the implication that an object of inquiry is not the same as an empirical phenomenon (Alexander 1982). We do not study societies as they are; we study them with the help of one or another theoretical frame of reference. The second claim of relativism is less often discussed but equally significant. Its assertion is that criteria of explanation no longer can be reduced to any definitional formula; instead, wholly alternative potentially viable kinds of explanations can be brought to bear on the same puzzle (Miller 1987; Hall forthcoming). For example, narratives have their ways of explaining that differ from theoretical explanations, which differ yet again from so-called "factor" explanations sometimes employed in analytic history. Each alternative kind of explanation may tell us something different about the English Revolution or racial discrimination. Moreover, even working with one general kind of explanation (for example, narrative), there is no single criterion of explanatory adequacy for any given empirical puzzle. Instead, considerations beyond logic and empirical observation affect criteria of explanation. To take an example concerning social inequality, sociologists might find the discovery of workable programs to reduce poverty quite important, even if the researchers lacked any theoretical understanding of why the programs worked or what fundamental processes contributed to the existence of poverty in the first place. Social values may suggest that certain knowledge is important, even if incomplete. Moreover, even if value issues are set aside, disciplines and research programs tend to establish well defined boundaries of inquiry. If the "infinite regress" of the next question is to be avoided, there must be pragmatic limits to inquiry. These limits are established by what Richard Miller (1987) calls "stopping rules" – conventional standards of explanation that designate the adequacy of explanations for one purpose or another, within one discipline or another, for the purposes of one research program or another.

In short, accounts of relativity identify its sources both in criteria of explanation and in conceptualization and measurement procedures that construct objects of inquiry. Of course, such accounts of relativity could be disputed. But I propose instead to suspend judgment and ask, "what does socio-historical inquiry look like if we acknowledge the relativistic possibilities?" The broad consequences are simple but significant. Objects of inquiry may be constituted in multiple ways out of the manifold flux of empirical socio-historical phenomena. Not only is there no single, warranted way of constructing an object of inquiry about any given empirical phenomenon, neither is there any single strategy for making sense of a given constructed object of inquiry. For example, whatever any specific constructed object of inquiry called "social stratification" may be, it is something different than the intricacies of social activities in the "lifeworld" – the spatially and perceptually available everyday world available in unfolding socially lived time (Schutz and Luckmann 1973; Habermas [1984] 1987) – out of which data about stratification are generated. Moreover, what counts as explanation about social stratification as an object of inquiry may vary depending on whether the theoretical interest is in: ordered relationships within a bounded community constituted through face-to-face interaction, the differentiation of social groups within a society considered as an objective totality, economic inequality among individuals, and so forth. In this light, social stratification is not either a "thing" in the world, or even a set of attributes about a thing: it is an orienting concept that can be used to consolidate objects of inquiry through measurement rules that categorically colligate (that is, group together) and distinguish between various aspects of socio-historical phenomena. With alternative rules of colligation and distinction, the conceptual object "stratification" can be constituted differently in a Marxist inquiry versus a structural-functional one, much less a feminist or intertextual approach – all in relation to "the same" worldly phenomena.

The basic issues of relativism that I have described can be represented in a two-dimensional typology that identifies four ideal typical projects of socio-historical inquiry. One typological dimension asks whether *criteria of explanation* are held to be theory or value informed, or theory and value neutral. The question here is whether rules of explanation are taken to exist independently of theoretical framework and value preferences, or whether the adequacy of explanations is understood as relative to criteria (for example, value, disciplinary or theoretical criteria) that are not scientifically "universal." Analytically independent of explanation criteria, there is the problem of concept formation. The second dimension therefore distinguishes whether the conceptual *object* of inquiry is held to be constituted "objectively" or in a theory and value relative way. Table 10.1 depicts the four basic projects of inquiry described by the resulting typology – *Interpretative Understanding* as relativized explanation of a perspectival object (for example, in the hermeneutic approach of Gadamer 1975), *Value-Objective Understanding* as relativized

Table 10.1   Projects of inquiry according to assumptions concerning the constructed object of inquiry and the possibility of objective criteria of explanation

		Criteria of explanation	
		Relative	*Universal*
Theory/value basis of object of inquiry	*Relative*	Interpretative Understanding	Value-Neutral Explanation
	Objective	Value-Objective Understanding	Positive Explanation

Source: from Hall (forthcoming)

explanation of an object of analysis somehow constituted "objectively" (for example, Habermas [1984] 1987), *Value-Neutral Explanation* as the objective explanation of a perspectively formed object of inquiry according to criteria of explanation that are somehow objective, or shared across otherwise contending points of view (for example, Weber),[2] and *Positive Explanation* as the development and evaluation of explanations according to objective criteria in relation to objectively constituted objects (that is, objects for which the salient properties for investigation do not depend on value orientations, but somehow inhere in the phenomena themselves). The typology illuminates the challenge of establishing a scientific sociology in the image of the natural sciences: the generally embraced goal of science – Positive Explanation – cannot be achieved insofar as *either* the criteria of explanation or the constitution of the object of inquiry is acknowledged to be theory or value dependent.[3]

Realism and the Attempt to Re-establish Positive Explanation

Relativistic critiques of science raise reasonable doubts about any privileged status of Positive Explanation, but relativism itself can be accused of self-contradiction. The alternative account of inquiry along the third path does not entail this self-contradiction; it recognizes Positive Explanation – like any other approach, including the present one – as a "cultural practice" of research that occurs within the historically located lifeworld of unfolding social activity, where efforts to achieve knowledge are necessarily incompletely rationalized.[4] Under the assumption that there are some regularities in the socio-historical realm, the question then becomes – what are the prospects for Positive Explanation in relation to other cultural practices of inquiry?

In terms of table 10.1, Positive Explanation would depend on both "universal" criteria of explanation and successive approximation toward "objective" construction of the object of inquiry, presumably through reliable and valid measurement that offered a basis to make decisions about the validity of any given hypothesis. The first issue – of whether universal explanatory criteria can be established – ultimately depends upon whether there can be translation between assertions made within heterogeneous theoretical perspectives and research practices (P. Roth 1987; Hall forthcoming). But the problem of translation cannot be addressed without first coming to terms with the relation of measurement to the constructed objects of inquiry.

Logical positivism in its classic form depended on theory-independent measurement and the refusal to make any metaphysical assumptions about the world being investigated (Halfpenny 1982). If the practicing sociologist could measure empirical variables while restricting assumptions to those concerning logic and theory testing, then secure knowledge of the socio-historical world's regularities could be built outward from this core without the circular reasoning entailed in assuming certain things that also are the subject of explanation. Socio-historical inquiry would be capable of testing assertions about the dynamics of social interaction or patterns of class conflict independently of any theoretical or ontological assumptions about the nature of the phenomenon under investigation. This, of course, is precisely the feature of positivism drawn into question by the problem of the "double hermeneutic" (Giddens 1976) – dealing with preinterpreted social realms – and by assertions about the theory-dependence of concept formation and measurement. It now seems that a concept such as "class" entails the baggage of both (contested) everyday meanings and one or another theoretical meaning, rather than corresponding to any ontologically "natural" and theoretically "neutral" referent.

In the face of such obstacles, "post-positivists" who seek to salvage a privileged status for science have sought to reaffirm the objective status of the (admittedly constructed) objects of socio-historical inquiry. To do so, they have drawn on three related approaches – *theoreticism*, *conventionalism*, and *realism*. The first approach, theoreticism, seeks to develop scientific propositions independent of empirical categories, within an *a priori* formal and internally consistent set of logically interrelated concepts that constitute a theoretical system or model. "Class," for example, might be defined within an *a priori* formal theory of social change without worrying about whether the term describes any empirically observable class category (for example, small-business entrepreneurs or manual workers). In its strongest versions (for example, Althusser and Balibar 1970; Hindess and Hirst 1975), theoreticism effectively amounts to a *logical idealism*, social theory as something akin to the mathematically specifiable relations between conceptual terms such as *pi* as the essential relationship between the diameter and circumference of a circle. In the second approach – conventionalism – a particular operationally defined measurement is asserted as the agreed basis upon which research is conducted. Class can be classified according to one or another standard system, "intelligence" can be defined as the score on one or another IQ test, and so forth. As efforts to re-establish conditions appropriate for Positive Explanation, theoreticism reaches an unsatisfactory end in abstracted idealism, and conventionalism serves only as a practical move that allows like-minded investigators to proceed, but without achieving any standard for resolving disagreements with investigators who reject the conventions. By contrast, in the third – realist – approach, "class" would be defined in relation to a posited real social process (such as class conflict), even if the process is not always superficially apparent.

Although realism, theoreticism, and conventionalism all seek to re-establish the epistemological privilege of Positive Explanation, each in its own way, they all construct objects of inquiry in relative rather than objective terms. They thus all amount to approaches of Value-Neutral Explanation, and they thereby force the question of what the prospects are for moving from Value-Neutral to Positive Explanation. These issues can be pursued efficiently by focusing on the approach of the three that has attracted the most recent interest – realism.

Realism is a resilient philosophical ontology that insists upon the reality of socio-historical phenomena. In the realist view, socio-historical phenomena amount to more than isolated events. Although the surface appearances of phenomena are ambiguous, realism posits that the phenomena themselves are generated by coherent processes or mechanisms. That is, even given qualifications about meaning, reflexivity, historicity, and so forth, there are ways in which social things happen that are somehow intrinsic to their nature. If this is so, the task of inquiry is to identify and describe the underlying processes and mechanisms by some empirical method.

This realist account might seem to offer grounds for salvaging objective concept formation and measurement. But I will argue that the power of realism is more apparent than real. Philosophical realism offers a basis for trenchant critique of conventionalist and empiricist strategies of concept formation and measurement. But when it comes to actual measurement, realism's solution turns out not to be realist after all. Instead, even if a realist ontological thesis is granted as a general assumption, concrete measurement practices of inquiry under so-called realism abandon the effort to capture any real essences of phenomena in favor of exploring "the real" as understood via a particular theory or explanatory viewpoint. For this reason, and in a way similar to theoreticism and conventionalism, realist measurement amounts to an activity that constructs out of manifold empirical phenomena an object of inquiry that is relative to its *particular* "realist" frame of reference.

By now, realist philosophies of inquiry have generated a considerable discussion that is a subject in its own right (for example, Bhaskar 1986; 1989; Outhwaite 1987; Harré 1990). Here, I concentrate on the most developed use of realism that actually confronts practical issues of quantitative sociology – Ray Pawson's *A Measure for Measures* (1989). Pawson rehearses phenomenological objections (but not post-structuralist ones) to quantitative measurement – namely that measurement tends to be irrelevant, arbitrary and artificial in relation to meaningful social phenomena. However, rather than rising to the phenomenological critique, he elects to sidestep it by defining sociology as a science with its own special language, that need not refer either to the subjective meanings of social actors or to their social constructions of reality (1989: 26–7). In effect, Pawson acknowledges that a phenomenological critique would pose serious difficulties for measurement *if* sociology were concerned with local, socially, and historically specific meanings of such things as class, power, or gender, and so he chooses instead to define sociology in a way that renders subjective and cultural meanings out of court.

This solution is highly problematic.[5] At the outset Pawson makes the very kind of metaphysical assumption about the nature of the phenomenon to be investigated that so worried the logical positivists. He decides that sociologists have no defensible way to develop measurements out of lifeworldly social meanings, and concludes that there must be no need to do so. But this move should not deter us from exploring Pawson's solution even though it advances a narrow (and self-privileging) definition of sociology. After all, it is for Pawson's sort of sociology that the threat posed by relativism is greatest and the stakes of measurement are the highest. Therefore, in order to take relativism seriously, this is the position on which to concentrate our attention.

At the core of Pawson's approach to measurement is the realist thesis that superficial events are the products of diverse underlying mechanisms and processes that sociologists may isolate and describe using their own, non-natural, language. In this view, the proper objects of inquiry are the underlying "real" processes and mechanisms, which have a "systemic" character. Pawson dismisses empiricist approaches that study correlations among variables independently of any integrated theory because they end up debating the surface correlations in their own terms and fail to make any headway in identifying underlying processes (1989, ch. 2). Such efforts to improve measurement of variables and their interrelationships are doomed, Pawson thinks, because they assume that aspects of phenomena can be measured independently of theory. In place of this misguided empiricism Pawson argues that social science must attempt a "holistic" analysis.

"The idea is to try and capture this idea [*sic*] that science is not the study of external relationships between discrete objects or events, but an investigation of a system of internal relationships brought about by the occurrence of an underlying mechanism which connects the parts of the system" (Pawson 1989: 134–5). This notion of holistic process, Pawson rightly connects up with inquiry organized through "research programs" of the sort described by Lakatos (1971). Specifically, Pawson describes the successful practices of measurement engineers working in the natural sciences who invent ever more sophisticated sensors to record temperature, velocity, and so forth (in this, he offers a seemingly *verstehende* analysis of the meaningful construction of measurement in the natural sciences!), and he suggests that sociology should follow the natural-science model by developing measures that serve to expand its explanatory domains. As Pawson rightly asserts, the trick is to disentangle the theories at stake in research-program expectations from those at stake in measurement practices, so that inquiry can be conducted without falling into the circularity of using a measure in a test of a theory when that very theory must be assumed as true for the measure to bear any validity. In short, Pawson seeks to separate the assumptions for particular measurements from the assumptions under test in a research program.

Pawson's account of realism has much to recommend in it, but there also is much to question. In the first place, his initial decision to sidestep situated meaning has its theoretical ramifications – limiting realism to the compass of only certain kinds of social theories. Table 10.2 shows four equally viable but crosscutting approaches to conceptualizing variable relations within cases that fulfill the general criterion of "holistic" theory upon which Pawson insists. The typology distinguishes on one axis between "meaningful" and "non-meaningful" case patterns of relations, and on its second axis between "structural" and "systemic" case patterns. But because two kinds of constructs – the "ideal type" and the "market system" – are based on meaningful constructions, they fall outside the domain of realist theorizing as delineated by Pawson. His sociological agenda thus is best understood as appropriate

Table 10.2 Types of holistic (case-pattern) concepts according to meaning
adequacy and basis of concept formation

| | | Basis of concept formation | |
		Structural	*Systemic*
Basis in meaning adequacy	*Present*	Ideal type	"Market" system
	Absent	Form	Functional/ dialectical system

Source: from Hall (forthcoming)

only to particular approaches to social theory, such as Marxian sociology,
Parsons' and Luhmann's functional systems theories, as well as Simmel's idea
of a "formal" sociology (that is, a project of identifying the underlying forms,
or coherent, non-meaningful properties of a phenomenon).

The examples that Pawson uses to illustrate his approach give evidence of
the limits to inquiry within his framework (1989: 171–85). He draws them
from diverse theoretical sources – Raymond Boudon's work on education and
inequality, Eric Olin Wright's *Classes* (1985), and Goldthorpe et al.'s study of
social mobility. But despite the different theoretical orientations, each example
constructs an object of inquiry as an external, rationalized, and objective
social system, that is, one that assumes social phenomena to have properties
appropriate to the version of realism that Pawson seeks to advance. These
approaches do not deny agency; they simply focus attention elsewhere – on
the study of social processes and mechanisms. Pawson's realist assumption
thus may serve as a basis for examining *some* theories that describe underlying
social dynamics, but it just as clearly *excludes* consideration of certain phenomena that are influenced by emergent social constructions of cultural
meanings. In his own way, by basing his realism on what amount to "social
facts," Pawson inherits Durkheim's dilemma of how to reconcile realist
conceptualization with constructs such as the *conscience collective* that refer to
meaningful phenomena (Parsons 1937).

It should by now be evident that Pawson's realism solves certain problems
of sociology by ignoring them. Whatever the benefits of the realist approach
within its domain, by sidestepping the question of local meanings in relation
to agency, it offers, at best, only half a sociology. But Pawson's inability to
reconcile realism and local meanings is understandable: social actions seem

likely to depend on actors' interpretations and efforts in ways that would create "meaningful slippage" in any mechanism or process defined in realist terms (Hall forthcoming). Pawson's realism is not a social realism – a realism of multiple, constructed and emergent realities in the lifeworld – of this moment, this place, these words. It is a realism that imports a particular (and disputed) natural-science ontology as the solution to sociology's difficulties. In this sense, it is a step backward, a resolution of the nineteenth-century *Methodenstreit* that chooses to ignore culture and meaning insofar as they cannot be reduced to "variables." Our task today, if we choose to accept it, is rather different: to develop socio-historical inquiry as something other than historicism, that nevertheless acknowledges the salience of meaning and culture.

Even if realism is accepted as a metaphysical possibility, even if we grant that there may be real and coherent social processes independent of any meaningful social construction, the gains do not seem particularly great. Why? Because it is one thing to posit realism in some general way uncommitted to any particular account of what is real, and another thing altogether to construct measurements aligned with some particular account of reality that is open to contention. In Pawson's realism, measurement proceeds within one or another research program. He rejects the alternative realism that would establish empirical measurement independent of theory. But as he correctly notices, with this move, the metaphysical assertion of realism offers little leverage for resolving theoretical disputes, for there are competing realisms (1989: 168). Marxists assert the significance of one reality, rational choice theorists, another, feminists yet another. For Pawson, this circumstance signals the need to push realism further, not to abandon it. Thus, he wants realists not just to assert the privileged status of their own analytic perspectives, but to *prove* the salience of their versions of realism by engaging in research programs that identify "generative models" – underlying mechanisms or processes that operate within empirical complexity. He thus shifts from the ontological assertion of realism to the epistemological problem of measurement as a research practice. Pawson is forced, in terms of Table 10.1, to offer measurement as a device by which to try to move away from the circumstance of competing Value-Neutral Explanations within alternative research programs, and toward Positive Explanation.

The Social Constructions of Measurement

Within the limits of its domain, Pawson's challenge to realists – go out and identify your generative models – is to be applauded. But even if we accept realism metaphysically, in practice, the relevant aspects of socio-historical phenomena are diverse, complexly interfigured with one another, and subject to historical and cultural emergence. These considerations raise the question of whether particular kinds of social phenomena are driven by any singular and identifiable generative mechanism with core properties and boundaries that can be isolated, or whether, alternatively, mechanisms and processes are both intertwined with one another, and "presaturated" with cultural and social significations that influence their properties and boundaries. That is, if multiple "real" processes are manifoldly structured by meaning and action, in the absence of culturally invariant real properties, there is no basis for isolating "essential" properties, and the tasks of concept formation and measurement become enterprises of meaningful signification intended to throw into relief ("real" or other) features of a phenomenon deemed salient on the basis of theoretical and value considerations. That is, measurement even in relation to realist social theories is oriented toward Value-Neutral rather than Positive Explanation.

This problem of value and theory relativity is already evident in the "realist" examples – about education, class, and social mobility – that Pawson discusses. From diverse theoretical starting points, Wright, Boudon, and Goldthorpe et al. were able to propose generative models about class that point to quite different salient aspects at work – domination, culture, action, resources, class boundaries, and so forth (Pawson 1989: 186). Let us assume some general similarities in results of efforts to measure "stratification" within a given society. Under this assumption, there are at least two broad possibilities. In one possibility, the realist position, there is at least one fundamental, generative and real process, which must be disentangled from externalities and described. Alternative theories are derivative or inferior ones – supported, if at all, by spurious data or incomplete analysis. But there is a second possibility. It may be that alternative measurements about stratification colligate the concept in divergent ways, in relation to heterogeneous aspects of any given set of phenomena. That is, there may be manifold mechanisms, processes, events, recipes of action, and other phenomena that are tapped by alternative measurements of stratification. Thus, there may be no definitive theoretical construct of stratification that describes a single and unambiguous real process or mechanism within a given case, much less across multiple cases. This account suggests that reality is more complex than any theoretical construction of it, and that different concepts and their measurements unevenly throw into relief one, another, or multiple and interconnected aspects of diverse dynamics and events.

In theory, it might be possible to sharpen the conceptual formulation and narrow the definition of a term such as stratification, to refine measurement of phenomena described by it, and on this basis, to isolate discrete mechanisms or processes, thus sustaining the realist thesis. But the sheer complexity of socio-historical phenomena undermines this agenda for at least three reasons: (1) seemingly real phenomena such as "stratification" may involve "configurations" of heterogeneous (real) processes that produce multiple coherent complexities to the point of chaos (in the scientific sense of that term) such that the identification of processes and mechanisms through any given focusing lens would be an incomplete and therefore inadequate basis of analysis; (2) the complexity of stratification may overwhelm our scholarly capacity to conduct inquiry about it, such that value interests (themselves diverse and historically shifting) would dictate conflicting research programs that change over time; and (3) the historically emergent character of processes and cultural structures salient to stratification may shift the dynamics of real processes in ways that outstrip any effort to identify their properties. Such difficulties cannot be ruled out in advance. Therefore, even granting the realist thesis as an ontological possibility, inquiry into real generative processes requires theoretical and value-based simplifying assumptions. It therefore must be tempered by the understanding that its measurements construct an object of inquiry in a way such that only selected aspects of phenomena are brought into view. A good sociological theory, as Lieberson (1992) has suggested, will not try to explain everything about an empirical phenomenon.

Relocating the realist thesis in relation to practices that construct objects of inquiry clarifies how what I have termed the third path moves beyond narrowly relativistic and scientific cultures of inquiry. In the first place, it revises Pawson's impoverished realist definition of what could count as real. Even if we grant the metaphysical assumption that some things happen in ways that are masked by the surface appearances of events, there is no reason to believe that those processes are necessarily of the kind anticipated in Pawson's realist approach to measurement. There is an equally plausible alternative to Pawson's account. The "substructures" of social processes may be socially constructed as "real" symbolic and meaningful connections in the emergent unfoldings of social interaction, that is, precisely the meanings that Pawson rules out of the court of sociological explanation within his approach. A second change concerns the status of realist accounts themselves. As I have argued, even for the generative mechanisms and processes anticipated by realism, measurement constructs an object of inquiry different from the manifold flux of socio-historical phenomena. No conceptualization of process or mechanism can be assumed to decisively represent or establish the generative centrality of any real social process or mechanism; such conceptualizations are only linguistic (even if mathematically linguistic) models. As Althusser had it in his apt quotation of Spinoza, "the concept 'dog' cannot bark" (Althusser and Balibar 1970: 105). A conceptual model is only a *construct* that analytically colligates and identifies aspects of a posited process or mechanism deemed of salience for describing the process in a coherent explanatory way. In these terms, even within a realist ontology, measurement is an activity that constructs its object as something other than the reality it is presumed to analyze.

Not only are "realist" objects of inquiry themselves social constructions, Pawson's account of measurement (1989: ch. 4) also is pushed in a constructionist direction precisely because he wants to avoid the circularity of positing a reality and measuring that reality under any procedure that assumes it (for example, avoiding defining social class through occupational categories which are in turn used to study class dynamics). To avoid this circularity, Pawson suggests that theoretical deductions from any particular realist premiss could identify some measurable consequence outside the defined theoretical domain as salient evidence of a generative process. That is to say, measurement may be relevant to the consideration of a realist theory not because it "corresponds" to some operative element of a process, but because theoretical discourse infers and predicts certain patterns of results from some particular unconfounded measurement procedure if the posited process is indeed operating. This is a reasonable effort to disencumber realism from the baggage of theory-dependent measurement, but it amounts to a retreat from the task of aligning measurement with realism. Pawson makes a good case for measurement as an activity of social construction based on theoretical reasoning that *produces* data, rather than an activity that *represents* posited aspects of phenomena by way of some autonomous concept. But this formulation means that Pawson's approach is best understood as something other than "realism," for the project of measurement construction that Pawson develops in relation to research-program realism potentially connects measurement with all kinds of hypotheses, not just realist ones.

Pawson seeks to transcend the circularity of realism by establishing other social constructions of measurement that do not depend on realist concepts, but for which implications of realist accounts can be identified. But this strategy does not depend on the realist status of theories and hypotheses. Insofar as Pawson's approach can be fulfilled, it helps resolve a fundamental problem of Value-Neutral Explanation more generally, namely, how to come to terms with the "hermeneutic circle." The problem that realists face –

conceptualizing the world in terms of a particular research program and then using those concepts to analyze the world – confronts any interpretative frame of reference, realist or not. For some investigators, the solution to this circularity of interpretation is to embrace the hermeneutic circle as the human condition of Interpretative Understanding, in which the readings and writings of texts are necessarily perspectival activities that nevertheless yield meaningful knowledge about the socio-historical world. But Value-Neutral Explanation seeks a different resolution: Max Weber (1949) acknowledged the constructed character of the objects of inquiry, but he nevertheless aspired to making valid assertions about objects of inquiry constructed via their cultural significance.

In the project of Value-Neutral Explanation, phenomena such as "organizations" are manifold in their qualities. Even within a limited theoretical domain of interest, say the analysis of contemporary business organizations, the range of analytic possibilities is sobering. Organizational analysts have investigated hierarchy and control, shifting occupational roles, interpersonal ties, interorganizational networks, social organization of finance, institutional cultures, civilizational differences, and so on. The very diversity of these equally plausible ways of construing organizational phenomena suggests that there is no fundamental key to organizational analysis; instead, wholly different insights may be developed within alternative research programs. The selection of characteristics to measure about them is based on addressing analytic issues of cultural significance, and the investigation of statements about relationships among concepts may reveal culturally significant information *whether or not* those relationships depend on some ultimately "real" social processes. Although such inquiry falls short of Positive Explanation, it nevertheless offers considerable opportunity for the practice of Value-Neutral Explanation as the structured and rigorous analysis of phenomena viewed from a particular perspective. Thus, we may want to know about things that we colligate as "anomie" in relation to things that we colligate as "hierarchy" (or Protestantism and capitalism, and so on) even if the referents of those concepts do not describe some deep formative structure of robust social processes.

Even under the non-realist assumption that objects of inquiry are socially constructed, the project of Value-Neutral Explanation only avoids the problem of circularity to the extent that it follows Pawson's proposal for the construction of measurements independently of theories. Conversely, the "realist" sociologies that Pawson embraces must be understood to have the same epistemological status as any other efforts at Value-Neutral Explanation. Given the diverse possible research programs of Value-Neutral Explanation and given the manifold potential of measurements about objects of inquiry to bring various aspects of socio-historical phenomena into the realm of theoretical reasoning, no research program can claim analytic priority over others on the basis of its ontological claims. That is, there is no *a priori* basis on which to distinguish realist from other approaches to concept formation. Instead, whether constituted topically or theoretically, research programs of Value-Neutral Explanation offer standards for adjudicating controversies within their domains. Even the solution of measurement construction that Pawson proposes only offers a basis for avoiding the problem of circularity within a particular frame of reference. It provides a way of exploring whether arguments *within* a particular culturally significant construction of a phenomenon are credible, but it does not yet deal with the issue of Positive Explanation – adjudicating among explanations derived from alternative frames of reference.

Sociologists sometimes accuse their protagonists in a different theoretical camp of improperly scaling or mismeasuring a particular variable, which when properly scaled and measured, gives rise to an altogether different (and presumably more theoretically adequate) set of relationships (for social class as an example, see Pawson 1989: 259–63).[6] Given the constructed character of concepts, whatever the existence and nature of social mechanisms and processes, arguments about the "correctness" of measurements take on a new dimension. Alternative measurements may simply reorganize perceptions about various aspects of a phenomenon deemed of interest, and patterns of relations between variables may become differentially meaningful on the basis of those measurements.

In short, although Pawson elaborates a procedure designed to avoid theory-dependent measurement within a realist framework, his approach can be folded into a more general neo-Kantian reconstruction of standard sociological measurement practice, in which no description or conceptualization can be assumed to reflect in any definitive sense aspects of the phenomenon posited as essential. Naming one way, measuring by a particular procedure, brings to light certain aspects of a phenomenon that alternative acts of apprehension and measurement would miss, even if they revealed other aspects. When this general circumstance is admitted, what Talcott Parsons (1937) once termed "analytical realism" has to be understood as "analytical constructionism." With this honesty about the circumstances of sociological concept formation and measurement, the often contradictory and conflicting research findings of socio-historical inquiry become more comprehensible.

Not unfortuitously, a broadly constructionist account of measurement aligns with recent investigations into culture and the historicity and social construction of measurement.[7] Unlike the narrower realist approach that shapes

Pawson's project, a more general constructionist conception of measurement does not deny the potential significance of local meanings for social processes. Instead, acknowledgment of the constructed character of the objects of inquiry opens out onto measurement of meaning configurations by use of ideal types, which are non-representational models by definition, constructed in order to throw into relief aspects of a socio-historical phenomenon deemed of cultural significance.[8] In turn, because measurement based on ideal types is oriented toward the analysis of meaning and culture, it is better equipped than Pawson's meaning-exclusionary realism to come to terms with the historicity and social constructed character of measurement itself, and thereby, to offer a reflexively adequate account of measurement. For example, the ideal type "legal–rational bureaucracy" does not correspond to any particular social phenomenon, but instead isolates the ways and degree to which an observer can meaningfully construe any such phenomenon as bureaucratic. In this account, measurement is a reconstruction of social phenomena that are not "naturally" real, but ideologically and socially constructed, categorically differentiated, and (with rationalization) statistically organized "realities" that are, on these bases, historically and cross-situationally unstable.

The consequences for measurement are twofold. In the first place, in that theoretical concepts such as "property" and "citizenship" themselves have social histories (see, for example, Somers 1992), their use in measurement amounts to a sort of "frame realism," adopting a particular social and cultural construction as defining "reality" for the purposes of conducting inquiry. Acknowledging this condition identifies the cultural constructedness of categories as both a neo-Kantian condition of inquiry and a topic of investigation. This admission may be unsettling to realist agendas, but it at least subjects socio-historical conceptualization and measurement to inquiry about its ideological and cultural sources.

Second, the historicist and cultural critiques of conceptualization and measurement render suspect any assumption that processes or mechanisms operate across cases or over time in ways that can be equilibrated through direct measurement. Pawson (1989: 219–20) admits to this condition of historicity, quoting Stanley Lieberson's (1985) example of how the measurement of racial discrimination against blacks must depend on historical period, since at certain points in time, blacks' long-standing exclusion from education would mask measurement of discrimination against them in high-status occupations. This point, like the problem of theory dependence, suggests to Pawson (1989: 223–4) the need to amend his account of measurement: identifying a generative process in realist terms must depend on *comparative* knowledge about how historical and social circumstances make one or another particular measure salient to understanding the real process. But finding or operationalizing historically conditional measurements salient to understanding generative mechanisms seems very much like an enterprise that entails constructing objects of inquiry, and a hermeneutic one at that!

Some scientists have readily admitted the constructed character of measurement. In the full swing of modernist science, Karl Pearson regarded arguments of causality as metaphysical. To quote Desrosières (1992a: 16): "Like the eighteenth century sensualists before him, [Pearson] said that we cannot know anything about *real things*, we can only know impressions on the brain, which constitute *perceptual routines* . . . which therefore constitute the *things* of the new sciences." For similar reasons, early inventors of social indicators resisted making strong claims about the meaning of actual numbers. In the debates over how to measure economic productivity during the late 1930s, for example, a National Research Project author demurred, "The position taken here is that no 'true' measure of productivity or production can be obtained for a group of diverse products, since no such thing exists in reality" (q. in Block and Burns 1986: 777).

Sociologists instrumental in the development of quantitative methods sometimes pay lip service to the constructionist account of measurement, but they seem to ignore the implications. To take one prominent figure, Hubert Blalock (1982: 21) readily admitted that "the real world can only be examined through our own perceptions of it." But in practice Blalock adopted a quasi-realist rather than a constructionist understanding of measurement. The problem, as he saw it, was to establish a "closer fit" between measured variables that serve as proxies for "latent theoretical" variables. But if the constructionist account has merit, the problem of measurement is not simply a matter of working toward a better fit between reality, theoretical variables, and indicators. In a constructionist understanding, concepts like "class," "revolution," or "organization" cannot be assumed to refer to empirically or analytically real phenomena. Instead, they serve as analytic constructs that help us gain explanatory leverage by bringing into view certain aspects of socio-historical phenomena that are of interest within a research program of Value-Neutral Explanation. It is not that this constructionist approach places in doubt the ultimate reality of socio-historical phenomena or the meaningful structure of statistical relationships between measured variables about "status," "power," or the like. Rather, in the absence of demonstration, it rejects any realist ontological assumption in favor of acknowledging the possibility that concepts only "fix" socio-historical phenomena statistically in one or another way that makes them differentially meaningful. It suggests that even though concepts do not represent reality, they may be more or less useful for asking about one or another theory or empirical explanation.

Most sociological measurement strategies still presume in various ways that their fundamental challenge is to refine conceptualization and measurement so as to get measured variables into closer and more predictable relations with objective phenomena – observable, latent, analytical, real, or empirical. These efforts presuppose some sort of external and apprehensible determinate reality with a form that can be ever more closely approximated by increasing the validity of concepts and reducing the "error" in measurements about it. In the constructionist vision of things, by contrast, concepts and their measurement for cases in statistical matrices become "texts." Like other cultural products, they lack any intrinsic or necessary relation to the objects of their reference.

As we all know, when concepts are operationalized and variables measured, data will be forthcoming, and it is likely that some relationships among variables (or patterns of parallel configurations among cases) will be "significant," others not – on the basis of nothing necessarily more than the artifactual consequences of measurement as a social activity. It is all too easy to measure. Perhaps the activity should be licensed. The artifactual and meaningful potentials of data imply that the improvement of "reliability" and "validity" – the conventional concerns of measurement – are issues subsidiary to the rationales that lead to naming and measuring in the first place. As much humility as the social construction of measurement suggests, however, we need not regard all naming as equally powerful. Instead, some naming will result in measurements that reveal suggestive relationships between the aspects of phenomena so named, while others show little or nothing. Understanding the significance of such statistical relationships is a broadly hermeneutic enterprise. How ought this enterprise be understood?

In constructivist terms, a research program amounts to one or another hermeneutic basis for exploring relationships between culturally significant (which includes theoretically significant) aspects of a phenomenon. Readings and writings of texts are not only first-order social activities, but also second-order ones of inquiry. This understanding transforms the status of data: knowledge is mediated for inquiry by the potentially multiple constructions (writings) of inquiry's objects, and by the multiple readings of those objects. In this regard, social scientists are in the same boat as literary critics. They no longer can aspire to decoding the definitive meaning of a text, for other social scientists are prepared to deconstruct and supplement any analytic project. Yet this post-modernist implication of the constructionist account of measurement still leaves substantial questions about the power of scientific sociological inquiry – how it ever produces results "on the ground."

One practical answer is that measurement works best in the statistical analysis of socio-historical phenomena that are preroutinized, that is, where public meanings are widely distributed and understood, where actions occur within "the same" cultural and historical circumstances.[9] But this account of measurement displaces conventional understandings of statistical analysis as the search for general laws and uniformities, in favor of the views advanced by David Haas (1982) and Clark Glymour (1983) that quantitative research typically involves a survey sampling logic and explanatory reasoning about historically specific populations. Though the rhetoric of generalization derived from the hypothetical–deductive model often gets invoked to legitimate statistical analysis, both Haas and Glymour hold, processes may be local and idiosyncratic, and susceptible to explanation with little or no reference to general laws. Given the local character of many efforts at explanation, for a general theory to be sustained, local hypotheses derived from it must withstand efforts at disconfirmation in a variety of settings. A research program institutionalized in its problematic questions and patterns of explanation can be considered successful to the degree that it can be extended to a wider and wider array of phenomena. On the basis of its theory-dependence, however, assessing an account within any such research program (optimally in non-circular terms) must be understood as an exercise in value-neutral, not objective, explanation.[10]

At this juncture, the possibility of Positive Explanation finally is begged. If a constructionist account of measurement is correct, multiple hypotheses about a phenomenon ought to be capable of avoiding rejection within the frames of reference of their respective research programs. This, of course, describes a circumstance that is widely recognized in socio-historical inquiry. However, in some quarters, responsibility for this state of affairs will be placed in the constructionist corner. Outhwaite (1987: 103–4) poses the issue in a central way: he questions Max Weber's account of ideal types as one-sided accentuations of reality, dictated by the topical interests of inquiry rather than any objective criterion of adequacy. What, Outhwaite asks, are the criteria for choosing among disparate claims that gain support within alternative regimes of Value-Neutral Explanation?

Positive Explanation under Constructionist Conditions

Admitting to the constructionist condition severs quantitative measurement from any simple understanding that it is "objective" simply because it employs standardized and replicable procedures. Instead, measurement involves value- and theory-dependent considerations that, in terms of table 10.1, locate it as a component of Value-Neutral Explanation (or, in the absence of explanatory standards, in a project of Interpretative Understanding). We are left to wonder whether there are any prospects at all for social science as Positive Explanation, or whether all knowledge is frame dependent. The third path leaves behind the quest for objective measurement of concepts describing phenomena independently of theoretical reasoning, with its hope for direct access to Positive Explanation. But it does identify one route to Positive Explanation. This route requires a practice that aligns research methodology with an overall theoretical logic that calibrates diverse issues in relation to any given inquiry (cf. Alexander 1982). Here, I can only sketch how such a theoretical logic might operate in relation to the relativity of concepts and measurement.

If the construction of inquiry's objects is a lifeworldly condition of research, then statistical discourses are not forged out of some purely coherent logic of numbers; they are not efforts to get at the inner harmony of society construed as "nature" or even socially constructed "nature." Instead, alternative statistical projects are potentially meaningful ways of arranging information about the socio-historical world. The task is to render measurements and statistical analyses meaningful in relation to particular practices of inquiry. The kind of inquiry of greatest concern to scientific sociologists is what I term "analytic generalization" – the search for, and attempt to explain in theoretical terms, observed patterns and regularities in data about socio-historical phenomena (Hall 1992). For this kind of inquiry, two central questions help crystallize a constructionist agenda: (1) Does constructionism deny the possibility or preclude the discovery of real social mechanisms and processes? (2) What might be entailed in distinguishing the causal adequacy of arguments tied to alternative research programs? The answer to the first question is simple: constructionism neither rejects nor accepts realist ontological claims; it suggests that they are matters for empirical investigation. However, by this standard, constructionism would rule out any privileging of realist explanations relative to other kinds of explanation – theoretical or otherwise.

In turn, the problem of an empirical standard is at the core of the second question. How can there be any empirical standard if evidence itself is constructed in value- and theory-dependent ways? How is it possible to adjudicate among explanations by use of concepts and measurements, when the capacity to get at empirical evidence is conditioned by concepts and measurements?[11] I have argued that in a constructionist response to such questions, research programs – realist or otherwise – amount to projects of Value-Neutral

Explanation that are theory- and value-dependent in their constructions of the object of inquiry. Such research programs are important for formulating and refining theories and explanations in their own terms, but they are necessarily bounded by their own frames of reference, even when they assess validity by non-circular means.

The adjudication of attempts at Positive Explanation therefore depends on locating Value-Neutral Explanations and measurements within a more encompassing theoretical logic that somehow transcends the differences among objects of inquiry by sorting through the possible contradictory implications of *alternative* perspectives and their theories. Such a challenge can be met only insofar as an "axial objectivity" can be established for competing perspectives. By axial objectivity, I mean to suggest a condition in which researchers operating within two different theoretical perspectives or research programs expect the same constructed measurement to yield different results. This circumstance does not occur "in nature" or through "testing a hypothesis" within any given research program; it happens because researchers puzzle through deductions from two different theories and their implications for certain measurements. In the constructionist account, measurement is theory-dependent, and therefore, its informed use depends on making explicit its relationship to theoretical reasoning. In the search for axial objectivity that bridges two or more social theories, theoretical reasoning is brought to bear on bridging two different Value-Neutral Explanations. In this task, theoretical reasoning must make explicit its rationales for the measures undertaken, its justifications for such measures as reasonable procedures to shed light on theoretical issues at stake, and its expectations about the measurement conditions under which theoretical arguments from competing research programs can be compared.[12] This move rejects any naive analytic empiricism and realigns the deductive procedures of logical positivism under conditions in which any attempt to establish axial objectivity depends on prior clarification of measurement stakes within contending research programs of Value-Neutral Explanation.

It should now be evident that I do not advocate a constructionist approach to understanding inquiry as cultural practice in order to suggest that either statistical analysis or scientific sociology is a hopeless enterprise. Instead, my view is that quantitative sociology's practices need to be reformed in relation to epistemological understandings of the reflexive, socially constructed, and historically embedded character of conceptualization and measurement. This is an ironic conclusion, for it means that concerns about the relativity of measurement push us in the direction of a working relation between the Value-Neutral Explanation of research programs and old-fashioned modernist positivism, the positivism that does not traffic in epistemological realism, that does not simply pretend to measure and analyze empirical variation, but instead adjudicates among alternative explanations by deducing predictions about aspects of the world for which measurable evidence might be sought.

The collapse of the hard distinction between science – as investigation – and "nature" – as phenomenon (Latour 1993) – erases sociology's old stigma of not being a "true" science. The "hard" sciences are in the same boat. Sociologists can belatedly reconstruct sociological practice in ways that acknowledge reflexivity and social constructedness, without sacrificing their science-like claims to an enterprise in which scholars watch over each other, and where the stronger argument ought to defeat the weaker. What then is lost? Only certain mystifying claims of scientific sociology – for measurement realism, for the autonomy of science, for its pre-eminence as the practice of sociology. Scientific sociology is located within the same extra-scientific circumstances of theory and value dependence and hermeneutic discourse that mark other kinds of socio-historical inquiry. Positive Explanation may be pursued as a goal, but its accomplishments are hard fought, not simply warranted by its procedures, and complexly related to Value-Neutral Explanation. This circumstance marks a brave new world, much more difficult to negotiate than the simpler modernist world where there were "two cultures" – of science and relativism – with a sharp line demarcating their territories. But that world is now upon us.

Notes

Revised version of a paper presented at the annual meetings of the American Sociological Association, August 17, 1993, Miami, Florida. While reserving to myself responsibility for this chapter, I wish to thank Marc Ventresca for encouraging me to take up these issues and Stephen Turner and Michael Hechter for their helpful comments.

1 On the diverse range of neo-Kantian positions and thinkers, see Köhnke (1991). For an introductory discussion of Weber and Simmel's approaches to the problem of values, and a delineation of alternative viable theoretical strategies of conceptualization, see Hall (forthcoming: chs 2, 4).

2 Briefly, Weber held, "In the *method* of investigation, the guiding 'point of view' is of great importance for the *construction* of the conceptual scheme which will be used in the investigation. In the mode of their *use*, however, the investigator is obviously bound by the norms of our thought just as much here as elsewhere. For scientific truth is precisely what is *valid* for all who *seek* the truth" (1949: 84, emphasis in original).

3 Given the alternative viable kinds of inquiry, there is no reason to assume that quantitative and formal methods of analysis are solely relevant to Positive Explanation. To the contrary, the other projects of inquiry identified in table 10.1 – even Interpretative Understanding – might benefit from quantitative analysis. Mohr (1992), for example, has used quantitative content analysis to identify gender-specific public meanings about welfare in late nineteenth-century New York. His analysis does not purport to explain the causes of differences in welfare discourse about men versus women. But it offers an intriguing look at the cultural constructions through which social welfare actions are oriented.

4 The long march under the modernist ethos of science was toward the rationalization (in Weber's sense) of research practices – measurement, experimental design, and so forth. Yet in the lifeworld, rationalization is always an incomplete process (cf. G. Roth 1987). More specifically, in inquiry, the sources of incomplete rationalization are inherent in the concatenation of heterologous discourses – theory, narrative, and so forth – within any single practice (Hall 1992).

5 It is a far cry from Outhwaite's (1987) ambitious but inconclusive effort to bring realism and hermeneutics into a common orbit. Nor does it come to terms with Bhaskar's (1989) attempt to offer a realist account of the relation between structure and agency. Bhaskar seems to have shifted positions on the problem of meaning objectivity, early on asserting the independence of meaning from the intention of an actor (1979: 108), later addressing the role of individuals in remaking meanings (1989: 76–7). In any event, Bhaskar's realism remains underdeveloped in grappling with the problem of meansurement, both in general and with respect to the problem of meaning. It is in confronting these very issues that Pawson beats a strategic retreat from cultural realism, because of what he regards as intractable difficulties embodied in the "double hermeneutic."

6 The language of deconstruction captures the interpretative stakes of controversies about measurement construction quite nicely: "Deconstruction demonstrates that, in any (our own) historical setting, it is always possible to construe any established schemata for analyzing and interpreting familiar phenomena as more restrictive, more distorting, more inadequate than another that can be generated, now, by submitting the one or ones in question to the process of supplementation" (Margolis 1985: 150, brackets in original).

7 Phenomenological and historicist critiques suggest both the social and constructed character of phenomena that are measured and the inadequacy of quantitative variables to the task of capturing salient features of meaningful social processes (Blumer 1956; Cicourel 1964; Hall 1984). Recent discussions elaborate these points. For example, Block and Burns (1986) point out that the production of buggy whips may serve as a reasonably meaningful leading economic indicator at one historical juncture, but not always. By extension, any depiction of, say, occupations depends upon a conventionalization that takes place under socially and historically shifting social circumstances of domination, rationalization, and so forth. What it means to be a barber, blacksmith, or secretary not only varies situationally, but also changes over time. Moreover, as Margaret Somers (1992)

has shown, seemingly straightforward concepts such as citizenship are (for example, western European) cultural inventions that may bear ideological baggage invisible to us because of our historical and social location.

In addition, there is the dual role that social statistics play – in the rationalization of social spheres, and in turn, in socio-historical inquiry about those constructed phenomena. Tests of psychological intelligence are notoriously culture bound, and consequential for social placement. The same holds for a seemingly more objective concept: as any demography student knows, the "population" of a given political territory is not simply the number of people in it at a particular moment; rather, that number must be "adjusted" to reflect what demographers and more importantly, politicians, think are the salient issues: sometimes slaves get counted some ways; sometimes Asians don't get counted at all. In Alain Desrosières's (1992a) evocative phrase, statistics help to "make things which hold together"; statistical monitoring and simulation are historically evolving practices integral to how and how well organizations work; the data are not "about" organizations, they are *part of* organizations (Desrosières 1992b). Statisticians face a quandary: to deny the salience of culturally established classifications and their uses (Desrosières discusses the example of occupations) by establishing independent measures is to ignore the socially constructed historical realities.

8 Ideal types are "ideal" in that they identify coherent meaning complexes independently of empirical complexities. Unlike formal concepts that posit deterministic mechanisms and processes, ideal types acknowledge the "shading off" of meaning (Spinoza's dog's bark, versus the ideal–typical "bark," versus the "growl" or the "howl") (cf. Blumer 1956: 688; Hall and Neitz 1993: 12–14). Ideal types thus are analytically precise, yet lend themselves to the situated analysis of socially constructed meanings in a way that transcends Pawson's realist program of measurement by including the culturally constructed meanings that interest Bhaskar (1989), but for which he has no strategy of measurement (for discussion of formal measurement of meaning in relation to ideal types, see Hall 1984). As useful as ideal types are for examining meaningful connections among socio-historical phenomena, however, if their use is to avoid the circularity of concept-dependent measurement, assessment of their Value-Neutral Explanations must depend on theory-independent measurement of the kind that Pawson describes (for an example of an explanation based on ideal types that uses such an independent criterion [organizational survival over time], see Hall 1988).

9 Thus, the relatively robust findings of Brustein (1991) and Griffin (1993).

10 Moreover, the research program as a popular warrant for socio-historical inquiry (Kiser and Hechter 1991) needs to be freed up from its supposed attachments to realist ontologies. A research program need not follow the realist formula of positing some underlying process or mechanism. A resilient pattern of explanation could just as easily be developed through the analysis of situation-specific social processes within alternative meaningful "cultural structures" (for example, Hall 1988) or by employing the practice of "configurational history" (Hall 1992) to investigate the idiosyncratic interaction of heterogeneous social events.

11 For a more detailed discussion of this topic, see Hall (forthcoming: ch. 8).

12 In this turn toward theoretical reason, constructionism finds common cause with Pawson's (1989) extension of realism. More precisely, if measurement – even in relation to putatively real mechanisms and processes is understood as constructed, and if research programs are severed from any necessary connection to the realist search for generative processes and mechanisms, Pawson's approach amounts to advocacy of deductive formal theorizing under the constructionist conditions of inquiry described here.

Part IV

The Reconstruction of Social Theory

The previous sections have been focused on the ways in which the classics are still meaningful for us and continue to be relevant to the project of social theory and sociology broadly construed. But what if one tries to wipe the slate clean and begin the whole thing over again? Is there a real alternative to the legacy, however patched up and extended, of the classics? Obviously the extent to which an alternative is genuinely radical or merely a different kind of patching up is merely a matter of degree. The "social thinkers" from Hammurabi to the present said a great deal indeed. One can never wipe the slate entirely clean, however much one might try. Indeed, the classics themselves did not do so. Contemporaries of the classics whose familiarity with the sources and context of the thought of the classics was far greater than our own wondered whether the innovations of the classics that we now celebrate were in fact anything more than verbal tricks or refinements of existing ideas, neatly packaged for a new and naive audience.

Nevertheless, there have been significant challenges to standard "classical" modes of theorizing in recent sociology. Fundamental theoretical developments in social theory have very often, and perhaps always, been discussions and revisions of fundamental ideas about human agency, that is about the nature of intentional action. Weber, for example, was trained as a lawyer and recognized that the categories of intentional action enshrined in the law were a kind of alternative framework within which actions could be categorized and this led him to recognize the ultimately arbitrary character of all frameworks for the explanation of action. His own sociological classification of action was thus presented not as the essential truth about, or the correct description of, human action but rather as a framework which could be assessed only in light of its utility in helping disciplines in the historical sciences in accounting for human action and making it intelligible. Durkheim attempted to revise the conception of the human agent by identifying an element of consciousness that was "collective" and operated in accordance with its own causal laws, and which produced (in a way that was not accessible to introspection) impulses that individuals struggled with in the course of making decisions. In particular, he argued that the sense of obligation that people feel and that guides action is the causal product of the collective realm, though it may not be and usually is not recognized as such by the agent. Parsons, of course, sought to construct a systematic account of logical structure of theoretical explanations of action. In part, this enterprise was directed at the model of action contained in classical economics which he considered to be insufficient because of its neglect of the "normative" element of action, an idea that is familiar from Durkheim's own revision of the notion of action.

The three approaches discussed in this part take quite different tacks. The thought of Pierre Bourdieu is perhaps the most important and influential challenge to conventional sociology. Bourdieu is more radically reflexive about the character of his project than Parsons and Merton were. He does not rely on an independent account of the nature of science which he strives to fulfill, but rather characterizes his own project in the same terms of struggle that he uses to characterize the intellectual projects of others. Bourdieu's approach identifies a set of purpose-like goals, especially the accumulation of "cultural capital," which can be attributed to agents and account for the activities which constitute the forms of consciousness and practices within which they act as intentional agents and which their actions as intentional agents presume. Bourdieu attempts to account for practices themselves in this way. In Woolgar's paper the model is actor-network theory. But the "actors" in this theory are not restricted to ordinary human agents involved in fully intentional action, making decisions, and so forth. The networks of "actors" include, in this case, machines, who function in the creation of human arrangements, such as the economic order, as well as in the constitution of the conditions of life as junior participants in or partners in networks who can be employed in struggles against other networks. In this case the concept of the intentional agent is extended and applied in such a way as to radically alter its character. Abell's paper discusses rational choice theory and the program of rational choice in sociology. In this case the model of intentional action is also changed, but it is changed by rendering it more parsimonious. The point of the strategy is to see how much can be accounted for, and particularly how much of the domain of facts traditionally accounted for in terms of other theories, such as Durkheim's, can be accounted for in terms of individual rational choice and its complex collective implications and expressions.

The idea which motivated Parsons in the middle of this century and various figures in the earlier history of sociology was that a single uniquely valid revision of the mundane model of intentional explanation and human agency was possible. If this were the case, we could contrast the "folk" and the "scientific" understandings of human action. The theoretical programs discussed in this section do not explicitly renounce these ambitions, though the reflexive character of the first two programs seems to limit the nature of their claims to unique intellectual authority. The rules governing intellectual ascendancy are, in these theories, part of the topic of the theory, and the way in which intellectual ascendancy is characterized in these theories does not lend itself to the kind of model of science as the uniquely valid description of reality.

Rational choice theory has an even more ambiguous methodological status. Key notions like "explanation" are employed in unusual ways. So the idea that rational choice theory explains anything at all must be accepted before the explanations themselves are. In a sense, this holds generally: the key methodological standards which are held to justify the claims of the theories are so closely bound up with the theory itself that selecting a viewpoint amounts to selecting the whole package of methodology, modes of description, and facts accepted as given and uncontroversial.

Alan Sica's concluding chapter evokes the atmosphere of delusion of grandeur that accompanied the last great attempt to provide a comprehensive theoretical understanding of the social world with a portrait of Parsons as a young man, riding on the waves of his own breathlessly announced "discoveries" and "solutions" to "theoretical problems." Parsons was certainly not the last social theorist to fall in love with his own creation, nor the last to radically mistake the significance of what he was doing. But the reminder of the great hopes with which his project advanced is salutary: social theory is a graveyard of simple insights and grand programs.

11

Toward a Reflexive Sociology: A Workshop with Pierre Bourdieu

Loïc J. D. Wacquant

Interest, Habitus, and Rationality

LOÏC J. D. WACQUANT: Your use of the notion of interest has often called forth the charge of "economism" (for example, Caillé 1987; Joppke 1986). What theoretical role does interest play in your mode of analysis?

PIERRE BOURDIEU: Building upon Weber, who utilized the economic model to develop a materialist sociology of religion and to uncover the specific interests of the great protagonists of the religious game, priests, prophets, and sorcerers (Bourdieu 1987b), I introduced the notion of interest − I prefer to use the term *illusio* since I always speak of specific interest, of interests that are both presupposed and produced by the functioning of historically delimited fields − in my analysis of cultural producers in reaction to the dominant vision of the intellectual universe, to call into question the ideology of the *freischwebende Intelligenz*. The notion of interest as I use it, which, paradoxically, as you indicate, has brought forth the accusation of economism against a work which, from the very outset (I could refer here to my first ethnographic pieces on the sense of honor among the Kabyles [Bourdieu 1965 and 1979]) was conceived in opposition to economism, is the means of a deliberate and provisional reductionism which allows me to bring the materialist mode of questioning into the cultural sphere from where it was expelled, historically, when the modern notion of art was invented and the field of cultural production won its autonomy (Bourdieu 1980d; 1987a).

This is to say that the concept of interest as I construe it has nothing in common with the naturalistic, transhistorical, and universal interest of utilitarian theory. (It would be otiose to show that Adam Smith's self-interest is nothing more than an unconscious universalization of the form of interest required and engendered by a capitalist economy.) Far from being an anthropological invariant, interest is a *historical arbitrary*, a historical construction that can be known only through historical analysis, *ex post*, through empirical observation, and not deduced *a priori* from some fictitious – and so naively Eurocentric – conception of "Man."

LW: This would imply that there are as many "interests" as there are fields, that each field simultaneously presupposes and generates a specific form of interest that is incommensurable with those that have currency elsewhere.

PB: Absolutely. There are as many practical understandings of the game, and thus interests, as there are games. Each field calls forth and gives life to a specific form of interest, a specific *illusio* as tacit recognition of the value of the stakes of the game and as practical mastery of its rules. Furthermore, this specific interest implied by one's participation in the game specifies itself according to the position occupied in the game (dominant vs. dominated, or orthodox vs. heretic) and with the trajectory that leads each participant to this position. Anthropology and comparative history show that the properly social magic of institutions can constitute almost anything as an interest, and as a realistic interest, that is, as an investment (in the double meaning the word has in economics and in psychoanalysis) that is objectively paid back by an "economy."

LW: Beyond interest and investment, you have "imported" from economic language a number of other concepts, such as market and capital (for example, Bourdieu 1985; 1986), all of which evoke the economic mode of reasoning. What sets your theoretical approach apart from the "economic approach" to social action?

PB: The only thing I share with neo-marginalist economists are the words. Take the notion of investment. By investment I mean the propensity to act which is born out of the relation between a field and a system of dispositions adjusted to the game it proposes, a sense of the game and of its stakes which implies both an inclination and an ability to play the game. The general theory of the economy of fields which emerges progressively from generalization to generalization enables us to describe and to specify the *specific form* taken by the most general mechanisms and concepts such as capital, investment, interest, within each field, and thus to avoid all kinds of reductionisms, beginning with economism, which recognizes nothing but material interest and the search for the maximization of monetary profit.

Thus my theory owes nothing, despite appearances, to the transfer of the economic approach. And, as I hope to demonstrate fully one day, far from being the founding model, economic theory (and Rational Action Theory which is its sociological derivative) is probably best seen as a particular instance, historically dated and situated, of field theory.

LW: Would the notion of habitus be the conceptual linchpin by which you rearticulate these apparently economic notions into a model of action that is radically different from that of economics?

PB: In double opposition to the objectivism of action "without an agent" of the Althusserians and to the subjectivism which portrays action as the deliberate pursuit of a conscious intention, the free project of a conscience positing its own ends and maximizing its utility through rational computation, I have put forth a theory of practice as the product of a *practical sense* (Bourdieu 1980a), of a socially constituted "sense of the game." Against positivistic materialism, the theory of practice as practice posits that objects of knowledge are *constructed*, and not passively recorded. And against intellectualist idealism, it reminds us that the principle of this construction is habitus, the system of structured and structuring dispositions which is constituted by practice and constantly aimed at practical – as opposed to cognitive – functions. In order to sidestep objectivism without relapsing into subjectivism and its demonstrated incapacity to account for the necessity immanent in the social world, it is necessary to return to practice as the locus of the dialectic between *opus operatum* and *modus operandi*, between the objectified and the embodied products of historical action, structures and habitus.

I could show that the concept of habitus, like that of field, is relational in that it designates a mediation between objective structures and practices. First and foremost, habitus has the function of overcoming the alternative between consciousness and the unconscious and between finalism and mechanicalism. Following the program suggested by Marx in the *Theses on Feuerbach*, it aims at making possible a materialist theory of knowledge which does not abandon to idealism the idea that all knowledge, be it mundane or scholarly, presupposes a work of construction, but a work which has nothing in common with intellectual work, a practical activity which sets into motion the practical inventiveness of habitus. (All those who used this old concept or similar ones before me – from Hegel's *ethos* to Husserl's *Habitualität* to Mauss's *hexis* – were inspired by a theoretical intention akin to mine, which was to escape from under the philosophy of the subject without doing away with the agent.)

In order to capture the gist of social action, we must recognize the *ontological complicity*, as Heidegger and Merleau-Ponty suggested, between the agent (who is neither a subject or a consciousness, nor the mere executant of a role or the "carrier" of a function) and the social world (which is never a

mere "thing" even if it must be constructed as such in the objectivist phase
of research). Social reality exists, so to speak, twice, in things and in minds,
in fields and in habitus, outside and inside of agents. And when habitus
encounters a social world of which it is the product, it finds itself "as fish in
water," it does not feel the weight of the water and takes the world about
itself for granted.

LW: All of this puts you in a frontal opposition to this wide, if heterogeneous,
current that has recently been gaining strength across the social sciences
under the label of Rational Action Theory or Rational Choice Theory.

PB: Without the shadow of a doubt. Forgetting all the abstractions it has
to effect in order to produce its theoretical artifact, Rational Action Theory
(RAT) typically substitutes the scientist for the practical habitus. It slips
from the model to the reality and does as if the action that its model accounts
for had this model as its principle. The social actor of RAT is nothing but
the imaginary projection of the *sujet savant* (knowing, scholarly subject) into
the *sujet agissant* (acting subject).[1]

Note also that this "imaginary anthropology" has nothing to tell us about
the social genesis of historically varying forms of interests since it postulates
ex nihilo the existence of a universal, preconstituted interest. Just as it ignores
the individual and collective *history* of agents through which structures are
formed and reproduced and which "live" in them. In reality, far from being
posited as such in an explicit, conscious project, the strategies suggested by
habitus as a "feel for the game" aim, on the mode of "protension" so well
characterized by Husserl in *Ideen*, toward the "objective potentialities" immediately given in the immediate present. Must we talk of "strategy," then?
The word is strongly associated with the intellectualist and subjectivist tradition which, from Descartes to Sartre, has dominated Western philosophy
and which is now again on the upswing with RAT, a theory well-suited to
satisfy the spiritualist *point d'honneur* of intellectuals. This is not a reason
not to use it, however, with a different theoretical intention, to designate
the objectively orientated lines of action which social agents continually
construct.

Moreover, the theory of habitus explains why the finalism of Rational
Choice Theory, although anthropologically false, may appear as empirically
sound. Individualist finalism, which conceives action as determined by
the conscious aiming at explicitly posed goals, is a well-founded illusion: the
sense of the game which implies an anticipated adjustment of habitus to the
necessities and to the probabilities inscribed in the field does present itself
under the appearance of a successful "aiming at" a future. Likewise, the structural affinity of habituses belonging to the same class is capable of generating

practices that are convergent and objectively orchestrated outside of any collective "conspiracy" or consciousness. In this fashion it explains many of those phenomena of quasi-teleology which can be observed in the social world, such as those forms of collective action or reaction which pose such insuperable dilemmas to RAT.

But the efforts of the proponents of some or other version of Rational Action Theory remind me of Tycho Brahe trying to salvage the Ptolemaic paradigm after Copernicus: it is the anthropological postulates of RAT concerning the nature of social action that are, in my view, irretrievably flawed. Both the kind of finalism represented by RAT, which wants to see nothing but choice (if under constraints: limited rationality, irrational rationality, "weakness of the will," and so on, the variations are endless – here again, anyone who recalls Sartre's analysis of bad faith or of oaths will quickly recognize the intellectual contortions of an Elster [1984] in *Ulysses and the Sirens* as the mediocre remake of a well-known show), and the mechanistic determinism taken to its extreme by structural Marxists equally mutilate the intrinsically double reality of human existence as a thing of the world for which there are things, a fundamental anthropological reality that Pascal captured brilliantly when he said: "*Le monde me comprend et m'anéantit comme un point mais je le comprends*" (in short, the world encompasses me but I understand it).

The proper object of social science, then, is neither individuals, this *ens realissimum* naively crowned as the paramount, rock-bottom reality by all "methodological individualists," nor groups as sets of concrete individuals sharing a similar location in social space, but the *relation between two realizations of historical action*, in bodies (or biological individuals) and in things. It is the double and obscure relation between habitus, that is, the durable and transposable system of schemata of perception, appreciation, and action that result from the institution of the social in the body, and fields, that is, systems of objective relations which are the product of the institution of the social in things, or in mechanisms that have the quasi-reality of physical objects; and, of course, of everything that is born out of this relation, that is, social practices and representations, or fields as they present themselves in the form of realities perceived and appreciated.

LW: What is the nature of this relationship of "ontological complicity" between habitus and field and how does it work itself out more precisely?

PB: The relation between habitus and field operates in two ways. On one side, it is a relation of *conditioning*: the field structures the habitus, which is the product of the embodiment of the immanent necessity of a field (or of a hierarchically intersecting set of fields). On the other side, it is a relation of knowledge or *cognitive construction*: habitus contributes to constituting the field as a meaningful world, a world endowed with sense and with value, in which it is worth investing one's energy. Two things follow: firstly, the relation of knowledge depends on the relation of conditioning that precedes it and fashions the structures of habitus; secondly, social science is necessarily a "knowledge of a knowledge" and must make room for a sociologically grounded phenomenology of the primary experience of the field or, to be more precise, of the invariants and variations of the relation between different types of fields and different types of habitus.

In short, the specificity of social science lies in the fact that its object of knowledge is a reality which includes agents who have this very reality as an object of knowledge. The task becomes, then, to construct a theory of prac- tice *as practice* and a theory of the practical mode of knowledge that is implied in it. Thus, if it is indispensable to break with the spontaneous knowledge of the social world, it is no less necessary to include in our theory the practical knowledge against which scientific knowledge is constructed and which continues to orient practices. The relation of practical knowledge is not that between a subject and an object constituted as such and perceived as a problem. Habitus being the social incorporated, it is "at home" in the field it inhabits, it perceives it immediately as endowed with meaning and interest. Practical action may be described by analogy with the *orthé doxa* of Plato in *Meno*, as the "right opinion": the coincidence between dispositions and position, between the "sense of the game" and the game, explains that the agent does "what he or she has to do" without posing it explicitly as a goal, below the level of calculation and even consciousness, beneath discourse and representation.

The theory of habitus, again, allows us to overcome a whole series of antinomies into which the theory of action routinely locks itself, those of consciousness and the "thingness" of social facts, of mechanicalism and finalism, of subjective teleology (as in all so-called theories of "rational choice") and objective teleology (which personalizes collectives, "the State," the "Bour- geoisie," and so on, and endows them with intentions and projects).

LW: Does the theory of habitus rule out strategic choice and conscious delib- eration as one modality of action?

PB: Not at all. The immediate fit between habitus and field is only one modality of action, if the most prevalent one ("We are empirical," said Leibniz, by which he meant practical, "in three quarters of our action"). The lines of action suggested by habitus may very well be accompanied by a strategic calculation of costs and benefits which tends to carry out at a conscious level the operations which habitus carries out in its own way. Rational choice may even become a *métier*, a profession, as in the trade of the historian, the economist, or the scientist. Times of crises, in which the routine adjustment of subjective and objective structures is brutally disrupted, constitute a class of circumstances when indeed "rational choice" often appears to take over. But, and this is a crucial proviso, it is habitus itself that commands this option. We can always say that individuals make choices, as long as we do not forget that they do not choose the principle of these choices.

The Refusal of "Theoretical Theory"

LW: Since we are talking "theory," let me bring up a puzzle. You are frequently billed, and certainly read, as a "social theorist" (and, as you well know, this is a very definite type in the gallery of possible sociological personas in the United States). Yet I keep being struck by how seldom, in your work, you make purely "theoretical" statements or remarks. Instead, you keep referring to particular research problems and mundane dilemmas you encountered while gathering, coding, or analyzing data, or thinking through a substantive issue. Even in your research seminar at the Ecole des Hautes Etudes en Sciences Sociales in Paris (Bourdieu and Wacquant, 1992, Pt 3), you warn your audience upfront that they shall not get from this course "neat presentations on habitus and field." You are also extremely reluctant to discuss the concepts that you have coined and use in your work in isolation from their empirical supports. Could you explicate the place that theory occupies in your work?

PB: Let me say outright and very forcefully that I never "theorize," if by that we mean engage in the kind of conceptual gobbledygook (*laïus*) that is good for textbooks and which, through an extraordinary misconstrual of the logic of science, passes for theory in much of Anglo-American social science. I never set out to "do theory" or to "construct a theory" *per se*, as the American expression goes. And it is a complete misapprehension of my project to believe that I am attempting some kind of "synthesis of classical theory" *à la* Parsons. There is no doubt a theory in my work, or, better, a set of *thinking tools* visible through the results they yield, but it is not built as such.

The ground for these tools – the notion of cultural capital,[2] for instance, that I invented in the early 1960s to account for the fact that, after controlling for class origins, students from more cultured families have not only higher rates of academic success but exhibit different modes and patterns of cultural consumption and expression in a wide gamut of domains – lies in research, in the practical problems and puzzles encountered and generated in the effort to construct a phenomenally diverse set of objects in such a way that they can be treated, thought of, comparatively or, more precisely, analogically. The thread which leads from one of my works to the next is the *logic of research*, which is in my eyes *inseparably* empirical and theoretical. I readily confess that I feel very little in common with the kind of rhetorical exercises in "theoretical theory" that are so common on your side of the Atlantic.

LW: What is the difference between "theoretical theory" and scientific theory as you conceive it?

PB: For me, theory is not a sort of prophetic or programmatic discourse which originates by dissection or by amalgamation of other theories for the sole purpose of confronting other such pure "theoretical theories." (I need not give examples of these endless and unassailable "conceptual melting pots" of neologisms, refurbished categories, and pseudo-theorems, generally closed by a call for future research or empirical application, preferably by others – Glaser and Strauss [1967] speak somewhere of "theoretical capitalists," perhaps rentiers would be a better image – whose paradigm remains, a decade after his death, Parsons' AGIL scheme that some today are trying to resurrect.) Rather, scientific theory as I conceive it emerges as a program of perception and of action – a scientific habitus, if you wish – which is disclosed only in the empirical work which actualizes it. It is a *temporary construct which takes shape for and by empirical work*.[3] Consequently, it has more to gain by confronting new objects than by engaging in theoretical polemics that do little more than fuel a perpetual, self-sustaining, and too often vacuous meta-discourse around concepts treated as intellectual totems. There is nothing more sterile than epistemology or theory when it becomes a topic for society conversation and a substitute for research.

To treat theory as a *modus operandi* which practically guides and structures scientific practice obviously implies giving up the somewhat fetishistic accommodativeness that "theoreticians" usually establish with it. It is for this reason that I never felt the urge to retrace the genealogy of the concepts I have coined or reactivated, like those habitus, field, or symbolic capital. Not having been born of theoretical parthogenesis, these concepts do not gain much by being resituated *vis-à-vis* previous usages. Their construction and use emerged in the practicalities of the research enterprise and it is in this context that they must be evaluated. The function of the concepts I employ is first and foremost to designate, in stenographic manner, within the research procedure, a theoretical stance, a principle of methodological choice, negative as well as positive. Systematization necessarily comes *ex post*, as fruitful analogies emerge little by little, as the useful properties of the concept are successfully tried and tested.[4]

Unfortunately, the socially dominant model sociology today is still predicated on a clear-cut distinction, and a practical divorce, between research (I think here in particular of this "science without a scientist" epitomized by public opinion research and of this scientific monster called "methodology") and the "theory without object" of pure theoreticians, presently exemplified by the trendy discussion raging around the so-called "micro-macro link" (for example, Alexander et al. 1987). This opposition between the pure theory of the *lector* devoted to the hermeneutic cult of the scriptures of the founding fathers (if not of his own writings), on the one hand, and survey research and methodology on the other is an entirely *social* opposition. It is inscribed in the institutional and mental structures of the sociological profession, rooted in the academic distribution of resources, positions, and competencies, as when whole schools (for example, conversation analysis or status attainment research) are based almost entirely on one particular method, and reinforced by the political demand for instruments of rationalization of social domination – and it must be rejected. I could paraphrase Kant and say that research without theory is blind and theory without research is empty.

The trick, if I may call it that, is to manage to combine immense theoretical ambition with extreme empirical modesty. The summum of the art, in social science, is, in my eyes, to be capable of engaging very high "theoretical" stakes by means of very precise and often very mundane empirical objects. We tend too easily to assume that the social or political importance of an object suffices in itself to grant importance to the discourse that deals with it. What counts, in reality, is the rigor of the *construction* of the object. I think that the power of a mode of thinking never manifests itself more clearly than in its capacity to constitute socially insignificant objects into scientific objects (as Goffman did of the minutiae of interaction rituals) or, what amounts to the same thing, to approach a major socially significant object in an unexpected manner – something I am presently attempting by studying the effects of the monopoly of the state over the means of legitimate symbolic violence by way of a down-to-earth analysis of what a certificate (of illness, invalidity, schooling, and so on) is and does. For this, one must learn how to translate very abstract problems into very concrete scientific operations.

Progress and Prospects for Sociology

LW: In a paper published in 1968 in *Social Research* (Bourdieu and Passeron 1968: 212), you expressed the hope that, "just as American sociology was able, for a time, by its empirical rigor, to act as the scientific bad conscience of French sociology," French sociology might, 'by its theoretical stringency, become the philosophical bad conscience of American sociology." Twenty years later, where does this wish stand?

PB: I think that it is the very distinction between theory and research implied by this statement that must be challenged. If French sociology is to become the scientific bad conscience of American sociology, then it must succeed in overcoming this separation by putting forth a new form of scientific practice founded at once upon a greater theoretical exigency and upon greater empirical rigor. The program of work that I recently completed on French elite schools in the field of power attempts, in its own partial way, to contribute to the maturing of such a form of research. In the book entitled *The State Nobility* (Bourdieu 1989) which grew out of it, I try to bring together the results of nearly twenty years of in-depth investigations, not of one but of some twenty Grandes Ecoles and of some two hundred corporations and their CEOs, based on surveys, direct observation, interviews of students, archival documents, and so on; a reflection on methods, including the problem of theoretical sampling; a phenomenology of the experience of being selected in or out of the elite; and a structural theory of modes of reproduction. Of course, I have no illusions that this work reaches all the lofty goals I just set but I believe that it does represent a genuine attempt at marrying theoretical and empirical rigor.

LW: In what sense can we speak of progress then? Can we say that sociology has moved forward, or are we still battling with the same evils of Grand Theory and Abstracted Empiricism as C. Wright Mills (1959) expressed it in the late 1950s?

PB: Instead of progress, I would rather speak of obstacles to progress, and of means of overturning these obstacles. There is undoubtedly progress, and sociology is a considerably more advanced science than observers, even its practitioners, are willing to grant. The reasons for this distrust of the scientific status of sociology are more social than epistemological: a truly scientific sociology, that is, a science of society that rejects the social demand for legitimation or manipulation, is a practice that is highly improbable sociologically speaking – and perhaps more so in the United States than in many other countries. Sociology is an especially difficult science because it uncovers things that are hidden and sometimes even repressed, and because its objects are the stakes of struggles in social reality itself.[5] Sociology denaturalizes, and thereby de-fatalizes the world, and the knowledge it produces is liable to exert a political efficacy every time it reveals the laws of functioning of mechanisms that owe part of their own efficacy to being misrecognized, that is, every time it reaches into the foundations of symbolic violence.

I have repeated often that one of the necessary conditions for progress is the autonomy of the scientific field. But this does not mean that each national sociology must remain aloof on the contrary. We need to engage in a collective reflection on the *institutional conditions of rational communication* in the social sciences. (It is an opportunity for such a reflection that I sought to promote in accepting to organize, along with James Coleman, the conference on "Social theory and emerging issues in a changing society" held at the University of Chicago in April of 1989, Bourdieu and Coleman 1993). What social scientists on both sides of the Atlantic must do is work to build and strengthen institutional mechanisms against isolationism, against all forms of scientific intolerance, mechanisms capable of promoting fair communication and a more open confrontation of ideas, theories, and paradigms. More than the positive and negative developments which have taken place in each national sociology in the last twenty years, what matters is the establishment of relations between American and Continental social scientists that make possible a greater unification of the field of world sociology and, most importantly, a *unification respectful of diversity*.

If there exist, *pace* Habermas, no transhistorical universals of communication, there certainly exist forms of social organization of communication that are liable to foster the production of the universal. We cannot rely on moral exhortation to abolish "systematically distorted" communication from sociology. Only a true *Realpolitik* of scientific reason can contribute to transforming structures of communication by helping to change both the modes of functioning of those universes where science is produced and the dispositions of the agents who compete in these universes, and thus the institution that contributes most to fashion them, the university.

LW: Isn't one of the conditions of scientific progress, then, to be capable of liberating oneself from the constraints of traditions of thought (and especially national traditions), which in turn presupposes a kind of "antinomic attitude" toward one's discipline: on the one hand you need concepts and theories to construct objects, thus you need to absorb and trust its heritage. But, on the other hand, these intellectual tools themselves are already (pre)constructions that carry over the accepted wisdom of our predecessors and create blinders that may hide as much as they reveal.

PB: Indeed, the sociologist is inescapably and endlessly faced with a sort of *double bind*, strapped in a Catch-22 situation of this sort. Without the intellectual instruments he owes his scholarly tradition, he or she is nothing more than an amateur, a self-taught, spontaneous sociologist – and certainly not the best equipped of all lay sociologists, given the generally limited span of the social experiences of academics. But, at the same time, there is the ever present danger that he will simply substitute to the naive *doxa* of lay common sense the no less naive *doxa* of scientific common sense which parrots, in the technical jargon and under the official trappings of scientific discourse, the discourse of common sense, which retranslates it in this terrible, half-concrete, half-abstract lingo that his training and the censorship of the sociological establishment impose on him.

It is not easy to escape the horns of this dilemma, this alternative between the disarmed ignorance of the autodidact devoid of instruments of rigorous scientific construction and this *half-science* which unknowingly accepts categories of perception directly borrowed from the social world. It is the task of research pedagogy to make students acutely aware of this double bind and to train them to resist its negative effects. (In this respect, I rest convinced that one of the chief obstacles to progress in the social sciences today lies in the ordinary teaching of sociology, and graduate students are no doubt its chief victim.) And it is the role of the reflexive return, of the social history of scientific practices, in a word, the objectivation of tools of objectivation, to remind us of it.

This being said, the social dispositions one brings into academia evidently play a crucial role here. Those best armed to avoid this dilemma are people who bring together an advanced mastery of scientific culture with a certain revolt against, or distance from, this culture (often rooted in an estranged experience of the academic universe which pushes one not to "buy it" at face value), or, quite simply, a *political* sense which intuitively leads one to reject or to resist the asepticized and derealized vision of the social world offered by the socially dominant discourse in sociology.[6] Needless to say, the more you consciously command the principles that lead you to challenge the accepted preconceptions of an intellectual tradition, the greater your chances of fully mastering your own thought and scientific products – in sum, to be the "subject" of the problems that can be posed about the social world.

LW: Since you evoked the process of becoming a sociologist, perhaps I could bring this dialogue to a close by asking you a more practical question: what advice would you give to young, aspiring sociologists, say, graduate students who are learning their trade and wish to escape this sterile opposition between "empty theory" and "blind research"?

PB: First and foremost: have fun! The craft of the sociologist is one of the most pleasant and enriching activities one can indulge in, spanning the whole gamut of intellectual practices and skills, from those of the novelist laboring to create emotions and character to those of the mathematician striving to capture the world in abstract models and equations. We must repel any unilateral, undimensional, and monomaniacal definition of sociological practice, as well as resist all attempts to impose one.

Consequently, and this would be my second point, apprentice sociologists need to question and constantly challenge methodological prescriptions and interdicts. Social research is something much too serious and much too difficult that we can allow ourselves to mistake scientific *rigidity*, which is the nemesis of intelligence and invention, for scientific *rigor*, and thus to deprive ourselves of this or that resource available in the full panoply of traditions of our discipline – and of the sister disciplines of anthropology, economics, history, and so on. In such matters, I would dare say that one rule only applies: "it is forbidden to forbid." So watch out for methodological watchdogs! Of course, the extreme liberty I advocate here (and which, let me hasten to add, has nothing in common with the kind of relativistic epistemological *laissez-faire* which seems to be much in vogue in some quarters) has its counterpart in the extreme vigilance that we must accord to the conditions of use of analytical techniques and to ensuring their fit with the question at hand. Instead of arbitrarily imposing this or that technology of measurement or analysis as the penultimate badge of scientificity, we must, whenever possible, mobilize and put to work all of the techniques which are relevant and practically usable given the definition of the problem under investigation. As the most rudimentary sociology of sociology reveals, methodological indictments are often no more than a disguised way of making a virtue out of necessity, of feigning to dismiss, to ignore in an active way what one is ignorant of in fact.

Thirdly, get your hands dirty in the kitchen sink: do not settle for the cozy and derealized experience of the social world fostered by those bureaucratic machineries of survey research that create a huge buffer between the social analyst and the universe he or she claims to dissect. Direct contact with the object not only has the virtue of helping preserve you from the fetishization of concepts and theories; it will also make you more attentive to the details of research procedures, to the built-in assumptions and consequences of apparently innocuous technical choices that are generally made unthinkingly. Most of all, you must adopt an active and systematic posture *vis-à-vis* "facts." To break with empiricist passivity, which rests content with ratifying the preconstructions of common sense, without relapsing into the vacuous discourse of grand "theorizing," you must tackle a very concrete empirical case with the goal of *building a model* (which need not be mathematical to be rigorous), by linking the relevant data in such a manner that they function as a self-propelling program of research capable of generating systematic questions liable to be given systematic answers, in short, to yield a coherent system of relations which can be tested as such. To be intelligent in the scientific sense is to put oneself in a situation that automatically generates true problems and true, productive, difficulties.

Fourthly, beware of words. Language poses a particularly acute problem for the sociologist because it carries along a "spontaneous" social philosophy which constitutes one of the most formidable "epistemological obstacles" to a rigorous science of society, to speak like Bachelard (1938). Common language is the repository of the accumulated common sense of past generations, both lay and scientific, as crystallized in occupational taxonomies, names of groups, concepts (think of all the ideological baggage borne by the apparently innocuous couple of "achievement" and "ascription," or consensus and conflict, or even individual and society), and so on. The most routine categories that sociologists borrow from it (for example, young and old; "middle class" and "upper-middle class") are naturalized preconstructions which, when they are ignored as such, function as unconscious and uncontrolled instruments of scholarly construction. One of the most powerful instruments of rupture with the *doxa* embedded in words lies in the social history of problems, concepts, and objects of inquiry. By retracing the collective work that was necessary to constitute such and such issue (the feminization of the work force, the growth of the welfare state, teenage pregnancy, or religious fundamentalism) into a visible, scientifically legitimate problem, the researcher can shelter him or herself from the social imposition of problematics. For a sociologist more than any other thinker, to leave one's own thought in a state of unthought (*impensé*) is to condemn oneself to be nothing more than the instrument of what one claims to think.

This is why, in my view, the history of sociology, understood as an exploration of the scientific unconscious of the sociologist through the explication of the genesis of problems, categories of thought, and instruments of analysis, constitutes an absolute prerequisite for scientific practice. And the same is true of the sociology of sociology: I believe that if the sociology I propose differs in any significant way from the other sociologies of the past and of the present, it is above all in that it *continually turns back onto itself the scientific weapons it produces*. It is fundamentally reflexive in that it uses the knowledge it gains of the social determinations that may bear upon it, and particularly the scientific analysis of all the constraints and all the limitations associated with the fact of occupying a definite position in a definite field at a particular moment and with a certain trajectory, in an attempt to master and neutralize their effects.

Far from undermining the foundations of social science, the sociology of the social determinants of sociological practice is the only possible ground for a possible freedom from these determinations. And it is only on condition that he avails himself the full usage of this freedom by continually subjecting himself to this analysis that the sociologist can produce a rigorous science of the social world which, far from sentencing agents to the iron cage of a strict determinism, offers them the means of a potentially liberating awakening of consciousness.[8]

Notes

This chapter is excerpted from a longer text written in the form of a dialogue to allow for more flexible and direct formulation of central problems raised in and by Bourdieu's theory of practice and knowledge. Both queries and answers are given a fuller, more systematic, expression in Pierre Bourdieu and Loïc J. D. Wacquant, *An Invitation to Reflexive Sociology* (Chicago, University of Chicago Press; Cambridge, Polity Press, 1992).

1 See Bourdieu (1980a: 71–86) for a thorough critique of Sartrian phenomenology and Elster's brand of Rational Choice Theory along these lines.

2 See Bourdieu (1979) on the "three forms" (embodied, objectified, and institutionalized) of cultural capital, and Bourdieu (1986) on the relations between cultural, social, economic, and symbolic capital.

3 See Bourdieu and Hahn (1970) and Bourdieu et al. (1968, part I) for elaborations.

4 For instance, it is only after utilizing the notion of "social capital" for a good number of years and in a wide variety of empirical settings, from the matrimonial relations of peasants to the symbolic strategies of research foundations to designers of high fashion to alumni associations of elite schools (see, respectively, Bourdieu 1977b; 1980a; 1980b; 1981; Bourdieu and Delsaut 1975), that Bourdieu wrote a paper outlining some of its generic characteristics (Bourdieu 1980c).

5 See especially "Une science qui dérange" and "Le sociologue en question" in Bourdieu (1980b: 19–60) for an elaboration of this point.

6 For instance, Skocpol (1988) shows that the recent rebirth of macro-historical sociology in the United States and its unique sensitivity to issues of conflict, power, and social transformation, are in part an effect of the academic maturing of an "uppity generation" of students trained during the rebellious 1960s who

came to academia with an experience of social and political activism that made it difficult, if not impossible, for them to believe in the consensual and falsely neutral vision of society promoted by structural functionalism and modernization theory.

7 The empirical demonstration of this argument is *Homo Academicus* (Bourdieu 1988).

12

Homo Sociologicus: Do We Need Him/Her?

Peter Abell

Until quite recently rational action or choice theory (spawned by *homo economicus*) had gained few adherents amongst those who struggle to find adequate foundational ideas for a sociological theory. Things now look more promising, however; Coleman (1990) has given us a truly remarkable work, and a number of journals are beginning to carry articles informed by a rational choice perspective.

For many, of course, the entire edifice of sociological theory rests upon assumptions, either that human actions are neither self-regarding nor rational (that is, not optimally chosen) or that such actions are of peripheral interest because human actors are propelled by Durkheimian structural forces beyond their control – thus at least one version of *homo sociologicus*. Yet for others, the vocabulary of action and motive provides only *post hoc* rationalizations, and all we are entitled to examine are the entrails of a rationalizing discourse. I suspect, however, that one reason why rational action theory is experiencing a new lease on life is precisely because these various approaches, when stripped of their verbal pretensions and quasi-philosophical veneer, appear to be rapidly leading us nowhere. Although it would not be prudent to claim that rational choice theory is likely to solve all the theoretical puzzles a sociologist might pose, in my view it must be given pride of place.

In the space available I cannot make a sustained case for this assertion. Rather I have chosen to concentrate upon one issue, namely the relationship between explanations of human action from (on the one hand) the precepts of rational action theory (RAT) and (on the other) from the constraint or facilitation of normative expectations. I take this route for a number of reasons: first, because for many, the most compelling mode of sociological explanation is in terms of social norms (that is, normative expectations);

second, because Coleman has argued that action compliant with social norms can be subsumed under RAT; and third, because Elster has argued to the contrary (1989). If Coleman is right and Elster wrong, then the case for at least one conception of *homo sociologicus* is undermined.

Elster makes several claims, as follows:

1 Social norms are to be distinguished from moral, legal, and private norms, and also from conventions (in the sense of conventional equilibria), habits, and traditional actions. Thus they stand apart as an independent category with their own defining characteristics.
2 Normatively compliant actions, as opposed to rationally optimal actions, are not evaluated in terms of their consequences. They are not instrumental or conditioned upon future states of affairs.
3 Normatively compliant actions characteristically are emotionally charged in the sense that their violation will lead to states of negative affect, guilt, shame, embarrassment, and so on (generally internal sanctions).
4 Normatively compliant action cannot be derived (is not determined by) self-interest. More generally, social norms have "an independent motivating power." This is called the "reality" of social norms.
5 Normatively compliant action is not a variety of optimal (rational) action, from either an individualistic or a collective standpoint. This is called the "autonomy" of social norms.

I shall argue that there are good reasons to doubt the exclusivity which these claims cumulatively build for the role of social norms.

It is useful, first of all, to distinguish between those individuals who "hold" or promote a social norm (that is, those who have a preference or expectation that the norm should be obeyed – usually in some specified circumstances and by designated actors) and those individuals whose actions comply (at least in part) with the norm in question. The two sets of individuals may or may not be coincidental or overlap. From an RAT perspective, there is a question as to the rationality of both the holders and those who are compliant. It is the ambition of the theory to make the actions of both fall under its precepts. If this effort is to be entirely successful, the theory would have to establish that:

1 the existence (genesis) of normative expectations can be accounted for by assuming (a) self-regarding, (b) optimally chosen, and (c) individual actions; and

2 the actions of both those who hold or promote and those who comply with normative expectations can be accounted for by the same three assumptions.

It is useful to keep (1) and (2) separate from each other because it may be possible to achieve a full RAT account of one but not the other.

It appears that RAT answers to (2) are achieved comparatively easily; the genetic question proves more problematic. It will be entirely in accord with the self-regarding interests of individuals to comply with the normative expectations of others if either (d) they are subject to credible threats and/or trustworthy promises, or (e) violation induces intraindividual ("psychic") costs that tip the expected utility appropriately. Within this framework, the calculation of internal cost–benefit ratios, derivative of the strength of the individual's normative conviction, counts toward the conception of self-regarding interest. Both mechanisms (d) and (e) are widely recognized and understood, and there is no *a priori* reason to suppose that assumptions (1) (a), (b), and (c) cannot achieve the necessary explanatory closure. The existence of internalized norms and the capacity to issue credible threats or trustworthy promises are each exogenous in this scheme of things; no doubt for many, it is these which require explanation. Endogenizing the existence of internalized norms, however, takes us to question (1).

Notwithstanding, much can be accomplished without taking this route. Elster says that "if some people successfully exploit norms for self-interested purposes it can only be because others are willing to let norms take precedence over self interest" (1989). But surely it is possible to make this claim only if we ignore the impact of internalized norms upon intraindividual cost–benefit ratios. Once again, the proper province for such inquiries is found under the auspices of question (1).

If we turn now to those who "promote" normative expectations, is there any sense in which we must surrender the assumptions of either self-regard or optimality on their behalf? Clearly if the promoter has internalized the norm (with respect to the actions of others), no *a priori* problem seems to arise. The net calculation of utility can lead her to rationally expect others to comply with a norm. If only external sanctions are involved, however, then (as Elster recognizes) things are not likely to be as straightforward. In the unlikely world bereft of normative internalization, A will comply with a norm either because it reflects her interests or because of the credible threats and/or trustworthy promises issued by B. But why does B so back a normative expectation? The obvious answer, of course, is because the norm enshrines B's self-regarding interests. Marxism's theory of norms, for instance, takes this simple form.

Yet it might be that B promotes the norm because of potential sanctions (threats and promises) on the part of a third actor, C (consider, for example, hierarchies of sanctioning authority). We may conceive of metanorms (that is, norms that take the ungainly form – sanctions of those who fail to sanction others who violate basic normative expectations). In the absence of cyclical sanctioning structures (which are not impossible – for example, some cooperatives), backward induction must produce a promoter of metanorms who does so irrespective of any threat of sanctions upon himself. Consequently, as Elster puts it, "some sanctions must be performed for motives other than the fear of being sanctioned" (1989: 133).

This is a rather tortuous point, but RAT will fail if indeed such a "prime mover" cannot be intellectually positioned so as to embrace the ultimate norm (and thus the derivative metanorm(s)) from a self-regarding standpoint. I believe, however, that this is empirically improbable. Thus the basic assumptions of RAT, in my view, are likely to hold up fairly well in examining action that is fashioned by institutionalized normative expectations.

Question (2) is altogether the more tricky. The first essential point of note about any RAT account of the genesis of normative expectations is that it cannot, from the start, invoke internalization and any associated psychic costs and benefits. These must necessarily come later. Thus it might very well be within the compass of my rational self-regarding interest both to promote and to comply with the fine-grained expectations of social etiquette, given the likely opprobrium, shame, embarrassment, and so on, consequent upon any violation on my part.

But is the genesis of these self-same expectations explicable in RAT terms? Or, to take another example – of which I have implicitly made extensive use – can RAT precepts (net of any normative internalization) explain the norms of "keeping promises" and "delivering threats" that underlie the existing normative expectations in any social system? These latter issues, of course, have been debated widely by economists because Pareto-improving voluntary exchange of goods and services is usually dependent upon the *prior* existence of norms that promote both promise keeping the respect for property rights (Rowe 1989).

Despite Elster's claim to the contrary, following Coleman (1990) and the intellectual traditions he draws upon, it is possible to see the broad shape of a general rational theory of the genesis of normative expectations. Such expectations will emerge where: (1) individuals' encounters are repeated, and (2) their actions (constitutive of the interaction) have external effects, so that individual and collective optimization do not generally coincide. It is well known, for instance, that norms of "promise keeping" can be conceived and modeled by a sequential game with the same ranking of payoffs as in the prisoner's dilemma. The second mover, by making trustworthy promises to play the cooperative strategy (for example, to complete the exchange at a later date), is able to promote normative expectations about her own action in the mind of the first mover and thus to increase the likelihood of co-operation by the first mover (Schelling 1960), leading to a Pareto optimum. Notice that the causal direction in the theory runs from an individual voluntarily establishing a normative expectation of her own action in the minds of others – not, as in many "sociological" theories, in the opposite direction, where normative constraint supposedly is causally operative.

Of course, there would be no *rational* grounds for the second mover to keep a promise in any single encounter, and indeed no rational grounds for the first mover to *expect* the second mover to honor any such promise. Each will play the dominant strategy rationally, procuring a Nash outcome. With indefinite encounters, however, there is some likelihood that normative expectations will arise. The strength of this sort of framework results from the fact that it predicts an absence of normative expectations where encounters are non-recurrent. No doubt, with exchanges that manifestly start from very unequal points, any normative expectations would have to be buttressed rapidly by credible threats whose imposition would have an almost identical logical structure.

Elster perhaps would accept all this but still would resist the conclusion that RAT precepts can account for the origin of all social norms. Consider, for instance, the norms of social etiquette. Elster thinks we are all worse off because of these (net of shame and such) – they are in no sense Pareto-functional. The argument that he uses against the standard RAT interpretation of their origin – namely that they serve *to support a social identity and to exclude outsiders* – is dismissed upon two grounds: first, their complexity (redundancy) – they appear to be far too elaborate for their supposed (rational) purposes; second, their appearance in low-status groups, which have no need to protect their boundaries against interlopers. "It is not clear," Elster argues, "why the working class as a whole would benefit from the fact that it contains an infinite variety of local subcultures" (1989).

Surely this is correct, but why should we require from our theory this sort of global constraint? Indeed, only if we are prepared to consider the "working class" as a theoretically relevant category would we be inclined to construct the problem in this way and ask for classwide optimality. The origin of the fine-grained structure of "working-class" social norms may be perfectly explicable in terms of rationally based local recurrent interactions, where local demarcations, rivalries, and such are of prime significance. I can see no good reason against adopting this perspective as a working assumption. Of course, as circumstances change and different patterns of recurrent interaction emerge, existing normative expectations will become redundant. Also, because by now they are invested with the emotions of internalized norms, they may persist and appear to be connectively suboptimal. Yet none of this counts against the RAT interpretation of what is going on.

Should we not be more inventive in trying to chart evolutions of this nature through the RAT perspective, rather than turning prematurely to a *homo sociologicus*?

13

Science and Technology Studies and the Renewal of Social Theory

Steve Woolgar

Introduction

The literature which attempts to diagnose the malaise associated with the current parlous state of social theory is extensive, and is hereby increased by one. A tempting way of approaching this issue is to formulate the nature of "the crisis" in social theory and then propose a particular package of solutions which, unsurprisingly, turns out to derive from the author's own sub-discipline. For the most part, this chapter follows this same approach. However, in one particular regard it is different. The discussion here is more concerned with the dynamics of change in social theory than with advancing one line of argument as the solution. The history of methodological fashion in social science is already full of disappointments, each once touted as a silver bullet in the service of overcoming obstacles to better social theory.

This chapter introduces, and discusses the salience for social theory of, some recent work within science and technology studies (STS).[1] Although social theorists have only rarely regarded STS as contributing to "mainstream" issues in social theory, an increasing number of writers have recently started to champion the relevance of the work (Law 1991a; Latour 1993; Lynch 1993b; Woolgar 1994; 1996). This arises, in part, from a growing emphasis in STS in recent years on "epistemic" questions (Coulter 1989; Lynch 1993a) and from attention to the reflexive implications of arguments about the social basis of explanatory adequacy (Ashmore 1989; Woolgar 1988). One important upshot of these emphases is that STS is no longer merely concerned to convey substantive findings about science and about technology, but instead finds itself involved in attempts to "respecify" key notions such as "social," "society" and "agency." It is in this spirit that the

discussion below aims to introduce, discuss, and evaluate the potential contribution of certain recent features of STS to social theory.[2]

The chapter is organized as follows. First, I identify the problems of social
theory with which I am concerned. Second, I recount certain recent developments[3] in STS, in particular those associated with "actor-network theory" or
"the sociology of translation." Thirdly, I argue that although "actor-network
theory" is unlikely to be a panacea for the problems of social theory, it provides a good example of the ways in which STS can offer a revitalization of
social theory. Fourth, I give a brief illustration of actor-network theory as
applied to a well known historical case – the story of the Luddites in the
British industrial revolution. The point here is to show how STS suggests an
alternative set of analytic categories for understanding the phenomena to
which social theory should address itself. Finally, an intriguing and, I suggest,
productive complication in the argument is that STS themselves purport to
be cognizant of the conditions of success of the kind of move being advocated. That is, STS are themselves in a position to assess the likelihood that
pleas for their relevance to social theory will be heard. Accordingly, a fifth
theme addressed below is the reflexive significance of the potential of STS.

Social Theory and the Transition to Democracy

I take it that social theory is quintessentially concerned to discuss and assess
different ideas about social organization. A key concern is the distribution of
resources and, relatedly, the distribution of power: how can society be organized, with what consequences for the division of the spoils; who dominates
who (and indeed to what extent is domination of any kind necessary?). An
important corollary to this central set of questions is the further question of
social change. Given the basic liberal premiss that "society could be otherwise," what are the prospects for social change? Under what conditions and
in what ways can significant social change take place? Moreover, I take it that
the "it could be otherwise" clause potentially has much wider import than
merely structural and organizational change. By "social" then, we can include
all aspects of life which are affected to a greater or lesser extent by social
arrangements. In other words, the "it could be otherwise" slogan should be
understood to refer in principle to intellectual change, changes in beliefs,
values, discourse and practice, and so on.

To the extent that social theory depends on the existence of plausible
empirical or imaginative alternatives to the modern capitalistic welfare state,
it has been suggested that events in recent years, particularly since 1989,
have significantly limited its scope.[4] Social theory originated in the reformist

project of nineteenth-century liberal thought. But does the end of communism as a viable universal ideological orientation suggest that the project of social theory – at least in its more radical depictions of alternative forms of societal organization – is now spent (Turner 1992)? The rationale for this suggestion is that there is now a reduced set of possible alternative societies. The collapse of communism is taken as evidence of the untenability of the ideas and arguments of Marxism and related ideologies.[5] Hence, so the argument goes, the "transition to democracy" entails the diminution of social theory.[6]

This line of argument has obvious problems. It is not clear that the demise of an institutional instantiation of an ideological system can be taken as evidence of the untenability of the ideas upon which it is based.[7] For example, the demise may turn out to be temporary: is some unexplicated Whiggishness at work here? This line of argument also underplays the considerable methodological difficulties in describing, let alone accounting for, what is allegedly happening in other societies.

Most importantly, this line of argument embodies an unnecessarily restricted (and unnecessarily pessimistic) conception of the sociological imagination. It suggests that the social theorist can only consider alternative forms of societal organization when confronted by their contemporary empirical reality. But this underplays the potential contribution of anthropological investigations – the cultural relativism that tells us that societies can be otherwise in other places.[8] It also tends to denigrate the potential contribution of social history – the historical relativism that tells us that societies can be otherwise at other times.

Quite apart from the accuracy of this diagnosis, the very suggestion – that the health and vitality of social theory is demonstrably tied to empirical changes in the world order – raises serious questions about the nature and scope of the sociological imagination. Where does social theory get its ideas from? Are changes in social theoretic thinking dependent on corresponding changes in actual social structure? To what extent do sociology's reformist origins constrain the range and type of phenomena it can treat? What are the prospects and opportunities for significant changes in the scope of social theory?[9] The interest of certain recent arguments in science and technology studies (STS) is that they provoke a reconsideration of (at least some of) these weighty questions.

STS and Social Theory

STS comprise a loose affiliation of disciplinary interests including sociology, philosophy, history, anthropology, and political science among others, committed to fashioning a new understanding of science and technology. The excitement and energy of this work lies in its double significance. On the one hand, it addresses issues and problems arising from the fact that science and technology are, arguably, the most pervasive and significant forms of cultural artifact in our societies. On the other hand, STS are important because they urge a reconceptualization of what, in fact, the practice of science and technology entail. This in turn is particularly important for interrogating long-standing pretensions (both within and beyond academia) about what is to count as scientific method. In this treatment, science and technology are the focus of attention for ideas drawn from a whole series of intersecting intellectual currents: relativism, feminism, constructivism, discourse analysis, semiotics, cultural studies, and others. The work is as energetic and prolific as it is epistemologically contentious.[10]

The recent claims of a certain species of STS – treated here under the rubric of "actor-network theory" – are tantamount to offering an entirely new source of possible alternative societies for social theory. These alternative societies are, in a sense, elaborated below, the societies presented by technology.[11] Recently, some of the actor-network literature has begun to make explicit the potential connections between STS and social theory.[12] For example, Law (1991b) argues that a major finding of STS is that the social – the glue that keeps things together – is not purely social at all. To the extent that society is held together, this is achieved by heterogeneous means. In other words, "the social world would not hang together if the natural, the corporeal, the technological, the textual and the topographical were taken away" (Law 1991b: 7). Law's point is that although sociology is centrally concerned with distribution – the division of resources between classes, race, ethnicity, gender – it systematically overlooks the significance of distribution between, say, machines on the one hand, and people on the other. Moreover, its practice takes for granted the distinction between categories like technology and society, such that its analysis is tantamount to a form of specism.

> Sociologists . . . tend to switch registers. They talk of the social. And *then* (if they talk of it at all which most do not) they talk of the technical. And, if it appears, the technical acts either as a kind of explanatory *deus ex machina* (technological determinism). Or it is treated as an expression of social relations (social reductionism). Or with difficulty the two are treated as two classes of objects which interact and mutually shape one another. (Law 1991b: 8)

The problem stems from the failure of sociology to investigate how the great distributions, such as those between humans and machines, are laid down and sustained.

> The very dividing line between those objects that we choose to call people and those we call machines is variable, negotiable and tells us as much about the rights, duties, responsibilities and failings of people as it does about machines. (Law 1991b: 17)

The complaint is that although sociology has put much effort into investigating, criticizing, and deconstructing the constitution of dividing lines with respect to class, race, gender, and so on, it has yet to attend to the dividing lines between machines, animals, plants, people. The central dictum of the sociological imagination – that any apparently "natural" order of things could be otherwise – is not applied to these categories.

Latour similarly notes how the great divide between humans and non-humans has been unproblematically adopted by social theorists[13]: "There is, social theory insists, a real, useful, and important difference between those who deal with the human and those who deal with the nonhuman" (Latour 1991a: 4). Latour suggests this dichotomy can be traced to a defensive strategy on the part of nineteenth-century social theory in the face of the emerging success of reductionist beliefs in positivistic scientific method. It was then that the ground was divided between nature and culture: the non-human and the human. And the distinctly different hermeneutic of social theory became a fiercely defended professional boundary marker.[14]

Latour claims that recent empirical ethnographic studies of science and technology subvert this divide since they direct social science away from studies of the peripheral and marginal phenomena and toward the hard core of society: technology and the natural sciences. According to Latour, this should not simply be a reductionist move. The important claim is not that scientific and technical knowledge is socially determined (although this clearly is the import of some other arguments in STS) as a kind of symmetrical counter to the claim that scientific knowledge is determined by nature.[15] As Callon and Latour (1992: 349) describe it, the preferred move is to an analytic dimension which lies orthogonal to the familiar continuum between the opposite poles of the technical and the social. The idea is not to determine the relative influence of nature and society, but instead to understand how these entities mutually constitute each other. It thus no longer makes sense to differentiate between them: the "key discovery of science studies [is that] we are confronted neither with society nor with nature." We have to transcend "these two impossible groupings: things in themselves, and humans among themselves" (Latour 1991a: 9).

By way of a historical deconstruction of the distinction between humans and non-humans, Latour enrolls the work of Shapin and Schaffer (1986).

According to these authors, the origin of the distinction was fabricated – accomplished not given – largely through the efforts of Robert Boyle and Thomas Hobbes. Their seventeenth-century disputes were precisely about the questions now taken as set in stone: which entities have what rights, capacities, obligations, and effects? In brief, they settled the new moral order by defining and establishing the rules of experimental method. In so doing, they coinvented the "political constitution of truth ... the very dichotomy between human political representation and nonhuman scientific representation" (Latour 1991a: 13) and it is this distinction which is the very basis of modernism.

Having established the historical contingency of the distinction, Latour berates those who now uncritically take it for granted:

> Do you see now the enormous deadly mistake of those well-meaning social theorists when they defend the hermeneutic by the so-called commonsense argument that humans speak and have intention while nonhumans are deaf and dumb? They accept as a given the result of a political constitution of truth that has first dispatched speech, deafness and dumbness. They pride themselves for being critical on the political side but they swallow it hook line and sinker when the politics of things is involved. (Latour 1991a: 14)

The central thrust of the argument, then, is against the uncritical adoption by social theory of a historically contingent distinction between humans and non-humans. This negative argument is fairly clear. But what precisely are the advantages of construing technology as a new source of ideas for social theory?

Technology as Alternative Societies

What does it mean to say that technologies offer alternative forms of possible society?[16] The idea derived from actor-network variants of STS is that the reconceptualization of technology and society offers different ways of thinking about the problem of social order. As the discussion so far suggests, the central theme is a revision of conventional ideas about agency: entities other than humans should also be included in the sociological purview.

How does this work? It is a basic lemma of much STS that technology embodies the antecedent circumstances of its production and use. In some versions this amounts to the claim that social circumstances are built into the technology. The apposite slogan is that "technology is congealed social interests." The central notion here is that the effects of technology are a reflection of the antecedent circumstances implicated in design, production, marketing, and so on. Well known examples include the inculcation of social class bias and racial prejudice in the case of Moses' bridges on the Long Island freeway (Winner 1980); political and military interests in the case of technologies of missile accuracy (MacKenzie 1990); gender bias in household technologies (Cowan 1983) and in information and communication technologies (Cockburn 1985; Cockburn and Ormrod 1993).[17]

The inculcation of antecedent circumstances can be interpreted in terms of the technology fashioning, altering, or merely enhancing social relationships between producers (suppliers) and users (consumers): users respond to the antecedent circumstances presented to them in and through their use of the technology (cf. Cooper and Woolgar 1993). When you use Wordperfect 3.1 you are tacitly agreeing to act and behave in accordance with the software writers' preconceptions about you. You can behave differently from (the designers') expectations but one result may be that the machine will not do what you want it to. Since the social relationship between designer and user is enshrined in material form, non-conformity with these expectations is consequential in the sense that alternative actions are costly. We could say that in and through the use of a technology, its designers' expectations are sanctioned both technically and socially.

A somewhat richer sense of sanctioned social relationship is captured in the slogan that "technology is society made durable" (Latour 1991b). The sense here is that technology constitutes a particular system/pattern of associations between heterogeneous entities: both humans and non-humans. The implication is that technology constitutes an especially robust network of such associations. It is not so much that exogenous social variables or influences are "built in" as that the technology comprises and is constituted by a novel set of heterogeneous relationships. To speak of these relationships as "social" seems now to miss the point, since they are associations between entities – both human and non-human – which seem to involve more than what sociologists traditionally focus upon. In particular, the fact of inclusion of non-human elements, the notion for example that scallops are willing (or not) to be caught by the fishermen of St Brieuc's Bay (Callon 1986), asks us to re-examine our assumptions about the distribution of attributes and capacities which we take for granted.[18] A new technology thus comprises a new set of associations between heterogeneous elements. And it is in this sense that these new technologies offer an alternative form of society: new kinds of relationships between a new cast of human and non-human entities.

This method of conceptualizing technology seems to resonate with our mundane apprehensions in at least three ways. First, access to a technology can be understood as tantamount to access to a new set of associations. To become part of this new society, one needs to become socialized and to demonstrate one's competent membership, most often by way of presenting oneself as an adequately configured user (cf. Woolgar 1991; 1993). Second, the very concept of technical can now be understood as a societal/community/network boundary marker. When something is said to be a "technical problem," the claim is that the problem lies within the provenance of a particular designated set of associations and expertises. Often, though not always, this turns out to be a device for excluding outsiders, for displaying and sustaining a boundary between entities who/which are and are not members of the heterogeneous network (cf. Low and Woolgar 1993). Third, and relatedly, this means of conceptualizing technology goes some way to explaining the remarkably futuristic tenor of much talk about new technologies. This is the "problem of tenses" (Friedman and Cornford 1989), the fact that talk about technology is usually talk about what this technology will bring. Technology offers future courses of action: or, sometimes, it offers to a specific set of potential users those future courses of action which are already available to others. If the "past is another country," then with technology the future is also another country. It is a country comprising novel and previously unimagined sets of associations between unexpected elements. It is a projected system of novel actions, behaviors and relationships to which we can obtain access, of which we can, at some point in the future, become a part.

More important than any of these particular advantages of reconceptualizing "technology," however, is the general point that STS is also offering new ways of conceptualizing "the social." This possibility stems directly from the fact that "scientific" and "technical" have been (and are) normatively defined in opposition to each other. The commonsense apprehension of science and technology is precisely of a realm of activity and achievement which excludes the social. This apprehension is deeply entrenched in the discourse and practice of many areas of academia, including social theory, and can be found to inform the writing of even the most sophisticated proponents of relativism and constructivism. It follows that any profound challenge to conceptions of technology (or science) is also a profound challenge to conceptions of the social. It is for this reason that STS, unlike other sub-disciplines, has the unusual capacity to impact upon social theory. Specifically, it suggests that alternatives to the traditional analytic categories of social explanation may be usefully employed in making sense of the world around us. In order to illustrate how STS can suggest a new focus for analytic attention, we consider below an application of actor-network theory to an infamous episode in the industrial revolution in Britain: the Luddites.

It is worth noting the extent to which the exposition below draws upon and demands unusual uses of descriptive language, in particular the application of predicates normally associated with human actions to those of machines and other inanimate objects. This resulting oddity of language use is, of course, theoretically consistent with the ambitions of the enterprise noted earlier. If it is the case that sociology has by and large adopted a language of description and explanation that takes for granted a particular form of distribution (between humans and machines) of rights, duties, responsibilities, and failings; and if it is also the case that conventions of language embody, constitute, and display deeply entrenched assumptions about this distribution of attributes; then we would expect to experience "awkwardnesses" in any attempt to furnish a description which challenges the accepted distribution. Nonetheless, as we shall discuss later, this kind of theoretical justification still leaves the problem of how to convince one's readers.

An Actor-network Interpretation of the Luddites

Many of the contending interpretations of the events associated with Luddism either presume the inherently progressive character of the machinery (in both establishment and Marxist accounts) or its irrelevance (in the machine as a symbol account).[19] These approaches implicitly assign technical capacities to technology or deem it merely coincidental to events unfolding for other, non-technical reasons. As I have already indicated, actor-network theory attempts to finesse this implicit dualism between technical and social factors. This section therefore describes and evaluates an actor-network account of Luddism. Without wishing to suggest that it captures all the nuances and variations of actor-network theory, this brief exposition aims to convey the main themes. The nub of the case is that the arrival of new machinery – the teasling and cropping machines and the gig mills – was tantamount to the insinuation of a whole new cast of actants into an existing set of networks. The arrival of this machinery presented a potential disruption to a relatively stable balance of power. By the end of the eighteenth century, the social organization of cropping in England was well established, organized as it was around allies such as hand shears and wire brushes. Such allies had proved their loyalty to the croppers and their families. So the key question for all involved was whether, to what effect, and for whom, could the new actants be enrolled as allies?

At the time, the organization and process of cloth production in the west of England differed from that in the north and in Nottinghamshire. In actor-network terms, the woolen industry of the west of England comprised a more heterogeneous network: more and different actors were involved. By contrast, the actor networks of the north and Nottinghamshire comprised a smaller number of different actors. In particular, the focal point of the latter was the croppers, who enjoyed a relatively dominant position in their network. This arose in part from the croppers' ability to define the key attributes of the work (and hence of membership of the network) in terms of skill (a five-year apprenticeship was required) and physical strength, and from their control over the selection of a limited number of apprentices (new human actants). In other words, this latter network was less heterogeneous.

It follows that the acquisition or loss of any one ally was likely to be more disruptive of networks in the north and Nottinghamshire than for the west of England, and this proved to be the case with the eventual mass desertion of the machines. The violence in the West Country (the "Wiltshire outrages") was relatively successful in stopping the spread of machinery (and in eventually undermining the textile economy in that part of the country altogether). This fits the fact that much of the resistance in the West Country came from individuals only indirectly affected by threat of the machinery. These latter actants provided a further source of heterogeneity in the more robust West Country network.

Few of the histories of Luddism contend the existence and use of some of the disputed machines years before the outbreak of violence and civil disobedience. So the mere presence of the new technology was insufficient as a cause of Luddism (cf. Randall 1991: 43–8). Instead, as numbers grew, the precise nature of the alliance being offered by these new actants came gradually to be questioned. It is likely that accounts of what the machines could achieve featured centrally in deliberations over the likely loyalty of these new actants. New technologies have often become the focus of considerable myth making about their supposed qualities and capacities. When construed as a significant source of possible change to the status quo, stories about what technologies can achieve are often played out in terms of the dire consequences of transgressing established moral boundaries (see, for example, Woolgar and Russell 1990). Indeed, it is precisely one historian's argument that the factory system was regarded by textile workers "as an approaching flood which threatened to submerge them all" (Randall 1991: 46). "Fears of the impact of the factory on the morals of the community, exaggerated or not, were deep-rooted" (p. 48). We can thus speculate that accounts of what the new allies (machines) could achieve became a source of focused discussion. Stories about their potential disruptive effects would have spread especially quickly (cf. Randall 1991: 50). Fuelling this were the manufacturers' accounts of what, for example, cropping machines could achieve: the promise that the machines could make savings for the owners particularly excited questions about which network these machines were supporting.

Actor-network theory provides a (re)description of subsequent events in a way designed to enforce a symmetry between the perspective of the human actants on the one hand, and that of the non-human actants on the other. The first element is unexceptional: The potential loss of an ally which, it seemed, might turn out to be treacherous, spurred the protesters into action. From their point of view a pre-emptive strike would prevent the machines being of use. If they were, after all, putative allies of rival networks, their destruction would ensure that they provided little support.

The second element is deliberately counter-intuitive. The machines themselves were persuaded (or "seduced," as the croppers would have it) by the futuristic rhetoric of the manufacturers: they were promised a future world full of machines, unimpeded by the demands of the croppers; a world in which there were far fewer anxieties and moral qualms about the "status" of machines. Consequently, deserters began to go over to the networks of the capitalists. This in turn exacerbated the reaction of the croppers which, needless to say, further persuaded the machines that they needed to desert. Once they found themselves being beaten up, those machines wanted out of there!

Part of the reason for the extremities of the confrontation between the networks, both in terms of the Luddites' violence and in the retributions which followed, is that both networks commanded considerable support. The desertion of the machine allies thus tipped the balance of power but did not provoke the immediate collapse of the croppers' network. In the course of the very bitter struggle, the capitalists came to recognize the croppers as a "reverse salient" (Hughes 1987); that is, they proved a particularly stubborn source of opposition around which it was necessary to maneuver. As part of their strategy, the manufacturers set out to enroll the machinery of the state to their cause. The government was not initially disposed against the croppers, having long before institutionalized some constraints on machinery, for example, in the form of laws preventing the use of gig mills.[20] But the manufacturers' case was that croppers were unworthy allies; it was implied that their motives were no different from those of other preeminent bogeymen (bogey-actants?) of the time – the French revolutionaries supporting the national network with which England was then at war. Thus, activities such as administering secret oaths were to be understood as the activities of enemies of the state, hell bent on anarchy and confusion. Moreover, these enemies of the state were just the kind of actor who would perpetuate crimes such as violence and burglary.

It did no harm to this (manufacturers') portrayal of the character of cropper actants, to exaggerate and extend the degree of violence perpetrated by the croppers. It was probably this phase of the proceedings which was crucial to transforming the key actants from croppers into Luddites. However, the Luddites themselves had a very solid community support system. Even under threat (and the actuality) of torture, very few of their number revealed information until right at the end of the struggle. They enjoyed a particularly strong domestic network embedded in, and reinforced by, local working culture. Even with the machines on their side, the manufacturers' was the weaker network. However, at the point where violence broke out, the solidarity of the Luddite actor network became critical: the Luddites had to ensure that none of their allies – the stores, guns, weapons, houses, lost bits of paper, and footprints – gave away any secrets. The final resolution of the dispute hinged on the manufacturers' ability to recruit, in addition to the legislature, the army (with its special artillery unit – the Rocket Corps) and the gallows. Certainly in Yorkshire, the beginning of the end stemmed from a few individuals being persuaded to give King's Evidence (Reid 1986: 208– 19). With the importance of solidarity for the Luddites, the desertion of these few "traitors" led very quickly to the unraveling of the Luddite actor network. The ensuing triumphal definition of Luddism was sufficiently robust to have become engrained in vernacular usage over 150 years later: a Luddite is now "any opponent of industrial change or innovation" (*Collins English Dictionary*, 1979).

In line with our earlier discussion of actor-network theory, this analysis eschews rigid distinctions between the "technical" and the "social" dimensions of the affair. By refusing the conventionally restricted conception of "social," actor-network theory tries to escape the implied oppositional pairing between the "technical" (understood as the "non-social") and the "social," which is characteristic of most traditional sociological analyses. Instead, the focus is on the formation and re-formation of networks wherein the capacities, rights, obligations, and interests of all parties (actants), both human and non-human, are mutually constructed and deconstructed. This means in particular that the Marxist category of "social class" is at best unnecessary and, at worst, a distraction. The idea of "social" is instead redefined to include different sorts of relationships between a wide variety of entities; "class" is now replaced by alignments and networks. In particular, machines can now become members of an analytically significant category. This in turn means that the Luddites, far from exhibiting the "irrational" behavior born of false consciousness, understandably reacted to the potential loss of allies by attempting to destroy them.

A further ramification is that in the actor-network account, power is not merely the possession of one group of humans over another (cf. Latour 1988). It is instead the effect of a particular alignment of humans and non-humans, the character and capacity of which changes as alliances are disrupted and reformed. The power of a network is equivalent to the cost of dismantling it. In this way the attempt by the actor-network account to transcend the social–technical divide makes redundant the Marxist need to rely on (one particular version of) the "actual" technical capacity of the machines (that is, that they can destroy the livelihoods of the workers). In actor-network theory, technical capacities are the (temporary) upshot of network building and disruption, rather than its cause.

We see that although actor-network theory reworks traditional conceptions of terms like power, in some other respects it adopts rather traditional notions current within social theory. Thus, for example, notions such as alliance, solidarity and (implicitly) trust and social bond all serve as fairly standard explanatory notions in redescribing the Luddites episode, and are not treated as needing explication. The novelty, of course, is in the attempt to apply them symmetrically to both humans and machines.

The "It Could Be Otherwise" Clause and the Dynamics of Theoretical Change

The way in which the actor-network variant of STS offers a conceptualization of technology as a new form of future heterogeneous society, brings a novel sense to the argument that technical change is also social change (and vice versa). This description of (simultaneously technical and social) change is an extension of the "it could be otherwise" clause which is central to liberal social theory. Instead of an imagined (or actual) alternative concatenation of "social" relationships between humans, actor-network theory posits an alternative set of associations between human and non-human entities. In the process, this variant of STS proposes a transformation of existing explanatory categories such as "social" and "power."

Of course, the actor-network interpretation of Luddism just given is by no means without its problems.[21] Of greater relevance for our purposes, however, are some more general objections raised against actor-network theory. For, as we shall see, these general objections to this particular variant of STS can be understood as symptomatic of a dynamic process of criticism and change within STS. Two main interrelated objections concern us here: first, that the appeal of actor-network theory is merely rhetorical and, second, that it projects a course of action which abrogates certain moral and ethical responsibilities.

The first objection is that the proposal to equate humans and non-humans is ludicrous since it is merely metaphorical. This stems from the counter-intuitive sound of the claims for actor-network theory. Against this, it should be said that STS (and particularly its component, the sociology of scientific knowledge), has a distinguished history of advancing and working through ideas and propositions which initially seem counter-intuitive, but which in hindsight seem almost commonplace. A good example is the very idea of a sociology of science itself. Before Kuhn, the term sociology of science was almost a contradiction in terms: what was it that could possibly be said to be social about science. Wasn't science precisely that which did not admit the social?

The difficulty of (or refusal to) understand(ing) calls to break down the human–non-human divide is a measure of entrenchment within the current ideology of representation. Because of their commitment to a conventional moral order of representation, critics will interpret the attribution of "human" capacities to "non-humans" as mere metaphor. It is for this reason that critics hear Callon's (1986) description of scallops being willing to be caught as merely involving a "figure of speech" or as the deployment of "imaginative resources." It would seem to be just a matter of dressing up the account differently: the language changes but the story remains the same. This is an interesting criticism because it shows that despite their professed commitment to the argument that language is socially constitutive of phenomena, some sociologists are still tempted to try to find *one preferred story* behind all. In this view, different ways of conveying the (actual) story then become distractions, fancy talk, unnecessary and sometimes dangerous embellishments.[22] There is the supposition that Callon must be joking, or talking metaphorically; he cannot *mean* that the scallops are actually willing to comply. Interestingly, even some sympathizers also unwittingly support the thrust of this complaint. Thus, for example, the recent accounts of several historians of science and technology contain references to "actors" and "networks," but it turns out that these terms are often applied exclusively to humans. Such attempts to follow actor networking fail to grasp its central (and most radical) point. What is vividly clear is that these asymmetric assessments depend on profoundly entrenched commitments to the "actual character" of the natural–social divide.

A second, related objection is that the radical symmetry proposed by actor-network theory undermines the humanistic potential of the sociology project. Construed as an effort to (re)assert the primacy of humankind, the application of sociology to science has in the past had the virtue of bringing scientific knowledge within the purview of sociological explanation, thereby demonstrating the uniquely human character of even the most technical achievement. To upholders of this view, actor-network theory seems bent on blurring the distinction which a humanistic sociology should be defending. This particular objection is related to the previous one in that the commitment to a particular conventional moral order of representation is enshrined in what counts as a "sensible" – that is, socially sanctionable – use of language attributes and terms.

This latter objection resonates with a more general complaint that the epistemological–analytic wing of STS (see note 12) has little to contribute to the important political tasks of informing the citizenry about science and technology, involving them in the policy process, ameliorating the adverse effects of new innovations and developments and so on.[23] The "action–political" concerns which inform this objection to actor-network theory perhaps stem from the same origins of the reformist vision for social theory in general. We thus see that traditional pretensions to liberal reform are premissed on a commitment to existing conventions of representation. In other words, in its traditional handling, the "it could be otherwise" clause of liberal reform carries with it an implicitly restricted sense of the "it" and the "otherwise" which are admissible. Although initial efforts to develop a sociology of things are only just now under way,[24] actor-network theory is a good example of a recent development in STS which asks social theory to explicate, reassess and perhaps modify some of the implicit assumptions of its reformist agenda.

It is important to understand the objections just mentioned in the context of the evolution of perspectives in STS. The actor-network interpretation of the "it could be otherwise" clause is the latest in a series of arguments which propose the extension of analytic symmetries. This succession of arguments can be traced back (at least) to the efforts of Mannheim (1936) in extending the application of the sociology of knowledge beyond Marx's concentration on ideology as a source of distorted knowledge; for Mannheim, at least in his programmatic arguments, both true and false knowledge should be treated symmetrically. In a separate tradition, Merton (1973) subsequently proposed that the specific knowledge generating institutions of science should be treated on a symmetrical par with other social institutions. The "strong program" in the sociology of scientific knowledge took up the Mannheimian theme, extending it in particular to mathematics (a domain neglected by Mannheim) and insisting upon the symmetrical treatment of scientific knowledge whether deemed true or false (Barnes 1974; Bloor 1976). More recently, the reflexive and ethnographic approaches to scientific knowledge have problematized the relation between the analyst and the scientist, for example by insisting on a symmetry between the textual roles of the observer and the observed (Ashmore 1989; Latour and Woolgar 1986; Woolgar 1988). Actor-network theory proposes a semiotically informed variant of this general reflexive dynamic. The call to transcend the human–non-human distinction is the latest in a series of radical symmetries, this time with respect to agency.

The recent history of research in STS is thus characterized by successive attempts to challenge prevailing analytical asymmetries (for a full discussion see Woolgar 1992). So we see that the call for breaking down the human–non-human divide is one instance within a larger dynamic: the successive rooting out and dismantling of fearful asymmetries. When social theory becomes complacent about the presumed scope of its sociological imagination, where its capacity to imagine the "otherwise" becomes sluggish, STS acts as its analytic conscience. STS is the hit squad on behalf of social theory: the cavalry coming to save sociology from itself. It is in this vein that Latour describes the partition between the social and natural sciences as a "shameful Yalta Pact that keeps all of us, hard and soft scientists, with all our family resemblances, trapped on two sides of one of the only Iron Curtains that remain" (Latour 1991a: 7).

STS thus promises the successive identification and deconstruction of a series of Iron Curtains. Indeed, a whole series of other divides begin to suggest themselves: we need to eliminate the great divides between science/society; macro/micro; rational/irrational; technology/science and so on. All to be dismantled in a glorious bonfire of the dualities.

So How Will STS Win (New) Friends and Influence Social Theory?

It is tempting to conclude the argument on this note. We have articulated the strength of the call by STS for the attention of social theory; an argument that social theory can gain the revitalization it needs by attending to the ways in which STS suggests it should revise some of its basic analytic categories. In the face of such an argument how can social theory resist?! Proponents of actor-network theory do occasionally lapse into unreflexive tirades about the need to redress the "errors" being committed by social theory, forgetting for the moment that their own "truth" (of actor-network theory) is merely contingent and temporary.[25] All sub-disciplines, to paraphrase Lévi-Strauss, overestimate the objectivity of their own thought.[26] However, as is well known by students of intellectual change, from Lewis Caroll's Achilles and the Tortoise to practitioners in STS, the sheer force of an argument is, by itself, insufficient guarantee that its recipients will be swayed. We need instead to recall the basic tenet of STS that the basis for intellectual change is social, and to put this to work in assessing on what basis a closer alliance between STS and social theory might be realized. Certainly, we need to ask more prosaically what advantages accrue to social theorists if they agree to follow actor networkers around? Why exactly should they want to buy this stuff?

The work of actor-network theory and of some recent ethnographic research on the development of technical artifacts provides a schematic answer. It is suggested, for example, that the uptake and use of technical artifacts depends on establishing new social relationships between producers and consumers (Woolgar 1991). Consumers are not swayed merely by the "intrinsic merit" of the black boxes they are being asked to purchase, but by a whole series of alliances and alignments into which they are being encouraged to enter. In particular, in a way which reflects the actor-network notion of enrollment and translation, users are taught what to want (Woolgar 1993). This involves, for example, the establishment of mechanisms whereby the boundary between producers and consumers can be managed. Hence, to the extent that one can fashion an analogy between the development of technical artifacts and the production of (other) cultural artifacts (Cooper and Woolgar 1993), STS could do worse than adopt a similar strategy; it should examine the possibilities for encouraging new forms of social relationship with the practitioners of social theory, whereby its own cultural artifacts (that is, the fruits of science and technology studies) become more attractive.

It follows from this general point that STS needs to understand more of the dynamics of its relation with its potential users. How might this apply to the particular case of the acceptance of actor-network theory by social theory? We saw earlier how some objections were based on an adverse reaction to perceived oddities of language in actor-network descriptions. We said that such oddities bespoke a difference in deeply entrenched assumptions about the distribution of attributes between humans and non-humans, and noted that these objections came from those unable to prise themselves from the constraints of convention. But the stylistic difference is also historically rooted. Since the origins of social theory lie in propaganda, the appeal of particular ideas about social organization often depends on their simplicity and directness. Truth is truth for everyone, not just for a specific set of intellectuals and academics. This in turn can mean that "oddities" of language use can easily be viewed as deliberately perverse or obscurantist, too clever, arch or frivolous.[27] Hence, efforts to be provocative and explore alternative ideas about social organization always need to take into account the preconceptions of possible audiences for these ideas.

Conclusion

Social theory is about possibilities. At its most general level, social theory tries to understand why one rather than another possible social scenario has come about, or to assess the likelihood of social change. Central to this effort is the "it could be otherwise" clause of liberal intellectual inquiry. A general dissatisfaction with the current state of social theory, coupled with the observation that various forms of alternative society (notably socialism and communism) have – in the recent wholesale transition to democracy – been "shown to be untenable," has led to the speculation that the scope and potential of social theory is coming to an end.

This chapter has tried to offer an alternative diagnosis. Social theory is not so much exhausted as merely undergoing a period of stagnation, whereby we have become too willing to accept a particularly restricted conception of the "it could be otherwise" clause. We have somehow got ourselves in a situation where we find it difficult to see beyond the end of our noses. The ideal of social theory as a form of universal historical self-consciousness is not dead. However, it is, perhaps, in severe danger of becoming ossified if we fail to consider imaginative possibilities in terms other than radical socialism. We could say that although a "transition to democracy" may be happening in a relatively confined arena concerning the reorganization of relations between humans, specism still abounds.

For a variety of reasons – its relativist–constructivist currents, its relevance to "epistemic" issues, its attention to the reflexive dynamics of explanatory adequacy and the basic point that "science" and "technical" are conventionally defined in opposition to "social" – work in recent science and technology studies (STS) is increasingly engaging the key theoretical notions of "social" and "agency." Actor-network theory is one example of STS which offers a reconceptualization of science and technology and which thereby requires us to reconsider these key concepts.

So does actor-network theory provide the answer to all the problems of a severely stagnated social theory? Probably not! But it does provide a good example of how moves within STS can provide an important provocation. Through its particular focus upon phenomena (science and technology) which are central to modernity, recent work in STS promises no less than new ways of conceptualizing (social) organization. The key clause of a liberal social theory is still "it could be otherwise." By responding to the provocation of STS we can perhaps ensure that social theory can extend the application of this basic premiss to new and unexpected domains.

Notes

1 In this chapter, "science and technology studies" is preferred to "sociology of technology" or "sociology of science." The latter designations imply the application of a perspective (sociology) to a preconceived object (technology or science), whereas I want to argue that one potentially attractive outcome of this work is its re-evaluation of what might count both as sociology and as technology/ science.

2 Of course, more general arguments for the "renewal" of social theory stem from movements such as post-modernism, feminism, post-structuralism, and continental philosophy. For a rare attempt to assess the salience of some of these currents for social theory *vis-à-vis* that offered by science and technology studies see Ward (forthcoming).

3 For reasons interesting in themselves, developments in STS have (thus far) almost always taken place outside mainstream sociology and social theory.

4 Lipset, in his presidential frontispiece to the program for the 1993 ASA meetings notes "the expansion of political democracy, first to southern Europe, then to Latin America, Eastern Europe and the Soviet Union, and most recently to much of Africa, including South Africa."

5 For a comprehensive critical assessment of the coherence of Marxist theories of the state and of Marxist theorizing in general, see Van den Berg (1988).

6 Clearly, much more can be said about the various ways in which "the crisis" in social theory can be formulated and about the ways in which it manifests itself. For example, a recurrent theme is that with the increasing globalization of social and cultural phenomena, it no longer makes sense to understand societies as unitary phenomena. Technology plays a major part in this globalization, even to the extent of its implication as a major factor in the events of 1989. See, for example, Deudney and Ikenberry (1991).

7 A point discovered, for example, in dialogues between Marxists and Christians.

8 Perhaps some unexplicated assumption that such societies are "underdeveloped" is at work here.

9 For an interesting series of attempts to address these questions historically, see the contributions to Halliday and Janowitz (1992).

10 However, by contrast with the abstract treatment of similar issues in the (much maligned) arguments of "post-modernism," most contributions to STS are notable for their commitment to careful detailed empirical investigation. Even though they remain theoretically skeptical about empiricism, contributors to STS acknowledge the power of persuasion through empirical demonstration. The use of detailed case studies is also one of the best ways of rigorously assessing some complicated theoretical arguments.

11 One could equally well use the phrase "science and technology." For purposes of clarity, this discussion will concentrate on "technology."

12 It would be wrong to infer a monolithic or even very consistent position within STS on the issues discussed here. Just where some of the most interesting divergences occur, we see a split along the lines of the likely contribution to social theory. Two such splits: (1) between pro-humanist sociologists of science like Collins, for whom the distinction between humans and non-humans is not just given but one which – in line with the Winchean inspired critique of positivism in social sciences – requires both quintessentially distinct (= non-natural scientific) methodology and a moral defence (Callon and Latour 1992; Harry M. Collins 1990; Collins and Yearley 1992; Restivo 1992; Woolgar 1992); (2) between those who view STS as primarily action–political rather than epistemological–analytic.

13 Much of the following argument, taken from Latour (1991a) subsequently appears in Latour (1993).

14 Latour notes Habermas' ([1985] 1987; 1989) arguments in this regard although Winch (1958) is also a familiar source for debates about positivism in the 1960s and 1970s.

15 For a discussion of ways in which actor-network theory "goes beyond" social constructivism see, for example, Akrich (1992a; 1992b).

16 It should be clear from the discussion so far that the prime interest of this version of STS in technology is as an analytic entity, not for its emancipatory potential. However, although the interest in technology's alternative forms of society is not a utopian claim about the potential benefits for society of life enhancing technologies (the alternative society), the appeals for this way of looking at technology do include appeals to its emancipatory potential, as we discuss below.

17 For a critique of the essentialist currents in much feminist and constructivist social analyses of technology see Grint and Woolgar (1995).

18 This is, importantly, as much an inquiry into why we are so generous in attributing capacity for intention and so on to humans, as it is a complaint about how mean we are in withholding similar attribution from non-humans. See, for example, Woolgar (1991; 1994).

19 This account is taken from a more sustained attempt to understand the events of the Luddite rebellion from a variety of perspectives in the social analysis of technology, see Grint and Woolgar (forthcoming).

20 In line with the general point about the contingency of interpretation of technical attributes, there is some ambiguity about which precise aspects of gig mill

usage were prohibited by these earlier legal statutes. Randall (1991: 120) discusses how the Luddite clothiers pressed their own retrospective interpretations.

21 For example, despite its efforts to transcend the dualism between social and technical, this detailed description of actor networks still seems to require a type of residual or textually embedded technicism. Thus, for example, the persuasiveness of the argument that a key turning point in the affair was the manufacturers' recruitment of the state and the army, depends on the textually adequate rendering of the (actual inherent) capacity of the army, even though it is also axiomatic to actor-network theory that no entity possesses (actual inherent) capacities, independent of their configuration within a network. Similarly, there is some ambiguity about the apparent "newness" of the machinery described in this account. It was suggested that the arrival of "new" machinery provoked fears about the potential disruption of established networks, but the account is unclear about whether and how the perception of its "newness" arose from the machines' enrollment in changing networks. For a fuller discussion of the specific weaknesses of this attempt to provide an actor-network analysis of Luddism see Grint and Woolgar (forthcoming).

22 Thus we find comments like "it is sometimes hard to know when Latour is being entirely serious" (Collins and Yearley 1992: n. 15).

23 It has been pointed out by Brown and Lee (1993) and by Shapiro (1993) that many of the appeals on behalf of actor-network theory are couched in quasi-emancipatory terms, where the subjects deserving of empowerment are those entities which traditional social theory has (thus far) tended merely to treat as things. Cf. Woolgar (1991: 90): "Let's hear it for machines, for a change!"

24 See, for example, Ashmore (1993), Ashmore et al. (1994) and Woolgar (1994).

25 Law (1991b) laments the reciprocal accusations of myopia between STS and social theory, but then baldly accuses social theory of committing a fundamental "mistake" in adopting the distinction between humans and non-humans. Latour (1991a: 17) says that this mistake is "paralysing all efforts at understanding and modifying our world," no less. Surely we would expect proponents of STS to be far more sophisticated about the contingency of truth and error production than to portray breaking down the human–non-human divide as a crusade against error – a way of helping root out sources of inconsistency or of deviation from the true path toward ultimately correct (error-free) social theory?

26 In the original: "All civilisations overestimate the objectivity of their own thought" (Lévi-Strauss 1966).

27 Compare, for example, the initial reactions to other movements in sociology such as ethnomethodology or reflexivity.

14

Theory Then/Theory Now
(or, "The Sociology is about to Begin, Said the Man with the Loudspeaker")

Alan Sica

The epigraph

In proportion as men know more and think more, they look less at individuals and more at classes. They therefore make better theories and worse poems. They give us vague phrases instead of images, and personified qualities instead of men.

Macaulay's Essay on Milton (1825)

The prefatory note

My assignment in this chapter is to assess social theory's current situation and give some thought to likely developments. There being a well-known formula for pronouncements of this kind, herewith a bald forewarning of its constituents: (1) *theory*: rhetorical, narratological retrospection; (2) *method*: hermeneutic reappropriation; (3) *data*: topical articles and books by Parsons, Merton, and others between 1935 and the mid-1960s, with particular emphasis on the 1940s and early 1950s; other chapters of this book; manuscripts submitted to *Sociological Theory* between June, 1989 and December, 1994, when I edited the journal. (4) Findings: TBA.

The tale

I

When Eliot sent Pound his draft of *The Waste Land* in 1921, it was divided into two sections, each called "He do the police in different voices," I and II. These subheads were later eliminated, perhaps at the instigation of Pound, who reworked the poem from top to bottom (Eliot 1971: 10). Even allowing for Pound's legendary sense for the *bon mot*, this particular aesthetic judgment now seems almost a mistake given the history of the poem – its canonical role in "modernism" – and the trajectory of culture and language since it appeared. There is a clangy ever-newness to Eliot's initial version that is lost in the emendation, a fun-with-words quality too easily surrendered to the staid, Tennysonian title immortalized (until lately!) in American literature textbooks. Modernist literary prose – via Stein, Woolf, Musil, Joyce, Eliot, Ford, Dos Passos, and all the rest – was rapidly overturning Henry James's and Hardy's word-worlds, and putting something in its place that had as much to do with theories of the self and self-expression as with pure story-telling. Gertrude Stein's oddball brilliance in William James' psychology courses at Harvard is the best known marker for this sort of link (Mellow 1974: 30–4).

Just when Eliot (as well as Joyce) gave the world their masterpieces, Parsons was about twenty years old, and most likely oblivious to the literary avant-garde, immersed as he was in the serious study of chemistry, biology, and institutional economics at Amherst, and enough involved in genteel political commentary to inaugurate his FBI file soon thereafter (Camic in Parsons 1991: vii–xvii). Though students of Parsons claim he cared for the arts – by one personal account, paying them to attend plays in Boston and to write reports for him about what they learned regarding "expressive symbolization" – his awareness of aesthetics as displayed in language seems never to have developed very far, and after he began dictating his "writings," it permanently atrophied. For the young Parsons, "aesthetics" was apparently something Kant thematized while destroying idiomatic German – thereby giving license to the young neo-Kantian to wreak similar havoc on English as his theory "matured." And since with carefully tuned aesthetic conscious-ness often comes wit, for which Parsons' prose was not known, it is surpris-ing to find a public utterance in which he lets out not only a laugh, but a self-deprecating moment of apperception that nearly brings humane charm to an otherwise brittle analysis.

As with all intellectual chronicles that bear on Parsons – *vide* the scrupulously complete auto-bibliographies attached to most of his books since 1949 – there is to this tale some belabored background. Building on the nascent authority accorded him by *The Structure of Social Action*, Parsons published a set of articles (Parsons 1938; 1945; 1948; 1950; 1959), in which he repeatedly tried to redefine theory to suit himself and his confederates, in obvious opposition to a number of competitors and detractors – most of whom, surprisingly enough, are little known today (for example, Howard P. Becker, Robert Lynd, Robert MacIver, Pitirim Sorokin), while Parsons still rides high. One of these papers was prompted by a talk at the December, 1947 American Sociological Society annual meeting (Parsons 1948), where Parsons delivered "The position of sociological theory" as required by his role as chair of the association's theory section (followed by pointed rebuttal from Robert K. Merton). He was forty-five and on the verge of exploding the boundaries of American social theory, and of graceful prose, with *The Social System*, four years later. (Being myself also forty-five and the chair-elect of the ASA theory section, it is unfortunately impossible not to make some comparisons between that era and our own, strictly, of course, "at the analytic level," as Parsons was fond of saying.) Two years later, at the 1949 meeting, and this time as President of the society, he loosened his tie a bit by colloquializing his earlier talk in "The prospects of sociological theory" (Parsons 1950). The unlikely moment of Parsonsian hilarity occurred when he broke with his standard rhetoric of scientific astringency, and told this mundane story:

> Some fifteen years ago two young Americans, who, since they were my own children, I knew quite intimately, and who were aged approximately five and three respectively at the time, developed a little game of yelling at the top of their voices: "The sociology is about to begin said the man with the loud speaker." However right they may have been about their father's professional achievements up to that time, as delivering a judgment of the state of the field as a whole I think they were a bit on the conservative side. (Parsons 1950: 3)

And he ended this hortatory occasion by recalling this scene once more: "'The sociology,' as my children called it, is not *about* to begin. It has been gathering force for a generation and is now really under way" (p. 16). Parsons' signature optimism and faith in scientifically derived theory, and theoretically guided science, is as robust on this ceremonial occasion all those years ago, as it continued to be until his death in 1979.

The general sameness of *Standpunkt* that obtained in 1947 and 1949, between Parsons and those skeptical colleagues to whom he pitched the need for theory, and the continuing tension between ideas and fact-gathering that holds today, cannot be missed. He offered to abet "science," announcing and insisting that "general theory" will make for better research practice and result, and will legitimate the social sciences among their elders and betters in the academy. (His little-known 1939 article on Comte, published in the celebrated Berlin/Vienna outlet, *Journal of Unified Science*, is pertinent in this regard.) And yet overall, what a world removed we are today, nearly five decades after he spoke to his small New York audience: American Sociological Society (ASS) membership numbered 1,370 (even after an unprecedented increase of several hundred from the previous year), the society's annual income totaled $19,741, disbursements were $16,029, and the annual meeting cost $483 (sic) (*ASR*, 13(2) [April 1948], 207, 209). A comparison with current figures – with a ten-fold increase in membership, a 500-fold enlargement in annual meeting costs, and a total budget that is 226 times that of 1947 – is instructive, though probably at some "pre-theoretical" level (*Footnotes*, 22(6), summer 1994, 11; figures in unadjusted dollars).

If there was a single overwhelming difference between his posture, rhetoric, and conceptual didactics, and our own post-modern, hesitant cogitations, it lies in his favorite words, "fruitful" and "hope." Naturally, with the war won, everyone deserved some relieved cheeriness, not least Parsons himself, considering his political and intellectual labors surrounding Nazism (see Gerhardt 1993: 1–78). But there's more to it than that, particularly in view of the canny retort by 36-year-old Robert Merton, published in 1948 along with Parsons' address. This exceedingly polite, even friendly, argument between student and teacher, then peer with peer, persisted for another fifteen years, so that Parsons, in the late 1950s, laughingly lets us in on the state of the family squabble by way of a footnote to the first page of another set-piece in the series: "I find it very gratifying that Professor Merton, in his most recent statement, seems to have gone rather farther than before in recognizing the probable *fruitfulness* of at least a few sociologists' giving serious attention to the general-theory level" (Parsons 1959: 3, n. 1; emphasis added). The charming datedness of this kind of remark is revealed, for example, in the equivocal apostrophe following "sociologists," which today would probably be dropped by copyeditors, even if thought to be inserted by writers in the first place, since the possessive case *seems*, at first glance, ambiguous and unnecessary. A sentiment of this kind – gentlepersonly disagreement among colleagues sharing warm mutual admiration, all within the context of a burgeoningly "fruitful" science – produces in today's reader a sensation similar to passing, in the opposing traffic, a perfectly restored '57 Cadillac, when US cars were spectacularly comforting, capacious, and unapprehensively bullish on the future. Not only is nostalgic peace attached to writings of this kind – particularly for those many of us who were small children in the back seat of those wombish cars, when parents up front seemed permanently attached to each other, and gasoline cost twenty-five cents per gallon – but a happy certainty that sociology and its theories had come of age, was headed in the right direction, and had gained the ears of government and the public it hoped to serve.

The story I want to tell this half-century after Parsons bemused his ASS audience concerns scientific aspirations, the magic of language, cultural apparatus, and the empirical conditions that gave rise to the sociological *Weltanschauung* from that earlier day compared with what we face in this ass-end of a century – our own unjubilant *fin de siècle*. And if Gadamer, following and elaborating Heidegger, is right in saying that we do not so much speak language, as language speaks us (Gadamer 1975: 397–414) – if the most significant human-ness revolves more around its reality-crushing use of talk and writing than any of its other salient features – then listening carefully to earlier theorists' special way of talking to each other and about the world becomes not only worthwhile, but a foremost theoretical concern.

II

To warm up for this foray into hermeneutic recovery, consider the kind of sentiments Max and Marianne Weber heard in St Louis as participants in the "Universal Exposition of 1904," as voiced by David K. Francis, the mastermind and chief organizer/financier behind that stupendous operation:

> The Universal Exposition of 1904 was conceived in a sense of obligation on the part of the people of the Louisiana Purchase Territory to give expression of their gratitude for the innumerable blessings that have flowed from a century of membership in the American Union, to manifest their appreciation of the manifold benefits of living in a land, the climate and soil and resources of which are unsurpassed, and of having their lots cast in an age when liberty and enlightenment are established on foundations broad and deep, and are the heritage of all who worthily strive. To rise to the full measure of such a sentiment required an undertaking of comprehensive proportions and the participation of all races and of every clime. Six years of preparation preceded the opening of the gates . . . The magnitude of the enterprise was never lost sight of by its promoters. The mammoth proportions, constantly increasing,

never for a moment shook the confidence, weakened the energies or diverted from their well defined purposes those who had been entrusted with the responsibility and the work ... By bringing together hitherto remote and unacquainted peoples, and thereby promoting mutual respect, it was an important step towards establishing that universal peace for which all right-minded people are striving.

   The Exposition of 1904 holds a place in history more conspicuous than its projectors anticipated. For the opening decade of this century it stands as a marker of the accomplishments and progress of man. So thoroughly did it represent the world's civilization that if all man's other works were by some unspeakable catastrophe blotted out, the records established at this Exposition by the assembled nations would afford the necessary standard for the rebuilding of our entire civilization (Francis 1913: v–vi).

Only one (fairly frivolous) lawsuit arose from the dozen years of preparation and recovery that the Exposition entailed, and this in the context of a $4.6m loan, quickly repaid, from Congress (out of the $11.2m needed), with 100,000 delegates and 19.7 million visitors attending, and "not a single case of sunstroke" (Francis 1993: 629). Francis' joyful remembrance of humankind's celebration at the Exposition, and his suggestion that the social world could be recreated from its very blueprints even if some "unspeakable catastrophe" erased humanity's earthly presence, has to be wondered at, given the events of August, 1914, and the load of irony thereby heaped on felicitous notions of the sort Francis apparently held. And, of course, with little imagination, one could rewrite Francis' prefatory remarks in keeping with today's point of view. (It goes without saying that labor costs, zoning ordinances, and liability insurance would make any such undertaking impossible, and that TV would reduce the potential audience probably by 90 percent.) The noble sentiments would evaporate, the optimism dimmed, and the hearty self-congratulations omitted entirely. It might say: "We staged a massive/awesome PR event, lost many millions, were sued by dozens of the aggrieved, and got bad notices in the press for neglecting any number of constituencies who might have liked representation but could not afford the pavilion construction costs, and needed a government subsidy. If we had it to do over again, we wouldn't."

   Or consider these opening words from the anthropologist and theorist, Elsie Clews Parsons, to her *Social Freedom* monograph, published two years after Francis' Rotarian bombast: "The modern Chinaman, however feminist he may be, cannot avoid referring to darkness or cold or the evil side of the world by the same word he uses for woman – all for *yin*" (Elsie Parsons 1915: 1). What does she mean by the peculiar clause "however feminist he may be"? Did feminism exist in China in 1915? Was she tossing a stinging sarcasm in the direction of Chinese phallocentrism? Did her notion of "feminism" entail what ours does? What does "ours" entail? Why in Chinese was the feminine "yin" correlated with evil and darkness to begin with? Were Chinese women – by virtue of structural location or linguistic machination – more wily and dangerous than Ango-Saxon women, in that the English "woman" shares no etymological ancestry with "evil"? Did Elsie Parsons think for a minute, while writing this uncharacteristic book some eighty years ago, that her opening line would later perplex an interested audience, that her scholarly and human intention could possibly be misconstrued or become a hermeneutic puzzle? If language truly does speak to us more than we it, what is language saying to us now in the frail, old voice of Elsie Parsons?

This long way round the barn falls under the rubric of "contextualization," making up one small part of a complete hermeneutics as recommended and practiced by the classical (Schleiermacher, Dilthey) and contemporary (Hirsch, Gadamer, Ricoeur) exemplars of that craft (see Shapiro and Sica 1984; Sica 1981). Naturally, a satisfying hermeneutic assessment of the materials in question would occupy the better part of a monograph (see, for example, Heath [1970], which analyzes *two* years in the literary relationship between Wordsworth and Coleridge). Without the luxury of such space at my disposal, I will compare, in compressed form, the theoretical climate which seemed to be operating in the 1930s and 1940s with today's orientations as revealed in other chapters in this book, along with similar materials that lie beyond its pages. That this portrait will be instructed more by Cézanne's aesthetic than Courbet's may not, perhaps, eliminate its usefulness altogether.

III

At sixty-three, the one-time engineer, missionary, theologian, and psychologist, Ellsworth Faris (Faris 1970: 30–5, 158), opened "The promise of sociology" (his December, 1937, Presidential Address to the ASS) by mulling over sociology's perennial inferiority complex *vis-à-vis* physics, on the grounds of being a less precise science. But in making this point he did not invoke Einstein or Heisenberg, but rather [Albert Abraham] "Michelson," by quoting a sonnet in his honor by one "Lewis," which begins: "He gathered up the iris from the plunging planet's rim / With Bright precision of fingers that Ariel envieth him" (Faris 1938: 1). Not only was this poor poetry, even in 1937, but it suggests what Parsons was up against that same year when he published *The Structure of Social Action (SSA)* and tried to bring social theory into the conceptual/language orbit of the natural sciences, neo-Kantianism, economics, and very decidedly away from the sylphic vectors swirling about in Faris' speech. While Parsons wrote of theory as the road to scientific truth, Faris' desires for the discipline were much closer to the social uplift that had inspired David Francis' remarks in 1913, and far removed from Parsons' push for a quasi-Weberian "objectivity" – that chimerical aloofness from the quotidian and its disturbing passions.

Consider, for instance, Faris' concluding paragraphs alongside the theoretical asperity Parsons was beginning to utilize:

> Some years before the organization of the society I went up to the university as a student of theology. My teachers were presenting theology as founded on philosophy and, after a year, I transferred to the department of philosophy, hoping to get at the heart of the matter. The philosophy lectures, at that time, were insisting on the importance of a foundation in psychology and after a year I went over into that department, seeking the basis and a sure foundation. In psychology, in those days, the emphasis was on a strong physiological and neurological foundation, and eventually I put on a white coat and enrolled in the medical school and began to dissect the brains of rats and men. But the foundation there recommended was physiological chemistry, and so I gave up the merry-go-round, coming to the conclusion that the metaphor was ill chosen; that the sciences are not founded on each other, and that there is none that is fundamental or basic. It is no longer helpful to erect a hierarchy of the sciences. (Faris 1938: 11–12)

The easy humanness of this parable – which probably reminded many in his audience of their own sophomoric quests for ultimate truths ca. 1900 – sits very awkwardly beside the Parsons article that follows Faris' in the same issue of *ASR*, wherein, at 35, he scales the ramparts of survey research (at Chicago), demanding a suitably dignified role for theorizing (Parsons 1938). Once again, we turn to Faris' parting shot:

> If in the past sociology was a daughter in her mother's house, today she is mistress in her own . . . Our age imagines no utopia nor does it look for a millennium. The quest for certainty [as in his teacher, Dewey?] has been succeeded by a desire for a greater measure of security . . . we can define our proximate goals and we can enjoy the prospect of separate triumphs of the human reason . . . The triumphs of the age of physical science give us confidence in the power of the human reason. The forces of human nature may be used and controlled to satisfy and increase the wants of man. Ours is a profession of the highest dignity. There is every reason to hope that by our efforts human welfare may be advanced. (Faris 1938: 12)

Presidential speeches at such occasions typically run to the inspirational, perhaps especially during the 1930s when good news was hard to come by, though noticeably less today, when the individual scholar's research is embellished before the attending mass of colleagues. But despite the intrinsic limits to such performances, does it not seem unsettling that virtually every notion Faris expressed in his last lines has turned out to be quite wrong some sixty years later – or worse, silly and childish? His inspirational vocabulary – the power of reason, the triumphs of science, the control of nature, the great dignity of sociology, the chance to hope for societal improvement based on sociology's "discoveries" – could be read aloud today as its own parody. And the ironic smirk that attaches itself to recognition of intellectual and political failure – since perfected as art in Adorno's *Minima Moralia* or Karl Kraus' *In These Great Times* – seems to humble Faris's noble hopes like yellowed photographs taken of adolescent lovers when seen, afresh, through the bleary eyes of middle age.

IV

Some time ago Alexander observed, in his most quoted line, that "If sociology could speak it would say 'I am tired'" (Alexander 1982: xiii). More to the point today, if sociology speaks, who, we must ask, is still listening – aside from sociologists? The messianic passion that moves unconcealed and uninhibited throughout Faris' address was banished from polite theoretical discourse with Parsons and Merton. In fact, Sorokin (their colleague and teacher respectively) lost his hold on the sociological fraternity in large part precisely because of his oracular statements concerning the place of theory and other theorists in his firmament. The measured tones of scientific prose and analysis, particularly of the lifeless sort Parsons perfected, fit nicely into the bland language-world of "organization man," and made heated prose (of Lynd, Mills, and other "engaged" writers) appear ridiculous, even juvenile, in its blunt moralizing. No social "scientist" interested in high academic position during the 1950s wanted to be taken for another Vance Packard (despite the wide public appeal of his work) if they might be mistaken instead for a "rocket scientist" – that enduring cliche signifying rarefied intellectual mastery.

Put another way, theory – most particularly, Parsons' – can be viewed, in its earlier, more imperialistic and "hopeful" period (say, between 1930 and 1960), as the product and prisoner of an affectless, de-magicalized (*entzaubert*) prose style which transmitted its message through a host of disembodied concepts, while striding briskly away from the very rhetoric that had promoted its birth at the turn of the century. (Parsons' father and mother were vocal proponents of this peculiarly American religio-political inspirational language, and were similar in age and disposition to Faris, whose stance Parsons was working to displace in the late 1930s.) Although dismantling Parsons' verbiage has been a parlor game among humanists since the 1950s, serious analysis of his language-making *as itself principally a theoretical enterprise* has not progressed very far, with a few exceptions (for example, Martel 1971, whose title outdistances the actual analysis, or Lanham 1974, which rehashes and elaborates Mills' critique). It is this project that I want momentarily to pursue for the larger purpose of assaying theory's current position in general.

When Parsons spoke before the Society for Social Research in 1937, he came to them "with due humility," not wanting to appear "presumptuous." These are terms and tones he seldom later used, especially as he developed into what Camic calls a "cosmopolitan local" (embellishing Merton's famous distinction), that is, one who generalizes the significance of the privately meaningful into global proportions – not at all unlike Parsons' *bête noire*, Hegel. Parsons then alluded to a Faris-like "fundamental unity of outlook and purpose which I think almost all of us feel should actuate the workers in a field of science." He urged everyone "to attempt seriously, objectively, and respectfully to learn from each other's work, thought and experience . . . If the *trouble* [is] taken to get to the bottom of other people's problems, there will turn out to be far more unity on fundamentals than appears at first sight" (Parsons 1938: 13; emphasis his unless noted otherwise). Many of Parsons' later pre-theoretical themes are here: the need for unity, if not unanimity among scientific laborers, happy reciprocity between theory and research, and a search for fundamental principles around which to build a robust discipline.

These organizing principles (or "domain assumptions," as Gouldner named them) and the terms and phrases he carefully selected to convey them throughout his career, were first stated for broader public consumption in "The place of ultimate values in sociological theory" (1935), an ambitious advertisement for *SSA*, and one which bristles with Parsons' own ultimate values – a fact of which he was probably only partly aware (see Camic's indispensable introduction to Parsons 1991 for necessary details). As his former teaching assistant, Leon Mayhew, expressed it while introducing an important Parsons anthology, "What we have here is a theory of social order that clearly stresses the importance of deeply rooted motivation to conformity with social norms"

(Parsons 1982: 14). Yet from the other side entirely, he observes: "That human beings can be socialized seems to strike Parsons as not far short of miraculous" (p. 16). This gives in short compass the two principal antinomic features of Parsons' theoretical/moral imagination, the one stipulating that social order is normatively constituted by reasonably willing societal members, the other worrying that "chaos" and "pessimism" lurk by the unprotected door; namely:

> In so far, however, as individuals share a *common* system of ultimate ends, this system would, among other things, define what they all held their relations ought to be, would lay down norms determining these relations and limits on the use of others as means, on the acquisition and use of power in general. In so far, then as action is determined by ultimate ends, the existence of a *system* of such ends common to the members of the community seems to be the only alternative to a state of chaos – a necessary factor in social stability. (Parsons 1982: 87–8)

Without pushing it too far, one might note that Parsons, the youngest of five children, might well be expected to harbor such wishful notions sheerly on the basis of birth-order and resulting family dynamics (see, for example, Ernst 1983; Toman 1993), even prior to a close examination of Parsons' early life – which, without an extant detailed biography, is not yet feasible in any case. How else can one comprehend a statement like this coming from a cosmopolitan family man in his mid-thirties who had lived through the First World War, the dissipated, violent 1920s (here and in Europe), and the Depression?: "Partly a priori and partly empirical considerations lead to the view that these ultimate ends do not occur in random fashion, but that both in the case of the individual and of the social group they must be thought of as to a significant degree integrated into a single harmonious *system*" (p. 91). And most astonishing of all, given the daily news we receive from city streets and boardrooms (as it were) in the US and elsewhere:

> it may be argued in general and abstract terms that this random variation of systems of ends would be incompatible with the most elementary form of social order. For there would be no guaranty that any large proportion of such systems would include a recognition of other people's ends as valuable in themselves, and there would thus be no necessary limitation on the means that some, at least, would employ to gain their own ends at the expense of others. The relations of individuals then would tend to be resolved into a struggle for power – for the means for each to realize his own ends. This would be, in the absence of constraining factors, a war of all against all – Hobbes's state of nature. (p. 87)

At one level at least, this dread image of barbarism – an essential ingredient in Parsons' theoretical imagery – and the correlated call for normative unity and the civility it fosters, is the plea of the smallest child in a large, multivalent family for harmonious relations, and as such, shares the pathos, romanticism, and fantastic quality that makes children's pronouncements along these lines both endearing and sorrowful to their elders.

Martel's "official" analysis of Parsons' ideas (the book in which it appears being dedicated to Parsons) supplements this view by wisely contrasting Weber's with Parsons' *Weltanschauungen*:

> Weber had feared that rationalization could pervade the entire modern social fabric and threaten all spontaneous human relations with destruction. Instead, Parsons argued that rationality as a principle has limits just as kinship values have, and he posited that kinship and personal relations still will be maintained, cherished, and protected in the private sphere . . . In extreme contrast to cultural relativism, Parsons believed in the cultural unity of man. (Martel 1979: 620)

Here Parsons clearly presages Lasch's "conservative" portrait of the family as "haven in a heartless world." Seen from still another vantage point, Parsons' sentiments originate in Protestant, communitarian, social gospelism, even if fitted in neo-Kantian academic regalia. Simple substitution of sacred for key secular terms makes this almost too obvious to warrant comment. Mayhew documents this repeatedly: "In candor I must concede that Parsons's [Harvard 1960s] lectures on American society often seemed to present views somewhat akin to religious conviction," neatly bound up with "Parsons's faith [sic], evident from the beginning of his career, that modernity unleashes forces of creativity . . . without moving us down an inexorable spiral toward either anarchy or totalitarian control" (Parsons 1982: 55, 41). After sixty-two pages of analysis, Mayhew ends an astute portrait of his former teacher with this remarkable claim: "In Parsons's own technical terms, acceptance of his vision of contemporary society is ultimately a matter of whether one accepts his value commitments – his moral leadership [!] – or whether one believes that there are no interpretations of our obligations to modern society that will allow us to survive with our values intact" (p. 62). Furthermore, a circumspect reading of Parsons' on "Christianity" illustrates, despite his half-hearted attempts at concealment, how closely tied to its ultimate *societal* values he remained, particularly as he aged (Parsons 1968). There is, then, in Parsons' most important theorizing an irreducible core of Christian utopianism and fear of Hobbesian disorder that, simultaneously, makes it a palliative for the anxious, and a bitter laughing-stock for the world-weary.

During the mid-1930s, while the country languished in Depression, Parsons struggled to legitimate his presence at Harvard by writing a great deal, composing his first and most lasting book, *The Structure of Social Action*, apparently between early 1934 and late 1935 (Camic in Parsons 1991: lxv [Merton recalls in a letter to me that Parsons taught Sociology 21, "Sociological Theories of Hobhouse, Durkheim, Simmel, Tönnies, Max Weber," already in 1932, clearly the background to his book]). On the penultimate page of this *tour de force*, Parsons registers a level of passion that more resembles Marcuse, Ellul, or Roszak than the resolute neutrality of the natural scientist or the lofty remove of his Heidelberg mentor, Jaspers, both of whom Parsons strove to emulate in different ways. It is in this unguarded moment – when "that good old term 'passion'" is heard, "something to which we succomb, in the presence of which we feel helplessly carried along by forces beyond control" (Parsons 1937: 584, n. 5) – that he most unambiguously reveals himself and the motor of his nonstop theorizing:

There has been of late a strong current of pessimism in the thought of students of the social sciences, especially those who call themselves sociologists. We are told that there are as many systems of sociological theory as there are sociologists, that there is no common basis, that all is arbitrary and subjective. To the present writer this current of sentiment has two equally unfortunate implications. On the one hand, it encourages the view that the only sound work in the social field is detailed factual study, without benefit of theory. On the other hand, for those who refuse to be satisfied with this, it encourages a dangerous irrationalism which lets go of scientific standards altogether. We are told sociology is an art, that what is valuable in it is to be measured by the standards of intuition and inspiration, that it is not subject to the canons of rigorous logic and empirical verification. It is to be hoped that this study may contribute to the combating of both these dangerous tendencies. (Parsons 1937: 774)

In order to understand the full weight such a statement had for Parsons, one must consider not only, as mentioned earlier, his persistent deafness to aesthetic meaning, which he pits here against science in a very un-Whiteheadian manner; but, even more importantly, his loaded use of "dangerous" "irrationalism." Earlier in the book he attacked this bogy while protecting Weber:

the "irrationality" of human action may be attributed to freedom of the will – an argument of good Kantian origin . . . This Weber answers [with] a very interesting argument. If this were true, he says, we should expect the sense of freedom to be associated primarily with "irrational" actions, those involving emotional outbreaks and the like. On the contrary, however, the reverse is much more nearly true. It is when we act most rationally that we feel most free . . . There can be no doubt about the correctness of Weber's point and its significance is far-reaching. (Parsons 1937: 584)

There is little point in chastizing Parsons for voicing a philosophical anthropology that now sounds as outdated as Tommy Dorsey's dance music. That his attachment to "good Kantian origins" was profound cannot be doubted, particularly when one considers his education at Amherst, where he studied Kant in depth, and then again under Jaspers' tutelage several years later (Camic in Parsons 1991: xiv, xx); he fixed quite naturally on the Kantian strain in Weber, while repudiating the Hegelian moves of Marx. But how ludicrous it seems now – imagine "selling" this notion to contemporary youth – to hold, *as if it were self-evidently true*, that "it is when we act most rationally that we feel most free," that calculated action promises freedom, but "emotional outbreaks and the like" offer humiliating bondage. If this were even slightly accurate, how could one begin to analyze the "post-modern" world? How would advertising and consumerist frenzy work, or the culture industry which supports it? Sadder still, how could one begin to understand nationalist and ethnic barbarity that now springs up worldwide like the immortal Hydra? It is when expressing these sorts of wishes, disguised to be sure as "objective/analytical theorizing," the inevitable "convergence" of all past thought, that Parsons followed his Protestant, ministering heart into a zone of axiology and ethical reflection for which there is flimsy sociological grounding. Perhaps his passion carried him away.

Related observations have been made before, if with a different critical vocabulary. Merton's early responses to Parsons (1945; 1948) made a strong case against those Kantian ambitions for universal theoretical coverage that obsessed the young Parsons: "We cannot expect any individual to create an architectonic system of theory which provides a complete *vade mecum* to the solution of sociological problems. Science, even sociological science, just isn't that simple" (Merton 1948: 165). "Architectonic" is synonymous with Kant-scale theoretical inclusiveness, a term Merton invariably used disparagingly, even as Parsons thrived "under its sign," as literary critics might put it. (In fact, the word itself did not appear in English-language metaphysics until 1801 [*OED*], following its redefinition by Kant in the first *Kritik* [Kant 1929: 653–5].) My point harmonizes with Merton's, but moves in a somewhat different direction – as one might expect, given the many years that separate our two responses. His dialectical reaction to Parsons' global scope (aside from writing as lucidly as his teacher did not – Merton's Schiller to

Parsons' Kant?) says more about the proper, most "fruitful" road to credible
theorizing than about its fundamental purpose or plausibility. My arguments
are more basic, and as much inspired by some of Merton's senior colleagues
as by his own elegant adjustments to Parsons' insistent agenda.

V

The May, 1945 *AJS* celebrated its first fifty years: "the editors thought it
fitting to devote the present anniversary issue to an analysis and evaluation
of the developments during the past half-century in important areas of sociological interest" (*AJS*, 50(6), 421). In addition to Merton's reflections
on theory, articles were solicited from Faris, Willard Waller and Mirra
Komarovsky, Burgess, Wirth, Ross, Lundberg, Kimball Young, Znaniecki,
L. L. Bernard, and others. Some of these pieces deserve careful rereading now
that *AJS* has published its 100th volume, but it's symptomatic of our time
that they will very likely not receive the kind of scrutiny which, for instance,
Small's early reports were given by the 50th anniversary party. Their over-
riding tone was of intelligently modulated optimism, even pride, in the
discipline's achievements to date. All of the authors, even the epistemologically
subtle Znaniecki, subscribed to a philosophy of science that made sociological truths *theoretically* attainable, and, more tellingly, morally incumbent
upon its practitioners to discover and then publicize. In short, they believed
their field had a "product" of knowledge that was worth society's investment,
because its "laws," when named, would improve the social order at any
juncture of concern. In this belief, at least, though often with markedly less
optimism than that of the minister's son from Colorado Springs, they were
at one. And their analytical language – from the rough handling of Lundberg's
scientism to the nuances of Merton's careful theory-prolegomenon – reflects
this confidence.

If it is indeed true that Parsons believed in the desirability of normative
unity across a multivalent social order, and if he further thought that
socialization, "properly" carried out, would produce, in the great majority of
cases, comfortable conformity to a set of values that seemed (*vide* Mayhew)
increasingly to mirror those evident in Cambridge, Massachusetts, then his
project of the early 1930s was absurd from the start, and became progressively more so as anomia slid into that warm-hearthed home wherein normative order once was thought to reside. He has often been characterized as a
lovely person with generous regard for his students and colleagues, all of

which is revealed in his utopian scheming (particularly in his final ontology, "A paradigm of the human condition" [Parsons 1978: 352–433]). This partly explains the uncritical loyalty he enjoyed among many sociologists in the 1950s and 1960s: he told a story of eventual salvation from societal calamity and individual despair, and, unlike the fascist or Stalinist line, it did not require that anyone die in the process.

Contemplating Parsons remains a useful way to answer the question before us: What is theory now, and tomorrow? Whereas he asked mockingly, when young and in need of theoretical space, who still reads Spencer, we can ask (as have many since he died), who now reads Parsons? For just as he rediscovered Spencer's merits late in life and was beginning to believe "that there is a precise analogy between the social process of institutionalization and the biological process of natural selection" (Parsons 1982: viii), we might once again turn to his language-world in order to see how righteous theorizing was constructed before the advent of the post-modern, deconstructive onslaught upon certitude that has disheartened social thought in the years since his death. (One might even reflect on how Parsons might have dealt theoretically with our Age of Heroic Greed, which began to take hold in 1980, just as he'd permanently stopped writing, and by its nature inexorably undermines his axiology.)

It is impractical for reasons of space, and impolite as well, to subject the other chapters in this book to dissection, amicable or otherwise, since (according to Gadamer) the hermeneutic interchange is necessarily dialogical; one voice cannot a helpful dialogue make – something Parsons never quite realized. Yet taken as a group, and representing many if not all current theoretical standpoints most often heard among leading practitioners of the craft, there are common distinctions between today's theory-speakers and those mentioned above – from Elsie Clews Parsons to Faris to the young Talcott Parsons and Merton and still others of the century's first half. This difference lies in the given theorist's posture *vis-à-vis* the world under inspection and the perceived reliability of theoretical language in laying bare its constitutive processes.

First of all, note that Parsons and a number of others during that period of theory-creation paid precious little attention to others' specific ideas. *Explication de texte* did not interest them very much, least of all Parsons after he turned forty or so. His self-referential and reverential texts are notoriously safe from too close an affinity with anyone else's, except for his closest allies'. Not so today's writers. Among the most noteworthy theorists, only Bourdieu is capable of writing on various topics with meager attention to the relevant work of his predecessors or contemporaries – and much of this mannerisn can be attributed to the French obsession with fashion and newness, especially in the realm of ideas, where patrimony and lineage is ritually disguised. For better or worse, most of the authors in this volume write with copious reference to their peers and predecessors. So when Alexander pointedly argues for the lasting importance of the classics, it is not a particularly hard case to sell *among theorists*, even if for most non-theorists scrupulous attention to "dead Germans" is viewed with pitying scorn. Whereas anyone with modest intelligence and training can compose a questionnaire and ask the populace how it "feels" about this or that, not everyone can read Weber, Simmel, or even Durkheim with thorough comprehension, so it's just as well that not everyone tries. That said, though, it has become a much more serious problem today for theorists on one side of the court, data analysts on the other, to find common ground than it seemed to be when Parsons spoke to such folk in 1937 (see Sica 1989). The scholarly cost of admission to theory debates has become prohibitively high for many potentially interested parties, just as debate about advanced methods has been left in relatively few hands. The basic culture of learning that was held in common by members of the ASS in 1938 has long since evaporated, and in its place nothing intellectually respectable or analytically useful has appeared, nor seems likely to. What debate there is turns around questions of technique on one side, hermeneutic dispute on the other, and the "world out there," to which Parsons and his peers turned with eager analytic eyes, whirls its way toward apparent societal entropy. It's worth recalling that very near the end of *SSA*, Parsons noted that "there is a further interesting parallel between Weber's process of rationalization and the second law of thermodynamics" (Parsons 1937: 752). But rather than dealing with the implications of this alarming realization in forthright terms, he takes refuge in the handy "fallacy of misplaced concreteness," and claims to have run out of space! He peered into the maelstrom and ran for home.

Some of today's theorists argue for a new sociological epistemology that acknowledges the sanctity, the "privileging," of social position, cultural heritage, or gendered ontology when box seats are allocated for the Truth Show in the Virtual Social Science Pavilion. Others claim that the postmodern has reorganized "the social" to such a determinate extent that the lexicon from pre-Derridean days now has strictly historical value. The concepts that continue to hold together, however delicately, introductory textbooks – family, stratification, self, norms, deviance, sex roles – are viewed by many in the avant garde as exhausted heuristics in dire need of replacement. Such words recall a social world that's since been converted to video-experience, and is remembered only in taped re-creations of imagined pasts. Consider, for example, the term around which Parsons built everything else: "socialization." What does this word mean today, when "homes" – what does *that* word mean, aside from Giddens' "storage container" for matériel? – cannot afford to exist, are emptied of socializing agents, and are "watched over"/monitored by television screens? Is ours the first society that expects its children to perform auto-socialization – perhaps as practice for the auto-eroticism which AIDS has urged on them and their "parents"?

Perhaps because the authors in this book have already played most of their Human Comedy Arcade tokens, the chapters are securely adult in direction and tone, and as such, speak with even less authority to video-culture than Parsons' friendly fantasies spoke to his world. As is common to the genre, some refer comfortingly to history, others to hypothetical, unlikely scenarios of events or intellectual development, and, as always, new words abound for well-recognized processes. Missing from all this is the self-confidence of theory 50 years ago, the certainty then entertained about the salutary relation among theorizing, social research, and the creation of an improved social sphere, however defined. The theory chorus, aping the socio-cultural world, has become exhaustingly querulous, and the close harmonies Parsons pleaded for unimaginable. Due both to multiculturalism's ideology of inextinguishable difference, and deconstruction's epistemological coup de grace to the apodictic, consensus – societal or theoretical – if pursued at all, is viewed as not only factually wrong, but morally evil. The slippery slope on which theorists now must pitch their tents has very little in common with the "strong empirical foundations" that *seemed* reasonably attainable to earlier generations. It is, alas, a good time to theorize – for those who are warmed by the uncertain and entropic.

Bibliography

Abbott, Andrew (1988) "Transcending general linear reality," *Sociological Theory*, 6, 169–86.

Abrams, Phillip (1982) *Historical Sociology*, Ithaca, NY: Cornell University Press.

Adorno, Theodor (1973) *The Jargon of Authenticity*, Evanston: Northwestern University Press.

—— (1974) *Minima Moralia: Reflections from Damaged Life*, trans. E. F. N. Jephcott, London: New Left Books.

Agulhon, Maurice (1992) *1848, Ou l'apprentissage de la République, 1848–1852*, nouv. éd. révisée et complétée. Paris: Ed. du Seuil.

Akrich, M. (1992a) "The de-scription of technical objects." In W. Bijker and J. Law (eds), *Shaping Technology/Building Society*, Cambridge, MA: MIT Press.

—— (1992b) "Beyond social construction of technology: the shaping of people and things in the innovation process." In M. Dierkes and U. Hoffman (eds), *New Technology at the Outset: Social Forces in the Shaping of Technological Innovations*, Boulder, CO: Westview.

Alexander, Jeffrey C. (1982) *Theoretical Logic in Sociology, Vol. I: Positivism, Presuppositions, and Current Controversies*, Berkeley: University of California Press.

—— (1987a) "The centrality of the classics." In Anthony Giddens and Jonathan H. Turner (eds), *Social Theory Today*, Stanford, CA: Stanford University Press.

—— (1987b) *Twenty Lectures: Sociological Theory Since World War II*, New York: Columbia University Press.

—— (1988a) *Action and Its Environments*, New York: Columbia University Press.

—— (1988b) "Culture and political crisis: Watergate and durkheimian sociology." In Jeffrey Alexander (ed.), *Durkheimian Sociology and Cultural Studies Today*, New York: Columbia University Press.

—— (1990) "Analytic debates: understanding the relative autonomy of culture." In Jeffrey Alexander and Steven Sieidman (eds), *Culture and Society: Contemporary Debates*, New York: Cambridge University Press.

—— (1992a) "Recent sociological theory between agency and social structure," *Revue Suisse de Sociologie*, 18, 7–11.

—— (1992b) "The promise of a cultural sociology." In Richard Munch and Neil Smelser (eds), *Theory of Culture*, Berkeley: University of California Press.

Alexander, Jeffrey C., Bernhard Giesen, Richard Münch, and Neil J. Smelser (eds) (1987) *The Micro–Macro Link*, Berkeley: University of California Press.

Alexander, Jeffrey and Philip Smith (1993) "The discourse of American civil society: a new proposal for cultural studies," *Theory and Society*, 22(2), 151–207.

Almond, Gabriel A. and Sidney, Verba (1963) *The Civic Culture: Political Attitudes and Democracy in Five Nations*, Princeton: Princeton University Press.

Althusser, Louis (1977) *For Marx*, London: New Left Books.

Althusser, Louis and Etienne Balibar ([1968] 1970) *Reading Capital*, London: New Left Books.

Anzaldua, Gloria (1987) *Borderlands/La Frontera*, San Francisco: Spinsters/Aunt Lute Press.

Archer, Margaret (1988) *Culture and Agency*, Cambridge: Cambridge University Press.

Arendt, Hannah ([1954] 1977) *Between Past and Future*, New York: Penguin.

Ashmore, Malcolm (1989) *The Reflexive Thesis: wrighting the sociology of scientific knowledge*, Chicago: Chicago University Press.

—— (1993) "Behaviour modification of a catflap: a contribution to the sociology of things." In *Kinnis et Methode X*.

Ashmore, Malcolm, Wooffitt, Robin and Stella Harding (eds) (1994) *Humans and Other Agents: Objects, Discourses, Selves*, Special issue of *American Behavioral Scientist*, 37(6).

Bachelard, Gaston (1938) *La formation de l'esprit scientifique. Contribution à une psychanalyse de la connaissance objective*, Paris: Libraire Philosophique J. Vrin (4th edn 1965).

Bakhtin, Mikhail (1981) *The Dialogical Imagination*, Austin: University of Texas Press.

Balzac, Honoré de (1898) *The Village Cure*, Philadelphia: George Barrie and Sons.

Barnes, Barry (1974) *Scientific Knowledge and Sociological Theory*, London: Routledge & Kegan Paul.

Bastid, Paul (1953) "La théorie juridique des Chartes," *Revue internationale d'histoire politique et constitutionelle*, n.s., 3(11), 63–75.

Bauman, Zygmunt (1992) *Intimations of Postmodernity*, London: Routledge.

Beck, Ulrich (1992) *Risk Society: Towards a New Modernity*, London/Newbury Park, CA: Sage.

Berger, Peter L. (1992) *A Far Glory: The Quest for Faith in an Age of Credulity*, New York: The Free Press.

Berger, Peter and Thomas Luckmann (1966) *The Social Construction of Reality*, Garden City, NY: Doubleday.

Bhaskar, Roy (1979) *The Possibility of Naturalism*, Atlantic Highlands, NJ: Humanities Press.

—— (1986) *Scientific Realism and Human Emancipation*, London: Verso.

—— (1989) *Reclaiming Reality*, London: Verso.

Bijker, Wiebe B. and John Law (eds) (1992) *Shaping Technology/Building Society*, Cambridge, MA: MIT Press.

Bijker, Wiebe B., Thomas Parke Hughes, and Trevor J. Pinch (eds) (1987) *The Social Construction of Technological Systems*, Cambridge, MA: MIT Press.

Blalock, Hubert M., Jr (1982) *Conceptualization and Measurement in the Social Sciences*, Beverly Hills, CA: Sage.

Blau, Peter M. (1977) *Inequality and Heterogeneity*, New York: Free Press.

Blau, Peter M., Terry C. Blum, and J. E. Schwartz (1982) "Heterogeneity and intermarriage," *American Sociological Review*, 47, 45–62.

Bloch, Maurice (1989) *Ritual, History and Power: Selected Papers in Anthropology*, London: The Athlone Press.

Block, Fred and Gene A. Burns (1986) "Productivity as a social problem: the uses and misuses of social indicators," *American Sociological Review*, 51, 767–80.

Bloor, David (1976) *Knowledge and Social Imagery*, London, Boston: Routledge & Kegan Paul.

Blumer, Herbert (1956) "Sociological analysis and the 'variable'," *American Sociological Review*, 21, 683–90.

Boltanski, Luc and Laurent, Thévenot (1991) *De la justification: les économies de la grandeur*, Paris: Gallimard.

Bonald, Louis de ([1802] 1988) *Législation Primitive Considérée par la Raison*, Paris: Ed. Jean-Michel Place.

Bordo, Susan (1987) *The Flight to Objectivity: Essays on Cartesianism and Culture*, Albany: State University of New York Press.

Bourdieu, Pierre (1965) "The sentiment of honour in Kabyle society." In J. G. Peristiany (ed.), *Honour and Shame: The Values of Mediterranean Society*, London: Weidenfeld & Nicolson.

—— ([1972] 1977) *Outline of a Theory of Practice*, New York: Cambridge University Press.

—— ([1972] 1977) "Marriage strategies as strategies of social reproduction." In R. Foster and O. Ranum (eds), *Family and Society: Selections from the Annales*, Baltimore: Johns Hopkins University Press.

—— (1979a) "The sense of honor." In *Algeria 1960*, Cambridge: Cambridge University Press.

—— (1979b) "Les trois états du capital." *Actes de la recherche en sciences sociales*, 30, 3–6.

—— (1980a) *Le sens pratique*, Paris: Editions de Minuit. (Trans. (1990) *The Logic of Practice*. Cambridge: Polity Press).

—— (1980b) *Questions de sociologie*. Paris: Editions de Minuit.

—— (1980c) "Le capital social," *Actes de la recherche en sciences sociales*, 31, 2–3.

—— ([1977] 1980d) "The production of belief: contribution to an economy of symbolic goods," *Media, Culture and Society*, 2 (July), 261–93.

—— (1981) "Epreuve scolaire et consécration sociale. Les classes préparatoires aux Grandes Ecoles," *Actes de la recherche en sciences sociales*, 39, 3–70.

—— (1984) *Distinction*, Cambridge: Harvard University Press.

—— ([1971] 1985) "The market of symbolic goods," *Poetics*, 14 (April), 13–44.

—— ([1983] 1986) "The forms of capital." In John G. Richardson (ed.), *Handbook of Theory and Research for the Sociology of Education*, New York: Greenwood Press.

—— (1987a) "The historical genesis of a pure aesthetics," *The Journal of Aesthetics and Art Criticism*, Special issue (ed. Schusterman), 201–10.

—— ([1971] 1987) "Legitimation and structured interests in Weber's sociology of religion." In Sam Whimster and Scott Lash (eds), *Max Weber, Rationality, and Modernity*, London: Allen & Unwin.

—— ([1984] 1988) *Homo Academicus*, Cambridge: Polity Press; Stanford: Stanford University Press.

—— (1989) *La noblesse d'Etat: Grandes Ecoles et esprit de corps*, Paris: Editions de Minuit. (Trans. (1996) *The State Nobility*, Cambridge: Polity Press).

—— (1990) *In Other Words: Essays Toward a Reflexive Sociology*, trans. M. Adamson, Cambridge: Polity Press; Stanford: Stanford University Press.

—— (1991) "Genesis and structure of the religious field," *Comparative Social Research*, 13, 1–44.

Bourdieu, Pierre, Jean-Claude Chamboredon, and Jean-Claude Passeron (1968) *Le Métier de Sociologue. Préalables Épistémologiques*, Paris and The Hague: Mouton.

—— (1991) *The Craft of Sociology: Epistemological Preliminaries*, trans. R. Nice, New York and Berlin: Aldine de Gruyter.

Bourdieu, Pierre and James S. Coleman (eds) (1993) *Social Theory for a Changing Society*, Boulder, CO: Westview Press.

Bourdieu, Pierre and O. Hahn (1970) "La théorie," *VH 101 2*, (Summer), 12–21.

Bourdieu, Pierre and Yvette Delsaut (1975) "Le couturier et sa griffe. Contribution à une théorie de la magie," *Actes de la recherche en sciences sociales*, 1, 7–36.

Bourdieu, Pierre and Loïc J. D. Wacquant (1992) *An Invitation to Reflexive Sociology*, Chicago: The University of Chicago Press.

Brebner, J. Bartlett (1948) "Laissez-faire and state intervention in nineteenth-century Britain." *The Tasks of Economic History*, (a supplemental issue of the *Journal of Economic History*), 8, 59–73.

Brock, Ditmar (1991) *Der schwierige Weg in die Moderne*, Frankfurt/M: Campus.

Brown, S. and N. Lee (1993) "System and network: thinking the place of the human in a non-human world." Paper presented to conference on "Non-human agency: a contradiction in terms?", University of Surrey, September 23–4.

Brunot, Ferdinand (1937) *Histoire de la langue française des origines à 1900, IX: La Révolution et l'Empire*, 2e Partie: *Les événements, les institutions et la langue*, Paris: Lib. Armand Colin.

Brustein, William (1991) "The 'red menace' and the rise of Italian fascism," *American Sociological Review*, 56, 652–64.

Burns, Gene (1992) "Culture, ideology, and ambiguity: the revolutionary process in Iran." Paper presented at the annual meeting of the Social Science History Association, Chicago.

Buxton, William (1985) *Talcott Parsons and the Capitalist Nation-State: Political Sociology as a Strategic Vocation*, Toronto: University of Toronto Press.

Caillé, Alain (1987) *Critique de Bourdieu*, Lausanne: Université de Lausanne, Institut d'anthropologie et de sociologie ("Cours, séminaires et travaux," n. 8).

Calhoun, Craig (1991) "The problem of identity in collective action." In J. Huber (ed.), *Macro–Micro Linkages in Sociology*, Beverly Hills, CA: Sage, 51–75.

—— (1992a) "Beyond the problem of meaning: Robert Wuthnow's historical sociology of culture," *Theory and Society*, 21, 419–44.

—— (1992b) "The problem of identity in collective action." In Joan Huber (ed.), *Macro–Micro Linkages in Sociology*, Newbury Park, CA: Sage.

—— (1993a) "Nationalism and civil society," *International Journal of Sociology*, 8(4), 387–411.

—— (1993b) "Nationalism and ethnicity," *Annual Review of Sociology*, 19, 211–39.

Calhoun, Craig and W. Richard Scott (1990) "Introduction." In C. Calhoun, M. W. Meyer, and W. R. Scott (eds), *Structures of Power and Constraint*, Cambridge: Cambridge University Press.

Callon, Michel (1986) "Some elements of a sociology of translation: domestication of the scallops and the fisherman of St. Brieuc's Bay." In John Law (ed.), *Power, Action and Belief: A New Sociology of Knowledge?*, *Sociological Review*, Monograph 32, London: Routledge.

Callon, Michel and Bruno Latour (1992) "Don't throw the baby out with the bath school! A reply to Collins and Yearley." In Andrew Pickering (ed.), Chicago: Chicago University Press.

Calvino, Italo (1986) *The Uses of Literature: Essays*, San Diego, CA: Harcourt, Brace, Jovanovich.

Cantimori, Delio (1948) "1848 en Italie." In F. Fejtö (dir.), *Le printemps des peuples: 1848 dans le monde*. Paris: Ed. du Minuit, I, 255–318.

Castoriadis, Cornelius (1990) *Le Monde Morcelé*, Les Carrefours du Labyrinthe III. Paris: Seuil.

Cecil, Lord Hugh (1912) *Conservatism*. London: Williams & Northgage.

Cicourel, Aaron (1964) *Method and Measurement in Sociology*, New York: Free Press of Glencoe.

Cockburn, Cynthia (1985) *Machinery of Dominance: Women, Men and Technical Know-How*, London: Pluto Press.

Cockburn, Cynthia and Susan Ormrod (1993) *Gender and Technology in the Making*, London: Sage.

Cohen, G. A. (1978) *Karl Marx's Theory of History: A Defense*, Princeton, NJ: Princeton University Press.

Cole, G. D. H. (1953) *A History of Socialist Thought*, I: *Socialist Thought: The Forerunners, 1789–1850*, New York: St. Martin's Press.

Coleman, James Samuel (1980) "The structure of society and the nature of social research," *Knowledge*, 1, 333–50.

—— (1990) *Foundations of Social Theory*, Cambridge, MA: Belknap.

Collingwood, C. (1940) *Metaphysics*, Oxford: Clarendon Press.

Collins, Harry M. (1990) *Artificial Experts: Social Knowledge and Intelligent Machines*, Cambridge, MA: MIT Press.

Collins, Harry M. and S. Yearley (1992) "Epistemological chicken." In Andrew Pickering (ed.), *Science as Practice and Culture*, Chicago: Chicago University Press.

Collins, Patricia Hill (1990) *Black Feminist Thought: Knowledge, Consciousness and the Politics of Empowerment*, Boston: Routledge.

Collins, Randall (1981) "On the micro-foundations of macro-sociology," *American Journal of Sociology*, 86, 984–101.

—— (1988a) "The durkheimian tradition in conflict sociology." In Jeffrey Alexander (ed.), *Durkheimian Sociology: Cultural Studies*, New York: Columbia University Press.

—— (1988b) "The micro contribution to macro sociology," *Sociological Theory*, 6, 242–52.

—— (1989) "Sociology: proscience or antiscience?" *American Sociological Review*, 54, 124–39.

Condliffe, John B. (1951) *The Commerce of Nations*, London: George Allen & Unwin.

Cooper, G. and Steve Woolgar (1993) "Software is society made malleable: the importance of conceptions of audience in software and research practice," *PICT Policy Research Paper* no. 25, Brunel University.

Coulter, Jeff (1989) *Mind in Action*, Cambridge, MA: Polity.

Cowan, Ruth Schwartz (1983) *More Work for Mother: The Ironies of Household Technology from the Open Hearth to the Microwave*, New York: Basic Books.

Darnton, Robert (1984) *The Great Cat Massacre and Other Episodes in French Cultural History*, New York: Basic Books.

Dawe, A. (1978) "Theories of social action." In T. Bottomore and R. Nisbet (eds), *The History of Sociological Analysis*, New York: Basic Books.

Desrosières, Alain (1992a) "How to make things which hold together: social science, statistics and the state," Paris: Institut national de la statistique et des études économiques, unpublished manuscript.

—— (1992b) "Official statistics and business: history, classifications, uses," Paris: Institut national de la statistique et des études économiques, publication no. 43/G305.

Deudney, D. and G. J. Ikenberry (1991) "Soviet reform and the end of the Cold War: explaining large scale historical change, *Review of International Studies*, 7, 225–50.

Dilthey, W. (1976) "The construction of the historical world in the human studies." In his *Selected Writings*, ed. H. P. Richman, Cambridge, England: Cambridge University Press.

DiMaggio, Paul and Walter Powell ([1983] 1991) "The iron cage revisited: institutional isomorphism and collective rationality in organizational fields." In Powell and DiMaggio (eds).

—— (1991) "Introduction." In Powell and Di Maggio (eds).

Drabek, Thomas E. (1986) "Taxonomy and disaster: theoretical and applied issues." Paper presented at the Symposium on "Social structure and disaster: concept and measurement," College of William and Mary, Williamsburg, Virginia.

—— (forthcoming) *Human System Response to Disaster: An Inventory of Sociological Findings*, New York, Heidelberg and Berlin: Springer Verlag.

Durkheim, Emile (1893) *The Division of Labor in Society*, New York: Free Press.

—— (1965) *The Elementary Forms of Religious Life*, New York: Free Press.

Ehrman, Bart (1993) *The Orthodox Corruption of Scripture: The Effect of Early Christological Controversies on the Text of the New Testament*, New York: Oxford University Press.

Eisenstadt, Shmuel N. (1962) *The Political Systems of Empires*, Glencoe, IL: Free Press.

—— (1964) *The Decline of Empires*, Englewood Cliffs, NJ: Prentice-Hall.

Eisenstadt, Shmuel N. and Miriam Curelaru (1976) *The Forms of Sociology – Paradigms and Crises*, New York: Wiley.

Eliot, T. S. (1971) *The Waste Land*: A facsimile and transcription of the original drafts, including the annotations of Ezra Pound, ed. Valerie Eliot, New York: Harcourt, Brace, Jovanovich.

Elster, Jon (1984) *Ulysses and the Sirens*, Cambridge: Cambridge University Press.

—— (1985) *Sour Grapes: Studies in the Subversion of Rationality*, Cambridge, London and New York: Cambridge University Press.

—— (1989) *The Cement of Society: A Study of Social Order*, Cambridge/New York: Cambridge University Press.

Ernst, Cecile (1983) *Birth Order: Its Influence on Personality*, Berlin/New York: Springer Verlag.

Evers, Adalbert and Helga Nowotny (1987) *Über den Umgang mit Unsicherheit. Die Entdeckung der Gestaltbarkeit von Gesellschaft*, Frankfurt/M: Suhrkamp.

Faris, Ellsworth (1938) "The promise of sociology," *American Sociological Review*, February, 3(1), 1–12.

Faris, Robert E. L. (1970) *Chicago Sociology 1920–1932*, Chicago: University of Chicago Press.

Feyerabend, Paul (1975) *Against Method*, London: New Left Books.

Foucault, Michel (1970) *The Order of Things*, London: Tavistock Publications.

Francis, David R. (1913) *The Universal Exposition of 1904*, (2 vols.) St. Louis: Louisiana Purchase Exposition Company.

Fraser, Nancy ([1986] 1989) "What's critical about critical theory: the case of Habermas and gender." In *Unruly Practices*, Minneapolis: University of Minnesota Press.

Frazer, Elizabeth and Nicola Lacey (1993) *The Politics of Community: A Feminist Critique of the Liberal–Communitarian Debate*, Hemel Hempstead: Harvester Wheatsheaf.

Friedland, Roger and Robert Alford (1991) "Bringing society back in: symbols, practices, and institutional contradictions." In Powell and DiMaggio (eds).

Friedman, A. L. with D. S. Cornford (1989) *Computer Systems Development: History, Organization, and Implementation*, New York: John Wiley.

Frisby, David and Derek Sayer (1976) *Philosophical Hermeneutics*, Berkeley: University of California Press.

—— (1986) *Society*, Chichester: Horwood and London: Tavistock.

Gadamer, Hans-Georg (1975) *Truth and Method*, New York: Seabury.

—— (1976) *Philosophical Hermenentics*, Berkeley: University of California Press.

—— (1981) *Reason in the Age of Science*, Cambridge, MA: MIT Press.

—— (1989) *Truth and Method*, trans. and ed. Joel Weinsheimer and Donald Marshall, New York: Crossroad Publishing Co. (2nd revised edn).

Garfinkel, Harold (1963) "A conception of and experiments with 'trust' as a condition of concerted stable action." In O. J. Harvey (ed.), *Motivation and Social Interaction*, New York: Ronald Press.

—— (1967) *Studies in Ethnomethodology*, Englewood Cliffs, NJ: Prentice-Hall.

Gash, Norman (1951) "Peel and the party system, 1830–50," *Transactions of the Royal Historical Society*, 5th series, 1, 47–70.

Geertz, Clifford (1964) "Ideology as a cultural system." In D. Apter (ed.), *Ideology and Discontent*, New York: Free Press, 47–76.

—— (1973) *The Interpretation of Cultures*, New York: Basic Books.

Gerhardt, Uta (ed.) (1993) *Talcott Parsons on National Socialism*, New York: Aldine de Gruyter.

Giddens, Anthony (1976) *New Rules of Sociological Method*, New York: Basic Books.

—— (1977) *Studies in Social and Political Theory*, New York: Basic Books.

—— (1984) *The Constitution of Society: Outline of the Theory of Structuration*, Berkeley, CA: University of California Press.

Gilbert, Claude and Marc Guillaume (1985) "L'acharnement politique ou l'effort de représentation." In François d'Arcy (ed.), *La représentation*, Paris: Economica.

Glaser, Barney G. and Anselm L. Strauss (1967) *The Discovery of Grounded Theory*, Chicago: Aldine.

Glymour, Clark (1983) "Social science and social physics," *Behavioral Science*, 28, 126–34.

Goffman, Erving (1959) *The Presentation of Self in Everyday Life*, New York: Doubleday.

Goody, Jack (1967) *The Social Organization of the Lo Wiili*, Oxford: Oxford University Press.

Goonatilake, Susantha (1992) "The voyages of discovery and the loss and rediscovery of the 'other's' knowledge," *Impact of Science on Society*, 167, 241–64.

Gouldner, Alvin (1979) *The Two Marxisms*, New York: Seabury Press.

Griffin, Larry J. (1993) "Narrative, event-structure analysis, and causal interpretation in historical sociology," *American Journal of Sociology*, 98, 1,094–133.

Griffin, Larry J. and Larry W. Isaac (1992) "Recursive regression and the historical use of 'time' in time-series analysis of historical process," *Historical Methods*, 25, 166–79.

Grint, K. and Steve Woolgar (1992) "Computers, guns and roses: what's social about being shot?", *Science Technology and Human Values*, 17(3), 366–80.

—— (1995) "On some failures of nerve in feminist and constructivist analyses of technology." In S. Woolgar (ed.), *Feminist and Constructivist Perspectives on New Technology*. Special issue of *Science, Technology and Human Values*, 20(3), 286–310.

—— (forthcoming) *The Machine at Work: Technology, Work and Organisation*, Cambridge: Polity Press.

Haas, David (1982) "Survey sampling and the logic of inference in sociology," *The American Sociologist*, 17, 103–11.

Habermas, Jurgen (1972) *Knowledge and Human Interests*, Cambridge, England: Polity Press.

—— (1973) *Theory and Practice*, trans. John Viertel, Boston: Beacon Press.

—— (1984) *Theory of Communicative Action, Vol. 1: Reason and the Rationalization of Society*, Boston: Beacon Press; Cambridge, England: Polity Press.

—— ([1984] 1987) *The Theory of Communicative Action, Vol. 2: Lifeworld and System: A Critique of Functionalist Reason*, Boston: Beacon Press.

—— ([1985] 1987) *The Philosophical Discourse of Modernity*, Cambridge, MA: MIT.

—— (1988) *On the Logic of the Social Sciences*, trans. Shierry Weber Nicholsen and Jerry A. Stark, Oxford, UK: Polity Press.

Hagstrom, Warren O. (1965) *The Scientific Community*, New York: Basic Books.

Halévy, Elie (1949) *A History of the English People in The Nineteenth Century, I: England in 1815*, London: Ernest Benn (2nd revised edn).

—— (1950) *A History of the English People in the Nineteenth Century, III: The Triumph of Reform, 1830–1841*, London: Ernest Benn (2nd revised edn).

Halfpenny, Peter (1982) *Positivism and Sociology*, London: Allen & Unwin.

Hall, John R. (1984) "Temporality, social action, and the problem of quantification in historical analysis," *Historical Methods*, 17, 206–18.

—— (1988) "Social organization and pathways of commitment: types of communal groups, rational choice theory, and the Kanter thesis," *American Sociological Review*, 53, 679–92.

—— (1990) "Epistemology and sociohistorical inquiry," *Annual Review of Sociology*, 16, 329–51.

—— (1992) "Where history and sociology meet: forms of discourse and sociohistorical inquiry," *Sociological Theory*, 10, 164–93.

—— (forthcoming) *Cultures of Inquiry: Discourse and Practices in Historical, Social and Cultural Studies*.

Hall, John R. and Mary Jo Neitz (1993) *Culture: Sociological Perspectives*, Englewood Cliffs, NJ: Prentice Hall.

Halliday, Terrence C. and Morris Janowitz (eds) (1992) *Sociology and Its Publics: The Forms and Fates of Disciplinary Organization*, Chicago: Chicago University Press.

Hannerz, Ulf (1958) "The world in Creolisation," *Africa*, 57, 546–59.

—— (1992) *Cultural Complexity: Studies in the Social Organization of Meaning*, New York: Columbia University Press.

Harding, Sandra (1983) "Why has the sex/gender system become visible only now?" In S. Harding and M. Hintikka (eds), *Discovering Reality: Feminist Perspectives on Epistemology, Metaphysics, Methodology and Philosophy of Science*, Dordrecht: Reidel/Kluwer.

—— (1986) *The Science Question in Feminism*, Ithaca: Cornell University Press.

—— (1991) *Whose Science? Whose Knowledge? Thinking from Women's Lives*, Ithaca: Cornell University Press.

—— (1992) "Rethinking standpoint epistemology: what is 'strong objectivity'?" In L. Alcoff and E. Potter (eds), *Feminist Epistemologies*, New York: Routledge.

—— (ed.) (1993) *The "Racial" Economy of Science: Toward a Democratic Future*, Bloomington: Indiana University Press.

—— (1994) "Is science multicultural?" In *Configurations*, 2(2), and in David Theo Goldberg (ed.), *Multiculturalism: A Reader*, London: Blackwell.

—— (1996) "Is modern science an ethnoscience? Rethinking epistemological verities." In Terry Shinn, Jack Spaapen, Rolant Waast (eds), *Sociology of the Sciences Yearbook: Sciences and Technology for the South*, Dordrecht: Kluwer.

Harré, Rom (1990) "Exploring the human umwelt." In Roy Bhaskar (ed.), *Harré and His Critics*, Cambridge, MA: Basil Blackwell.

Hartsock, Nancy (1983) "The feminist standpoint: developing the ground for a specifically feminist historical materialism." In Sandra Harding and Merrill Heldke (eds), *Discovering Reality: Feminist Perspectives on Epistemology*.

Hayek, Frederick A. von (1952) *The Counter-Revolution of Science: Studies on the Abuse of Reason*, Glencoe, IL: Free Press.

Heath, William (1970) *Wordsworth and Coleridge: A Study of Their Literary Relations in 1801–1802*, Oxford: Clarendon Press.

Hennessy, Rosemary (1993) *Materialist Feminism and the Politics of Discourse*, New York: Routledge.

Hesse, Mary (1966) *Models and Analogies in Science*, Notre Dame: University of Notre Dame Press.

Hindess, Barry (1991) "Imaginary presuppositions of democracy," *Economy and Society*, 20(2), 173–95.

Hindess, Barry and Paul Q. Hirst (1975) *Pre-Capitalist Modes of Production*, London: Routledge & Kegan Paul.

Hobhouse, L. T. (1911) *Liberalism*, London: Oxford University Press.

Hobsbawm, Eric J. (1962) *The Age of Revolution, 1789–1848*, New York: World Publishing, A Mentor Book.

Holquist, Michael and Clark, Katarian (1986) *Bakhtin*, New Haven: Yale University Press.

Holton, Gerald J. (1973) *Thematic Origins of Scientific Thought: Kepler to Einstein*, Cambridge, MA: Harvard University Press.

hooks, bell (1983) *Feminist Theory From Margin to Center*, Boston: South End Press.

Hughes, Thomas Parke (1987) In Bijker et al. (eds), *The Social Construction of Technological Systems*, Cambridge, MA: MIT Press.

Hunt, Lynn (1984) *Politics, Culture, and Class in the French Revolution*, Berkeley: University of California Press.

Hwang, Jin Lin (1993) "Changing the sacred: discourse in early republican China 1915–23," Ph.D. thesis, University of California, Los Angeles.

Iggers, Georg G. (1958) *The Cult of Authority: The Political Philosophy of the Saint-Simonians. A Chapter in the Intellectual History of Totalitarianism*, The Hague: Martinus Nijhoff.

Isaac, Larry W. and Larry J. Griffin (1989) "Ahistoricism in time-series analyses of historical process," *American Sociological Review*, 54, 873–90.

Jacobs, Ronald (1996, forthcoming) "Civil society and crisis: culture, discourse, and the Rodney King beating," *American Journal of Sociology*.

Jaggar, Alison (1983) "Feminist politics and epistemology." In A. Jaggar, *Feminist Politics and Human Nature*, Totowa, NJ: Rowman & Allenheld.

Joas, Hans (1987) "Symbolic interactionism." In Anthony Giddens and Jonathan H. Turner (eds), *Social Theory Today*, Cambridge: Polity (now reprinted as "Pragmatism in American sociology." In Joas (1993) *Pragmatism and Social Theory*, Chicago: University of Chicago Press).

—— (1993) "An underestimated alternative: América and the limits of 'critical theory'," *Pragmatism and Social Theory*, Chicago, University of Chicago Press.

Joppke, Christian (1986) "The cultural dimension of class formation and class struggle: on the social theory of Pierre Bourdieu," *Berkeley Journal of Sociology*, 31, 53–78.

Kane, Anne (1991) "Cultural analysis in historical sociology: the concrete and analytic autonomy of culture," *Sociological Theory*, 9, 53–69.

—— (1994) "Culture and social change: symbolic construction, ideology, and political alliance during the Irish Land War," Ph.D. thesis, University of California, Los Angeles.

Kant, Immanuel ([1787] 1929) *The Critique of Pure Reason*, trans. Norman Kemp Smith, London: Macmillan.

Katznelson, Ira and Aristide R. Zolberg (eds) (1986) *Working-Class Formation: Nineteenth-Century Patterns in Europe and the United States*, Princeton, NJ: Princeton University Press.

Kermode, Frank (1985) *Forms of Attention*, Chicago: Chicago University Press.

Kertzer, David (1988) *Ritual, Politics, and Power*, New Haven: Yale University Press.

Kiser, Edgar and Michael Hechter (1991) "The role of general theory in comparative historical sociology," *American Journal of Sociology*, 97, 1–30.

Köhnke, Klaus Christian (1991) *The Rise of Neo-Kantianism: German Academic Philosophy between Idealism and Positivism*, New York: Cambridge University Press.

Kolakowski, Leszek (1978) *Main Currents of Marxism: Its Rise, Growth, and Dissolution*, 3 vols, Oxford: Clarendon Press.

Kraus, Karl (1976) *In These Great Times: A Karl Kraus Reader*, ed. Harry Zohn, Montreal: Engendra Press.

Kuhn, Thomas ([1962] 1970) *The Structure of Scientific Revolutions*, Chicago: Chicago University Press (2nd enlarged edn).

Kully, Hannah (1994) "Where is agency and meaning in neo-institutionalist theory?" Paper presented at annual meeting of the American Sociological Association, Los Angeles.

Labrousse, Ernest (1949) "1848–1830–1789: comment naissent les révolutions," *Actes du Congrès historique du Centenaire de la Révolution de 1848*, Paris: Presses Univ. de France, 1–20.

Lakatos, Imre (1971) "History of science and its rational reconstructions," *Boston Studies in the Philosophy of Science*, 8, 91–136.

Lanham, Richard A. (1974) *Style: An Anti-Textbook*, New Haven: Yale University Press.

Latouche, Serge (1985) "La fin de la société des nations," *Traverses*, 33(4), 36–43.

Latour, Bruno (1988) "The prince for machines as well as for machinations." In B. Elliott (ed.), *Technology and Social Progress*, Edinburgh: Edinburgh University Press.

—— (1991a) "Technology is society made durable." In John Law (ed.) (1991a).

—— (1991b) "The impact of science studies on political philosophy," *Science Technology and Human Values*, 16(1), 3–19.

—— (1993) *We Have Never Been Modern*, Hemel Hempstead: Harvester Wheatsheaf; Cambridge: Harvard University Press.

Latour, Bruno and Steve Woolgar ([1979] 1986) *Laboratory Life: the Construction of Scientific Facts*, Princeton, NJ: Princeton University Press.

Law, John (ed.) (1991a) *A Sociology of Monsters: Essays on Power, Technology, and Domination*, London: Routledge.

—— (1991b) "Introduction: monsters, machines and sociotechnical relations." In J. Law (ed.) (1991a).

Law, John and Michel Callon (1992) "The life and death of an aircraft: network analysis of technical change." In Wiebe B. Bijker and John Law (eds) (1992).

Leiss, William (1972) *The Domination of Nature*, Boston: Beacon Press.

Lévi-Strauss, C. (1966) *The Savage Mind*, Chicago: University of Chicago Press.

Levine, Donald (1985) *The Flight From Ambiguity*, Chicago: Chicago University Press.

Lieberson, Stanley (1980) *A Piece of the Pie*, Berkeley and Los Angeles: University of California Press.

—— (1985) *Making It Count*, Berkeley: University of California Press.

—— (1992) "Einstein, Renoir, and Greeley: some thoughts about evidence in sociology," *American Sociological Review*, 57, 1–15.

Liebes, T. (ed.) (1994) *Dramatizing the Facts: The Narratives of Journalism*, special issue of *Journal of Narratives and Life Stories*, 4.

Lloyd, Genevieve (1984) *The Man of Reason: "Male" and "Female" in Western Philosophy*, Minneapolis: University of Minnesota.

Low, John and Steve Woolgar (1993) "Managing the social–technical divide: some aspects of the discursive structure of information systems development," *CRICT Discussion Paper no. 33*, May. Also in P. Quintas (ed.), *Social Dimensions of Systems Engineering*, Chichester: Ellis Horwood.

Luhmann, Niklas (1979) *Trust and Power*, New York: Wiley.

—— (1984) *The Differentiation of Society*, New York: Columbia University Press.

Lukes, Steven (1973) *Individualism*, Oxford: Basil Blackwell.

Lynch, Michael (1993a) *Scientific Practice and Ordinary Action: Ethnomethodology and Social Studies of Science*, Cambridge: Cambridge University Press.

—— (1993b) "'When is Giddens going to talk to us?' Implications of sociology of scientific knowledge for textbook sociology." Paper presented to 4S conference, Purdue, November 18–20.

Lyotard, Jean-François ([1979] 1984) *The Postmodern Condition*, Minneapolis: University of Minnesota Press.

—— (1985) "Une ligne de résistance," *Traverses*, 33–4, 60–5.

MacKenzie, Donald A. (1990) *Inventing Accuracy: A Historical Sociology of Nuclear Missile Guidance Cambridge*, Cambridge, MA: MIT Press.

MacKinnon, Catharine (1982) "Feminism, Marxism, method, and the state: an agenda for theory," *Signs*, 7(3), 515–44.

Maffesoli, Michel (1996) *The Time of the Tribes: The Decline of Individualism in Mass Society*, London: Sage.

Manicas, Peter (1987) *A History and Philosophy of the Social Sciences*, Oxford: Blackwell.

Mannheim, Karl (1936) *Ideology and Utopia*, trans. L. Wirth and E. Shils, New York: Harvest Press.

Manning, D. J. (1976) *Liberalism*, London: J. M. Dent & Sons.

Manuel, Frank E. (1956) *The New World of Henri Saint-Simon*, Cambridge, MA: Harvard University Press.

Margolis, Joseph (1985) "Deconstruction; or the mystery of the mystery of the text." In Hugh J. Silverman and Don Ihde (eds), *Hermeneutics & Deconstruction*, Albany: State University of New York Press.

Marshall, Alfred (1921) *Industry and Trade: a Study of Industrial Technique and Business Organization: and of Their Influences on the Conditions of Various Classes and Nations*, London: Macmillan.

Martel, Martin U. (1971) "Academentia Praecox: the aims, merits, and scope of Parsons' multisystemic language rebellion (1958–1968)." In Herman Turk and Richard L. Simpson (eds), *Institutions and Social Exchange: The Sociologies of Talcott Parsons and George Homans*, Indianapolis: Bobbs-Merrill Co.

—— (1979) "Talcott Parsons," *International Encyclopedia of the Social Sciences, Biographical Supplement*, Vol. 18, 609–30, ed. David Sills, New York: Free Press.

Marx, Karl and Frederick Engels ([1848] 1973) *Manifesto of the Communist Party*. In Karl Marx, *The Revolutions of 1848: Political Writings*, Vol. I, Harmondsworth: Penguin.

Mason, E. S. (1931) "Saint-Simonism and the rationalisation of industry," *Quarterly Journal of Economics*, 45 (August), 640–83.

Mayer, Karl and Nancy Tuma (eds) (1990) *Event History Analysis in Life Course Research*, Madison, WI: University of Wisconsin Press.

Mead, George Herbert (1934) *Mind, Self, and Society*, Chicago: University of Chicago Press.

Mellow, James R. (1974) *Charmed Circle: Gertrude Stein and Company*, New York: Praeger.

Merchant, Carolyn (1980) *The Death of Nature: Women, Ecology and the Scientific Revolution*, New York: Harper & Row.

Merton, Robert K. (1945) "Sociological theory," *American Journal of Sociology*, 50(6), 462–73.

—— (1948) "Discussion [of Parsons' remarks]," *American Sociological Review*, 13(2) 164–8.

—— (1959) "Notes on problem-finding in sociology." In Robert K. Merton, Leonard Broom, and Leonard S. Cottrell, Jr (eds), ([1959] 1965).

—— (1968) *Social Theory and Social Structure*, New York: The Free Press.

—— (1973) *The Sociology of Science: Theoretical and Empirical Investigations*, Chicago: University of Chicago Press.

Merton, Robert K., Leonard Broom, and Leonard S. Cottrell, Jr (eds) (1959) *Sociology Today: Problems and Prospects*, New York: Basic Books (reprinted 1965 as Harper & Row Torchbook in 2 vols).

Meyer, John and Brian Rowan ([1977] 1991) "Institutionalized organizations: formal structure as myth and ceremony." In Powell and DiMaggio (eds).

Meyssonier, Simone (1989) *La Balance et l'horloge. La genèse de la pensée libérale en France au XVIIIe siècle*, Montreuil: Ed. de la Passion.

Miller, Richard W. (1987) *Fact and Method: Explanation, Confirmation and Reality in the Natural and the Social Sciences*, Princeton: Princeton University Press.

Mills, C. Wright (1959) *The Sociological Imagination*, New York: Oxford University Press.

Minogue, K. R. (1963) *The Liberal Mind*, London: Methuen.

Mohr, John (1992) "People, categories and organizations: making sense out of poverty in New York City, 1888–1917." Paper presented at the annual meeting of the American Sociological Society, Pittsburgh, PA.

Moore, Sally and Barbara Myerhoff (1977) "Introduction: secular ritual: forms and meanings." In Sally Moore and Barbara Myerhoff (eds), *Secular Ritual*, Amsterdam: Van Gorcum, Assen.

Mudimbe, V. Y. (1988) *The Invention of Africa*, Bloomington: Indiana University Press.

Nisbet, Robert A. (1944) "De Bonald and the concept of the social group," *Journal of the History of Ideas*, 5, 3, 315–31.

—— (1952) "Conservatism and sociology," *American Journal of Sociology*, 58(2), 167–75.

—— (1956) *The Sociological Tradition*, New York: Basic Books.

—— (1966) *Contemporary Social Problems*, NY: Harcourt, Brace and World (2nd edn).

—— (1976) *Sociology as an Art Form*, London: Oxford University Press.

Noiriel, Gérard (1991) *La tyrannie du national: le droit d'asyle en Europe 1793–1993*, Paris: Calmann-Lévy.

Offe, Claus (1989) "Fessel und Bremse. Moralische und institutionelle Aspekte 'intelligenter Selbstbeschränkung'." In Axel Honneth et al. (eds), *Zwischenbetrachtungen. Im Prozess der Aufklärung*, Frankfurt/M: Suhrkamp.

Outhwaite, William (1987) *New Philosophies of Social Science: Realism, Hermeneutics, Critical Theory*, New York: St. Martin's Press.

Parsons, Elsie Clews (1915) *Social Freedom: A Study of the Conflicts Between Social Classifications and Personality*, New York: G. P. Putnam's Sons, The Knickerbocker Press.

Parsons, Talcott (1935) "The place of ultimate values in sociological theory," *International Journal of Ethics*, 45 (partially reprinted in Parsons 1982, and entirely in Parsons 1991).

—— (1937) *The Structure of Social Action*, New York: Free Press.

—— (1938) "The role of theory in social research," *American Sociological Review*, 3(1), 13–20.

—— (1939) "Comte," *Journal of Unified Science*, 9, 77–83.

—— (1945) "The present position and prospects of systematic theory in sociology," 42–69. In Georges Gurvitch and Wilbert E. Moore (eds), *Twentieth Century Sociology*, New York: Philosophical Library.

—— (1948) "The position of sociological theory," *American Sociological Review*, 13(2), 156–64.

—— (1950) "The prospects of sociological theory," *American Sociological Review*, 15(1), 3–16.

—— (1959) "General theory in sociology." In Robert K. Merton, Leonard Broom, and Leonard S. Cottrell, Jr (eds), *Sociology Today: Problems and Prospects*, New York: Basic Books (reprinted 1965 as Harper & Row Torchbook in 2 vols).

—— (1968) "Christianity," *International Encyclopedia of the Social Sciences*, Vol. 2, ed. David Sills, New York: Macmillan/Free Press.

—— (1978) *Action Theory and the Human Condition*, New York: Free Press.

—— (1979) "Karl Jaspers," *International Encyclopedia of the Social Sciences, Biographical Supplement*, Vol. 18, ed. David Sills, New York: Free Press.

—— (1982) *Talcott Parsons on Institutions and Social Evolution*, ed. Leon Mayhew, Chicago: University of Chicago Press.

—— (1991) *The Early Essays*, ed. and intro. Charles Camic, Chicago: University of Chicago Press.

Pawson, Ray (1989) *A Measure for Measures*, New York: Routledge.

Pearson, Karl ([1892] 1911) *The Grammar of Science*, New York: Macmillan.

Pettijean, Patrik, Catherine Jami, and Anne Marie Moulin (eds) (1992) *Science and Empires: Historical Studies About Scientific Development and European Expansion*, Dordrecht: Kluwer Academic Publishers.

Pickering, Andrew (ed.) (1992) *Science as Practice and Culture*, Chicago: Chicago University Press.

Plamenatz, John (1952) *The Revolutionary Movement in France, 1815–1870*, London: Longman, Green.

Polanyi, Karl ([1944] 1975) *The Great Transformation*, New York: Farrar, Straus & Giroux.

Pollner, Melvin. (1987) *Mundane Reason: Reality in Everyday and Sociological Discourse*, Cambridge: Cambridge University Press.

Powell, Walter and Paul DiMaggio (eds) ([1983] 1991) *The New Institutionalism in Organizational Analysis*, Chicago: University of Chicago Press.

Procacci, Giovanna (1993) *Gouverner La Misère*, Paris: Seuil.

Quine, W. V. O. (1953) "Two dogmas of empiricism." In *From a Logical Point of View*, Cambridge, MA: Harvard University Press.

Rae, J. (1993) "Repair mechanisms and the 'procedural infrastructure of interaction': modems, faxes, email – intersubjectivity for all practical purposes?" Paper presented to conference on "Non-human agency: a contradiction in terms?," University of Surrey.

Ragin, Charles C. (1987) *The Comparative Method*, Berkeley: University of California Press.

Rambo, Eric and Elaine Chan (1990) "Text, structure and action in cultural sociology," *Theory and Society*, 19, 635–48.

Randall, Adrian (1991) *Before the Luddites: Custom, Community and Machinery in the English Woollen Industry 1776–1809*, Cambridge: Cambridge University Press.

Redfield, Robert (1957) *The Little Tradition*, Chicago: University of Chicago Press.

Reid, Robert W. (1986) *Land of Lost Content: The Luddite Revolt 1812*, London: Cardinal.

Restivo, Sal (1992) "Zen and the art of science studies," *Science Technology and Human Values*, 17(3), 402–5.

Ritzer, George (1993) *The Mcdonaldization of Society: An Investigation into the Changing Character of Contemporary Social Life*, Newbury Park, CA: Pine Forge Press.

Roemer, John (1982) *A General Theory of Class and Exploitation*, Cambridge, MA: Harvard University Press.

—— (1992a) "Can there be socialism after communism?," *Politics and Society*, 20, 261–76.

—— (1992b) "A future for socialism" (unpublished).

Rorty, Richard (1979) *Philosophy and the Mirror of Nature*, Princeton, NJ: Princeton University Press.

—— (1989) *Contingency, Irony, and Solidarity*, Cambridge: Cambridge University Press.

Rose, Hilary (1983) "Hand, brain and heart: a feminist epistemology for the natural sciences," *Signs*, 9(1), 73–90.

Rossi, Pietro (1982) "La sociologia nella seconda metà del'ottocento: dall'impiego di schemi storico-evolutivi alla formulazione di modelli analitici," *Il pensiero politico*, 15(1), 188–215.

Roth, Andrew (1994) "Ethnomethodology." In Frank Magill (ed.), *Survey of Social Science: Sociology*, Pasadena: Salem Press.

Roth, Guenther (1987) "Rationalization in Max Weber's developmental history." In Scott Lash and Sam Whimster, *Max Weber, Rationality, and Modernity*, London: Allen & Unwin.

Roth, Paul A. (1987) *Meaning and Method in the Social Sciences*, Ithaca, NY: Cornell University Press.

Rowe, Nicholas (1989) *Rules and Institutions*, Hemel Hempstead.

Rueschemeyer, Dietrich and Theda Skocpol (eds) (1996) *Social Knowledge and the Origins of Social Policies*, Princeton and New York: Princeton University Press and Russell Sage Foundation.

Sahlins, Marshall (1981) *Historical Metaphors and Mythical Realities*, Ann Arbor: University of Michigan Press.

Said, Edward (1976) *Orientalism*, London: Edward Arnold.

—— (1978) *Orientalism*, New York: Pantheon.

Saussure, Ferdinand de (1985) "The linguistic sign." In Robert Innis (ed.), *Semiotics: An Introductory Anthology* (reprinted from *Course in General Linguistics* 1959), Bloomington: Indiana University Press.

Schapiro, J. Salwyn (1949) *Liberalism and the Challenge of Fascism: Social Forces in England and France (1815–1870)*. New York: McGraw-Hill.

Schelling, Thomas (1960) *The Strategy of Conflict*, Cambridge, MA: Harvard University Press.

Schroeder, R. (1993) "Virtual humans and other non-human actors in the emergence of virtual reality research." Paper presented to conference on "Non-human agency: a contradiction in terms?," University of Surrey.

Schutz, Alfred (1967) *The Phenomenology of the Social World*, Evanston, IL: Northwestern University Press.

Schutz, Alfred and Thomas Luckmann (1973) *The Structures of the Lifeworld*, Evanston, IL: Northwestern University Press.

—— ([1973] 1976) *The Structures of the Lifeworld*, Evanston, IL: Northwestern University Press; London: Longman.

Seidman, Steven (1983) *Liberalism and the Origins of European Social Theory*, Oxford: Blackwell.

Seidman, S. (1986) "Models of scientific development in sociology," *Humboldt Journal of Social Relations*, 15(1), 119–39.

Selten, Reinhard (1975) "Re-examination of the perfectness concept for equilibrium points in extensive games," *International Journal of Game Theory*, 4, 25–55.

Sewell, William H., Jr (1980) *Work and Revolution in France: The Language of Labor from the Old Regime to 1848*, New York and Cambridge: Cambridge University Press.

—— (1985) "Ideologies and social revolutions: reflections on the French case," *Journal of Modern History*, 57, 57–85.

—— (1990) "Collective violence and collective loyalties in France: why the French revolution made a difference," *Politics and Society*, 18, 527–52.

—— (1991) "Three temporalities: toward an evenemental sociology." In Terrence McDonald (ed.) (1996, forthcoming), *The Historic Turn in the Human Sciences*.

—— (1992) "A theory of structure: duality, agency, and transformation," *American Journal of Sociology*, 98, 1–29.

Shapin, S. and S. Schaffer (1986) *Leviathan and the Air-Pump*, Princeton, NJ: Princeton University Press.

Shapiro, Gary and Alan Sica (eds) (1984) *Hermeneutics: Questions and Prospects*, Amherst: University of Massachusetts Press.

Shapiro, S. (1993) "Caught in a web: STS, ecology and non-human agency." Paper presented to conference on "Non-human agency: a contradiction in terms?", University of Surrey.

Sherwood, Steven (1993) "Narrating the social: post-modernism and the drama of democracy." In T. Liebes (ed.) (1994).

Shils, Edward A. (1970) "Tradition, ecology, and institution in the history of sociology', *Daedalus*, 99: 798–820.

Sica, Alan (1981) "Hermeneutics and Social Theory: The contemporary conversation," *Current Perspectives in Social Theory*, 2, 39–54.

—— (1989) "Social theory's 'constituency'," *American Sociologist*, 20(3), 227–41.

Simon, Walter M. (1956) "History for utopia: Saint-Simon and the idea of progress." *Journal of the History of Ideas*, 18(3), 311–31.

Skinner, Quentin (1969) "Meaning and understanding in the history of ideas," *History and Theory*, 8, 3–52.

Skocpol, Theda (1979) *States and Social Revolutions*, New York: Cambridge University Press.

—— (1984) "Sociology's historical imagination." In Theda Skocpol (ed.), *Vision and Method in Historical Sociology*, Cambridge: Cambridge University Press.

—— (1988) "An 'uppity generation' and the revitalization of macroscopic sociology: reflections at midcareer by a woman from the 1960s." In Matilda White Riley (ed.), *Sociological Lives*, Newbury Park: Sage Publications.

Smelser, Neil J. (1959) *Social Change in the Industrial Revolution*, Chicago: University of Chicago Press.

Smith, Dorothy (1987) *The Everyday World as Problematic: A Feminist Sociology*, Boston: Northeastern University Press.

—— (1990) *The Conceptual Practices of Power: A Feminist Sociology of Knowledge*, Boston: Northeastern University Press.

Smith, Phillip (1993) "The semiological foundations of media narratives: Hussein and Nasser." In T. Liebes (ed.) (1994).

Sohn-Rethel, Alfred (1978) *Intellectual and Manual Labor*, London: Macmillan.

Somers, Margaret R. (1992) "The political culture concept: the empirical power of conceptual transformations." Presented at the annual meeting of the American Sociological Association, 1991. Working paper no. 88, Ann Arbor: University of Michigan Comparative Study of Social Transformations Working Papers.

Somers, Margaret and Gloria Gibson (1994) "Reclaiming the epistemological other: narrative and the social constitution of identity." In Craig Calhoun (ed.), *Social Theory and the Politics of Identity*, Oxford: Blackwell.

Sorokin, Ptirim (1957) *Social and Cultural Dynamics*, Boston: Porter Sargeant (abridged edn).

Sternhell, Zeev (1994) *The Birth of Fascist Ideology: From Cultural Rebellion to Political Revolution*, Princeton, NJ: Princeton University Press.

Stinchcombe, Arthur (1968) *Constructing Social Theories*, Baltimore: Johns Hopkins University Press.

Strauss, Anselm (1978) "A social world perspective," *Studies in Symbolic Interaction*, 1, 119–28.

Swidler, Ann (1986) "Culture in action: symbols and strategies," *American Sociological Review*, 57, 273–86.

Taylor, Charles ([1971] 1985) "Interpretation and the sciences of man." In *Philosophy and the Human Sciences: Philosophical Papers, II*, Cambridge: Cambridge University Press.

—— (1989a) *Sources of the Self. The Making of the Modern Identity*, Cambridge, MA: Harvard University Press.

—— (1989b) "At cross-purposes: the liberal–communitarian debate." In Nancy L. Rosenblum (ed.), *Liberalism and the Moral Life*, Cambridge, MA: Harvard University Press.

—— (forthcoming) *Selected Essays*, Cambridge, MA: Harvard University Press.

Thompson, E. P. (1963) *The Making of the English Working Class*, New York: Vintage Books.

Tiryakian, Edward A. (1979) "The significance of schools in the development of sociology." In W. E. Snizek et al. (eds), *Contemporary Issues in Theory and Research*, Westport, CN: Greenwood Press.

Todorov, Tzvetan (1993) *On Human Diversity: Nationalism, Racism and Exoticism in French Thought*, Cambridge, MA: Harvard University Press.

Toman, Walter (1993) *Family Constellation: Its Effects on Personality and Social Behavior*, New York: Springer Publishing Co.

Touraine, Alain (1985) "An introduction to the study of social movements," *Social Research*, 52(4), 749–87.

—— (1992) *Critique de la Modernité*, Paris: Fayard.

Trevor-Roper, H. R. (1965) "Religion, the Reformation and social change," *Historical Studies*, 4, 18–45.

Tudesq, André-Jean (1964) *Les grands notables en France (1840–1849): etude historique d'une psychologie sociale*, 2 vols, Paris: Presses Univ. de France.

Tuma, Nancy B. and Michael T. Hannan (1984) *Social Dynamics: Models and Methods*, Orlando: Academic Press.

Turner, Charles (1990) "Lyotard and Weber: postmodern rules and neo-Kantian values." In Bryan S. Turner (ed.), *Theories of Modernity and Postmodernity*, Newbury Park, CA: Sage.

Turner, Jonathan (1985) "In defense of positivism," *Sociological Theory*, 3, 24–30.

—— (1986) "Review: the theory of structuration," *American Journal of Sociology*, 91, 969–77.

Turner, Stephen P. (1980) *Sociological Explanation as Translation*.

—— (1992) Personal communication.

Turner, Stephen P. and Mark L. Wardell (1986) "Epilog." In Mark L. Wardell and Stephen P. Turner (eds), *Sociological Theory in Transition*, Boston: Allen & Unwin.

Turner, Stephen P. and Jonathan H. Turner (1990) *The Impossible Science: An Institutional Analysis of American Sociology*, Newbury Park, CA: Sage Publications, Inc.

Turner, Stephen P. and Regis A. Factor (1994) *Max Weber: The Lawyer as Social Thinker*, London: Routledge.

Turner, Victor (1969) *The Ritual Process*, Chicago: Aldine.

—— (1974) *Dramas, Fields, and Metaphors*, Ithaca: Cornell University Press.

Vanberg, Viktor and James M. Buchanan (1988) "Rational choice and moral order," *Analyse & Kritik*, 10, 138–60.

Van den Berg, A. (1988) *The Immanent Utopia: From Marxism on the State to the State of Marxism*, Princeton, NJ: Princeton University Press.

Van der Veen, Robert and Van Parijs, Phillipe (1986) "A capitalist road to Communism," *Theory and Society*, 15, 635–55.

Van Fraassen, Bas and Jill Sigman (1993) "Interpretation in science and in the arts." In George Levine (ed.), *Realism and Representation*, Madison: University of Wisconsin Press.

Van Parijs, Phillipe (ed.) (1992) *Arguing for Basic Income: Ethical Foundations for a Radical Reform*, London: Verso.

Wagner, Peter (1991) "Science of society lost: the failure to establish sociology in Europe during its 'classical' period." In Peter Wagner, Björn Wittrock, and Richard Whitley (eds), *Discourses on Society. The Shaping of the Social Science Disciplines*, Dordrecht: Kluwer.

—— (1992) "Liberty and discipline: making sense of postmodernity, or, once again, towards a sociohistorical understanding of modernity," *Theory and Society*, 22, 467–92.

—— (1994) *A Sociology of Modernity. Liberty and Discipline*, London: Routledge.

Walby, Sylvia (1986) *Patriarchy at Work*, Lodnon: Macmillan.

Wallace, Walter L. (1971) *The Logic of Science in Sociology*, Chicago: Aldine.

Wallerstein, Immanuel (1991) "The French Revolution as a world-historical event." In *Unthinking Social Science: The Limits of Nineteenth-Century Paradigms*, Cambridge: Polity Press, 7–22.

—— (1992) "The concept of national development, 1917–1989: elegy and requiem." In G. Marx and L. Diamond (eds), *Reexamining Democracy: Essays in Honor of Seymour Martin Lipset*, Newbury Park, CA: Sage Publications, 79–88.

Walzer, Michael (1983) *Spheres of Justice. A Defense of Pluralism and Equality*, New York: Basic Books.

—— (1990) "The communitarian critique of liberalism," *Political Theory*, 18(1), 6–23.

Ward, S. (forthcoming) "In the shadow of the deconstructed metanarratives: Baudrillard, Latour and the end of realist epistemology." *History of the Human Sciences*.

Warnke, Georgia (1987) *Gadamer*, Stanford: Stanford University Press.

Watson, George (1973) *The English Ideology: Studies in the Language of Victorian Politics*, London: Allen Lane.

Wearne, Bruce C. (1989) *The Theory and Scholarship of Talcott Parsons to 1951: A Critical Commentary*, Cambridge/New York: Cambridge University Press.

Weber, Marianne (1975) *Max Weber*, New York: Wiley.

Weber, Max (1949) "'Objectivity' in social science and social policy." In Edward A. Shils and Henry A. Finch (eds and trans.), *Weber, The Methodology of the Social Sciences*, New York: Free Press of Glencoe.

—— ([1946] 1958) "Politics and a vocation." In H. H. Gerth and C. Wright Mills (eds), *From Max Weber: Essays in Sociology*, London: Routledge & Kegan Paul.

—— ([1904–5] 1958) *The Protestant Ethic and the Spirit of Capitalism*, New York: Scribners.

—— (1967) *Ancient Judaism*, New York: Free Press.

—— ([1946] 1976) "Science as a vocation." In H. H. Gerth and C. Wright Mills, *From Max Weber: Essays in Sociology*, New York: Oxford University Press.

—— (1978) *Economy and Society*, Vol. I. Guenther Roth and Claus Wittich (eds), Berkeley: University of California Press.

—— ([1919] 1989) "Science as a vocation." In P. Lasseman and I. Velodny (eds), *Max Weber's "Science as a Vocation"*, London: Unwin Hyman.

Weintraub, Jeff (1994) "Introduction." In Jeff Weintraub and Krishan Kumar (eds), *Public and Private in Thought and Practice*, Chicago: Chicago University Press.

Wertsch, James (1990) *Vygotsky*, Cambridge, MA: Harvard University Press.

White, Reginald J. (ed.) (1950) "Introduction." In *The Conservative Tradition*, London: Nicholas Kaye.

Wieder, D. Lawrence (1974) *Language and Social Reality: The Case of Telling the Convict Code*, The Hague: Mouton.

Wilson, William Julius (1982) *The Declining Significance of Race*, Chicago: Chicago University Press.

—— (1987) *The Truly Disadvantaged*, Chicago: Chicago University Press.

Winch, Peter (1958) *The Idea of a Social Science*, London: Routledge & Kegan Paul.

Winner, L. (1980) "Do artefacts have politics?," *Daedalus*, 109(1), 121–36.

Woolgar, Steve (ed.) (1988) *Knowledge and Reflexivity: New Frontiers in the Sociology of Knowledge*, London: Sage.

—— (1991) "Configuring the user." In John Law (ed.), 1991a.

—— (1992) "Some remarks on positionism." In A. Pickering (ed.), *Science as Practice and Culture*, Chicago: Chicago University Press.

—— (1993) "The user talks back," *CRICT Discussion Paper* no. 40, Brunel University.

—— (1994) "Re thinking agency: recent moves in science and technology studies," *Mexican Journal of Behavior Analysis*, 20, 213–40.

Woolgar, Steve and G. Russell (1990) "The social basis of computer viruses," *CRICT Discussion Paper* no. 17, December, Brunel University.

Wright, Erik Olin (1985) *Classes*, London: Verso.

—— (1992) "The noneffects of class on the gender division of labor in the home," *Gender and Society*, 6(2), 252–82.

Wright, Erik Olin, et al. (1989) *The Debate on Classes*, London: Verso.

Wright, Erik Olin, Andrew, Levine, and Elliott, Sober (1992) *Reconstructing Marxism*, London: Verso.

Wuthnow, Robert (1987) *Meaning and Moral Order*, Berkeley: University of California Press.

—— (1989) *Communities of Discourse: Ideology and Social Structure in the Reformation, the Enlightenment, and European Socialism*, Cambridge, MA: Harvard University Press.

Zucker, Lynn (1983) "Organizations as Institutions." In S. B. Bacharach (ed.), *Research in the Sociology of Organizations*, Greenwich, CT: JAI Press.

Newspapers

Connaught Telegraph, Castebar, Ireland.

Freeman's Journal, Dublin, Ireland.